Compassion and Responsibility

Compassion and Responsibility

Readings in the History of Social Welfare
Policy in the United States

Edited by
Frank R. Breul and Steven J. Diner

THE UNIVERSITY OF CHICAGO PRESS
Chicago and London

The essays in this volume were originally published in various issues of *Social Service Review*. Acknowledgments of the original publications can be found on the first page of each chapter.

The University of Chicago Press, Chicago 60637
The University of Chicago Press, Ltd., London

Library of Congress Cataloging in Publication Data
Main entry under title:

Compassion and responsibility.

"The essays . . . were originally published in various
issues of Social service review."
 Bibliography: p.
 Includes index.
 1. Public welfare—United States—History—Addresses,
essays, lectures. I. Breul, Frank R. II. Diner,
Steven J., 1944–   III. Social service review
(Chicago, Ill.)
HV91.C6754   361'.973   79.56040
ISBN 0-226-07413-7

Contents

Preface   vii

Part I. General Concepts in Social Welfare History

Introduction   1

Compassion and Protection: Dual Motivations in Social
Welfare   5
   Ralph E. Pumphrey

Social Service and Social Reform: A Historical Essay   14
   Clarke A. Chambers

**Part II. Social Welfare in Colonial Times and the Early
National Period**

Introduction   29

The Development of Poor Relief in Colonial Virginia   36
   Marcus Wilson Jernegan

The Puritan Background of the New England Poor Laws   54
   Elizabeth Wisner

The Patchwork of Relief in Provincial New York, 1664–1775   64
   David M. Schneider

Poor Relief in a Massachusetts Village in the Eighteenth
Century   95
   Eleanor Parkhurst

Poverty and Its Relief in American Thought, 1815–61   114
   Benjamin J. Klebaner

The "Benevolent Fair": A Study of Charitable Organization
among American Women in the First Third of the
Nineteenth Century   132
   Mary Bosworth Treudley

The Early Days of the Magdalen Society of Philadelphia   146
   Negley K. Teeters

The Federal Government and Social Welfare in Early
Nineteenth-Century America   156
   Walter I. Trattner

The Tragedy of the Ten-Million-Acre Bill 169
  Seaton W. Manning

**Part III. Late Nineteenth-Century Reform and Early
Twentieth-Century Social Welfare Progress**

Introduction 177

Public Welfare in the South during the Reconstruction Era,
1865–80 183
  John Hope Franklin

"Scientific Philanthropy," 1873–93 197
  Robert H. Bremner

Raymond Robins: The Settlement Worker as Municipal
Reformer 203
  Allen F. Davis

Social Settlements and Immigrant Neighbors, 1886–1914 214
  George Cary White

Chicago Social Workers and Blacks in the Progressive Era 226
  Steven J. Diner

Consensus for Reform: The Mothers'-Pension Movement in
the Progressive Era 244
  Mark H. Leff

Prelude to Welfare Capitalism: The Role of Business in the
Enactment of Workmen's Compensation Legislation in
Illinois, 1905–12 265
  Joseph L. Castrovinci

Isaac Max Rubinow: Pioneering Specialist in Social Insurance 288
  J. Lee Kreader

Women and the Anti-Child Labor Movement in Illinois,
1890–1920 312
  Lynn Gordon

The Chicago Playground Movement: A Neglected Feature of
Social Justice 333
  Benjamin McArthur

Contributors 353

Appendix 357

Index 367

Preface

This volume brings together for social welfare and history students a group of scholarly articles on the history of American social welfare policy. In preparing the fiftieth anniversary issue of *Social Service Review* which appeared in March of 1977, we were impressed with the large number of important articles on the history of social welfare that had appeared in the *Review* over the years. We felt that these articles should be made available to students in a relatively inexpensive form, so that the volume could be used as supplementary reading in courses on social welfare policy and on American history. Therefore, these articles are reproduced as they appeared originally.

Of course, only a small number of the history articles that the *Review* has published could be included in this volume. In making the selection, we limited ourselves to articles on the United States. We also tried to give approximately equal space to the years before and after the Civil War. The volume starts with two outstanding historical interpretations of the nature of American social welfare and of the social work profession. A complete list of the history articles that have appeared in the *Social Service Review* since its inception in 1927 is published at the end of the book.

Edith Abbott and Sophonisba P. Breckinridge, the founders of the *Review*, believed deeply that students of social work and public policy must understand the past. Today, teaching and research in social welfare history is showing new vigor. We sincerely hope that this volume will prove useful to students and instructors in social welfare and history classes.

PART I

General Concepts in Social Welfare History: Introduction

This volume brings together historical articles on American social welfare history that have appeared in *Social Service Review* over the last half century. Contemporary discussions of such recurring concerns as the relief of poverty, the treatment of juvenile delinquency, or the rehabilitation of criminals too often portray these problems, or at least the efforts to solve them, as unique to our own times. American social welfare policy has a long history, however, and it is impossible for the contemporary student of social welfare policy to understand the forms our social welfare programs have taken without understanding the circumstances surrounding their development.

The concept of social welfare is very amorphous, and therefore it is difficult to delimit those aspects of the past which constitute a history of social welfare policy. Most scholars agree that social welfare concerns the material and emotional well-being of individuals and groups of people. Few things adversely affect human well-being so much as war, yet military and diplomatic history are not considered integral to the study of social welfare in the past. Advances in medical knowledge and technology have likewise profoundly affected human well-being, but the history of medical science remains peripheral to the study of social welfare. Indeed, almost all written history deals with aspects of the past that have in some way affected the physical or emotional condition of people.

Frank R. Breul defined social welfare in *The Encyclopaedia Britannica* as "the attempts made by governments and voluntary organizations to help families and individuals by maintaining incomes at an acceptable level, by providing medical care and public health services, by furthering adequate housing and community development, by providing services to facilitate social adjustment, . . . by furnishing facilities for recreation . . . [by protecting] those who might be subject to exploitation, and [by caring] for those special groups considered to be the responsibility of the community."[1] As this definition suggests, social welfare scholars have been concerned primarily with the organized activities of government and of voluntary associations. Throughout human history, people have helped each other in times of material or emotional crisis, through informal arrangements within their family, church, or village. In traditional societies, where most people engaged in subsistence agriculture, few formal institutions provided assistance to people, but people assisted each other. The rise of modern commercial and industrial society since the end of the Middle Ages has produced vastly more complex systems of social organization. Formal institutions have developed, both within government and apart from it, to deal with the problems of human well-being. Social welfare historians have been concerned primarily with the rise of these formal institutions.

The earliest European colonists in North America established formal social welfare institutions, and these institutions grew modestly after American independence. At the end of the nineteenth century, the modern profession of social work developed, and simultaneously the number and complexity of formal governmental and voluntary institutions for human welfare increased dramatically. Some of the new professional social workers argued that the profession could avoid past mistakes by examining how formal institutions had cared for homeless or delinquent children, the poor, the aged, the physically handicapped, the mentally ill, or others with problems *before* the advent of professional social work.

Social Service Review, the social work profession's first scholarly journal, published numerous articles detailing how private and governmental institutions had attempted to cope with social problems in the past. Edith Abbott, one of the founding editors, argued that history "is of first-rate importance because experiments involving the lives of human beings are very costly and ought never to be unnecessarily repeated. Moreover, it is by building on the knowledge of the past that we shall go forward and not backward. . . . So little do people know of the social reformers of the past and of their work," she insisted, "that old experiments are wastefully repeated and outworn theories accepted."[2] For Edith Abbott, then, social welfare history was the history of those activities now performed by social workers to provide guidance for the present and the future.

Social Service Review has always published history articles, written by either social welfare scholars or by professional historians. In time, scholars began to examine also the founders of the social work profession and their institutions. Thus, many of the articles in this volume on the early twentieth century analyze the activities of early professional social workers like Edith Abbott. The authors of these articles commonly left it to their readers to draw appropriate lessons for the present from the past. When you read these articles, consider the extent to which they actually enhance our capacity to solve today's social welfare problems. Does the past provide sufficiently close analogies to the present to give us guidance in attempting to deal with contemporary problems? One of the striking features of our social welfare history, as many of the articles in this volume suggest, is the extent to which problems like poverty or crime persist despite the efforts of government, voluntary social agencies, and reformers. If this is the case, then the contemporary student of social welfare must consider why these problems do persist. Consider also the extent to which real progress has been made in protecting human well-being in this country since the seventeenth century, and how much of that progress has been the result of the work of institutions explicitly devoted to social welfare.

Should you conclude, as many scholars have, that the study of past social welfare policies and institutions provides little or no guidance for present action, there is still a good reason for you to study social welfare history. Today's complex web of government social welfare programs and voluntary social welfare agencies has evolved over time; it was not created as a single piece. A full understanding of our social welfare system requires an understanding of how and why particular institutions or programs developed as they did. For example, the much maligned program of Aid to Families with Dependent Children grows out of the assumptions and experiences of the Elizabethan Poor Laws as transplanted to the American colonies, and the adaptation of this tradition to industrialization and urban growth in the early twentieth century through state mothers' pension laws. Only by examining the history of modern social welfare policies can one understand why certain programs are federal responsibilities and others the responsibilities of the states, why some social welfare activities continue to be the province of voluntary associations, and why social welfare agencies provide for some kinds of social welfare needs more completely than for others.

Most of the articles reprinted in this volume consider a special aspect of the history of organized efforts to enhance material and emotional well-being in America. The essays in this introductory section, however, attempt to construct a comprehensive framework for understanding the details of American social welfare history. Ralph E. Pumphrey argues that two motivations have characterized organized social welfare activities in the American past—compassion, by which he means "the effort to alleviate present suffering, deprivation, or other undesirable conditions . . . "; and protection, which he defines as "endeavors to prevent unwanted developments." Clarke A. Chambers likewise suggests that the history of the social welfare profession has been characterized by a tension between concern for the individual client (social service) and concern with alleviating the conditions which produced the problems of individuals (social reform). Social workers today are still assessing the relationship between these two objectives. These twin concerns are reflected in the distinction most social work curricula make between courses in social treatment and those in social policy. Short of a utopia in which there is no human suffering or deprivation, persons concerned with social welfare will have to remain interested in both remedying the causes of social problems and in treating those who suffer from them. By understanding this issue in historical perspective, individual social workers will be better equipped to work out the relationships of their particular activities to the broader objectives of their profession.

Notes

1. *Encyclopaedia Britannica,* 14th ed., S.V. "Social Welfare."
2. National Conference of Social Work, *Proceedings,* 1928.

COMPASSION AND PROTECTION: DUAL MOTIVATIONS IN SOCIAL WELFARE[1]

RALPH E. PUMPHREY

THE range of "causes," activities, and institutions which make up the overlapping fields of philanthropy and social welfare is so vast, and the different parts are so isolated from each other, that it is difficult to comprehend the whole. This is equally true for the historian and the professional practitioner, such as the educator or social worker. There is a lack of recognition of common elements that can be analyzed, whatever the form of organization or the object of the activity, regardless of the time or place at which they occur.

Historians have not attempted to relate such diverse items as the movement for universal education and the Social Security Act of 1935, the founding of the Pennsylvania Hospital and the research in the field of child labor once conducted by the Russell Sage Foundation. In this, they are merely reflecting the lack of unity between operating fields, but the result has been that existing histories, mostly institutional, usually fall short of their potentialities in relating their immediate subjects to the whole of American life.

Finding common elements in organizations and activities which, on the surface, have little relation to each other would not only forward historical research but would contribute to the philosophic understanding and perspectives of the professions and institutions that are responsible for current operations.

MOTIVATIONS FOR PHILANTHROPIC EFFORT

One thread running through much of our philanthropy is the effort of benefactors to make life in the immediate present better for the beneficiaries than would otherwise be the case. This is frequently accomplished through institutions which put those motives into slogans such as the Boy Scout injunction to "Do a Good Turn Daily" and the CARE appeal that "Hunger Hurts!" But these institutions are essentially extensions of such spontaneous individual acts as rescuing a child from a well, dropping a coin in a beggar's cup, or helping some young person through college. Examples of such individual efforts are found in very early colonial records. Winthrop noted in his journal during a smallpox epidemic among the Indians:

Mr. Maverick of Winesmeet is worthy of a perpetual remembrance. Himself, his wife, and servants, went daily to them, ministered to their necessities, and buried their dead, and took home many of their children. So did other of the neighbors.[2]

This aspect of philanthropy may be designated as *compassion:* the effort to alleviate present suffering, deprivation, or other undesirable conditions to which a segment of the population, but not the benefactor, is exposed. It characteristically results in direct physical services to meet an obvious present need without necessarily relating the services to the

[1] Paper presented at a meeting of the Mississippi Valley Historical Association, Minneapolis, April 25, 1958.

[2] *Winthrop's Journal,* ed. James Kendall Hosmer (New York: Charles Scribner's Sons, 1908), I, 115 (December 5, 1633).

extent of the need or to ways of preventing it.

Another thread found in the pattern of philanthropy is typified in current life by such commonplaces as school crossing guards, chlorinated water, and the Scout motto: "Be Prepared!" This, too, can be found in the earliest colonial records, as when, during the "starving time" in Jamestown, John Smith found it necessary to tell his disorderly band:

> I will take a course you shall provide what is to be had. The sick shall not starve, but equally share of all our labours; and he that gathereth not every day as much as I doe, the next day shall be set beyond the river, and be banished from the Fort as a drone, till he amend his conditions or starve.[3]

This is *protection,* in which the promoters, not only on their own behalf, but on behalf of their group or of the whole community, endeavor to prevent unwanted developments. It may result either from fear of change or from fear of what may happen if existing conditions are not changed. Characteristically it involves reasoning, and it results in institutionalized action designed to forestall the need for compassion.

Compassion and protection represent two more or less consciously determined purposes that may be served by any given philanthropic enterprise. They become crystallized in institutional patterns, and hence are precursors of social policy. They are usually found in combination, rather than in pure form. John Smith, for instance, probably felt compassion for the sick who could not care for themselves. But his greatest concern appears to have been for the survival of the entire company; and he may well,

too, have wished to insure himself not only against starvation but against bodily harm from his followers and against the wrath of the promoters in London who would hold him accountable for failure.

Some problems in using compassion and protection to analyze the inception, development, and impact of philanthropic enterprises may be mentioned. One may well be confused by the wide differences in the objects of concern of the benefactors. Disaster relief calls forth a compassionate outpouring on behalf of utter strangers. At the other extreme is the self-protective benevolence of real estate promoters who give land for schools, churches, and parks to increase the attractiveness of their developments. Consider, too, the mixture of motives of persons who give buildings to colleges and have them adorned with their own names.[4]

Time and place also occasion confusion. In the mid-nineteenth century, most associations for improving the condition of the poor had as a major objective the financial protection of givers and society at large through better coordination of the activities of the many small relief agencies of that day. Yet, over the years, these associations tended to minimize their protective function while maximizing the compassionate activity of almsgiving.[5] Also, Charles

---

[3] John Smith, *The Generall Historie of Virginia, New England and the Summer Isles* (London: Printed by I. D. and I. H. for Michael Sparkes, 1624), p. 87.

[4] An extreme example of this is Ogden Hall, Miami University, Oxford, Ohio, where each entrance bears a brass tablet reading: "Laura Louise Ogden Whaling, donor of Ogden Hall, named this apartment thereof ...., in honor of ...." One entrance is modestly named "Whaling, in honor of herself."

[5] See annual reports of the New York Association for the Improvement of the Condition of the Poor, 1845–1900, esp. first (1845), pp. 14, 15; ninth (1852), p. 43; and fifty-sixth (1899), pp. 90–105. See also annual reports of the Baltimore Associ-

Loring Brace and the promoters of the New York Children's Aid Society were apparently largely influenced by an urge to protect society against the "dangerous classes."[6] However, in placing the children snatched from the streets of New York in homes throughout the middle west, the agency relied upon the very different motivations of compassion and cupidity on the part of the receiving families.[7]

The sponsoring group itself may be an artificial assemblage representing a variety of individual and group motivations converging on a single objective. The published appeals of a community chest, directed to groups of givers, may be quite distasteful to those dealing directly with recipients of service. An intensive historical analysis of the different groups which have been involved in chests—big and small givers, boards and staffs of beneficiary agencies, public officials, the combined giving and beneficiary group represented by labor unions—might well reveal that the variety of their motivations has been a major source of internal conflicts in the movement for unified fund-raising.

Disparity between what people do

and what they say is a familiar phenomenon to behavioral scientists. Often it is an indication of deep-seated emotional involvements. Even in those expressions of motivation which find their way into institutional pronouncements and behavior, usually on a quite conscious level, people may talk compassion and act out self-protection, or vice versa. A desirable campsite was made available rent free to a struggling youth organization in a northern city. The public saw youngsters who otherwise would have been on the city streets given a chance for a camp experience. But suppose the donor had required the agency, which had a substantial number of Negro members, to refuse to permit any Negro to set foot on the camp grounds. Would this raise the question whether the donor was using a gift with compassionate elements to erect a dike against an unwanted social change, while the agency, in its compassionate desire to provide camping opportunities to some of its members, was allowing economic pressure to force it into a partial negation of some of its objectives?[8]

One further problem is the danger of false identification of differences in motivational concepts with such familiar dichotomies as conservative and liberal, public and private, treatment and prevention, or services to individuals as against services to the community at large. Motivational concepts are entities in themselves, and examples of both compassion and protection can be found aligned with both elements of all these dichotomies. The basic distinction is that in compassion the benefactor identifies with and seeks to alleviate the present pain which another person feels; in pro-

ation for the Improvement of the Condition of the Poor, 1851–1900.

[6] This term, which was later made famous by the title of Brace's best-known book, *The Dangerous Classes of New York,* was emphasized from the start. See *First Annual Report of the Children's Aid Society* (New York, 1854), p. 12. The idea had been expressed in the "First Circular of the Children's Aid Society" (1853): "These boys and girls ... will help to form the great multitude of robbers, thieves, and vagrants who are now such a burden upon the law-respecting community." Quoted in Emma Brace, *The Life of Charles Loring Brace Chiefly Told in His Own Letters* (New York: Charles Scribner's, 1894), Appendix A, p. 490.

[7] Hastings Hart, "Placing Out Children in the West," *Proceedings of the National Conference of Charities and Correction, 1884,* pp. 143–50.

[8] Such a situation has come within the professional cognizance of the author.

tection he guards against painful consequences to himself, his group, or his community in the future.

THE COMPASSION OF
DOROTHEA DIX

How may these ideas be applied? The story of Dorothea Dix and her campaign for the humane treatment of the insane is a familiar one.[9] Her memorials to one state legislature after another were masterpieces in the art of assembling incontrovertible facts calculated to shock and shame lawmakers into taking the action demanded. Ultimately, in 1854, her clamorous appeals led Congress to authorize the distribution of public lands to the states for the care of the insane. This measure was vetoed by President Pierce on the grounds that if Congress could provide for the indigent insane it could provide for all indigent, and thus the federal government would "enter into a novel and vast field of legislation, namely, that of providing for the care and support of all those, among the people of the United States, who, by any form of calamity, become fit objects of public philanthropy."[10]

The Pierce veto may be regarded as a significant turning point in American constitutional history. For eighty years, until the passage of the Social Security Act, the country was bound by its identification of the care of the indigent as compassionate activity and therefore a matter of individual and local, rather than federal, concern. One might speculate on the "ifs" of social welfare and the effect on national life had the Dix bill been enacted, but it is not speculation that Miss Dix's essentially compassionate motivation and her appeal to the compassion of others fixed the form for the provision of care to the insane throughout most of the country down to the present. Miss Dix saw suffering human beings inhumanly confined in jails, barns, and sties. When asked if she had investigated the causes of insanity, she said: "I have not. . . . Shall man be more just than God? . . . Have pity on those who . . . 'unto themselves are more grievous than the darkness.' "[11] She promoted institutional care on a state-wide basis as the means of providing clean, warm, safe surroundings, whether or not the patients were treatable.

It would have been entirely possible for her to direct her energies to the furtherance of efforts to find and extend the use of improved methods of treatment in order to reduce future suffering, but she responded to the compassionate urge to see that the immediate conditions of the victims were more comfortable, and she impressed this pattern on the country. Protection through research and treatment received secondary attention. It was two generations later before another crusader,[12] with a compassionate focus on treatment, began to alter the pattern, but it persisted.

[9] Albert Deutsch, *The Mentally Ill in America* (2d ed.; New York: Columbia University Press, 1949), chap. ix; Helen E. Marshall, *Dorothea Dix, Forgotten Samaritan* (Chapel Hill: University of North Carolina Press, 1937), esp. pp. 87–91; Francis Tiffany, *Life of Dorothea Lynde Dix* (Boston: Houghton Mifflin Co., 1891).

[10] James B. Richardson, *A Compilation of the Messages of the Presidents, 1789–1897* (Published by Authority of Congress, 1901), V, 249.

[11] *Memorial to the Legislature of Massachusetts, 1843* (Old South Leaflets, Vol. VI, No. 148), p. 17.

[12] Clifford Whittingham Beers, *A Mind that Found Itself* (New York: Longmans, Green & Co., 1908), pp. 295–96; Albert Deutsch, "The History of Mental Hygiene," in *One Hundred Years of American Psychiatry* (New York: Published for the American Psychiatric Association by Columbia University Press, 1944), pp. 356–59; Deutsch, *The Mentally Ill in America,* chap. xv.

In recent years those concerned with mental hygiene have emphasized protection. In contrast to the pattern which Miss Dix bequeathed to us, the amount of purely custodial care is being minimized, while increasing effort is being put into research into the causes and cures of mental illness and into education and auxiliary services designed to prevent the expansion of the problem. In 1945 a federal official stated:

> Neuropsychiatric disorders constitute one of our most serious health problems, and call for prompt and energetic action if we are to avoid an even more serious situation than that in which we find ourselves. . . . It is necessary to find the cause, provide treatment for those who are ill, reduce the incidence of new cases, and show the public how they can help in combatting the disease.[13]

After such testimony Congress enacted the National Mental Health Act and launched the government on its present vigorous protective mental hygiene program.

Many other institutions and movements started out as purely or largely compassionate responses to immediate need. There were the movements for the institutional care of other groups of the handicapped. For example, Samuel Gridley Howe's education of the blind, deaf Laura Bridgman stands out as one of the great examples of individual compassionate action within an institutional setting.[14] Orphanages throughout the land were expressions of compassion, as

such a name as "New England Home for Little Wanderers"[15] still testifies. Sarah Josepha Hale, working through the Boston Seaman's Aid Society, was far ahead of her time in the quality of the compassion which she bestowed on the women whom she employed at living wages instead of giving them alms.[16] The travelers'-aid and the visiting-nurse movements, as well as disaster relief,[17] are other examples.

It seems probable that historical examination would show that, when they have endured, institutions originating in compassion have changed their programs usually to reflect a protective urge to forestall the need for the sort of service which they had been providing.

JOHN GRISCOM EXEMPLIFIES PROTECTION

The motivation of a person like John Griscom, on the other hand, was primarily protection. An older contemporary of Dorothea Dix, he is known as "the father of all chemistry teachers."[18]

---

[13] Letter from Watson Miller, acting administrator, Federal Security Agency, September, 1945, in *Hearings before a Subcommittee of the Committee on Interstate and Foreign Commerce, on H.R. 2550, National Neuropsychiatric Institute Act, September 18, 19, and 21, 1945* (House [79th Cong., 1st sess.], Washington, D.C.: Government Printing Office, 1945), p. 5. The National Mental Health Act (outgrowth of these hearings) was enacted in 1946.

[14] Harold Schwartz, *Samuel Gridley Howe, Social Reformer, 1801–1876* (Cambridge: Harvard University Press, 1956), chaps. v, vi, x.

[15] A prominent Boston agency. For the development of orphanages, see Henry W. Thurston, *The Dependent Child* (New York: Published for the New York School of Social Work by Columbia University Press, 1930), chap. v, esp. pp. 45, 53, 61.

[16] Mrs. Hale, president of the Seaman's Aid Society, Boston, 1833–37, wrote the annual reports of the agency during that period. This phase of her career is dealt with briefly in Isabelle Webb Entrikin, *Sarah Josepha Hale and Godey's Lady's Book* (Philadelphia, 1946), pp. 60–67, 83–89, 137, 151.

[17] Bertha McCall, "History of the National Travelers Aid Association, 1911–1918" (mimeographed; New York: National Travelers Aid Association, 1950), pp. 206; Lillian D. Wald, *The House on Henry Street* (New York: Henry Holt & Co., 1915), esp. pp. 7 ff. and 40 ff.; J. Bryon Deacon, *Disasters* (New York: Russell Sage Foundation, 1918), pp. 39, 40, 54, 56, 106.

[18] Edgar F. Smith, *John Griscom, Chemist* (Philadelphia: University of Pennsylvania Press, 1925), p. 14, cited in Araminta W. Anthony, "John Griscom, His Life Experiences, Philosophy, and Contribution to Social Work" (unpublished Master's

He devoted considerable time to teaching science to people not ordinarily reached by such education. As a redoubtable advocate of free, universal public education, he made notable contributions to the philosophy and techniques of education; as a philanthropist, he was the founder of the New York Society for the Prevention of Pauperism, a short-lived organization which cast a long shadow. When he moved to New York, Griscom, appalled to find poverty and ignorance on a scale such as he had never experienced, saw the two—poverty and ignorance—as interrelated threats to the well-being of the whole social structure. While he expressed his compassion in many ways, including his science lectures, his concern for the individual was, in large part, subordinated to his protective concern for society.

In his *Discourse on the Importance of Character and Education in the United States*, he asked:

> Where learning is only a thing of patrician acquirement . . . is it surprising that these [chosen few] should be crushed by the tumultuous passions which impel the vulgar breast?

Not only does the safety of our form of government depend upon . . . universality of instruction, but the wisdom of its measures and the whole concatination of its policy. . . . If then Americans are wise, will they not cherish with peculiar affection, and with surpassing liberality, their seminaries of learning, and every institution which renders useful knowledge accessible to all.[19]

In the same protective vein, in his "Report on the Subject of Pauperism," prepared in 1818, he said:

We were fully prepared to believe, that without a radical change in the principles upon which public alms have been usually distributed, helplessness and poverty would continue to multiply—demands for relief would become more and more importunate, the numerical difference between those who are able to bestow charity and those who sue for it, would gradually diminish, until the present system must fall under its own irresistible pressure, prostrating, perhaps, in its ruin, some of the pillars of the social order.[20]

Having this sort of background, Griscom saw as principles for systematic charity:

> *First*, amply to relieve the unavoidable necessities of the poor; and *Secondly*, to lay the powerful hand of moral and legal restriction upon every thing that contributes . . . to introduce an artificial extent of suffering; and to diminish . . . a reliance upon . . . powers of body and mind for an independent and virtuous support.[21]

Thus, Griscom saw the importance of relieving the immediate needs of the poor, but, unlike Miss Dix who made care an end in itself, he saw this as only one aspect of a total program of protection, on behalf of which he appealed to the fear of what might otherwise happen to society. Here Griscom utilized his own scientific background to attempt an approach to the problems of poverty. Throughout the rest of the century, in England and America, we see these same ideas recurring—in Thomas Chalmers, the Scottish divine whose writings so greatly influenced the charity organization movement; in Robert Hartley and the New York Association for the Improvement of the Condition of the Poor; in Charles Loch and the London Charity

---

project, New York School of Social Work, Columbia University, February, 1958), p. 8. See also John H. Griscom, *Memoir of John Griscom, L.L.D.* (New York: Robert Carter & Bros., 1859).

[19] John Griscom, *Discourse on the Importance of Character and Education in the United States* (New York: Mahlon Day, 1823), pp. 11, 13.

[20] "Report on the Subject of Pauperism, on Behalf of the Committee, John Griscom, Chairman," in *First Annual Report of the New York Society for the Prevention of Pauperism* (New York, 1819), p. 12.

[21] *Ibid.*, p. 13.

Organisation Society; and in such American charity organization leaders as Josephine Shaw Lowell and Mary Richmond. In its essence, Griscom's concept of the twofold protection of society through adequate relief and through environmental controls is deeply embedded in most modern American social welfare legislation and organization.

However, every generation has had difficulty maintaining this protective approach. Griscom himself, after a trip to Europe during which he imparted to Dr. Chalmers his ideas about the necessity to protect society against pauperism,[22] became eager to do something for the poor waifs who were getting into trouble on the streets of New York. The Society for the Prevention of Pauperism took up his ideas, and the energies of that organization were soon drained off into the establishment and operation of a new institution, the House of Refuge, the first home for delinquents in this country. From the start, and throughout the hundred years of its history, this agency, which had its nurture in protection, functioned primarily according to the concept of compassion.[23]

The historian who examines institutions from this point of view may well find even more clear-cut illustrations of institutions in which protection was the primary motivation. Such a possibility seems to be particularly good with respect to the social hygiene, tuberculosis, and Americanization movements; such specialized police activities as the Police Athletic League and juvenile aid bureaus; and such ideological efforts as the American Heritage Foundation appeals on behalf of Radio Free Europe.

A BLENDING OF MOTIVATIONS

The founding of the Pennsylvania Hospital in 1750 shows the combination of compassion and protection from the start. There was no American precedent for Franklin and his friends when, moving beyond a merely ameliorative infirmary in which the ill might be cared for, they envisioned an institution that would supplement the "many compassionate and charitable provisions for the relief of the poor" and would make it possible for the ill, "by the judicious assistance of physick and surgery . . . to taste the blessings of health, and be made in a few weeks useful members of the community, able to provide for themselves and families."[24]

Note the identification with both the poor person and the donor which is conveyed in this excerpt from the 1761 report:

Let it be considered that . . . poor people are maintained by their labour, and, if they cannot labour they cannot live, without the help of the more fortunate. We all know, many mouths are fed, many bodies clothed, by one poor man's industry and diligence: should any sudden hurt happen to him, which should render him incapable to follow the business of his calling, unfit him to work, disable him to labour but for a little time; or should his duty to his aged and diseased parents or his fatherly tenderness for an afflicted child, engross his attention and care, how great must be the calamity of such a family! How pressing their wants! How moving

[22] John Griscom, *A Year in Europe: Comprising a Journal of Observations* [1818–19] (New York: Collins & Hannay, 1824), p. 261.

[23] *House of Refuge for Vagrant and Depraved Young People: Report of a Committee Appointed by the Society for the Prevention of Pauperism in the City of New York on the Expediency of Erecting an Institution for the Reformation of Juvenile Delinquents* (New York: Mahlon Day, 1824); "Vacating the House of Refuge," *Correction Magazine* (Albany: New York State Department of Correction, March, 1935).

[24] Benjamin Franklin, *Some Account of the Pennsylvania Hospital* (Philadelphia: B. Franklin & D. Hall, 1754), p. 5. This quotation is from the petition to the provincial House of Representatives.

their distress! And how much does it behove the community to take them immediately under their guardianship and have the causes of their misfortunes as speedily remedied as possible! Experience shows, this will be more effectually and frugally done in a publick hospital than by any other method whatever.[25]

Whereas the uncured sick person and his family were a drain, the one who was restored to health was a contributing member of the community. The corollary, that the best results would come from the best physicians and that opportunity should be afforded to train them, was embodied in the rules for the operation of the hospital.[26] Hence, from the start, this was no mere custodial institution, but one for cure, research, and training—an embodiment of compassion that also extended protection to the donor and the community at large. Further, the fact that the hospital was to be open to paying patients only if there were beds available after all public cases were taken care of[27] established a relationship that was salutary to the standards of public service.

For such an institution it was possible to appeal to people with many different motivations—pity for the afflicted, worry over the expense to the taxpayer of inadequate care, concern over danger from little-understood diseases, and self-seeking publicity. To get the colonial assembly to provide the building, Franklin played on all of these, proposing a contingent appropriation requiring private subscription of a like sum. He tells us the result in his autobiography:

This condition carried the bill through; for the members who had opposed the grant, and now conceived they might have the credit of being charitable without the expense, agreed to its passage; and then, in soliciting subscriptions among the people, we urged the conditional promise of the law as an additional motive to give since every man's donation would be doubled; thus the clause worked both ways.[28]

USE AS ANALYTICAL TOOLS

There are other significant motivations, such as religion, and other concepts, such as responsibility, which might be developed similarly. Here compassion and protection have been developed in a very limited way as samples of the sorts of unifying ideas that need to be identified and utilized in the analysis of historical materials in the wide area of philanthropy and social welfare, just as nationalism and the frontier have been identified and utilized in other aspects of history. Their usefulness can only be suggested.

First, the historian of a single agency is likely to be puzzled by sudden modifications in program, frequently associated with new leadership. In such cases, did motivation change and, if so, did the new leadership reflect or precipitate the shift in emphasis between protection and compassion? Did internal struggles reflect changing attitudes in society at large? What changes in skill and training of staff were required as the agency's prevailing purposes changed?

On the other hand, in the study of the long-range effects of new technical skills or institutional mechanisms, one may find instances in which, with little change in form, the technique is used to accomplish varying purposes at differ-

[25] *Continuation of the Account of the Pennsylvania Hospital* (Philadelphia: B. Franklin & D. Hall, 1761), pp. 113–14.

[26] Franklin, *Some Account of the Pennsylvania Hospital*, p. 49.

[27] *Ibid.*, pp. 47–48.

[28] *The Life of Benjamin Franklin, Written by Himself*, ed. John Bigelow (Philadelphia: J. B. Lippincott & Co., 1874), I, 298.

ent times. For example, the idea of the exchange of information about individual clients, represented in institutional form in most cities by the social service exchange, has been a battleground for generations between those who see this device as a way of protecting givers and taxpayers against fraudulent appeals for help, those who see it from the compassionate point of view of providing more information about, and therefore better service to, the individual client, and those who see it as an undesirable activity because of their compassionate desire to shield the person in trouble from any intrusion into his affairs.[29]

Again, in the analysis of relations between agencies, and indeed between major fields, such as education, medicine and social welfare, the historian might find the ideas of compassion and protection helpful in understanding some of the recurring affinities and rivalries such as those seen in the current acrimonious exchanges between courts, police, schools, social agencies, and other groups dealing with juvenile delinquency. Would this type of analysis help to explain some of the fratricidal criticism of each other among philanthropic groups as "hard boiled," "impersonal," or "soft," a well-known aspect of the competition for the philanthropic and tax dollar?

For the biographer, who may wish to probe rather deeply the inner motivations of his subject, external manifestations such as compassion or protection still provide focuses for analysis. What was there about Mrs. Hale that led her to direct her great compassion for the families of sailors toward enabling them to be as much like other people as possible, rather than toward providing alms or institutionalization? What, on the other hand, made Mrs. Lowell, in her urge to protect society against pauperism, feel it necessary to set relief recipients completely apart from other people?[30]

Finally, might not historical examination of compassion and protection give some further clue to philanthropists and professional workers regarding the nature of the components of a successful institution? A hypothesis that might well be tested is that no matter what their auspices or sources of support, those social welfare institutions which have proved enduringly useful to society as a whole have embodied in a balanced relationship both compassion, that is, a desire to do something for the benefit of unfortunate people in the present, and protection, a concern for the well-being of the donor's group both now and in the future.

GRADUATE SCHOOL OF PUBLIC ADMINISTRATION
AND SOCIAL SERVICE
NEW YORK UNIVERSITY

Received April 30, 1958

[29] For the evolution of social service exchange philosophy see Associated Charities of Boston, *First Annual Report* (1880), p. 5; *Third Annual Report* (1882), pp. 12–13; Margaret F. Byington, *The Confidential Exchange: A Form of Social Cooperation* (New York: Charity Organization Department of the Russell Sage Foundation, Publication No. 28, 1912); Beatrice R. Simcox, "The Social Service Exchange, Part II: Its Use in Casework," *Journal of Social Casework*, XXVIII (1947), 388–90; Stephen L. Angell and Frank T. Greving, "A New Look at the Social Service Exchange," *Social Work Journal*, XXXVI (1955), 16–17.

[30] Seaman's Aid Society, Boston, *Third Annual Report* (1836), pp. 12–13; Josephine Shaw Lowell, *Public Relief and Private Charity* (New York: G. P. Putnam's Sons, 1884), pp. 67, 106.

SOCIAL SERVICE AND SOCIAL REFORM: A HISTORICAL ESSAY

CLARKE A. CHAMBERS

The author is a member of the faculty of the Department of History at the University of Minnesota. Substantial parts of this paper were first given at the Annual Program Meeting of the Council on Social Work Education in January, 1962, under the title, "Political Action versus Individualized Treatment in Social Welfare Work," and as a lecture, "The Historical Role of Social Work in the Formation of Public Policy," given under the auspices of the School of Social Welfare of the University of California at Berkeley in June, 1962.

FROM the beginning the profession we identify now as social work or social welfare has been engaged in two main lines of activity—more often mutually supportive than antagonistic or competitive—service to people in need, on the one hand, and social reform or the formation of public policy, on the other.[1] Even in pioneer days —when the National Conference chose to name its concern for "charities and correction," when caseworkers were simply "friendly visitors," when psychiatric counseling, unknown by name, was practiced by priests, pastors, and rabbis —the dedication was both to assistance for the individual and his family in making the best of a bad situation and to reconstruction of the social environment.

[1] Many social workers have wrestled with these issues. Particularly illuminating in more recent literature are Bertram M. Beck, "Shaping America's Social Welfare Policy," in *Issues in American Social Work*, ed. Alfred J. Kahn (New York: Columbia University Press, 1959), pp. 191–218; and Donald S. Howard, "Social Work and Social Reform," in *New Directions in Social Work*, ed. Cora Kasius (New York: Harper & Bros., 1954), pp. 159–74. Nathan E. Cohen's *Social Work in the American Tradition* (New York: Dryden Press, 1958) and Frank J. Bruno's *Trends in Social Work, 1874–1956* (New York: Columbia University Press, 1957) are works to which all social welfare historians are indebted.

Care of the individual client, whatever his needs may be, has always been a central and legitimate function of social work. To provide assistance so that the client and his family can move away from dependency and need toward independence and self-direction has been for decades a fully accepted function of welfare work. Care and the removal of the causes of dependency may require financial support, provision of health or recreational services, vocational guidance, family counseling, cash relief, a lead to a new job, an insight into the sources of marital conflict, two weeks at a vacation camp, the placement of an illegitimate child, prolonged psychiatric sessions, or a new set of teeth. In any case the focus of such work is upon helping the client to help himself, seeing him through a time of crisis when his own resources, financial or psychological, are inadequate to the demands made upon him, liberating him from dependency, enriching his life, or helping him to make satisfactory adjustments to his environment or to reconstruct it as far as possible.

Here then are represented the service functions of social work: assistance to individuals in the context of existing circumstances, whatever the means utilized, whatever the special skills employed, whatever the subdivision of task. The stress—although not the exclusive emphasis—is upon assisting the individual to make a reasonably satisfactory adjustment to his environment. If once, in a more primitive age, these procedures involved only (or at least primarily) care and perhaps cure, if they amounted to patchwork amelioration—what some called "scavenger work"—those days have long since passed. The goals, over time, have become more comprehensive, more positive, though still focused on the individual, his well-being, his adjustment to life as it actually is. This is social work (especially in its casework phase) in its retail, client-centered, service-oriented aspects. If, over the past forty or fifty years, it has been inspired more by St. Sigmund than by St. Karl, so be it.

But, traditionally, professional social work has had a responsibility to society and to public welfare as well as to the individual client. Even those workers whose daily routine necessarily forced a nearly exclusive concern with the adjustment of the individual to the givens of his environment have rarely been unaware of the direct and overwhelming influence of the health of society upon the health of the client. Grace Coyle summed it up in her presidential address before the National Conference at the end of the depression decade of the 1930's: "There is no reasonable doubt that poverty itself is responsible for increased illness, that unemployment breeds unemployability, that crowded housing undermines family life, that undernourished children will grow into incompetent workers."[2]

Social workers are scavengers, of course they are, said Sidney Hollander in 1937, and so are doctors; and both must move from amelioration to cure to prevention and finally to positive measures to assure physical and social health. Social work must struggle to lift burdens from those who suffer (so often through no failing of their own) and seek also to correct "the basic maladjustments to which this wreckage bears witness."[3] When the limits of personal assistance were reached, Mr. Hollander continued, then social work has the obligation to promote measures, through political and social action, that will lighten the external handicaps and create opportunities for fuller and richer lives for all.

Helen Hall put it in the specific terms with which settlement workers habitually dealt: It was acceptable casework method, she said in 1936, to assist a torn and deprived family to get out of objectionable quarters for the sake of both health and morale. "But in the long run," she continued, "it is both poor case work and poor health work merely to move particular families and do nothing toward changing the conditions out of which you have taken them and into which others will move." Social workers must drum up support for housing reform, slum clearance, and public housing and must assist other groups to work effectively toward these ends. "Social action for change and advance is inescapable," she concluded, "unless we are willing to drift along eternally patching up the consequences of social neglect and industrial breakdown."[4]

[2] "Social Work at the Turn of the Decade," in *Proceedings of the National Conference of Social Work, 1940*, pp. 22–23 (hereinafter cited by year as "*Proceedings*").

[3] "A Layman Takes Stock of Public and Private Agency Functions," in *Proceedings, 1937*, p. 190.

[4] "The Consequences of Social Action for the Group-Work Agency," in *Proceedings, 1936*, pp. 235, 237.

So over and over again, as social workers pressed up to the limits of what a given situation permitted in the way of adequate individual assistance, leaders from the profession pressed forward with proposals to break down those external limitations or to push them back. Effective service always required social action. Even though the temptation persisted to rely upon "methods of individual treatment without a companion concern and activities for corrective measures," Rudolph Danstedt warned, social workers were forced to recognize that "family-centered social work services, psychiatric services, and programs for control and prevention of juvenile delinquency" were effective only in a society in which the evils of squalor, idleness, ignorance, sickness, and want had been rooted out.[5]

Thus the two overlapping phases of social work continue to exist, not always harmoniously, but certainly in interdependence—the one focused on the individual and his welfare, strongly influenced by the psychological disciplines, introspective, dealing in personalized, retail services; the other concerned with reform, with reconstruction, informed primarily by the social sciences, extroverted, dealing in group or community or wholesale services. Professor Pumphrey recently suggested the terms "compassion" and "protection"—the former referring to "direct physical services" aimed at making "life in the immediate present better for the beneficiaries," the latter moved by the desire for security or stability (of self or of community) and engaged in "institutionalized action designed to forestall the need for compassion."[6]

[5] "An Assessment of Social Action," in *Social Welfare Forum, 1958*, pp. 203–4 (hereinafter cited by year as *"Forum"*).

Perhaps a metaphor borrowed from organized religion will sharpen the distinction. A minister may be priest or prophet; at best he is both, but rarely are these talents combined in one holy person. As priest, as shepherd, he serves, he counsels, he comforts, he reconciles, he listens, he accepts, he judges not, he plays out a ritualistic role, he bears witness to a transcendent concern. As prophet, as preacher, he has a harder, more demanding, and more lonely role to play. In the world, if not of it, he holds up absolute standards against which the sins of man and the shortcomings of the world may be measured and judged; his cry is less for charity and compassion than for justice; he is not content merely to stand and to serve; repentance and reform or doom is his prophesy. It may be safe to note that the vast majority of professional social workers are properly engaged in what we may call priestly functions. The actionists—the prophets, if you wish—are exceptional leaders, impatient with ameliorative measures, demanding social justice through social reform.

To extend the metaphor just a bit further, the prophets have often been scornful of the priests—of the scribes and the Pharisees. Thus, in 1930, a labor educator chided an assembly of

[6] The two, Pumphrey clearly sets forth, are overlapping and intertwined functions, and both involve mixed motives: "In compassion the benefactor identifies with and seeks to alleviate the present pain which another person feels; in protection he guards against painful consequences to himself, his group, or his community in the future." Pumphrey also notes the tendency of the compassionate response to lead to action designed to eliminate "the need for the sort of services" which compassion institutionalized had offered ("Compassion and Protection: Dual Motivations in Social Welfare," *Social Service Review*, XXXIII [March, 1959], 23–24).

social workers for having "gone psychiatric in a world which has gone industrial."[7] A contemporary, Isaac M. Rubinow, prophet of social security, bitterly attacked those social workers for having "substituted the concept of personal inadequacy and individual maladjustment for the theory of the responsibility of the environment." Social action, aimed at liberation from economic dependency, not personal readjustment, was the need.[8] And so—selecting almost at random—one can find supporting illustrations of social-action leaders appalled with what they take to be the apathy, passivity, downright shameful neglect of the great body of social workers to enlist in reform causes, to see the vision of the good society, to lift their eyes above the routine of the day's work. There was contempt for those who could consider social reform to be but one of several divisions of social work; so to hold, Gaynell Hawkins wrote, rather than to see that reform was the fundamental basis of the whole process, "is analogous to the legal profession's saying that the administration of justice is one of the divisions of that profession."[9] Thus Grace L. Coyle in 1937 lashed out at all those who continued "to pick up the pieces without ever attempting to stop the breakage." She thought caseworkers were particularly guilty of adjusting the client to "deprivation" without seeking to correct injustice. She wrote: "The real situation which faces us as social workers includes a society, potentially rich but actually poor, wasteful of its material and human resources, torn by class and racial conflicts, its cultural life on the whole meager, vulgar and disintegrated."[10] Or recall the tone of Harry L. Lurie's protest against the failure of his profession militantly to seek reform even in the reform-oriented New Deal years. The habit of impartiality, the conservative influence of agency board members, the fear that change would disrupt familiar ways—all contributed to a peculiar passivity. "As a professional group," he wrote, "we are in general tied up with the reactionary rather than with the advancing forces of social change." A sweeping realignment of the whole profession, both in philosophy and in program, he warned, would have to precede any effective change.[11]

Between the "movers and shakers," on the one hand, and the "seekers and sojourners," on the other, there has often been misunderstanding and bad blood.

POLITICAL ACTION AND SOCIAL WORK
FROM THE TURN OF THE CENTURY

We know—with that advantage that hindsight affords—what a truly crucial role was played by those whom we

---

[7] A. J. Muste, quoted in Mary Ross and Paul U. Kellogg, "New Beacons in Boston," *Survey*, LXIV (July 15, 1930), 344.

[8] "Can Private Philanthropy Do It?" *Social Service Review*, III (September, 1929), 369.

[9] *Education for Social Understanding* (New York: American Association for Adult Education, 1940), p. 25.

[10] "Social Workers and Social Action," *Survey*, LXXIII (May, 1937), 138–39.

[11] "The Part Which Social Workers Have Taken in Promoting Social Legislation in New York State," in *Proceedings, 1935*, p. 503. See also Mary Van Kleeck, "Our Illusions Regarding Government," in *Proceedings, 1934*, pp. 473–85; Karl Borders, "Social Workers and a New Social Order," in *Proceedings, 1933*, pp. 590–96; Charles I. Schottland, "Social Work in the 1960's," in *Forum, 1960*, pp. 20–41; Daisy Lee W. Worcester, *Grim the Battle* (New York: Exposition Press, 1954), a semi-autobiographical account of social work and its failure, as she sees it, to seek reform militantly and persistently.

would now consider practitioners of social work in elaborating programs of reform during the years of the Progressive Era. To cite Professor Bremner's brilliant study of the "discovery of poverty" is sufficient documentation for our purposes. We find their names and careers conjured up for us in social welfare literature, particularly by those who are nostalgic for the good old days when social workers were first crusaders: Jane Addams, beloved lady, and her many associates—Lillian Wald; Graham Taylor; Mary McDowell; the Abbott sisters, Grace and Edith; Edward T. Devine; Paul U. Kellogg; Owen Lovejoy; Homer Folks; and the indomitable and irrepressible fighter for all good causes, Florence Kelley. These pioneer figures have come to stand for the social-reconstruction-through-political-action phase of welfare work— "pure and simple" reformism—at its best (which is to say its most direct and militant).

There is no denying that to those whose commitment is to democratic, humane, welfare liberalism their vision and their techniques are enviable. Tested pragmatically, social-welfare-as-social-reform worked. Look at the evidence: the prohibition or severe regulation of child labor, together with compulsory school-attendance laws; reduction of hours and increase in wages for exploited women workers; workmen's compensation; mothers' pensions; new standards of public sanitation and health; special courts for juvenile offenders; visiting nurses and visiting teachers. Welfare reforms spilled over into other areas as well: municipal housekeeping, immigrant protection, woman suffrage, direct democracy, civil liberties, international peace. This surge of reform culminated in the great platform, "Social Standards for Industry," adopted by the delegates to the 1912 National Conference acting as individual citizens, not as members of a professional association. This statement strongly influenced Theodore Roosevelt's confession of faith, and parts of it were incorporated in the platform of his Progressive party. These actions established the ideal of community or public responsibility for the welfare of the disadvantaged and disinherited, men and women and children in need through no inherent fault of their own. Upon these foundations of philosophy and program rest the superstructure of welfare liberalism.[12]

If welfare work, over the decades that spanned either side of 1900, moved from care to cure to prevention, the traditional functions of care and support, individual and family assistance, did not lapse—indeed, under the surpassing influence of Mary Richmond they were being given a more scientific basis, as friendly visiting gave way to casework. It was this retail phase of social work that emerged ascendant in the postwar decade of normalcy and prosperity. Legislative success in the prewar years had nearly exhausted reform objectives; implementation, modification, extension of hard-won goals was now to be the order of the day. Prosperity (unevenly distributed, as many social workers were quick to point out) seemed to offer, together with reforms already won, a way to remedy the dependency that came from social poverty. The perfectly legitimate longing for

[12] The committee report and platform are found in *Proceedings, 1912*, pp. 376–95. The story has often been told, but see especially Allen Davis, "Spearhead for Reform: The Social Settlements and the Progressive Movement, 1890–1914" (doctoral dissertation, University of Wisconsin, 1959).

professional status to be accorded social work, just coming of age, created new concerns in the fields of education, graduate training, research, accreditation, refinement of diagnostic and therapeutic tools. Furthermore, the 1920's proved generally inhospitable to reconstruction measures; when the courts knocked down protective legislation, particularly in the fields of child labor and the employment of women, reformers were frustrated in their attempts to seek new paths to re-establish familiar goals. America generally seemed more excited by contemplation of the internal landscape of the person than of the external landscape of society; Fitzgerald and Hemingway pushed out Dreiser and Sinclair; George Luks, Robert Henri, and John Sloan gave way to Georgia O'Keefe, John Marin, and Arthur Dove. So, too, in social work the excitement was primarily in exploring the tangled wilderness of the human psyche rather than the jungle of modern industrial and urban society. As Paul U. Kellogg, having in mind the ascendancy of casework, observed in 1930, social workers, in "recoil" from progressivism and war, had turned away from reform toward "individual readjustment." As he put it, "the drama of people's insides rather than the pageantry of their group contacts and common needs" was foremost.[13]

It may be that the speed with which psychoanalytic concepts and devices were incorporated into social work practice can be attributed to the profession's receptivity to a process that was "profoundly democratic . . . in its studied permissiveness and self-choice" for the client, and because both analysis and

social work dealt with specific cases in action, as Weston La Barre has observed; or because such concepts reflected certain inherent biases in American social work tradition, such as the commitment to the "uniqueness of each individual," to "emotional factors in experience," to "unity of personality and the necessity for dealing with the whole person," and to the "need of each person to be self-determining," as Grace Coyle has suggested.[14] In any case, psychology, psychiatry, psychoanalysis offered ways to assist the individual to make a partially satisfactory adjustment to conditions over which, acting alone, he had little or no control. The methods of assistance, moreover, required a high level of sophisticated self-understanding on the part of the worker and required as well that the client participate actively, not merely as a passive recipient, in the processes of rehabilitation. Particularly did the insights that modern psychology offered open up new and remarkably valid techniques for workers engaged in child welfare or child-saving agencies and in the understanding and correction of delinquent behavior.[15]

The charge that social actionists made against social work in the 1920's —that it "turned away from large social issues and placed its main emphasis upon 'individualizaton' "—is, however,

[13] Ross and Kellogg, "New Beacons in Boston," op. cit., p. 341.

[14] Weston La Barre, "The Social Worker in Cultural Change," in Forum, 1957, pp. 179–93; Coyle, "Social Work at the Turn of the Decade," op. cit., p. 13.

[15] On these and related points see Helen Harris Perlman, "Freud's Contribution to Social Welfare," Social Service Review, XXXI (June, 1957), 192–202; and the brilliant and classic book by Virginia P. Robinson, A Changing Psychology in Social Case Work (Chapel Hill: University of North Carolina Press, 1930).

but another partial truth.[16] As I have suggested elsewhere, the decade of the 1920's was marked by a continuation of antiquated care and preventive programs, to which were added new techniques in social casework and new constructive measures that aimed beyond prevention toward the positive creation of a freer, fuller, more secure life for all, including those who lived above the line of poverty. If most social workers were still legitimately engaged in care and cure, and if the subtle shift in emphasis from preventive to constructive measures was not immediately or widely recognized, the two phases of social welfare were nonetheless mutually interdependent and overlapping phases of a common enterprise.[17]

Well before the great panic ushered in a decade of depression, the old progressive alliance between social reformer and social worker was being joined again, particularly in the movement for social insurance against the hazards of economic dependency, unemployment, and old age—a crusade that the settlement leaders helped to initiate, a cause in which hundreds of social workers enlisted until the great Social Security Act of 1935 (with all its shortcomings) was enacted. Porter Lee, in his presidential address of 1929, saw with perfect clarity that social work was both "cause" and "function." Any "movement directed toward the elimination of an intrenched evil" called for zeal and enthusiasm; "cause" institutionalized into "function" required the more "hum-

drum and routine" qualities of intelligence and efficiency. Civilization demanded from social work "the capacity to develop new ideas as well as to insure the permanence and efficacy of those to which it has given corporate life."[18] I. M. Rubinow put it more simply: social action dealt in wholesale, casework in retail, reform. Both were essential.[19]

As World War I broke the ascendancy of political action, panic turned the emphasis once more from the person to the environment. Social work was soon forced to recognize that retail methods no longer sufficed to meet the desperate needs of millions of citizens. Hard-won professional gains were soon set back by the tens of thousands of untrained amateur workers enlisted to administer government relief and public welfare projects. Prolonged depression switched the questions and transformed the answers. Social workers may not have played exactly the same role that pioneer reformers had in prewar years when the line between social reform and social work was blurred, but they performed similar functions in sometimes different ways. The role of direct agitation was often left largely to voluntary reform associations, to politicians, to labor leaders (playing, in the New Deal years, an aggressive role that had rarely been countenanced in the days of Gompers); social workers were more often now found working in and through government, on the staffs of numerous commissions, committees, bureaus, and agencies, than as voices crying in the wilderness. Some were highly visible—

[16] The quotation is from Katherine D. Lumpkin and Dorothy W. Douglas, *Child Workers in America* (New York: R. M. McBride & Co., 1937), p. 264, but one can find similar remarks elsewhere.

[17] Clarke A. Chambers, "Creative Effort in an Age of Normalcy, 1918–1933," in *Forum, 1961,* pp. 252–71.

[18] "Social Work: Cause and Function," in *Proceedings, 1929,* pp. 3–20.

[19] "Social Case Work: A Profession in the Making," *Journal of Social Forces,* IV (1925), 286–92.

Harry Hopkins, Frances Perkins, Aubrey Williams, Molly Dewson, Edith and Grace Abbott, Katharine Lenroot, Josephine Roche. Others were less visible, but nonetheless influential—Helen Alfred, J. E. Alloway, Mollie Ray Carroll, C. C. Carstens, Courtenay Dinwiddie, John Lovejoy Elliott, Abraham Epstein, John Fitch, Abraham Goldfeld, Helen Hall, Olive E. Henderson, William Hodson, Caroline Hogue, Joel D. Hunter, Robert F. Keegan, Dorothy Kenyon, Stanley Mathewson, William H. Matthews, Royal Meeker, John O'Grady, John A. Ryan, Mary Simkhovitch, Lea Taylor, Warren J. Vinton, Richard W. Wallace—social workers all, who labored, each in his own way, within and without government, in season and out, for social security, slum clearance and public housing, adequate standards of relief, public works, industrial minimums (maximum hours, minimum wages, prohibition of child labor), the right of labor to organize and bargain collectively.[20]

The professional social work leader necessarily engaged in all these measures to "mend, alter, rebuild." The words were those of John A. Fitch, speaking at the end of the depression decade, who went on to observe that the obligation of political action in no way meant that the social worker "should be engaged in a general, undifferentiated onslaught on social wrongs." As a private citizen he possessed the same responsibility as all citizens to participate in the strengthening of the general welfare, but beyond that he had the obligation to bring, in co-operation with others, his own special competence to the solution of terribly complex issues, to present the evidence of need derived from his experience, to participate in public discussion.[21]

But if social action again constituted the mainstream, there was no neglect of refined methods of individual assistance. If reform persisted in the years of normalcy, personal care survived in the New Deal decade. The differences were those of degree of emphasis, but they made a profound difference in the whole structure, organization, procedure, and source of support for welfare activities. The assumption on the part of government (local, state, and particularly national) of the major responsibility in the whole welfare field implied a drastic

---

[20] The list, both of social workers engaged in political action and of the measures they secured, is meant to be suggestive and illustrative and in no way a definitive statement. In addition to secondary accounts of the New Deal, few of which have stressed the role of social workers, one can follow these affairs in the *Proceedings*, in the *Social Service Review*, and in the *Survey* for these years.

[21] John A. Fitch, "The Nature of Social Action," in *Proceedings, 1940*, p. 491. For variations on the theme, the following pieces are particularly revealing of social work's concern with political action from many different points of view: Porter Lee, *Social Work as Cause and Function* (New York: Columbia University Press, 1937), pp. 177–200; Antoinette Cannon, "Recent Changes in the Philosophy of Social Workers," in *Proceedings, 1933*, pp. 597–607; Monsignor Robert F. Keegan, "Social Work Marches On," in *Proceedings, 1934*, pp. 98–108; Harry L. Lurie, "Summary of National Conference," *Social Service Review*, VIII (September, 1934), 552–53; Katharine F. Lenroot, "Social Work and the Social Order," in *Proceedings, 1935*, pp. 25–37; Elizabeth Magee, "Opportunities for Social Workers To Participate in Social Legislation," in *Proceedings, 1935*, pp. 487–96; Monsignor Robert F. Keegan, "Democracy at the Crossroads," in *Proceedings, 1936*, pp. 7–26; Edith Abbott, "Public Welfare and Politics," *Social Service Review*, X (September, 1936), 395–412; Dorothy Kenyon, "Technique of Utilizing American Political Machinery To Secure Social Action," in *Proceedings, 1936*, pp. 412–20; Paul U. Kellogg, "Employment Planning," in *Proceedings, 1936*, pp. 454–69; Dorothy C. Kahn, "Social Action from the Viewpoint of Professional Organizations," in *Proceedings, 1940*, pp. 498–507; Audrey M. Hayden, "Organizing the Community for Social Action," in *Proceedings, 1942*, pp. 584–93.

reorientation of methods and goals, means and ends. The place of voluntary or private agencies had to be reassessed; the relevance of taxation policies to social welfare took on an importance never before evidenced; the field of welfare administration necessarily took on new significance as skilled executives were required to oversee gigantic welfare bureaus. Bigness of operation brought problems of control, of impersonality for which the past offered insufficient guidance. At times, so it seemed to many, the possibilities for either reform or individual assistance had become unmanageable. Life had become too complex, issues too involved, demand for specialization too intense. War and postwar confusions only added to the burdens of an already overburdened profession.

THE CRISIS OF SOCIAL POLICY IN THE POSTWAR WORLD

In this context, it became increasingly difficult to define the legitimate sphere and proper role of social work in social action. Certain long-standing forces persisted to retard the social-reform impulse. The growing demand for professional specialization in the service phases of welfare work made it difficult for the ordinary practitioner to see social problems whole. The understandable tendency of social workers was to place their loyalty to clients and to agency before concern for the general welfare of community or society, which often seemed entirely too general and abstract. The ambiguous position of public welfare workers, particularly under the Hatch Act, regarding criticism and amendment of programs which they themselves were delegated to administer was not conducive to independent political action; while the general reluctance of private agency boards or politicians to inaugurate, encourage, or even countenance new programs acted as a damper, particularly if they involved, as they usually did, enlarged contributions or increased taxation and changes in established routines and relationships.

The oft-times paralyzing consequences of objective, sober scholarship with its inclination to see things as they really are—complex and ambiguous—constituted still another cautionary force. The demise of Paul U. Kellogg's *Survey* magazine, for nearly a half-century the primary organ of information and exhortation in the field of social policy and reform, left a vacuum that no other publication could fill. When it ceased publication in 1952, the attachment of the profession as a whole to broad social action was irrevocably weakened. Then there was the widespread frustration of reform by public indifference and ignorance, and, of larger significance, one senses the recognition that some problems seemed to proliferate faster than society could possibly handle them: decay at the heart, sprawl at the periphery of modern urban complexes; pollution of water and air; delinquency and crime. Feelings of personal inadequacy, futility, and impotency marked leaders of other professions as well as social work. Here were problems so many, so diverse, so beyond control that one observer, Dr. Charlotte Babcock, a psychiatrist addressing a social work audience, could suggest that the advance from care to cure, prevention, and constructive measures was now being reversed. "How have we come upon such a situation," she cried out in 1951, "that we speak not of prevention and cure but of mitigation?"[22]

Above all else must certainly be listed the priority assigned to the one overriding anxiety of this present age—sheer survival of the human race—a concern before which marginal advances in the field of welfare often seemed irrelevant. To one group of social workers it seemed that men lived "in apprehension which feeds on itself, balancing between fear of annihilation and fear of threats to ideological values, of not surviving at all and of surviving with humanity lost."[23] A world divided against itself, a world in ferment and rebellion, a world in which everything not nailed down was coming loose; a nation shaken by fears and suspicions and frightful rumors of conspiracy hardly offered a climate hospitable to social criticism.

Or (let us be honest), perhaps it would be instructive still to listen to the incisive indictment made by an experienced leader, speaking a generation ago of the "timidity and indecision," the "uncertainty and confusion," the overlapping and duplication of effort that he saw typical of social work in the 1930's. Sidney Hollander's diagnosis of its sickness concluded: "hardening of the arteries, creeping paralysis, premature senility, heart failure (especially heart failure), sleeping sickness—almost everything except growing pains."[24]

Whatever the causes, those whose commitment was to social welfare as opposed to social work were uneasy with the apparent reluctance of professional leaders to press forward in the field of social policy. Why had not the guild been more aggressive in seeking decent housing, health insurance, and civil rights? Why did professional schools stress personal and family therapy to the neglect of "social administration" and "social research"? Why had sustained criticism of social security been left to economists and politicians? These were the pointed questions that Eveline M. Burns asked of the delegates to the Conference on Social Policy and Social Work Education in 1957.[25] Most of the delegates tended to agree with her diagnosis; and, if no explicit recommendations for correction were immediately forthcoming, there seemed to be general agreement on the need to introduce social-policy materials into every phase of the curriculum rather than to set up still another separate field of specialization.

Perhaps political action was too often identified with good, old-fashioned (and for its own generation entirely valid) direct action, of which the Conference platform of 1912 was a pure and perfect example. Social workers have labored in ways far less spectacular, but with no less efficacy, to push back environmental restraints in order that the welfare of the individual could better be served. May not a "short course" for probation officers or for judges of juvenile courts be a perfectly appropriate

---

[22] Charlotte G. Babcock, M.D., "The Social Worker in a World of Stress," *Social Service Review,* XXV (March, 1951), 1.

[23] *Challenge in Crisis* (four-page printed leaflet in observance of the Tenth Anniversary of the Council on Social Work Education [St. Louis: George Warren Brown School of Social Work of Washington University, 1962]).

[24] Sidney Hollander, "A Layman Takes Stock of Public and Private Agency Functions," *op. cit.,* p. 181.

[25] The conference at Arden House was sponsored by the New York School of Social Work, and its "Papers and Proceedings" were made available in mimeographed form. Mrs. Burns's remarks can be found in the Introduction, pp. 1–7, and in her paper, "Social Policy and Social Work Education," pp. 54–79.

form of social action? Where is one to draw the line between political action and individualized service?

Take the Urban League, for example. It engages in many service-oriented functions for non-whites: individual and group counseling for young people to stimulate and assist them in career selection; educational encouragement and scholarship aid (the Tomorrow's Scientists and Technicians program); information and assistance to individuals and families in solving problems of adjustment in the community and problems of financial assistance, family disorganization, and discrimination. But it has its political-action programs as well—expert testimony on fair employment and open-occupancy ordinances, and public-information campaigns designed to break down discrimination in employment and housing and to promote neighborhood betterment and urban renewal.[26] Is it possible to distinguish sharply between service on the one hand and political action on the other? I think not. At least it can be said that the various programs of this social agency are mutually supportive and not in any way competitive. Every institution requires both its priests and its prophets, clerical and lay, professional and amateur.

THE INTERACTION OF SOCIAL SERVICE AND SOCIAL POLICY

If I read correctly the discussion of these matters over the past ten or fifteen years, it appears that social work at its best has clearly comprehended what are called the "psychosocial" factors of human existence, taking the in-

ternal and the external together as one organic (if not harmonious) whole, providing services where needed, and working for "those changes in our social institutions which will reduce social dislocations and make possible healthier and more constructive relations."[27]

So the advice runs from one division of social work to another. Fern Lowry, summing up current concepts in social casework practice nearly a quarter of a century ago, defined her field as "nothing more or less than a method of helping individuals to meet such needs as are derived from the impoverishment of the environment or the limitations of individual capacity." The caseworker had necessarily to begin with the individual client in his given setting and could not afford to "dissipate energy" in frustrating attempts to change the environment, but clearly caseworkers had "an obligation to direct some . . . efforts toward the elimination of elements inimical to the best interests of the individual."[28] Even Mary Richmond, a generation earlier, had clearly seen the relevance of both social reform and individual treatment to effective casework practice.[29]

[26] This description is from a letter of Ernest C. Cooper, executive director of the St. Paul Urban League, dated January 4, 1961.

[27] Grace L. Coyle, "The Social Worker and His Society," *Social Service Review*, XXX (December, 1956), 395.

[28] Fern Lowry, "Current Concepts in Social Case-Work Practice," *Social Service Review*, XII (September, 1938), 370. Also see: Gordon Hamilton, "The Role of Social Casework in Social Policy," *Selected Papers in Casework* (New York: National Conference of Social Work, 1952), pp. 66–83; Marjorie L. Smith and Eileen Younghusband, "Exporting Casework to Europe," *Education for Social Work, 1953,* (New York: Council on Social Work Education, 1953), pp. 86–94; "Notes and Comment," on the death of James Mullenbach, *Social Service Review*, IX (June, 1935), 313–14, which include his observation that "the natural effect of good social case work is to reveal the need of social justice."

[29] Muriel Pumphrey, "Mary E. Richmond—The

Group work, too, while stressing the interpersonal relations, was from the beginning dedicated to both "socialization of individuals and . . . improving the quality of social relations."[30] From their earliest days over seventy years ago down to the present moment, the settlements have combined both phases, not always in perfect equilibrium and sometimes in tension and with varying emphases: "to be of service to the people in their neighborhoods, and . . . to change those conditions which made life in slum areas a bitter and squalid experience."[31] The service functions covered every possible line of activity—education, recreation, arts and crafts, drama, personal hygiene and public health, family relations; while settlement leaders were in the vanguard of every major reform movement in the twentieth century—industrial and labor reform in the Progressive Era, social security and housing reform in the interwar era, and, most recently, community attacks on juvenile delinquency and urban blight.

In the field of community organization the most casual glance at the literature suggests its dual concern with

both service and reform.[32] The social work historians and philosophers Karl de Schweinetz and Gisela Konopka have followed both lines during their varied careers.[33] So did many social work educators—Helen R. Wright, for example, who proclaimed the guild's dual responsibility for efficient, competent service to client and community and "for social action or social reform, for community planning, in short for creating or helping create conditions that make good service possible, or, even better, that obviate the need of such services."[34]

Even psychiatric social work occasionally became fatigued with the introspective quality of its concern with

---

Practitioner," *Social Casework,* XLII (October, 1961), 375–85, and Charlotte Towle, "Social Work: Cause and Function, 1961," in *Social Casework,* XLII (October, 1961), 385–97.

[30] Clara Kaiser, "Group Work Education in the Last Decade," in *Group Work: Foundations and Frontiers,* ed. Harleigh B. Trecker (New York: Whiteside, Inc., 1955), p. 356. In the same anthology, see the contributions of Helen Northen, "The Place of Agency Structure, Philosophy, and Policy in Supporting Group Programs of Social Action," pp. 236–47, and Lucy P. Carner, "Assignment in Social Action" (the report of a national committee of the American Association of Group Workers), pp. 247–56.

[31] Grace L. Coyle, "The Great Tradition and the New Challenge," *Social Service Review,* XXXV (March, 1961), 6.

[32] See, for example, Violet M. Sieder, "The Community Welfare Council and Social Action," in *Proceedings, 1950,* Part II: *Selected Papers,* pp. 22–41. For an early symposium on community and individual factors in juvenile delinquency, see Louis McGuire and John Slawson, "Social Work Basis for Prevention and Treatment of Delinquency and Crime: Community Factors . . . Individual Factors," in *Proceedings, 1936,* pp. 579–99. The dedication of the *Social Service Review* under all its editors was to both service and reform and to the need of social workers to acquire "a broad intellectual grasp of basic social issues" (Wayne McMillen, "The First Twenty-six Years of the *Social Service Review,"* *Social Service Review,* XXVII [March, 1953], 1–14). Nathan E. Cohen's "Revising the Process of Social Disorganization," in Kahn, *op. cit.,* pp. 138–58, is a recent criticism of the elevation of social work over social welfare.

[33] See especially Karl de Schweinitz, "Social Values and Social Action—The Intellectual Base as Illustrated in the Study of History," in *Education for Social Work, 1956,* pp. 55–68; for a good summary of her point of view, see Gisela Konopka, who spoke for herself as well as for the subject of her biography, when she insisted that social work must seek "to help individuals in the framework of existing conditions as well as to help change social institutions" and to lift the burden of oppressive institutions (*Eduard C. Lindeman and Social Work Philosophy* [Minneapolis: University of Minnesota Press, 1958], pp. 194–99).

[34] Helen R. Wright, "Social Work Education and Social Responsibility," in *Education for Social Work, 1954,* p. 15.

intrapersonal and interpersonal hanky-panky. At least, one catches a glimpse of good-natured despair in a commentary on the news item, recorded in 1954, that a course in interpersonal communication through music therapy was to be inaugurated jointly by the New England Conservatory of Music and the Boston State Hospital. The reader was asked to contemplate the psychiatric social worker and his interpersonal communication: "He must relate to the psychiatrist, the psychologist, the physiatric nurse, the group therapist, the occupational therapist, the psychotherapist, the bibliotherapist, the psychodramatist. . . . And now the music therapist. Well—music hath charms—welcome to the Team!"[35] Within the psychiatric field of service, as within its other branches, social work operated "variously to reform, to restore, and to reinforce human powers and human institutions."[36]

It may have been the recognition of the increasing complexity of "psychosocial" events that turned social work statesmen, time and again over the past generation of crisis, to a consideration of the guild's dual commitment to service and action. The more skilled and sophisticated research and practice became, the faster both dimensions of experience, the internal and the external, got out of hand. So it seemed. And so social work suffered the ironic dilemma of the nation itself—the greater its ap-

parent powers, the larger its frustrations! Together with these worries has gone a constant concern for the revitalization of democratic and humane values and the elaboration of means appropriate to these goals.[37]

Kenneth L. M. Pray explored the issues in a series of papers delivered toward the end of World War II and the beginning of uneasy and precarious peace. Professional social work, in his view, could not jeopardize its service responsibilities by indiscriminate and undisciplined action, but neither could it avoid the obligation "to apply its knowledge and skill to the end of adjusting social institutions and arrangements to the needs of human beings" while at the same time "helping people find the utmost of satisfaction and achievement within the social circumstances that surround them." The two functions could never arbitrarily be separated. Indeed, in the very process of offering individual service, the client could be led "to discover and release strength and energy," which in concert with others might voluntarily be channeled toward the promotion of desirable so-

---

[35] H. H. P., in "Notes and Comment," *Social Service Review*, XXVIII (September, 1954), 332.

[36] Perlman, "Freud's Contribution to Social Welfare," *op. cit.*, p. 193; Lloyd E. Ohlin, "The Development of Social Action Theories in Social Work," in *Education for Social Work, 1958*, pp. 77–87; Preface to *Proceedings, 1950*, Part I, pp. vii–viii.

[37] Social work statesmen have always been so engaged, of course, but in an age of depression, war, and revolution the problem became more acute. A prescient sense of the changes that were coming and the challenges they would entail can be seen, for example, in Coyle, "Social Work at the Turn of the Decade," *op. cit.*, and in Hawkins, *op. cit.* See also, by way of illustration, Marshall E. Dimock, "The Inner Substance of a Progressive," *Social Service Review*, XIII (December, 1939), 573–78; John A. Fitch, "The Nature of Social Action," in *Proceedings, 1940*, pp. 485–97; Marion Hathaway, "Social Action and Professional Education," in *Proceedings, 1944*, pp. 363–73; Chester I. Barnard, "A Nonprofessional View of the Opportunities and Mission of Social Work," in *Proceedings, 1943*, pp. 6–14; Leonard W. Mayo, "The Future for Social Work," in *Proceedings, 1944*, pp. 25–34.

cial change. Beyond that, social workers must testify publicly to their knowledge of needs and their satisfaction. No one expected that social work should come forward with detailed blueprints for social reconstruction. The profession after all was no more omnicompetent than those others with which it strove for the broadening of welfare; but there was no area of life for which some division was not competent to offer constructive advice on social policy, whether in "health, work, play, education, . . . family life, parenthood, [or] childhood." In serving individual welfare and in working for the "progressive improvement" of community life, social work was obliged to use democratic means, to work through voluntary rather than coercive actions, to seek self-determination and co-operation which were marks of an open society.[38]

Many others took up the challenge, and what may have begun as a debate soon evolved into a consensus. The social worker had a responsibility as a citizen and as a professional person, not only to join with others in support of welfare measures, but to seize the initiative in seeking the elimination of specific social ills. Whether they were acting in a service or a reform capacity, social workers were not to manipulate but to assist others in appraising alternative courses and choosing constructively from among them. Together they worked through "practice and policy, psychological individualization and so-

cial reform, improvement of social conditions, direct rendering of services and broader programs of prevention, personal therapy and social leadership."[39] In 1957, the National Conference, having earlier passed beyond "charities and correction," left behind its more prosaic and professional reference to "social work," and dedicated itself to "social welfare," while the bylaws of the National Association of Social Workers stated the profession's dual obligation to use its professional skill both "by social work methods and by social action" to alleviate or prevent "deprivation, distress and strain." Thus social work aimed at "a better ordering of our basic social institutions and the widening of opportunities of all to contribute to the utmost of their capacity." To these ends, delegates to the 1958 Delegate Assembly of NASW concluded, professional social work labored under the responsibility of identifying, analyzing, and interpreting social needs; of advancing standards against which the validity of public policies could be

[38] Quotations in the above passage are, in order, from Kenneth L. M. Pray, "Social Work and Social Action," in *Proceedings, 1945*, pp. 349, 354, 352; "Social Work in a Revolutionary Age," in *Proceedings, 1946*, p. 10. See also his piece, "Social Workers and Partisan Politics," *Compass*, XXVI (June, 1945), 3–6.

[39] Schottland, "Social Work in the 1960's," *op. cit.*, p. 39. See also Ellen C. Potter, "The Year of Decision for Social Work," *Social Service Review*, XIX (September, 1945), 297–309; Benjamin Youngdahl, "Social Workers: Stand Up and Be Counted," *Compass*, XXVIII (March, 1947), 21–24; Eveline M. Burns, "Social Action and the Professional Social Worker," *Compass*, XXVIII (May, 1947), 37–40; Donald S. Howard, "New Horizons for Social Work," *Compass*, XXVIII (November, 1947), 9–13, 28; Hertha Kraus, "The Future of Social Work: Some Comments on Social Work Function," *Social Work Journal*, XXIX (January, 1948), 3–9; Arthur J. Altmeyer, "Social Work and Broad Social and Economic Measures," in *Proceedings, 1948*, pp. 101–12; Jane Hoey, "Human Rights and Social Work," in *Proceedings, 1949*, Part II: *Social Work in the Current Scene*, pp. 3–9; Charles I. Schottland, "Social Work Issues in the Political Arena," in *Forum, 1953*, pp. 18–33; Grace L. Coyle, "The Social Worker and His Society," *Social Service Review*, XXX (December, 1956), 387–99.

measured; and of applying its special techniques and competence toward the orderly solution of complex social problems.[40]

Most practitioners were necessarily and properly engaged in service functions, but upon the profession as a whole and upon its leaders and prophets rested the responsibility to work unceasingly and imaginatively for the general welfare. The problem was to discover, by research and in practice, new means of meeting the dual obligation to person and to society. If the prophetic role was no longer a simple or a lonely one, all the more need to elaborate sophisticated insights and novel tactics and strategies, all the greater the need to illuminate its philosophic premises which Leonard Mayo listed as: "our concern for people; our respect for the dignity, integrity, and rights of individuals; our abhorrence of injustice as one of the greatest foes of freedom; our responsibility to speak and act with respect to the causes as well as the results of social maladjustment; and our major concern, not only for prevention, restoration, and rehabilitation, but for helping to create relationships, homes, neighborhoods, and nations in which human beings may live out their lives and develop their full potentials as free people."[41]

Certainly there was no shortage of work to be done; an affluent society was as rich in problems as in material plenty: urban congestion and sprawl; juvenile delinquency; pockets of poverty and a hard, irreducible core of unemployment; racial tension and animosity; substandard housing; crowded schools; asphalt jungles; mayhem on the highway; murder on the playground; national parks turned into littered tent slums; polluted streams; smog-palled cities; costs of health care rising faster than the meager resources of the aged could afford; a vast disparity between wealthy nations and deprived nations, the latter advancing faster in population than in the production of necessities.

Social work did not possess ultimately valid answers to all these problems; no one did. But upon the profession—as upon all citizens—rested the responsibility of working toward solutions of partial efficacy at least. And social welfare stood in a long tradition of service and action from which it could draw insight and inspiration for the harder tasks that lay ahead.

Received March 15, 1962

[40] Eveline M. Burns, "Social Welfare Is Our Commitment," in *Forum, 1958,* pp. 3–19; National Association of Social Workers, *Goals of Public Social Policy* (New York: Delegate Assembly of NASW. May, 1958), pp. 5, 11–13.

[41] Leonard W. Mayo, "Basic Issues in Social Work," in *Proceedings, 1948,* p. 24.

PART II

Social Welfare in Colonial Times and the Early National Period: Introduction

The articles in this section deal with social welfare developments in the colonies of British North America during the seventeenth and eighteenth centuries and in the United States prior to the Civil War. Although industrialization and the factory system did not begin to take hold in North America until the last three decades of this period, towns and cities played a vital role in the mercantile economy of British America from the start. In 1820, the United States contained thirteen cities with populations of 10,000 or more and by 1860 there were ninety-three such cities, including nine with populations of at least 100,000. These developments seem modest by comparison to the growth of massive industrial cities later on, and by 1860 the United States was still a predominantly rural society. Prior to the 1860s, social welfare services consisted primarily of the operation of the local poor law plus some little aid to selected disadvantaged persons by small, locally supported private and religious charitable organizations. This social welfare system suited the predominantly rural character of American life before the Civil War, although it proved grossly inadequate in the cities, where poverty and vagrancy were serious social problems almost from the start.

The early colonization of North America by the British and the development of the poor law in England were products of the same social and economic changes. As the feudal social and economic system with its emphasis on local government and reciprocal rights and duties and its concentration on subsistence agriculture broke down, people moved from farms not only to manufacturing centers but also to colonies abroad. If the development of poor laws can be considered an adequate criterion of such social dislocation, certainly by the middle of the sixteenth century there must have been a sizable number of families who were unable to obtain a satisfactory living on the land of their ancestors.

Although the first of the Tudor Poor Laws, enacted in 1531, did little more than declare idleness to be "the Mother and Root of all evil" and require that beggers be certified, it was a clear sign that the old order was passing and that modern society with its emphasis upon isolated individuals and their mobility must make some provision for those no longer able to depend upon their extended family and no longer legally attached to the land. The poor laws were amended regularly as the indigent became more numerous and moved about the countryside and from village to city seeking sustenance. Finally, in the year 1601, all the statutes of the previous seventy years were codified and brought together in the form generally designated as the Elizabethan Poor Laws.

That codification of 1601 became the basis for the poor law that continued in England until after World War II and which remains the basis of state and local public assistance programs in the United States until this day. The main principles of that legislation, which have guided the development of social welfare in the United States as well as in Britain and in other English-speaking nations, were as follows:

Necessary funds must be raised by taxation;

The smallest governmental subdivision, the parish, must be responsible for its administration;

Able-bodied persons with no means of support must be given jobs, not relief;

Poor children must be bound out as apprentices;

Children, parents, and grandparents must be mutually responsible for each other's support.

Clearly, then, the Elizabethan Poor Laws provided an unambiguous statement to the effect that responsibility for the poor belonged to the state, not to private charity or to the church, and that poor relief should be administered by the smallest and most local unit of government. The latter prescription, of course, raised fears in the more wealthy parishes that they might be asked to support the poor from other places. So, sixty years later, the Act of Settlement was passed that established severe and rigid residence requirements as one of many conditions for receiving aid. At the very time when the needs of the economy were causing people to move, the poor law, as it has done so often since that time, was trying to move the poor back to their feudal starting point.

The first permanent English settlement in North America was established just six years after the final Elizabethan statute was enacted. Since some form of the poor law had been operating throughout England since the middle of the previous century, all adults among the colonists must have had experience with its administration. However, since most of the leaders, in New England at least, were not members of the established church, they probably had not served as wardens of their parish or as overseers of the poor. On the other hand, many of the indentured servants and bonded workers undoubtedly had been recipients of poor relief in earlier years, and some of the apprenticeships may have been arranged by poor law authorities. In any case, the poor law was a familiar institution. When the need for such legislation arose in the colonies, the statute of Elizabeth was unwrapped and became the basis of all future social welfare developments.

One may wonder why a poor law was needed in the New World and, especially, why a poor law that was appropriate for a nation struggling to wrench itself from feudalism was considered suitable for scattered agricultural settlements and commercial towns along the eastern seaboard of what was to become the United States. Excess population certainly posed no problem. As David M. Schneider points out in his article, the whole colony of New York had a population of less than 12,000 when surrendered by the Dutch in 1664; by 1771 there were fewer than 170,000. Of these the number receiving poor relief during the eighteenth century, at least, was miniscule. But the colonists must have found the poor law to be a useful item in their statute books. The small, struggling localities of the seventeenth century had little food, clothing, and shelter to spare. Yet most of the colonists were religious men and willing to care for those in need who belonged to their community. Since in the seventeenth century there were probably few large accumulations of wealth among the colonists, private charity could not be depended upon. So the Elizabethan Poor Law with its compulsory rate on all householders was just what they needed. In addition, they must have welcomed the emphasis on required work and settlement provisions that assured the colonists they would care only for their own.

The first four articles in this section provide some details concerning the way in which poor relief and other social provisions were administered in colonial America. There is one article dealing with colonial Virginia and one with New England, since each major geographical area had some distinct problems and solutions. Those two articles are followed by two that concentrate on developments during the eighteenth and early nineteenth centuries, one dealing with New York and one with Massachusetts.

The first colony to be settled adopted not only the philosophy of the Elizabethan Poor Law but also its method of administration. Marcus W. Jernegan points out, in "The Development of Poor Relief in Colonial Virginia," that the colony, having been settled by members of the established church, adopted the English parish system. This involved governance by a vestry of twelve men who carried out the poor laws and in general cared for the religious, moral, and charitable affairs of the parish. The great numbers of orphans and illegitimate children and the prevalence of slaves and bonded workers concerned the vestrymen throughout the seventeenth century. In light of later disputes as to the form poor relief should take, the early proposals to build almshouses are of particular interest. The most common form of poor relief in Virginia was payment to a relative, friend, or neighbor of the indigent person.

Elizabeth Wisner in "The Puritan Background of the New England Poor Laws" reiterates the importance of public relief and the poor laws. She learned that there were many small private charities and mutual aid arrangements in New England, but they could not begin to cope with the need caused by such scourges as small pox and scarlet fever and the necessity for long-term care of the aged, disabled, and mentally ill. She also highlights the means employed to keep "undesirables" and potential indigents out of the colonies, showing the development of restrictions on mobility much like the English Act of Settlement.

From colonial times through the first quarter of the nineteenth century, the mainstream of social welfare development emphasized the care of indigent individuals in private homes, aided by funds granted by parish vestries or township overseers. As is apparent from the next two articles of this section, while the colonies frequently toyed with the idea of centralizing care for the poor in some sort of almshouse, little was done in that direction. After about 1815, however, both Englishmen and Americans began vigorously debating this issue. In England, the rising middle class believed locally controlled relief and wage supplementation in the recipient's home to be an extravagance and invitation to idleness. The 1834 English Poor Law Reform both centralized administration and required all recipients of public aid to submit to the degradation of having to live in a workhouse. The importance of the issue in America is apparent from Schneider's article, which describes the hiring of houses for the poor in Southhampton and New York City, and from Eleanor Parkhurst's, which reports the activities of a local commission in Chelmsford that was appointed to investigate the advantages and disadvantages of almshouse care.

The developments in Chelmsford that Parkhurst relates were part of a statewide, even national, movement. That town's commission must have been influenced by the 1821 Report on the Pauper Laws of Massachusetts by Josiah Quincy who apparently was in close touch with the events in Great Britain. The first two findings of the Quincy report were as follows: (1) That of all the modes of providing for the poor, the most wasteful, the most expensive, and the most injurious to their morals and destructive to their industrious habits is that of supply in their own homes. (2) That the most economical mode is that of almshouses having the character of workhouses or houses of industry, in which work is provided for every degree of ability in the pauper, and thus the able poor are made to provide, partially at least, for their own support and also to the support or, at least, the comfort of the impotent poor.

Similar recommendations were made in the 1823 report of New York's Secretary of State, J. V. N. Yates. He found that, in fact, few paupers were provided for in their own homes or in almshouses. Instead, the usual way of caring for them at that time was either by "farming them out" to contractors for stipulated prices or by auctioning them to those who would support them at the lowest cost. Considering that system to be both cruel to recipients and a waste of tax revenues, Yates recommended that an almshouse be established in each county and that all "outdoor relief" be discontinued. The Yates and Quincy reports, together with other state and local studies, such as that at Chelmsford, had a lasting effect on poor law administration. Benjamin J. Klebaner in "Poverty and Its Relief in American Thought, 1815–61" documents the poor law debate in which those reports were significant elements. Considering the virulence of the attack on the poor law by some influential persons, it is surprising that they were not entirely eliminated, as the disciples of Malthus urged. The debate, however, did open the variety of poor law practices to public view. In many instances, they were replaced by more uniform methods of administration centering on the almshouse in the public sphere and on organized charitable societies in the private domain.

Private charitable organizations, which were such important agents of social welfare services in the late nineteenth and early twentieth centuries, appeared first during the early days of the republic, and it was then that the principles of what later to be called "scientific philanthropy" were developed. The best known private charitable organizations of the period were the Associations for Improving the Condition of the Poor (AICP), which could be found in most large cities. The first one was founded in New York City in 1843. But there were many large and small charitable organizations operating long before then. Mary Bosworth Treudly in "The Benevolent Fair" discusses the role of women in setting up the many charitable societies that were a feature of towns large and small in early nineteenth-century America. They did not try to deal with the broad problems of general poverty but specialized instead in such areas as aid to widows with small children and "employing the female poor." Men, especially members of the clergy, also had a hand in setting up small charitable organizations with specialized aims. This is illustrated by Negley K. Teeter's article on the Magdalen Society. Its founders in Philadelphia were interested only in "unhappy females who have lost their virtue."

Two minor exceptions and an attempt at a major one served to prove the rule that responsibility for social welfare lay primarily with local poor relief authorities and organized private charities. The exceptions are reported in the last two articles of this section. The grants of public lands to Connecticut and Kentucky to help establish schools for the deaf and mute, as reported by Walter I. Trattner, were quite discreet events and did not serve as precedents for other national action. The fact that Congress drew back when requested to make similar grants to other states illustrates the narrow concept it had of its jurisdiction. That restricted view of the role of the national government was reinforced by President's Pierce's veto of the bill proposed by Dorothea Dix which would have made land grants to the states to help with the construction of institutions for the insane. Those episodes prove how strong the local-private tradition was, but they also indicate that the states had begun to take some responsibility for the mentally ill and some other disabled groups, and they provide some information about how the role of the federal government was conceived.

Whether, as Seaton W. Manning suggests, federal grants to the states would have come earlier if the charity workers and social reformers had agitated the cause of the mentally ill during the first Lincoln administration, is anyone's guess. Now, of course, Congress regularly grants funds to private agencies such as the Kentucky school. Our elaborate system of federal grants for mental health began after World War II. Unlike the wishes of Dorothea Dix, however, federal policy at present is to encourage the tearing down rather than the building up of state asylums. Considering recent complaints about the multiplication of "categorical grants," it was perhaps, fortunate that the federal government did not get started before the Civil War.

The articles that follow provide rich details which elaborate on the major themes of development outlined above. Prior to the Civil War, social welfare policy for preindustrial America concentrated on adjusting the poor laws of England to the requirements of both the new and mature settlements. The emphasis, as always, was on making sure that only the "deserving" received aid. Private agencies had their beginnings at this time but were of minor importance when compared with the large influential agencies discussed in Section III. Almshouses, rather than home relief, became the predominant method of providing for the needy.

The student of social welfare history must remember that the importance of the developments discussed above is not limited to the states and localities on which the articles concentrate. Just as the colonists brought the poor law with them from England, so the pioneers and settlers heading for the Midwest and on to the Far West brought along the poor law of their home towns. And so poor relief law and custom spread and developed a remarkable uniformity throughout the nation. It was replaced and augmented only gradually by the developments described in Section III. The English poor law was designed for an economy that was primarily agricultural, as was that of the United States until after the Civil War. But even in today's industrial society, remnants of the old poor law may be found at the core of such programs as Aid to Families with Dependent Children and General Assistance.

THE DEVELOPMENT OF POOR RELIEF IN COLONIAL VIRGINIA

I T IS well known that the humanitarian movement in the second quarter of the nineteenth century was one of the important social effects of the industrial revolution. That great outpouring of human sympathy for the unfortunate elements of society—the poor, defectives, sick, and other unfortunates—continues to bear fruit on an ever increasing scale. Never in the world's history have such unprecedented amounts of money been granted by private and public agencies to alleviate human suffering. While the modern historical development of this movement is well known, the colonial background of one phase, poor relief in America, is not so familiar. It is, therefore, proposed in this article to discuss some of the conditions that confronted colonial Virginia,[1] and the public agencies devised to solve problems of this character.

For the historical background of poor relief in Virginia one needs to call to mind important English economic and social changes in the sixteenth century.[2] With the expansion of England's foreign trade and increased demand abroad for woolen cloth, sheep-raising

[1] For economic and social conditions in Virginia consult P. A. Bruce, *Economic History of Virginia in the Seventeenth Century* (2 vols. New York, 1896), and *Institutional History of Virginia in the Seventeenth Century* (2 vols., New York, 1910).

[2] E. P. Cheyney, *Social Changes in England in the Sixteenth Century;* A. P. Usher, *Introduction to the Industrial and Social History of England.*

Social Service Review 3 (March 1929): 1–18

was stimulated. This was the important reason for the enclosure movement,[1] the fencing in of open fields for grazing, and in consequence the decline of an agricultural economy to pasture farming. There followed a surplus of unemployed agricultural laborers, for a few herders took the place of many farm laborers. Thus the number of unemployed and poor persons had been on the increase for a long period before American colonization began. In fact, at this date, 1607, relief of the poor was one of the most pressing questions of the day. Not only the unemployed but also the vagabonds, rogues, beggars, paupers, and the criminal classes increased rapidly.[2] Wages of farm laborers fell as low as a shilling a day, while rents and prices rose several fold.[3]

Previous to the confiscation of the church property by Henry VIII there had been little legislation with respect to the poor, for the guilds and monasteries had been active in poor relief.[4] With the confiscation of the main sources of supply, poor-relief legislation increased. Thus an act of Edward VI instructs collectors "to gently ask and demand of every man and woman what they of their charity will give weekly towards relief of the poor."[5]

The important act of 1562,[6] the Statute of Artificers, attempted to solve many of the problems mentioned above and others such as the wages and hours of labor, the checking of enclosures, the fixing of prices, unemployment, pauperism, and apprenticeship as a system for national welfare. Migrations from the rural districts to the towns, due to the conversion of arable to grazing land, led a contemporary preacher to lament thus:[7] "O, Merciful Lord! What a

[1] Harriett Bradley, "The Enclosure of Open Fields England," in *Columbia Studies in History*, Vol. LXXX.

[2] C. J. Ribton-Turner, *A History of Vagrants and Vagrancy and Beggars and Begging;* Frank Aydelotte, *English Rogues and Vagabonds.*

[3] J. E. T. Rogers, *History of Agriculture and Prices in England, 1259–1793,* 7 vols.

[4] E. M. Leonard, *The Early History of English Poor Relief;* Sir George Nicholls, *A History of the English Poor Laws,* 3 vols.

[5] 5 and 6 Edw. VI, c. 2. See also 5 Eliz., c. 3 "An Act for the relief of the Poor"; also in G. W. Prothero, *Select Statutes and Other Constitutional Documents,* pp. 41–45.

[6] 5 Eliz., c. 4. See also in Prothero, *Select Statutes,* pp. 45–54. Cf. J. F. Scott, *Historical Essays on Apprenticeship,* etc., chap. iii, "The Statute of Artificers"; O. J. Dunlop and R. D. Denman, *English Apprenticeship and Child Labour.*

[7] Scott, *op. cit.* p. 27.

number of poor, feeble, halt, blind, lame, sickly, yea with idle vagabonds, and dissembling catiffs mixed among them, lie and creep begging in the miry streets of London and Westminster." This movement was not to the liking of the craft guilds and town artisans, who wished to protect their calling from an oversupply of labor. In the country districts conditions were almost as bad. Sir Thomas More in his *Utopia*[1] (written in 1515) complains that sheep from being meek and tame now "consume, destroy, and devour whole fields, houses and cities"; that the husbandmen were forced out of their homes, or compelled to sell all for almost nothing and to depart away, poor, seyle [innocent], wretched fools, men, women, husbands, wives, fatherless children, widows, woeful mothers, with their young babes . . . . out of their known and accustomed houses, finding no place to rest in. . . . . And when they have wandered abroad . . . . what can they else do but steal, ... or else go about a begging. And yet then also they be cast in prison as vagabonds, because they go about and work not: whom no man will set to work, though they never so willingly profer themselves thereto."

The Statute of Artificers attempted to fix wages and hours of labor and, through the system of apprenticeship, raise the standard of skill in the industrial arts. But more than this it tried to solve the problem of pauperism and vagabondage by placing the worker of the nation in the occupation for which he was best suited. It dealt with the able-bodied poor not by giving alms but by forcing them to work, and through the apprenticeship clauses provided for children. Persons not otherwise employed between 12 and 60 were ordered to be servants in husbandry. Youths who refused to serve as apprentices might be imprisoned. Another clause forbade anyone below the rank of a yeoman to withdraw from an agricultural pursuit in order to be apprenticed to a trade. This doomed the farm laborer to his calling notwithstanding the scarcity of work.

The poor, however, increased, and in 1601 was passed the great Poor Law Act, which emphasized the system of apprenticing poor children. It attempted to "provide work for those who could work, relief for those who could not, and punishment for those who would not."[2] The Act of 1601 provided that overseers of the poor should

---

[1] *Utopia*, ed. Edward Arber (1869), p. 40.

[2] W. Cunningham, *The Growth of English Industry and Commerce*, II, 61.

be nominated for each parish by the justices, with the addition of the church wardens and several householders. Their duty was to set children to work whose parents were unable to maintain them, to raise by taxation sums necessary, and to place out poor children as apprentices. The desire to find someone to maintain the child rather than to teach him a trade was the important feature of this act.[1]

With this English background in mind, let us now turn to colonial Virginia. It will be found that those elements of society needing poor relief, as well as the agencies devised to support and administer funds for this purpose, were closely related to the conditions in England. As early as 1574 Sir Humphrey Gilbert declared:

> We might inhabit some part of those Countreyes (America) and settle there such needy people of our countrey which now trouble the commonwealth and through want here at home are enforced to commit outrageous offences, whereby they are dayly consumed with the gallows.[2]

Richard Hakluyt in his *Discourse on Western Planting* (1584) declared that many thousand of idle persons in England were without work,

> very burdensome to the commonwealthe, and often fall to pilferinge and thevinge and other lewdness, whereby all the prisons of the lande are daily stuffed full of them . . . . these pety thieves might be condempned for certen yeres in the westerne partes, especially in Newfounde lande, and set to work.[3]

So Velasco, the Spanish minister to England, wrote in 1611, "Their principal reason for colonizing these parts is to give an outlet to so many idle, wretched people as they have in England, and thus to prevent the dangers that might be feared of them."[4]

Those elements of Virginia society[5] that made a system of poor relief necessary may be described as follows. The chief dependence for a supply of labor in the seventeenth century was this large body of unemployed in England—the poor, paupers, vagabonds, and con-

---

[1] 43 Eliz. c. 2, also in Prothero, *Select Documents*, pp. 103–5. See p. 2, n. 4, and H. D. Traill, *Social England*, Vol. IV, chap. xiii, on "Pauperism, 1603–1642."

[2] The "Discourse" is in the *Publications of the Prince Society* (1903), p. 86.

[3] Hakluyt's "Discourse on Western Planting" (1584), *Maine Historical Society Collections*, II, 37.

[4] Alexander Brown, *The Genesis of the United States*, I, 456.

[5] See p. 1, n. 1.

victs, who were transported to Virginia mainly through the agency of the indentured servant system. In the eighteenth century the chief dependence was the Negro slave, though many indentured servants continued to arrive.[1] The children of the servant class and the freed servant, legitimate and illegitimate, were one important element of society calling for poor relief. Besides the presence of these two classes, many of the free whites who had descended from the poorer elements of the white servant class became objects of charity. There were complaints from an early date of "vagrant, idle, and dissolute persons."[2] Such persons often became the fathers of illegitimate children by both free white and white servant women. If they ran away, as frequently happened, their children were thrown on the parish for support. Such persons also often deserted their wives and children.[3]

Another class was made up of free Negroes and mulatto servants.[4] The latter, born of a free white mother or white servant, were indentured as servants and after a long period of service became free Negroes. Of course, there were other unfortunates, such as the defectives, the sick, idiots, etc. All these classes of society called for poor relief. In general, then, Virginia was confronted with a great problem, as in England, namely, how to protect the parish from a large number of paupers, and how to provide work in order to reduce idleness and unemployment on the one hand and on the other to train workers for the needs of a growing colony.

The machinery for administering poor relief was ready at hand —the English parish system, reproduced in Virginia.[5] The counties were laid off in Virginia in 1634 and in 1641 divided into parishes.[6]

[1] J. C. Ballagh, "White Servitude in the Colony of Virginia," *Johns Hopkins University Studies*, Series XIII, and "A History of Slavery in Virginia," in *Johns Hopkins University Studies*, extra Vol. XXIV; J. D. Butler, "British Convicts Shipped to American Colonies," in *American Historical Review*, II, 12–34. See also above, p. 1, n. 1.

[2] Hening, *Statutes of Virginia*, II, 248.   [3] *Ibid.*, IV, 208–12.

[4] J. H. Russell, "The Free Negro in Virginia, 1619–1895," in *Johns Hopkins University Studies*, Series XXXI.

[5] S. L. Ware, "The Elizabethan Parish in Its Ecclesiastical and Financial Aspects," in *Johns Hopkins University Studies*, Series XXVI; P. A. Bruce, *Institutional History of Virginia* I, chaps. vi–ix (Parish, Vestry, Church Wardens).

[6] Hening, I, 224, 433.

The governing body of the parish was the vestry, a group of twelve men,[1] after 1676 chosen by the freeholders,[2] whose duty it was to levy and collect parish tithes; appoint clergymen; investigate cases of immorality and disorder; administer the poor laws; and, in general, care for the religious, moral, and charitable affairs of the parish. The executive arm of the vestry was the church wardens, whose duty it was to administer the business of the parish, and present cases needing the attention of the vestry.[3]

While George Washington was for years a vestryman of Truro Parish, and while as a rule it was expected that the vestrymen should be "the most able and discreet persons of their Parish,"[4] not all vestrymen measured up to this high standard. The Assembly dissolved the vestry of Suffolk in Nansemond County because of "several unwarrantable practices in the misapplication of divers charitable donations given for the use of the poor of the said parish known by the name of the Lower Parish."[5]

Owing to the organization of new counties and parishes, due to the westward movement of population, and to the division of counties and parishes because of the increase of population, the number of parishes increased throughout the Colonial period. In 1722, there were 29 counties and 54 parishes.[6] In 1774 there were 62 counties and 95 parishes.[7]

The vestries of these parishes acted under general and special laws governing the care of the poor. Those having to do with the system of apprenticeship were designed to protect the parish from maintaining a large number of poor and illegitimate children; to reduce idleness and unemployment, and to stimulate the development of an artisan class skilled in the trades. In these acts there was also the notion of improving the religious, moral, and educational status of poor children.

[1] *Ibid.*, II, 25.   [2] *Ibid.*, p. 356.   [3] *Ibid.*, I, 433.

[4] *Ibid.*, V, 275. The vestry of Truro parish was dissolved by act of assembly in 1744 because some of the vestrymen were unqualified; several "pretending to act as vestrymen, are unable to read or write . . . . and imposed many hardships on the inhabitants of the parish" (*ibid.*, pp. 274–75).

[5] *Ibid.*, VII (1759), p. 303.

[6] F. L. Hawks, *Contributions to the Ecclesiastical History of the U.S.*, I, 84–86.

[7] *William and Mary College Quarterly*, V, 200–3.

A brief sketch of the legislation[1] affecting poor illegitimate, and orphan children will help in understanding the practice. At least eight important acts affecting poor children of various classes were passed between 1646 and 1769. That of 1646[2] gives as one motive for the act the necessity of avoiding "sloath and idlenesse wherewith such young children are easily corrupted, as also for the reliefe of such parents whose poverty extends not to give them breeding." It provided that justices of the peace should at their discretion bind out children, and for public flax houses to which two children from each county might be sent and taught to spin. Again in 1672[3] because of the increase of "vagabonds, idle and dissolute persons," justices of the peace were empowered "to place out *all* children whose parents were not able to bring them up apprentices." Again in 1727,[4] the act of that year complains of "divers idle and disorderly persons" able to work who "stroll from one county to another, neglecting to labour"; and vagabonds, "run from their habitations and leave either wives or children, without suitable means for their subsistence, whereby they are likely to become burthensome to the parish wherein they inhabit." Children of such parents, because of their "idle, dissolute and disorderly course of life," could be bound out by church wardens on certificate from the county court.

Besides the acts relating to poor children, several were passed affecting illegitimate children.[5] The number of illegitimate children increased with the increase of indentured servants. As early as 1642–43[6] laws were passed against fornication between servants and free men and servants. In 1657–58 the father of an illegitimate child was obliged to give security to indemnify the parish against keeping

[1] The legislation is summarized in its educational aspects by the author, in the *School Review*, XXVII (June, 1919), 405–25, and the workings of the laws in *ibid.*, XXVIII (February, 1920), 127–42.

[2] Hening, I, 336–37. The Act of 1668 also gave power to the county court "to take poore children from indigent parents to worke in those houses" (*ibid.*, II, 267).

[3] *Ibid.*, II, 298.

[4] *Ibid.*, IV, 208–14. This is a comprehensive act defining vagabonds and their treatment; poor and sick persons; the responsibilities of the vestry for the poor, and the method of caring for illegitimate children.

[5] See Bruce, *Inst. Hist. of Va.*, I, chap. v. ("Public Morals," "Bastardy and Slander"), for the seventeenth century. See also n. 1 *Supra*.

[6] Hening, I, 253.

the child.[1] If the father were an indentured servant, he could not of course indemnify the parish. So, in 1662,[2] it was provided that the parish should "take care to keepe the child during the time of the reputed father's service by indenture or custome, and that after he s free the said reputed father shall make satisfaction to the parish." Finally, in 1769,[3] because the laws in force were insufficient and because of the "great charges frequently arising from children begotten out of lawful matrimony," the church wardens were instructed to bind out illegitimate children of free single white women. If the illegitimate child were born of a convict[4] servant woman during the time of her service, the master of such servant was obliged to maintain the child until twenty-one or eighteen years of age, and was entitled to its service.

Still another problem for the parish was the increase of mulatto children. The act of 1691[5] complained that there was need of preventing "that abominable mixture and spurious issue which hereafter may increase in this dominion as well by negroes, mulattoes, and Indians intermarrying with English, or other white women, as by their unlawful accompanying with one another."[6]

Another problem was the care of orphans. No less than seventeen acts were passed by Virginia relating to this class, most of them having to do with the management of orphans' estates, but some providing for the binding out of poor orphans.[7]

It is of course true that the laws enacted by the assembly represent an ideal rather than actual practice. The administration of poor relief was indeed largely regulated by law, but on the other hand the vestries often acted from custom rather than law. This is clearly shown in the minutes of the vestries, several of which have

[1] *Ibid.*, p. 438.   [2] *Ibid.*, II, 168.

[3] *Ibid.*, VIII, 374.   [4] *Ibid.*, p. 377. See p. 5, n. 1.

[5] *Ibid.*, III, 86–87.

[6] Other acts provide penalties for fornication between servants and for the "destroying and murdering of bastard children," *Ibid.*, III (1696), 139; (1710), 510; IV (1727), 213.

[7] The act of 1756 provided that if orphans had an estate so "meane and inconsiderable that it will not reach to a free education," then he must be bound out as an apprentice (*ibid.*, I, 416). See p. 7, n. 1.

been published.[1] It is from these records that we can learn the actual practice and methods of poor relief in Virginia.

The most important function of the vestries was their duties as financial managers of the parish. Each year, in meeting assembled, they made up their budget[2] and divided the amount by the total number of tithables in the parish. The tithe was generally paid in kind, usually tobacco, but might in some cases be levied and paid in wheat or maize.[3] This method of payment made it necessary to appoint a collector, who worked on a percentage basis. He had power "to make, distress for the same," viz., to compel payment by selling the property in case of a refusal to pay the tithe.

It appears that in the period from 1720 to 1730, the vestry of Bristol Parish levied 370,982 pounds of tobacco, of which 34,415 were for poor relief.[4] The ratio was thus about 9 per cent. In St. Peter's Parish, for the year 1722, the percentage for poor relief was twenty-two, or nearly one-third of the total levy.[5] A typical year (1726) in the case of Bristol Parish shows a levy of 66, 789 pounds of tobacco, the number of tithables being 1,236, or 54 pounds per poll. Of this total, 6,124 pounds were for poor relief, and the number aided was eight.[6]

Parishes also received bequests from time to time. Thus in 1674 James Bennett of Nansemond gave the parish two hundred acres of land. The rents were to be received yearly by the church wardens and applied to the relief of poor, aged, and impotent persons forever.[7] Again, in 1707, a Mrs. Hill bequeathed by will 350 acres for

---

[1] *The Vestry Book of Saint Peter's Parish, New Kent County, Va., 1682–1758* (Richmond, 1905); C. G. Chamberlayne, *The Vestry Book and Register of Bristol Parish, Virginia, 1720–89* (Richmond, 1898); L. W. Burton, *Annals of Henrico Parish* contains *Vestry Book of Henrico Parish, 1730–1773*, ed. by R. A. Brock; "King William's Vestry Book, 1707–1750," is in *Virginia Magazine of History*, Vols. XI and XII; C. G. Chamberlayne, *The Vestry Book of Christ Church Parish, 1663–1767* (Richmond, 1928).

[2] See pp. 11–12.

[3] "King Williams's Parish V. B.," in *Virginia Magazine of History*, XII, 26, 243; XIII, 179.

[4] *Bristol Parish V. B.*, pp. 3–45.   [5] *St. Peter's Parish V. B.*, pp. 133–34.

[6] *Bristol Parish V. B.*, p. 30. Compare the budget of the *St. Peter's Parish, 1744*, on pp. 11–12, below.

[7] See *William and Mary College Quarterly*, VII, 222, 236, 255, for bequests to the poor; and Bruce, *Institutional History of Virginia*, I, 26–27.

the benefit of the poor of the parish.[1] Besides land, cattle, tobacco, and slaves were left for the support of the poor. Thus Mathew Godfrey of Norfolk County left by will, 1715–16, 1,000 acres and slaves, to be let out each year, the income to be used for the support of the poor of the county, and to be divided equally among three parishes.[2] In view of both public and private aid for the poor, Beverley's assertion (1722) that the poor of Virginia were well cared for seems fair. He says that some countries gave but just sufficient to preserve the poor from perishing, but in Virginia "the unhappy creature was received into some charitable planter's house where he was at the public charge boarded plentifully."[3]

The administration of poor relief for children rested largely on the apprenticeship laws, already discussed, and for adults on general laws. A petition[4] of 1641 complained that "Divers poore men have longe inhabited heere and nowe are growne decrepped and impotent." In 1642–43 a general law[5] defining the duties of vestries, states that the poor had been of long continuance in the colony, and that many were prevented from laboring because of sickness, lameness, or old age. On complaint to the vestry, such could be certified to the commissioners of the county court as to their poverty and freed from all public charges "except the ministers' and parish duties." Under their general powers, then, the vestries could apprentice poor children, administer bequests for the poor, make levies, and allot aid according to the needs of individual cases. The vestry, however, was under the supervision of the county court, and in case of neglect of duty, could be called to account. It was also of course subject to the general assembly.[6]

Plans for "farming out" all the poor to the lowest bidder were sometimes proposed but seldom carried out in practice. Thus, in 1719, in St. Peter's parish, it was voted that

Whereas, Capt. John Scott has made an offer to take all the Poor People of this Parish: It is ordered That he shall Receive all the poor people which shall

---

[1] *William and Mary College Quarterly*, VII, 254.   [2] Hening, VII, 418.

[3] Bruce, *op. cit.*, p. 88, and Robert Beverley, *History of Virginia*, 1722, p. 223.

[4] *Virginia Magazine of History* (1901–2), p. 55.

[5] Hening, I, 242.

[6] *William and Mary College Quarterly*, V, 219, 221.

be sent him by the Church Wardens. And to provide for them all such necessaries as Shall be Convenient (Except Apparrell) As the Church Wardens and he can agree.[1]

This plan, however, was not carried out, nor were similar votes of Bristol parish "That the Church wardens at the most Convenient place put up the Poor of this Parish to the lowest Bidder."[2] An elaborate plan for a poorhouse, to be supported by three parishes, Bristol, Martin's Brandon, and Bath was also proposed but this likewise failed to mature.[3]

The common method of administering poor relief was to have the poor cared for in different homes, by paying a sum agreed upon for each person. This involved either total support for those entirely disabled, or partial support for persons needing temporary relief, or for those not wholly without resources. This called for a grant of a specific sum for the time kept for service rendered. Thus the persons receiving aid and the kind of aid given were extremely varied. A typical budget[4] made up by the vestry of St. Peter's Parish, New Kent County, for the year 1744, reads as follows:

At a Vestry held for St. Peter's Parish September the 29th, 1744.

Present:

The Rev'd David Mossom, Min'r; Maj'r John Dandridgge, Capt. Rich'd Littlepage, Capt. Wm. Massie, Mr. Walter Clopton, Mr. Thomas Butts, Mr. Chas. Massie, Coll. Dan'll Parke Custis, Maj'r Jos. Foster, Mr. Ambrose Dudley, Vestrymen; Coll. Wm. Macon, Mr. Jos. Marston, Church Wardens.

St. Peter's Parish,   Dr.

To the Rev'd Mr. Mossom his Salary to September the 29th	16000
To Cask to Do. a 4 P. ct	640
To the Rev'd Mr. Mossom for the Deficiency of Glebe	1600
To Cask to Do. a 4 P. ct	64
To James Holmes his Salary to September the 29th	1800
To Stephen Broker, Sexton, his Salary	630
To Sarah Broker for washing the Surplice these 2 years	100
To James Ashcroft for keeping his Father	600
To Hugh Grindley for keeping Charles Goodwin	450
To David Patteson for keeping Mary Hazard	800

[1] *St. Peter's Parish V. B.*, pp. 125–26.

[2] *Bristol Parish V. B.* (1757), p. 168; (1762), p. 182.

[3] *Ibid.* (1757), pp. 165–66.   [4] *St. Peter's Parish V. B.*, pp. 194–96.

To Israel Asutin for keeping his Brother......................... 250
To John Phillips for his Support................................ 600
To Cornelius Matthews for the Support of his Mother.............. 500
To Samuel Bailey for keeping Mary Major........................ 450
To Henry Strange for keeping Marg't Grumbal.................... 700
To Phillis Moon for keeping her Son............................ 967
To George Heath for keeping John Vincent, an orphan child......... 600
To Sarah Broker for keeping Christ'r Bendall in his Sickness........ 300
To Maj. John Dandridge his acco't.............................. 380
To Mr. Ben. Waller for a copy of the List of Tithables............. 18
To Capt. Wm. Massie his L3, 3, 10, in Tobo. at 10 P. ct............ 638
To Rich'd Crump, Sen'r, his Acco't, L4, 2s., 0, in Tobo. at Do........ 419
To Coll. Macon his acco't, L8, 17, 4, in Tobo. at Do................ 1744

                                                                  30280
To George Taylor for keeping Catherine Taylor in Child bed......... 400
To Hannah Morgan for keeping Marg't Foster 4 weeks.............. 400
To Sarah Broker as part of her Fee for Bring Cath. Taylor to Bed.... 30

                                                                  31110
Ord'd that the Sume of 12750 lb. of Tobo. be Levyed for the use of the
    Parish... 12756

                                                                  43866
To the Coll'n at 6 P. Ct....................................... 2632

                                                                  46498
To a Rem'r due from the Coll'r................................. 54

                                                                  46552
                    Per Contra,   Cr.
By 1058 Tithables at 44 lb. Tobo. Pr. Poll...................... 46552

It will be noted that out of a total levy of 46,552 pounds of tobacco
no less than 7,040 pounds were for poor relief, involving thirteen
different persons; also that a father, brother, mother, and son were
"kept" by immediate relatives; also that aid was granted for the
care of an orphan, for women "in child bed," and for poor persons
in general.

The problem of total support may be illustrated by the following
cases:

Upon the petition of James Turner Setting forth that he has been visited
with Lameness and sickness severall years in So much that he hath spent all
his substance upon Phesitians and nessicaries, therefore, ordered that Samuell

Waddy keep the same James Turner during Life and to find him sufficient Clothing, meate, drink, washing and Lodging, and all nessicaries, and to be paid
twelve hundred pounds of Tobacco and Cask p annum. and soe proportionable
for a longer or a shorter time the said Wadde assuring to this vestry to keep the
said Turner for the Sume of 1200 lbs. of Tobacco, and bring noe Claime against
the parish for the same.[1]

This is a case where the vestry burdened itself with the maintenance of one person for his whole life, at a fixed sum per year, with
no further claim against the parish.

A widow, Elizabeth Faulkner, was a source of great expense to
St. Peter's parish for a number of years, 1690–1710. Let us follow
the history of the Widow Faulkner. First, in May 1690, five hundred pounds of tobacco were granted toward her maintenance for
one year.[2] In November, Lyonell Morriss agreed "to find her sufficient accomodations" at the rate of one thousand pounds of tobacco
a year.[3] In 1696 Thomas Minns was paid 1,040 pounds of tobacco
for "keeping" the widow Faulkner one year and "providing her a
pr. of shoes."[4] The next year he was paid 1,080 pounds for keeping
her and 30 pounds for another pair of shoes.[5] Two hundred and
ninety-two pounds were also paid Mr. Wyatt for her "Cloathes."[6]
This same amount, 1,080 pounds, was paid for the next few years,
1699–1706.[7] On May 8, 1707, however, Mr. Minns made a complaint. Perhaps the widow was either eating too much, or the cost
of living was rising. The record reads "Whereas Tho. Minns complains that his allowance for keeping Wid. Faulkner is too little, the
vestry have ordered it increased for ye future 1100 lbs. tobo. . . . .
if she lives."[8] The Widow Faulkner was thus supported by the
parish, in three different houses, for twenty years, at a cost of 20,619
pounds of tobacco.

In general the old, impotent, and lame were charges on the parish, as well as those who were temporarily or permanently disabled
by sickness or other causes.[9] The dreaded modern scourge of cancer
is reported in 1728.

[1] *Ibid.*, p. 67.

[2] *Ibid.*, p. 23.

[3] *Ibid.*, p. 26.

[4] *Ibid.*, p. 40.

[5] *Ibid.*, p. 43.

[6] *Ibid.*

[7] *Ibid.*, pp. 51, 56, 60, 66, etc.

[8] *Ibid.*, p. 92.

[9] *Bristol Parish V. B.*, pp. 5, 10, 17; St. *Peter's Parish V. B.*, p. 69.

Robt. Glidewell Being afficted With a Cancur in his face which hath made him unable to labour for his livelihood it is ord'red that the Church Warthen find him necessary Cloathin and likewise that John Browder find him necessary board and he to be allow'd one hundred pounds of tobo pr. month.[1]

These cases illustrate the method of total support. Persons not wholly without resources also received either permanent or temporary aid. Take the case of Anthony Burrass, "stricken blind," November, 1696.

Whereas Anthony Burrass of this parish is stricken blind & his wife is very ancient by what means they are incapable of getting their living & that ye s'd Anthony addressing himself to this vestry for a maintanence.

It is therefore ordered yt ye Church wardens forthwith cause ye s'd Anthony Burros to convey over unto them for ye use of this parish forever his plantation, Cattle, horses & hoggs & yt there be allowed to each of them five hundred pounds of Tob. & Casq's for their maintenence during their or either of their natural lives or till he may be recovered of his eye sight.[2]

Later he accepted 1,600 pounds of tobacco yearly for the maintenance of himself and his wife, and this agreement was carried out for some years.[3]

The parish helped the able-bodied poor by enabling them to help themselves. Robert Magrime could work, but apparently was in danger of becoming a parish charge. So

Mr. Gideon Macon offering to this vestry to take the said Magrime and keep him as long as he can work and pay levys and keep him from being a parish charge During his natural life, therefore ordered that the Sheriff sumon the said Magrine to appear at the next Court to answer what the Court shall therein order.[4]

Another type of poor relief was the provision for the partial support of, or aid to, the poor for a limited period, viz., occasional temporary relief. Margaret Butler, having petitioned that she "being disabled by Sickness is not Able to help herselfe," the vestry ordered that she live with Richard Butler "untill the vestry can Agree with A Doctor to cure her if possible he can." Mr. Butler was allowed

---

[1] *Bristol Parish V. B.*, p. 38.

[2] *St. Peter's Parish V. B.*, p. 41. In Henrico Parish, 1737, among others aid was given for two "impotent" persons, one old woman, one blind woman, and one "Ideot" (*Henrico Parish V. B.*, p. 42).

[3] *St. Peter's Parish V. B.* (1698), p. 49.   [4] *Ibid.*, p. 55.

eight pounds of tobacco a month for the time she lived with him, he "to find her diet, lodging and washing for the time."[1] The vestry also agreed with "Doct^r Thompson for the Cure of Jacob Butler and to Bring in their accm't at the laying of the nex parrish leavy."[2]

In case of accident relief was often given. Thus "Peter plantin being Much Burnt by acsident and he being poor and aged Not Able to pay for his Cure Mary hall is ord'red to take Care of the Sd plantine and to Do her Endeavour to Cure him and she to bring in her ac^{mt} at the laying the Next parrish leavy."[3] The practice of making a contract with a doctor to cure the sick was very common. Thus "Ordered that ye Church wardens Agree with Some Doctor to Cure Mary Wilde of her Ailement, & if she think herself able to undergo a Course of Phisic, The Church wardens are to agree w'th ye Doctor for ye same."[4] Parishes might even provide for the expense of taking a person to a health resort. Thus "Ordered that the Church Wardens Agree with some Person on the best terms they can to carry Richd Sentale to the Spring on New River for the Recovery of his health."[5] Another type of aid occurred when the church wardens were "impowered to give Thomas Ashcraft Credit in a Store for forty Shillings towards finding him in Cloathes for the ensuing year."[6] Still another method of aiding the poor was the distribution of fines. Thus the church wardens were ordered to distribute fines in their hands "among the Poor of the Parish."[7]

Another form of temporary aid was that of freeing persons from parish dues. Persons unable to pay might secure relief by petitioning the county court or they could apply directly to the vestry for relief.[8] Thus "Tho. Andrews being Ancient & Crasey & not Able to Work is Acquitted from paying P'ish Levies."[9] "Robt Glascock

---

[1] *Bristol Parish V. B.*, pp. 25–26.   [2] *Ibid.*, p. 45.

[3] *Ibid.* (1728), p. 37. So also "To Mary Harding for curing Mary Burnet of a Burn," *Henrico Parish V. B.*, p. 8.

[4] *St. Peter's Parish V. B.*, p. 108. See also *Bristol Parish V. B.*, p. 36.

[5] *Ibid.* (1744), p. 116. The Vestry of King William's Parish paid 150 pounds of tobacco "for burying a poor man," *Virginia Magazine of History* XIII, 269.

[6] *St. Peter's Parish V. B.* (1739), p. 181.

[7] *Ibid.* (1744), p. 194.

[8] Hening, I (Act of 1642–3), p. 242; III (1700), p. 201.

[9] *Bristol Parish V. B.*, p. 1. See also *St. Peter's Parish V. B.*, p. 148.

being upwards of 60 years old & lame is Acquitted from paying P'ish Levies."[1] "Upon the petition of Phillis Moore for to gett her Son John Moore levy free, Setting forth in her petition that her S'd Son is troubled with Convultion fitts & much burnt, It is ordered that the Said Jno. Moore be exempted from paying of parish Levy During his Infirmity."[2]

Generally speaking charity seems to have been given with some regard for the feelings of the recipient. In Bristol Parish, however, the church wardens ordered the pews numbered, and after four had been reserved "for the use of the Poor," ordered that they "lett the Same, to the highest Bidders."[3]

The binding out of poor, illegitimate, and orphan children, as provided for by law, was one of the important duties of the vestry, and their minutes contain numerous examples of the practice. Thus at one meeting of the vestry of Bristol parish, it was ordered that eight poor children, five from one family, should be bound out to various persons.[4] A specific case is that of "Agnes Tudora, poor Infirm Girl, being put upon this parish for a Charge and Rich'd & Sarah Brookes being willing to take the said Girl, Ordered that ye Church wardens bind the Said Agnes Tudor to the Said Rich'd & Sarah Brookes for Seven Years."[5]

The vestry was broadly speaking the moral sponsor for the parish. Accordingly the vestry books abound with records of illegitimate children whose maintenance might result in added burdens to the parish, and the prosecution of which cases was entrusted to the vestry. There are orders to support or bind out all types of illegitimate children, white and mulatto, born of free white women, and white servant women.[6] Thus "It is ordered that a thousand pounds of tobacco and cask be paid unto Mary Wilkinson for nursing a

[1] *Bristol Parish V. B.*, p. 2.   [2] *St. Peter's Parish V. B.*, pp. 157–58.

[3] *Bristol Parish V. B.*, p. 271.

[4] *Ibid.*, pp. 65–66. See *William and Mary College Quarterly*, V, 219–23, for binding out of poor children and orphans, and see above, p. 7, n. 1.

[5] *St. Peter's Parish V. B.*, p. 151.

[6] For the seventeenth century see, Bruce, *Inst. Hist. of Va.*, Vol. I, chap, v, "Public Morals: Bastardy and Slander." At one meeting of Henrico Vestry, grants were made for the support of three bastard children (*Henrico Parish V. B.* [Oct. 13, 1732], 11). See p. 7, n. 1.

bastard child belonging to a servant woman of Capt. Joseph Forster this ensuing year."[1] The process of binding out such a child is illustrated by the following entry:

Margaret Micabin serv't to Mr. David Crawley having a bastard Child Mr. Crawley prays the Gen[tle]men of this Vestry to bind out the s'd Child as they think fitt. It is ord[rd] by the Vestry that the Church-Wardens bind out the s'd Child named John Sadler born the 26th July last 1720. The fores'd Child is by indenture bound unto Mr. David Crawley to serve according to Law.[2]

There was a great increase of illegitimate mulatto children in the eighteenth century, born of free white women or white servant women. In either case the child was not a slave, but according to law must be bound out to service till of age. Thus in October, 1724, "Hen. Royall pettitioneth that he hath two Moll. children born in his house by Name Wm. and hannah may be bound to him & his heirs according to Law his pett. is granted."[3] At the meeting of June 28, 1725, three petitions were received to have two mulatto girls and one boy, born probably of white servant women, in three different houses, bound to the masters and mistresses of the servants.[4]

Orphan children also were bound out to relieve the parish of keeping them. The number of orphans is surprising. In Spottsylvania County, will book "B" contains a list of forty-five guardians bonds between 1749 and 1761, involving seventy children.[5]

The system of poor relief became more and more unsatisfactory in the latter half of the eighteenth century. Changes in Virginia

[1] *St. Peter's Parish V. B.*, p. 8.

[2] *Bristol Parish V. B.*, p. 2. An unusual case was "Mary Burnet's bastard child, she being an Idiot, and upon ye Parish" (*Henrico Parish V. B.* [1748], p. 83). At the same meeting aid was given "To John Jones, for keeping his Daughter, being a Fool" (*ibid*).

[3] *Bristol Parish V. B.*, pp. 18–19.

[4] *Ibid.*, p. 24. The following entries seem to indicate that the parish gave aid to mulatto and negro servants, or possibly free negroes: "To Robert Cooke for the care of Susannah a Mulatto 400" (pounds of tobacco); and "To Ryland Randolph, church-warden, for smallpox negro, £2, 17, 0" (*Henrico Parish V. B.* [1758], p. 109; [1763]). p. 123.

[5] W. A. Crozier (ed.), *Virginia County Records*, I, 72–76. "Mr. Tho. Bott haveing an orphant boy bound to him by his mother desires the same may be confirmed by this Vestry" (*Bristol Parish V. B.*, p. 2). See p. 7, n. 1.

society, the inefficiency of the Anglican Church, the westward movement of population, the formation of large back country parishes,
and the delay in the formation of parishes were some of the new factors. One complaint was made that because of the want of a vestry
in Botentourt Parish, the poor were likely to suffer "for want of
proper support and maintenance."[1] From 1780 to 1785, the assembly by a series of acts dissolved the vestries and provided for overseers of the poor in each county. The preamble of the act of 1780
reads, "Whereas great inconveniences have arisen from the mode
prescribed for making provisions for the poor" in seven western
counties named, the vestries of such were dissolved, and the sheriffs
were ordered to elect five freeholders as "Overseers of the Poor,"
with the powers and duties of vestries and church wardens.[2] In
1782, another act dissolved the vestries of five more western counties, because the former act "hath greatly removed the inconveniences for making provision for the poor."[3] Finally, in 1785, a general act was passed to provide for the poor in all the counties of the
state, by appointment of overseers of the poor who also were given
the same powers over bastards and vagrants, formerly exercised by
the vestries.[4] Thus the care of the poor passed out of the control of
the Anglican Church to that of the counties. This was one of the
consequences of the American Revolution and the separation of
church and state in Virginia.

MARCUS WILSON JERNEGAN

UNIVERSITY OF CHICAGO

[1] Hening, IX, 527.   [3] *Ibid.*, XI, 62.
[2] *Ibid.*, X, 288.   *Ibid.*, XII, 27–29

THE PURITAN BACKGROUND OF THE NEW
ENGLAND POOR LAWS

ELIZABETH WISNER

IT HAS become a commonplace to say that the New England colonies derived their basic poor laws from England, and with the overwhelming majority of the early population of English descent it could hardly have been otherwise. Not only were the early poor laws English in origin but the religious institutions, the arrangement of classes, and the law which bound the early colonists together were inherited from the mother-country and adapted to the New World. Even Puritanism, which has been described not only as a religion and a philosophy but also as a conception of the way in which all community life should be organized, was brought over by the seventeenth-century settlers and modified in the face of the new situation.[1] To say, however, that the New Englanders brought with them their conceptions and practices governing the care of destitute persons and to ignore the special pioneer conditions under which the Colonial poor law legislation was administered is to fail in our understanding of the subsequent development of such legislation.

Contrary to certain opinion during the 1930's, the essentially "American way" of aiding the poor was through legislative enactments and taxation rather than through reliance upon voluntary efforts, for the great growth of organized philanthropy did not take place until the nineteenth century. In fact, the struggling plantations of Massachusetts Bay, New Hampshire, Connecticut, and Rhode Island early developed the concept of the "town poor" and later the "state poor." Obviously, the endowed charities and the numerous hospitals and almshouses of the mother-country were lacking; and, although small bequests of £100 or so were made by some of the settlers from time to time, such gifts were not very important so far as any comprehensive support of destitute persons was concerned. Many of the governing group, particularly in Massachusetts and Connecticut, were men of substance, some with landed estates in England, while others were well-to-do merchants; but their funds were needed to develop a pioneer undertaking and to maintain as comfortable a living as possible under the circumstances. As trade flourished, some substantial fortunes were made in shipbuilding, shipping, brewing, and lumber and in the exports of furs and fish; but the great fortunes with which great philanthropies are associated were yet to be carved out of the wildness. Therefore, the New England "annals of the poor," which are neither short nor simple, are to be found largely in the account of the poor laws.

This does not mean that the charitable impulses toward the poor, which were closely bound up in the religious practices of the period, were absent; and, indeed, they found expression in many ways. In fact, the great importance of the church in New England and of the

[1] Charles Beard, *The Rise of American Civilization* (1937), pp. 124–26; Perry Miller and T. H. Johnson, *The Puritans* (1938), see esp. General Introduction, pp. 1–64, and chap. ii, "Theory of State and Society," pp. 181–94.

Social Service Review 19 (September 1945): 381–90

religious fervor which animated the daily lives and institutions of the early colonists immediately raises the question as to what was the Puritan attitude toward charity and problems of poverty. John Winthrop, first governor of Massachusetts Bay Colony and at all times a most influential personage in the colony, delivered a sermon to his fellow-passengers aboard the "Arbella" on the voyage to New England which expresses the point of view of the period. Speaking on "a model of Christian charity," he reminded the group that "God Almighty in His most holy and wise providence hath soe disposed of the condition of mankind, as in all times some must be rich some poore, some highe and eminent in power and dignitie; others meane and in subieccion."[2] While adjuring them in the ways of justice and mercy and moderation "soe that the riche and mighty should not eate upp the poore," neither were the poor and despised to rise up against their superiors or to shake off their yoke.

Social equality and religious freedom were no part of the mental climate of England in the 1630's and 1640's, and the Winthrops, Endicotts, Saltonstalls, and Eatons transplanted to Massachusetts and Connecticut the current conceptions of a stratified class society as well as religious intolerance. Even the struggles and leveling process of settling a wilderness did not quickly dissipate such conceptions; and William Hubbard, an eminent theologian and graduate of the first class at Harvard College, preaching in Boston on "The Happiness of a People" in 1676, believed that nothing was more remote either from reason or from true religion than that, because men were equal at birth and would become so at death, they were therefore equal throughout life. He urged that the

rich (i.e., the strong) and mighty must protect the poor; otherwise they "might starve with hunger and cold were they not fed with the morselles, and warmed with the fleece of the wealthy."[3]

To Cotton Mather the poor were divided into the "godly" and "ungodly," as they were later to be classified as "worthy" and "unworthy." Writing in his diary in January, 1707, he recounts his recent charitable efforts:

I have often taken some Care of the Poor, that have not a Character of Godliness upon them. So I found out ten or dozen such People and I carried them some Relief of money and I gave them the best Council I could, and I left also a good Book in their Hands to direct and excite the Practice of serious Religion in them. Who can tell but in this Way of Treating with such poor Creatures, they may be some of them won over to the Wayes of Piety.[4]

But it would be unfair to Cotton Mather if his charitable efforts were dismissed as merely opportunities for proselytizing the ungodly poor. One cannot read his diary, which was kept from 1681 to 1724, without sensing his genuine compassion for people who were suffering and in need and without admiration for his indefatigable efforts in their behalf. In many ways his strong sense of responsibility toward community problems is akin to that which gave rise to the great philanthropic efforts of the nineteenth century and which was so marked among certain leading citizens of Boston. Of all the men of thought and action in the New England Colonial period, he is, perhaps, the most interesting to the social worker. A member of a distinguished family of theologians, he typifies in many ways the best and the worst in the Puritanism of the middle

[2] Miller and Johnson, *op. cit.*, p. 195.

[3] *Ibid.*, pp. 247–50.

[4] *Diary of Cotton Mather* ("Massachusetts Historical Society, Collections," Vol. VII[7] [1911-12], p. 580).

period. For, like many of his colleagues, he supported the Salem witchcraft trials and executions, while in his later years he was an outstanding exponent of small-pox inoculation and fought valiantly for that cause. As a writer he was prolific, and his known published sermons, essays, and works total between four and five hundred. Throughout his life he was involved in many controversies; but, in spite of these and his heavy duties as minister of the North Boston Church, he still found time to devote to a variety of charitable undertakings. In fact, his diary bears almost daily witness to his activities on behalf of the poor. In *Bonifacius, or Essays To Do Good*, which he published in 1710, Mather imagines that "there is a City in the World where every House hath a Box hanging in a Chair, on which is Written, *Think* on the Poor,"—and undoubtedly he longed to see Boston become that city.

First among his many interests was the cause of education and the erection of charity schools for poor children. Not only did he give from his own purse, for several years being the sole support of a charity school for Negroes, but he interested himself in a similar school in the East Indies. As in the case of many private charitable efforts, interest waxed and waned; but to Cotton Mather "doing good" was an imperative which could never be ignored, and so expired charity schools must be revived and new ones started. True, the amount of education offered was very limited, and literacy was important mainly that the Bible might be read and the catechism taught; but, even so, at a time when general education was not provided, such efforts were as important in the new country as they were in the old.

The promotion of charity schools was, however, only one of his many activities,

and much of his time and interest was devoted to dispensing relief and caring for the sick, the aged, the widowed, and the orphaned and in finding employment for the able-bodied. In one entry in his diary he writes that his list of the poor to be cared for included about ninety persons—so numerous, in fact, were the poor around him that he struggled to find some way of deciding between those who seemed to have equal claims upon his alms. At one point he decided on an ingenious method, for, he writes in his diary, "why may I not write their Names on Papers, and looking up to Heaven, to dispense the Lott, then draw and give according? Doubtless the good Angels of Heaven would operate on this Occasion."[5] His name is also associated with that typically Boston institution, the "Quarterly Charity Lecture," for on March 6, 1720, he began the long series of lectures at which funds were collected for distribution to the poor.[6]

No attempt is made in this study to give a comprehensive account of the private charities of the New England colonies and states, but some further mention should be made of this subject. For the growth of innumerable societies and bequests to aid the poor, particularly in the city of Boston, cannot be wholly divorced from a consideration of the poor laws. In some instances the first almshouses were erected out of funds bequeathed by charitably minded individuals, as, for example, the Boston Alms House, which owed its origin to a legacy of £100 left by Mr. Henry Webb in 1660; and this gift apparently in-

[5] *Ibid.*, VIII[7], 66 and 152.

[6] T. J. Holmes, *Cotton Mather: A Bibliography of His Works* (1940); Ralph and Louise Boas, *Cotton Mather, Keeper of the Puritan Conscience* (1928); H. M. Dexter, "The Mather Family and Its Influence," *Memorial History of Boston*, Vol. II, chap. iv; and *Diary of Cotton Mather*.

spired others to leave small sums for the same purpose. Other trust funds, such as the Charlestown and Stoughton Poor Funds, the Boylston, Pemberton, and many other special bequests for the care of poor and aged persons and poor orphans, were added from time to time.

The Scots' Charitable Society, organized in 1674 by Boston merchants of Scotch descent for the purpose of aiding their destitute countrymen, is credited as being the earliest charity in that city and is perhaps the earliest in the New World, and it is of interest as typifying the large number of similar organizations for the aid of special groups. "Poor widows" funds and innumerable special charities and agencies grew apace especially during the latter half of the eighteenth and throughout the nineteenth centuries and illustrate the rapid rise of the philanthropic movement in Boston. Among the most notable and useful of these were the medical charities for the "sick poor" such as the Boston Dispensary and the Massachusetts General Hospital. By the latter half of the nineteenth century the *Directory* issued by the Boston Associated Charities was said to contain a list of charities covering over a hundred pages, showing, "like Homer's catalogue of the Grecian ships gathered for another warfare, how heartily and readily the men and women of Boston have joined with each other in the great siege, which has been bequeathed from sire to son, of the fortress of poverty, ignorance and crime."[7]

Private charities likewise flowered in Hartford and New Haven, especially during the 1800's, and the Charity Society of Hartford (1809) is an interesting illustration of the way in which private benevolence supplemented the poor law, for the act of incorporation specified that it was for the purpose of aiding the widowed, the orphaned, the aged, and the sick for whom the poor laws of the state did not provide relief "suitable to their conditions and circumstances, or adequate to their necessities."[8] A proviso was added that only persons known to be sober and industrious and not addicted to drinking or misspending their time at the gaming tables were to be aided by the society, and in the main it was the purpose of the private charitable societies to aid only the "worthy" poor. In the city of Providence, Rhode Island, local tax funds for the care of the poor were supplemented through the legacy of Ebenezer Knight Dexter, who bequeathed the city a valuable property which was used as an asylum for the poor and which yielded in addition over $4,000 in the year 1851.[9] Again it should be pointed out that, although private benevolence grew apace with the growth of population and wealth after the Revolutionary War, most of the private societies and trust funds were limited to aiding special groups mainly in the larger towns and that the total volume of expenditures was undoubtedly small in comparison with those spent by the poor-law authorities.

Another source of help to the early colonists which might be termed "mutual aid" should be mentioned. Scattered through the earliest town records are brief entries from time to time showing the degree of interest taken in the welfare of the inhabitants. As in all closely knit

---

[7] *Memorial History of Boston*, Vol. IV, "Charities of Boston," pp. 641–74; see also *A Manual for the Use of the Overseer of the Poor in the City of Boston, 1866.*

[8] S. A. Eddy (comp.), *Index to Private Laws and Special Acts of Connecticut [1789–1897]*, (Bridgeport, 1897), p. 321.

[9] T. R. Hazard, *Report on the Poor and Insane in Rhode Island* (Providence, 1851), p. 73.

communities, acts of mutual assistance and neighborly kindness such as persist today in a rural economy are recorded. Some of the poor received allotments of land for cultivation, and the common lands were used for pasturage. Individuals assisted in the sinking of wells and in providing food, shelter, and firewood to their less fortunate friends and neighbors. The Connecticut and Massachusetts records reveal that corn was distributed to those in distress and, in the latter colony, water and blankets to the less fortunate inhabitants. In Yarmouth, one of the old Plymouth colony towns, the court ordered that a cow and a heifer were to be assigned to the use of the poor.[10] Similar acts of mutual assistance are recorded in the Rhode Island town records and need not be repeated here.[11]

In any consideration of the legal provisions for the poor, the extent to which relief measures were necessary in a new country is of interest. In the small, sparsely settled towns and newly developing plantations, widespread destitution as it was known in the Old World was absent. Labor was in demand, and, although there is evidence that there were from time to time some unemployed able-bodied men, unemployment on the Old World scale or as it was to develop in the later periods was not a major social problem. The system of land tenure in contrast to the English gave encouragement to those without property to acquire land, while commonage or the joint possession of land for pasturage and tillage (in the very early days) added to the sources of livelihood. When life became difficult, migration to the outlying territories was always possible, and many of the more adventuresome among the colonists moved on to settle new lands and to found additional plantations and villages.

On the other hand, life was hazardous, and epidemics, accidents, shipwrecks, and drownings left in their trail numbers of dependent wives, children, and other members of the family to be cared for. And not even the opportunities afforded in a new country could in every instance provide against dependency in old age. Problems inevitably arose in connection with the "ideot and distracted," and there was also the illegitimate child needing protection and support. Strangers or unsettled persons constituted another group to which there is constant reference in the legislation and town records. At the same time conflicts with the Indians not only spread fear and death among the colonists but brought enslavement to the Indians. Later some of them must have become dependent upon public funds for support, for in 1748 the Massachusetts Council appointed a committee to prepare a bill for the relief and support of Indians who because of age, infirmity, or sickness were in want and incapable of providing for their own subsistence.[12]

The Negro slave was also a member of the household of the more well-to-do, and in respect to this group there are a considerable number of higher-court decisions which show that the question of their support and settlement were litigated by the respective towns. In fact, the early colonists were faced with a whole array of social problems which could not be wholly ignored and which called for some kind of public provisions.

If one major cause of dependency can be singled out, preventable illness would take first place. Physicians were scarce in the colonies, and tuberculosis and in-

[10] *Plymouth Colony Records*, II (1641–51), 972.

[11] Margaret Creech, *Three Centuries of Poor Law Administration* (1936), chap. ii.

[12] *Massachusetts Archives*, XXXI, 614 (Indians).

fant mortality enacted a heavy toll among all groups in the population, the well-to-do and poor alike. It was, however, the "pestilential and malignant ffevers" recurring frequently and decimating the small town and village populations that receive special mention in the early town histories. In reading these accounts, it is evident that, except in the case of smallpox, little was known as to the true nature of many of the epidemics, for they are referred to as "the great scourge," the "nervous fever," the "spotted fever," the "throat distemper," or the "New Milford Fever" in the instance of an epidemic that started in that Connecticut town. The terror and desolation caused by these mysterious visitations were, however, frequently recorded. No wonder that in 1685 the Massachusetts Court and six years later the Connecticut Court decreed that a day of solemn humiliation and prayer should be kept throughout the colonies to stay "the threatening hand of God" and that smallpox was linked with "antichristian enemies" as a cause of the Lord's anger.[13]

Actually, a "pestilential fever" was epidemic among the Indians living near Plymouth as early as 1621, and the fact that it had nearly depopulated the territory was regarded by one early historian as a fortunate incident, for he remarks philosophically: "Thus, in a sense as it was of old, God cast out the heathen to make room for his people, some parts of the country therebye made to look like a mere Golgatha."[14] But then, as

now, germs recognized few barriers, and in 1633 another epidemic brought death to many Plymouth colonists as well as to the Indian population. Again and again the New England towns mourned the loss of many of their leading citizens. The smallpox epidemic of 1721–22 was particularly severe in Boston. and its vicinity, and it was estimated that 5,889 persons, of whom 840 died, were visited with this scourge. Nine years later Harvard College dismissed its students owing to alarming violence of the disease, and the town selectmen met nine times within two weeks to devise some means to control the epidemic.[15] The prevalence of smallpox in Massachusetts also threatened the inhabitants of Rhode Island, where stringent measures were taken in 1721 and again in 1731 and 1739 to deal with the scourge. In 1735-37 the "throat-distempter," or scarlet fever, which according to one commentary was the severest of all the epidemics, swept up from New York scourging fourteen towns in New Hampshire and passing on to the Massachusetts towns. In Haverhill it was said that in October of that year more than half of the children under fifteen years of age died.

Almost every house was turned into a habitation of mourning and scarce a day passed that was not a witness of the funeral procession. Many a hopeful son, or lovely daughter, arose in the morning with apparent perfect health; but, ere the sun went down they were cold and silent in the winding sheet of the dead. In many families, not a child was left to cheer the hearts of the stricken parents.[16]

Throughout Maine more than five hundred persons were said to have died among a very small population, and in the town of Scarborough no one attacked

---

[13] N. B. Shurtleff (ed.), *Records of the Governor and Company of the Massachusetts Bay in New England (1628–86)* (1853–54), V, 509; *Town Records of Derby, Connecticut (1655–1710)* (Derby: Sarah Riggs Humphrey's Chapter Daughters of the American Revolution, 1901), II, 281–82.

[14] William Hubbard, *A General History of New England from the Discovery to MDCLXXX* (1848), pp. 194–95.

[15] R. L. Paige, *History of Cambridge, Massachusetts, 1630-1877* (1877), pp. 127–28.

[16] G. W. Chase, *History of Haverhill, Massachusetts, 1640–1860* (1861), pp. 306–7.

by the disease recovered.[17] Smallpox as well as dysentery raged among the soldiers during the Revolutionary War, and yellow fever was prevalent in most of the commercial towns between 1793 and 1799.

It was inevitable that the frequent arrival of sailing ships in various port towns along the New England coast line gave rise to the recurring epidemics, and the lack of adequate quarantine and public health measures was also inevitable for the period. Around inoculation for smallpox arose one of the interesting controversies in medical history, and again to Cotton Mather goes much of the credit for his vigorous advocacy of this treatment during the epidemic of 1721. He was opposed by the only physician in Boston who had graduated from a medical school and by others who disliked him for his views, and there was even an attempt made upon his life. Dr. Zabdiel Bolyston, who had no medical degree but who was widely respected as a practicing physician, became interested and after making inquiries among the Negroes who had used inoculation, thereafter became the leading advocate of this practice. Mather's tract, *Account of the Method and Success of Inoculating the Small-Pox in Boston in New England* was published anonymously in 1722 in England, where his claims were vigorously supported by the Royal Society, which had earlier made him a member.

Inoculating hospitals were also the subject of much controversy, and over and over again the various towns would refuse to allow such a "pest-house" to be opened. During a very violent epidemic in 1764, Boston and Chelsea entered into a debate over the selection of Point Shirley, a fishing station in or near the latter town, as a place for inoculation. The situation in Boston was so serious that the governor and council had acted in behalf of the citizens in designating the Point as a place for inoculation; but Chelsea, fearful that persons coming out from Boston to be inoculated would not only spread the disease but would become a burden upon the town of Chelsea, at first refused and only consented after considerable pressure had been brought to bear upon the local officials. Other towns frequently voted to open inoculating hospitals and gave physicians permission to carry on their work, only to reverse their decision at the next town meeting.

During the Revolutionary War, while Boston was in the hands of the British, smallpox was epidemic, and some three hundred of the town's poor were sent to Chelsea on General Howe's orders; and again the townsmen of Chelsea protested, this time to General George Washington. So serious was the problem that the General Court of Massachusetts sent an investigating committee to Chelsea and ordered that persons who had been "smoked and cleansed" were to be given certificates showing that they were "the poor of Boston and quite free from infection" and were then to be sent on to other towns that did not have their proportion of "such people." Those who could not be removed were to be cared for out of public funds, and the General Court agreed to reimburse Chelsea for such expenditures.[18]

The relation between illness and the poor laws is indicated very early, for the first poor law of the old Plymouth colony recognized the fact that persons in the settlement were moving about in order to secure the services of physicians or "chirurgeons" and specified how their

---

[17] Josiah Pierce, *History of the Town of Gorham, Maine* (1862), pp. 35–36.

[18] Mellen Chamberlain, *A Documentary History of Chelsea, 1624–1824* (1908), II, 389–406, 525–32.

relief was to be met in the event they became in need.

The general poor laws of Massachusetts, New Hampshire, and Rhode Island early specified the sick as those for whom the towns must provide relief if in need, and later legislation of Massachusetts and Connecticut recognized the danger to the public health in allowing the towns to send back to their places of settlement persons suffering from contagious diseases and therefore provided that their relief should be paid from state funds. In fact, the Massachusetts Poor Law of 1692 was in effect the earliest of the public health measures passed in the colony, for it gave the local authorities power to remove and isolate infected persons. Disease did not, of course, strike every New England town every year, and recurring epidemics often proved less virulent than the earlier ones. Moreover, the small communities showed remarkable recuperative powers, gradually crude public health measures were undertaken, and slowly the population increased. In addition to the epidemic diseases, tuberculosis, accidents, and many other illnesses took their toll, and to a considerable degree the need for public assistance in the colonies was directly related to the one important factor of illness.

The Puritan conception of charity has been mentioned, and some reference should also be made to the current attitudes toward personal behavior. It is apparent that Colonial legislation regarding the poor, the stranger, the idle, and the offender reflected the religious beliefs and the relentless search for the origin of sin which permeated the thinking of the governing group. Whether the common man felt such personal enthusiasm for religion is not so fully recorded, but undoubtedly he accepted the current pattern of thought; for in the colonies, as in England, the poor and lowly were expected to give obedience to the ruling class, and a severe discipline was exercised over the morals and manners of all the settlers. The famous Blue Laws of Connecticut were long the subject of controversy as to whether they actually existed, but any extensive examination of town records will illustrate the numerous admonitions and fines directed against those who deviated from the straight-and-narrow path not only in Connecticut but in the other New England states.[19]

In Massachusetts absence from public worship was especially noted, and the Salem court in 1667 fined several men 20s. and their wives and servants 10s. each for such an offense. The Cambridge records of 1665 reveal that three single men were brought before the selectmen to give an account of their abode and orderly carriage and thereby ordered to live in submission to family government.[20] "Bravery in dress" was strictly forbidden, and the two daughters of Hannah Bosworth of Haverhill were fined 10s. each for wearing silk, as this was contrary to law for persons in their station of life. Sam Weed was fined by the Hampton Court for his impertinent language when he said to the president of the court that "he might wear silver buttons if he paid for them as well as any man in the country," but the fine was remitted upon his humble petition and confession of his faults.[21] These

[19] W. F. Prince, "An Examination of Peter's Blue Laws," in *Annual Report of the American Historical Association, 1898*, chap. viii, pp. 95–139.

[20] Paige, *op. cit.*, p. 160; *Records and Files of the Quarterly Courts of Essex County, Massachusetts* (Salem, Mass.: Essex Institute, 1911——), III, 462.

[21] Chase, *op. cit.*, p. 122; *Records and Files of the Quarterly Courts of Essex County, Massachusetts*, V, 409.

penalties were in keeping with the prevailing law, for in 1651 the Massachusetts Bay Assembly had proclaimed their "detestation and dislike that men or women of meane condition, education and callings should take upon them the garb of gentlemen by wearing of gold or silver lace or buttons or poynte at their knees, to walk in great boots; or women of the same rank to wear silk or tiffany hoods or scarfs which . . . . [were] allowable to persons of greater estates or more liberal education." It prohibited persons or any of their relatives dependent upon them whose visible estate real and personal did not exceed £200 from wearing gold or silver lace.[22] Cotton Mather in his "Advice from the Watch Tower" furnished the inhabitants with "a Black List of some Evil Costums," which included not only absence from church but also sleeping in church, swearing, revels at weddings and at Christmas, and many other sins of the day. These few examples are offered as illustrations of the ways in which the leaders exercised discipline over many aspects of human behavior and conduct and to suggest the inevitable influence of Puritanism upon the social legislation of the earlier period.

Finally, in considering the poor-law legislation of the Colonial period, it is important to know who exercised the franchise and to what extent the economically less fortunate as well as the nonconformist in religion were represented. As has been pointed out, the New England fathers were little disposed toward democratic ideas, and a government in which the lowly participated would have seemed inconsistent with the rule of enlightened and pious men. Although the governing bodies were civil in character, the influence of

the clergy was strongly felt, and in Massachusetts the franchise in the beginning was limited to freemen who were members of the churches within the colony. This requirement "excluded from full rights of citizenship a steadily increasing number of excellent, upright and conscientious persons who for reasons suited to themselves could not or would not come into covenant with a church by prescribed methods."[23] Certain concessions were made gradually, and by 1652 all men of mature years who had taken the oath of fidelity to the government could participate to some degree in the management of local and colony affairs. But even as late as 1676 it was estimated that five-sixths of the men in Massachusetts were nonvoters because they were not church members, and consequently the many orders concerning the poor and the exclusion of strangers were passed by a minority of the inhabitants.

The Plymouth plantation did not limit the franchise to church members, and Rhode Island, as the refuge of religious nonconformists, naturally imposed no such restriction with the exception of the steps taken in 1729 to disfranchise the Roman Catholics. However, to be a freeman and therefore entitled to vote, one had to be a landowner, and this property qualification was not entirely eliminated until well into the nineteenth century and long after all the states except Connecticut had extended the franchise. In New Haven Colony prior to its absorption into Connecticut in 1665 only church members had the right to make the laws and to choose the public officials, and in the Connecticut Colony the right to vote was not dependent upon church membership but upon a carefully phrased oath of fidelity to the

[22] Shurtleff (ed.), *op. cit.*, III, 243.

[23] *Memorial History of Boston*, I, 150.

government which in effect excluded other than Trinitarians from taking the oath. The question of participation in government was further complicated by the distinction made between the "admitted inhabitant" and the "freemen." The former could vote and take part in local affairs and could elect the deputies to the general court (or legislature), but only the latter were deemed fit to fill the offices of deputy and of magistrate, and to them was left the general management of the affairs of the colony. Again, as in Massachusetts, the number of qualified voters was small, and it has been estimated that during the earlier years only about one-third of the admitted inhabitants were qualified as freemen. No attempt is made here to discuss fully the various steps taken to extend the franchise in the New England colonies but only to suggest some of the early limitations.[24]

Around the legislation governing pub-lic aid to persons becoming dependent arose many difficult legal questions. The most important one was whether the persons "belonged" to a town or had an "inhabitancy," by which was meant a legal right to dwell in the town. An inhabitancy further determined whether the destitute person was a "settled" person and therefore eligible for public aid from the selectmen or overseers of the poor. Altogether, it may be said that the right to dwell in the towns or plantations, the right to vote, to hold office, and to enjoy certain privileges and the question of public aid for persons becoming dependent, although separate questions, were closely related as they affected the status of the early colonists. For the clergy and those who because of position or substance assumed leadership in the government of the colonies the question of rights and obligations was clearly defined. But for the nonconformist in religion and the economically less fortunate the ways in which a foothold was to be secured and maintained in the New World were not always simple.

[24] *Ibid.*, pp. 148–59; cf. also C. M. Andrews, *The Colonial Period of American History* (1934), Vol. I, chaps. xiv and xx. For a comprehensive discussion of this question as it is related to Connecticut and Rhode Island, see *ibid.*, Vol. II, chap. i, iv, and v.

TULANE UNIVERSITY SCHOOL OF SOCIAL WORK

THE PATCHWORK OF RELIEF IN PROVINCIAL NEW YORK, 1664-1775[1]

DAVID M. SCHNEIDER

THE laws relating to the poor in New York province were largely "preventive" in character, concerned mainly with keeping indigent or potentially indigent persons from gaining settlement rather than with the actual relief of dependency. Poor-law administration in the province was lacking in uniformity—and in clarity, for that matter. It is significant that the poor laws invariably were drawn up for particular cities or counties and were studded with exemptions; general poor laws were rare. The administration of poor relief differed in many parts of the province in accordance with the varied backgrounds and needs of the inhabitants. Statutes attempting to regulate certain aspects of public welfare were frequently disregarded by localities where circumstances made it more convenient to adopt a contrary system.[2] In many districts, where the population was sparse and widely scattered, it was not necessary to adopt any definite poor-relief system, since occasions for relieving dependency were so few. Each case requiring public relief was dealt with independently as it arose, in a more or less haphazard manner.

Reports sent by various provincial governors to the mother-country, particularly in the last quarter of the seventeenth century, give the impression that the poor-relief problem in New York was negligible indeed. Governor Andros in 1678 informed the Lords of Trade in London that there were no beggars and that all the poor in the province were cared for. Eight years later Governor Dongan reported to the same body that "Every Town & County are obliged to maintain their own poor, which makes them bee soe careful that

[1] This article is a chapter from a forthcoming volume, *The History of Public Welfare in New York State, 1609–1866*, by David M. Schneider, to be published in November, 1938, as one of the "Social Service Monographs" by the University of Chicago Press.

[2] For example, the explicit directions contained in the first code of laws under the English, promulgated in 1665, ordering each locality to elect eight overseers and two churchwardens, were ignored by a number of towns.

Social Service Review 12 (September 1938): 464–94

noe Vagabonds, Beggars, nor Idle Persons are suffered to live here:"[3] Replying to a suggestion made by the Board of Trade and Plantations that a workhouse be erected in New York City, Governor Bellomont in 1699 expressed amusement at the idea, assuring the Board that "there is no such thing as a beggar in this town or country." We must take these statements with a grain of salt, of course, since they were written by men defending their administration and trying to paint the condition of the province in as rosy a hue as possible. Nevertheless, we may safely assume that poor-relief problems really did not reach any large proportions during the early colonial years. As the population increased and the social life grew more varied, however, these problems became more complex and the need for a permanent, carefully regulated poor-relief policy became more acute. When the Dutch surrendered the colony in 1664, the population was estimated at less than 12,000. In 1720 the estimate was 31,000; in 1731 it was 50,289; in 1771, 168,007. At the end of the Revolution it was given as 233,896.[4]

In spite of the harsh attitude manifested toward strangers, the relief of dependent persons actually settled in a locality was often characterized by generosity and neighborly warmth. Largely because of the rigid restrictions on settlement, persons dependent on the freeholders for support were few in the early days, and the cases that could be considered "unworthy" were fewer still. We are told that the town of East Hampton had for many years but one pauper, a woman friendless and alone. This single dependent was well cared for by the town, and when she subsequently fell sick the townspeople, who had no physician in the community, obtained medical attention for her from New York City and near-by towns, continuing their humane aid over a long period and at great expense.[5]

The English settlements on Long Island enjoyed autonomous government for some years prior to the first surrender of New Nether-

[3] *Documents Relative to the Colonial History of the State of New York*, ed. by E. B. O'Callaghan (New York, 1853–87), III, 415.

[4] Ellis H. Roberts, *New York: The Planting and Growth of the Empire State* (Boston, 1887), pp. 109, 232, 262, 343, 449.

[5] David Gardiner, *Chronicles of the Town of Easthampton, County of Suffolk, New York* (New York, 1871), p. 40.

land by the Dutch in 1664. Their methods of relieving the poor were simple and direct, as exemplified by an entry in the "First Book of Purposes" of the town records of Oyster Bay in 1661:

> All we whose names are heare under writen doe hereby Ingage our sellves that we will give frely towards the maintenans of the widdow croker so much Indian Corne for a yeare beginning at the first Day of February 1661 and to end the first of February 1662 provided we may be no more troubled with her more then the rent of the hous and that there be a person appointed to receiv it and to look to it and her that it may not be wasted. . . . .[6]

Fifteen freeholders of the town pledged to contribute from one to three bushels of corn each toward the widow Croker's relief. A year later, it appears, a tax was levied on all freeholders, "according as they have lots and rights in the Towne," for the maintenance of the poor widow.

Relief in kind was commonly practiced in many other parts of the province in those days, even in the city of New York. The accounts of Southampton for 1696 reveal how the town's first dependent, John Earl, was relieved in kind:[7]

> March ye 19th 1696. Account.
>
> Abraham Howell 12 loads of wood for Earl...... 1 lb. 10s.
> To half a bushel of wheat................... 3s.
> To 1½ bushels of corn....................... 7s.
> To a barrel of pork for Earl................. 3 lbs.
> Ellis Cook for a Steer for Earl.............. 4 " 3s.

The practice of boarding out paupers was also frequently resorted to in provincial New York. Thus, the town records of Huntington in the mid-eighteenth century contain such items as: "paid to ye widow Esther Titus for Sarah Chichester, 2 pounds, 6s., 8d." and "to Nath Wickes for keeping Mary Gunnery, 4 pounds."[8] In 1771, the South Precinct of Dutchess County (now Putnam County) paid a lump sum of 23 pounds to John Ryder for caring for the three-year-old orphans, Abigail and Levina Discomb, until they should "arrive to the age of eighteen years." In return for this

---

[6] Oyster Bay, N.Y., *Oyster Bay Town Records, 1655–1763* (New York, 1916–31), I, 3, 4, 9. Hereinafter referred to as *Oyster Bay Town Records*.

[7] *Records of the Town of Southampton*, V, 155.

[8] Huntington, N.Y., *Huntington Town Records, including Babylon, Long Island, N.Y.* (Huntington, 1887–89), II, 425–26.

payment, Ryder promised "to save the Precinct harmless from any further charge that may happen by said children" in the interim.[9] Before the poor law of 1773 made it mandatory for persons within certain degrees of consanguinity to provide for dependent relatives, paupers were often boarded out at public expense with their own parents, sisters, brothers, etc. In 1753, for instance, a blind dependent of Oyster Bay is recorded as being maintained by her father at the town's expense.[10]

Sometimes, when there were no permanent poorhouses, houses were hired temporarily to shelter the town's paupers. The practice of hiring a house for the poor was established in Southampton in 1724 and was continued for some years until the town secured an almshouse of its own.[11] The same custom, as will be shown, was followed in New York City for many years.

While certain aspects of provincial poor relief reflect a kindly and neighborly spirit, the prevailing attitude toward dependency was stern, cold, and strait-laced. In some parts of the province, a peculiarly harsh custom was adopted for branding the recipient of public relief with an unmistakable stigma. We refer to the practice of forcing the dependent to wear a badge of pauperism conspicuously upon his person, a custom derived from the mother-country. In 1696 a statute was enacted in England directing that each person receiving relief must wear on the shoulder of his right sleeve a badge or mark with a large letter "P," signifying "pauper," together with the initial of his parish. If the said pauper were a married man, his wife and children were also required to wear this pauper badge, to be cut in red or blue cloth. The same act authorized any justice of the peace to punish a poor person refusing to wear such badge by ordering his relief allowance reduced, suspended, or withdrawn altogether, or else to commit him to the house of correction, there to be whipped and kept at hard labor for a term not exceeding twenty-one days.[12]

---

[9] W. S. Pelletreau, *History of Putnam County* (Philadelphia, 1886), p. 153.

[10] *Oyster Bay Town Records*, VI, 367.

[11] *Records of the Town of Southampton*, V, 81.

[12] Sir George Nicholls, *A History of the English Poor Law* (rev. ed.; London, 1898), I, 341.

A decade after the passage of this English statute, the city of New York adopted a similar method for deterring dependency. The Common Council, in 1707, decreed that

The Church Wardens of this City put A Badge upon the Cloths of such poor as are Clothed by this City with this Mark N: Y in blew or Red Cloath att their discretion.[13]

That this practice survived late in the provincial period is indicated by the action taken at a town meeting at Oyster Bay held on April 1, 1755, when James Sands was "Chosen to Inspect Into the Poor and to See the Letter P: Sett on there garment as a Token of there Being Supported by ye Town."[14]

POOR RELIEF DEVELOPMENTS IN NEW YORK CITY

The unsteady, trial-and-error character of the development of colonial poor relief was nowhere so evident as in New York City, especially during the first quarter-century of English government.

Under Dutch rule, relief had been administered mainly through the congregational plan, with very little supervision by the civil authorities. In the score of years following the Dutch surrender, relief was dispensed in a haphazard manner, while authority for raising and disbursing poor funds remained vague and ill-defined. The provisions of the poor law of 1683, attempting to establish a uniform, secularized administrative pattern for the province, do not appear to have had any noticeable effect on the relief policy—or, rather, on the lack of such policy—in New York City. In November, 1683, the municipal authorities sent a petition to Governor Dongan explaining the government of the city, and recommending certain changes. They suggested, among other things, that overseers of the poor be elected, besides aldermen, in each of the six wards into which the city was divided. Governor Dongan approved of their plan, but the inhabitants do not appear to have carried it out. Consequently, Dongan found it necessary in 1685 to address a letter to the Common Council recommending that it take measures for the relief of the local poor.[15]

[13] New York City, Common Council, *Minutes of the Common Council of the City of New York, 1675 to 1776* (New York, 1905), III, 230. Hereinafter referred to as *N.Y.C., M.C.C., 1675-1776.*

[14] *Oyster Bay Town Records*, VI, 375.

[15] *N.Y.C., M.C.C., 1675-1776*, I, 104, 113, 167.

The Common Council responded in October of that year by directing the city aldermen to certify to the mayor the names of persons in their respective wards who "are poore and Wanting almse for their Susteanance," so that the operation of relief might be expedited. But the situation remained in an unsatisfactory, indefinite state, for in February, 1688, the Common Council again urged the aldermen to make inquiries in their several wards concerning persons in need of relief, and to present lists of such persons to the mayor. It was also ordered that the latter "Doe Releve the poore as hee hath don fformerly Vntill ffurther Ordor."[16] This arrangement seems to have placed an intolerable burden on the mayor, for two weeks later, on February 26, the Common Council made an important change in the administration of relief. It directed that thereafter the aldermen and the assistant aldermen were to "provide for theire poore in their Owne Ward & Bee paid out of ye Publick Tresury for what they disburst uppon ye Said accompt."[17] This practice of making the ward the relief unit in the city, and charging the alderman with the double duty of certifying and relieving dependents in his own ward, was to be revived from time to time during the succeeding centuries, with political consequences that may easily be imagined.

The raising of adequate relief funds through a central authority proved so difficult that in January, 1690, the Common Council, noting the absence of sufficient funds to meet the current relief needs, ordered the constables to collect voluntary offerings for poor relief from the residents of their respective wards.[18]

An attempt was made to establish some semblance of order in the municipal administration of relief in December, 1691, when two aldermen, Johannes Kip and Teunis de Kay, were appointed as overseers of the poor, who were empowered to act jointly in disbursing relief to all persons deemed "objects of charity."[19] It appears, however, that the other aldermen continued to administer relief to the poor in their several wards from their own purses, until reimbursed from the municipal treasury. Relief at this time was customarily given in the home in cash. A typical relief item from the city records dated September 17, 1691, reads:

[16] *Ibid.*, I, 193.   [17] *Ibid.*, I, 194.   [18] *Ibid.*, I, 212.   [19] *Ibid.*, I, 258.

Ordered that the Two Woemen and two Children without the gate in the House of John de La Vall the one called Topknott Betty the other one Stillwells wife with Children be prouided for as Objects of Charity & that four Shillings a weeke bee allowed them for one months time.[20]

On the same day, the Common Council directed that three shillings per week be paid to Mrs. Arthur Strangwich for the maintenance of her husband, who was "an object of charity." An identical weekly sum was ordered to be paid to a landlady for maintaining "the Widow Barbery," also an object of charity.

In 1693 the city came under the Act for Settling a Ministry. This statute provided for raising a maintenance for a Protestant ministry in the southern part of the province (with the Anglican church implicitly favored) and also for a poor rate. Poor relief was to be administered by ten vestrymen and two churchwardens to be elected by the freeholders. It does not appear that the terms of the act were carried out in New York City at the time. In 1695 the city experienced a critical emergency, and a temporary measure was enacted by the provincial assembly, entitled "An Act to Enable the City of New York to Relieve the Poor and defray their necessary and Publick charge." The preamble referred to the great distress of the poor, together with the fact that the city's public buildings were in a sad state of repair and "the highways streets and Lanes so Mirey and foul that they are Noysome to the Inhabitants of the said City as well as of his Majesties Liege Subjects resideing and travelling to and from the same," principally because no annual fund was being raised for these matters.[21] The statute provided for the annual appointment by the Common Council of "five good and Sufficient Citizens . . . . who shall be called overseers of the Poor and Public works and buildings." The overseers were empowered to raise an annual public tax for the public charges and for "the necessary reliefs of the Same impotent, old blind and such others being Poor and not able to work &c." We might infer from the dual responsibilities of the overseers, and the fact that poor relief and public works are mentioned together, that a public work relief program was intended

[20] *Ibid.*, I, 233.

[21] New York State, *Colonial Laws of New York from the Year 1664 to the Revolution* (Albany, 1894), I, 348–51. Hereinafter referred to as *C.L.N.Y.*

by this statute, although this intention is never made explicit in the wording of the law.

The Common Council named five overseers, as specified. Only four responded, however, and for some unexplained reason the Council failed to fill the existing vacancy. Directed to take a census of public dependents in the city and to estimate the poor rate needed for the following year, the overseers reported a rate of £100 for poor relief. But attempts to raise this sum through taxes proved unsuccessful, and during the year the overseers were forced to draw upon other city funds and to accept an advance of £10 from one of the aldermen, Jacobus Van Cortlandt, in order to meet relief needs.[22]

In 1702, the first year of Queen Anne's reign, a great epidemic of yellow fever broke out in New York City, causing the death of about 500 inhabitants out of a total population of approximately 4,400. This precipitated an emergency situation in poor relief. The city found itself bound by the provincial statutes limiting the annual poor rate to about £150, which had to be fixed on a certain day in the year. The fixed maximum was grossly inadequate to meet the crisis resulting from the epidemic, and the city fathers appealed to the legislature for aid. The assembly thereupon passed an "Act for the better Support and Maintenance of the Poor in the City of New York for the future," stating in the preamble that

. . . . the Mayor, Aldermen and Common Council of the City of New York, have represented unto the General Assembly of this province, that in the late Calamitous Distemper, which it please Almighty God to afflict the Inhabitants of the said City, the number and necessitys of the Poor were much increased; and the Sum of Money raised for the mainteinance of the Poor in the said City, was farr short of giving them a necessary Support in this Emergency.[23]

The act empowered the city authorities to raise special tax levies for relief purposes at any time in the year, should an emergency arise, instead of fixing the poor rate at a given time of the year, as previously required. The maximum poor rate permitted to New York City, which formerly had been restricted to a part of £300

---

[22] A scarcity of flour and a rise in bread prices in 1696 caused the poor of the city to petition the authorities for aid. It was at this point that the municipality was forced to seek a loan of ten pounds from one of its richest citizens, Alderman Van Cortlandt, to relieve the poor "in their Present Necessity" (*N.Y.C., M.C.C., 1675–1776*, I, 426, 429).

[23] *Ibid.*, I, 507–8.

allowed for *all* public charges, was raised to £300, with the proviso that the act was to be enforced for a limited period not exceeding two years.[24]

About this time a vigorous movement was in progress to give the Church of England a favored footing as the established church in New York City and elsewhere in the province. The city had previously resisted attempts to supersede the civil poor relief authorities with vestrymen and churchwardens, as had been ordered in the law of 1693 for settling a ministry. Now, however, the overseers of the poor disappeared from the picture. In the early 1700's it was the Common Council (and later the Mayor's Court) which, with the Anglican churchwardens and vestrymen, formed the administrative body in the municipal relief system.[25] The Dutch Reformed and Lutheran deaconry continued to be responsible for their respective congregational poor. The vestrymen were mainly responsible for levying the poor rate and supervising its collection. The churchwardens were charged with the actual distribution of the poor funds, usually upon specific orders from the Mayor's Court. Appeals for aid were made to the Mayor's Court, and, if applicants were considered deserving, the wardens were given specific instructions as to their relief. The Mayor's Court, an institution set up under Governor Nicolls in the cities of New York and Albany, consisted simply of the mayor and aldermen sitting as a court rather than as a legislative body.

In November, 1713, the justices and vestrymen of New York City informed the Common Council "that the poor of the said City are perishing for want of Cloths and Provisions and that there is an Absolute Nessessity for their Speedy relief." This emergency was met through the flotation of a loan of £100 for a period of six months, in anticipation of taxes.[26] Early in the same year a list of the city's poor had been entered in the minutes of the Mayor's Court. It comprised less than a score of names, and probably rep-

The poor rate rose steadily during the colonial period, reaching several thousand pounds in the later years.

[25] At first ten vestrymen were elected, but after 1745 there were fourteen, two being chosen from each ward.

[26] *N.Y.C., M.C.C., 1675–1776*, III, 52–53.

resented only those dependents who were considered permanent cases, since other entries at this time show many unlisted persons as recipients of relief for temporary periods.

A minor crisis in municipal poor relief occurred in November, 1720, when the churchwardens informed the Mayor's Court that funds were lacking to pay the minister's salary "or to Supply the dayly Occasions of the Poor," and that they—the churchwardens— had "disburst and Expended upwards of fifteen pounds of their own Moneys to preserve several Poor People from Perishing." In this instance the Court ordered that the churchwardens continue to disburse their own funds until a tax could be levied, and that they be repaid with interest from the receipts.[27]

Other crises, more or less severe, came in 1741, 1753, and during and after the French and Indian War, which ended in 1763. The difficulties of 1741 seem to have been occasioned largely by a particularly severe winter,[28] and gave rise to a notable venture in voluntary relief. Notices published in the *New York Journal* during the month of January, 1741, indicate that a fund of £500 was raised for the poor and placed for disbursement in the hands of Abraham Lefferts and Abraham Van Wycke, who probably constituted the first citizens' emergency relief committee in the city. These gentlemen proposed to make their headquarters at the house of Nicholas Roy, "opposite to the late Black Horse Tavern," three mornings each week, and there receive the applications and attend to the needs of the poor. The utmost discretion was promised respecting the relief of "any Credible Families [who] are in real Want, and scruple to make it known."

The hardships of 1753 were caused by the efforts of the city merchants to check the import of English half-pennies; they refused to accept such coins save at a reduced value. As a result the poor, who probably had few enough ha'pennies of any kind to start with,

[27] New York City, Mayor's Court, *Minutes*, Nov. 8, 1720. (Hereinafter referred to as *N.Y.C., M.M.C.*)

[28] "The winter of 1740-1 was remembered for many years as the 'Hard Winter.' The intense cold continued from the middle of November to the close of March. The snow was six feet on a level, the Hudson was frozen at New York, and great suffering was felt among the poor" (Mary L. Booth, *History of the City of New York* [New York, 1867], I, 353-54).

found their ability to buy essential goods seriously impaired. Clubs
and staves were flourished with much abandon in a protest demonstration which followed; the threat of violence was serious enough
to warrant a grand jury investigation.[29]

Poverty must have increased markedly in the city during the
French and Indian War. In January, 1759, the *New York Gazette*
carried news of "a very considerable Collection" having been made
for the poor, "all the necessaries of life at this time being at a much
higher price than was ever known in this City." In January, 1765,
it was necessary to borrow £200 from the general tax fund to carry
on poor relief, the money raised for this purpose having been completely expended. During the same month the *New York Gazette*
noted the existence of a severe post-war depression:

> The declining state of business in the city together with the high rents and
> prices of the necessaries of life, having reduced very many families and poor
> people generally to great distress especially since the late severe weather, con-
> tributions for their relief have been made by several humane gentlemen.

An order of the Common Council dated May 6, 1767, shows that
the distress of the past year had made it necessary to hire at least
two extra dwelling houses for the care of the poor.[30]

RISE OF INSTITUTIONAL RELIEF IN PROVINCIAL NEW YORK

The English poor law of 1601 (43 Elizabeth, c. 2), which served
as the foundation for the general poor-relief policy in Great Britain
and America, made a distinction between three classes of dependents: Those who cannot work, those who have no employment
though they are willing and able to work, and those who will not
work. Out of this distinction there developed a threefold system of
institution provision for dependents: (1) the poorhouse, for the "impotent" poor; (2) the workhouse, for the able-bodied poor who were
"worthy"; and (3) the house of correction, for the able-bodied poor
who were "unworthy"—that is, the types then known as "valiant
rogues" and "sturdy beggars."[31]

While these three institutional types were clearly defined in

---

[29] *New York Gazette*, January 14, 21, 1754.

[30] *N.Y.C., M.C.C., 1675–1776*, VII, 66.

[31] It should be noted that workhouses and houses of correction (or bridewells) existed
in England prior to the enactment of the Elizabethan poor law.

theory, no marked distinction was maintained in practice. In most instances it was highly impractical for a town to construct three separate institutions, or even two. A workhouse might be used as a place of punishment for vagrants and other "unworthy" able-bodied poor, and as a place for setting the "worthy" able-bodied poor to work. Sometimes it housed the latter and the impotent poor; occasionally it included all three types of dependents under its roof. It was this combination workhouse, poorhouse, and house of correction that was finally adopted in New York City.

Under Dutch rule there had been several poorhouses in the colony maintained by the Dutch Reformed church for its indigent members. There was apparently no stigma attached to inmates of these institutions, who were regarded as worthy poor. These congregational almshouses continued to function for many years after the colony came under British hegemony. In 1701 the consistory of the Dutch church in New York City auctioned off its old poorhouse at Broad Street, which had become dilapidated, and built a new one at the present site of 37 Wall Street.[32] In a petition requesting the incorporation of the Dutch church of Albany, presented to the provincial authorities in 1720, it is stated that the congregation had "purchased Certain two Tenements and Lotts of ground for a poor or alms house, and for a Minister's dwelling house."[33] However, it was not until 1735 that the first poorhouse under civil auspices was built in the province. Quite naturally, it was located in the most populous town, New York City. The erection of this institution marked the culminating point of a development dating back many years.

Institutional provision for the able-bodied poor had been recommended in instructions, couched in identical language, sent by the Crown to Governor Benjamin Fletcher in 1692 and to Governor Richard Bellomont in 1697:

> You are to endeavour with the assistance of the Councill to provide for the raising and building of Publick Work houses in convenient Places for the employing of Poor and Indigent People.[34]

[32] New York State, State Historian, *Ecclesiastical Records State of New York* (New York, 1901–16), III, 1,462.

[33] *Ibid.*, III, 2,148.   [34] *Docs. Rel. Col. Hist.*, III, 823.

But on April 27, 1699, Lord Bellomont reported to the Lords of Trade:

A Bill to enforce the building of publick workhouses (which is another instruction from his Majesty) to imploy the poor and also vagabonds I offered to the Assembly, but they smiled at it, because indeed there is no such thing as a beggar in this town or country; and I believe there is not a richer populace any where in the King's dominions than is in this Town.[35]

In 1714, however, the Common Council appointed a committee:

. . . . to Consult with the Mayor about the building of a poorhouse and house of Correction in this City . . . . [and to] Consider of A Convenient place to Erect the same, of the Demensions and Materialls and of ways & Means for Raising a fund for the compleating thereof.[36]

No record of the committee's report has been found; perhaps it was never made. Certain it is that the idea of constructing a permanent institution for paupers and vagrants was dropped for the time being. Instead, the city adopted the policy of sending indigent persons to a private dwelling-house, the mistress or keeper of which was paid for receiving and maintaining the poor. Thus, though the city as yet had no municipal poorhouse, a congregate method of housing public dependents was introduced. In August, 1714, one Samuel Garratt, being "very Sick and weak," was ordered into "the poor house" by the Mayor, and the Mayor's Court directed that he be supported "untill he be able to work for his living" and that the churchwardens pay the "woman of the poor house for his Support hitherto."[37]

It appears that the first "poor house woman" was one Elizabeth Burger. On July 5, 1715, the churchwardens were ordered to pay "to Elizabeth Burger Keeper of the poor house Six pounds New York Money for Supplying her with necessaries for the use of the poor and for her Care and trouble about them for one year."[38] The greater part of the poor continued to be maintained by relief in their own homes as before. It seems likely, from the records, that the population of the poorhouse at this time consisted almost exclusively of the friendless and helpless, for whom the incidental care available in ordinary private dwellings would not be adequate.

[35] Ibid., IV, 290.   [37] N.Y.C., M.C.C., August 31, 1714.
[36] N.Y.C., M.C.C., 1675–1776, III, 59–60.   [38] Ibid., July 5, 1715.

The need for municipal institutions for the dependent and mis-demeanant classes was more keenly felt as time went on and the population continued to increase. The charter of 1730 recognized this need by empowering the city to construct an almshouse and one or more houses of correction and workhouses.[39] Four years later the Common Council voted favorably on a resolution authorizing the erection of a building to serve all three purposes "on the unim-proved Lands of this Corporation on the North Side of the lands of Coll. Dongan, Commonly Called the Vineyard," which lay near the site of the present city hall.[40]

In March, 1736, the institution was completed and was given the all-embracing name of "House of Correction, Workhouse and Poor House." It was a two-story structure, 65 feet by 24, built of stone. In the same month plans for its operation were drawn up, and a committee of the Common Council was appointed "to enquire upon what terms this corporation may hire an able and sufficient person to be keeper of the House of Correction and overseer of the workhouse and poorhouse."

In order to set "such poor to work as are able to labour and to prevent their being a Charge and Burthen to the Publick by sloth and Idleness and for Carrying on Trades, Occupation and Manu-factures," the committee, in its report, recommended:

That the said house of correction Workhouse and poorhouse be furnished with all convenient speed with the following Tools and Utensils (to witt) four spinning wheels one or two large wheels for making of shoes, two pairs of wollen cards, some knitting Needles, twelve pounds of Flax, 500 pounds of old Junck, twelve pounds of wool, twelve pounds of Cotton, two or three Hatchells, and such other Tools, Utensils and Furniture as for the future shall be found needful and necessary from time to time. . . . . .[41]

John Sebring was selected as the first superintendent. His salary was fixed at £30 annually, with board for himself and his family. He was responsible to the city churchwardens, who were in turn responsible to the vestrymen and justices of the peace. His duties, as defined by the Common Council, were to:

[39] New York City, *Charter* (1730) (New York, 1819), pp. 73–74.

[40] *N.Y.C., M.C.C., 1675–1776*, IV, 240–41.

[41] *Ibid.*, IV, 308.

. . . . sett on Work all such poor as shall be sent or committed thither and able to labour; and also all disorderly persons, parents of Bastard Children, Beggars, Servants, running away or otherwise misbehaving themselves, Trespassers, Rogues, Vagabonds, poor persons refusing to work, and on their refusal to work and labour to correct them by moderate Whipping, and to yield a true Account to Every General Quarter Sessions of the peace to be held for this City and County of all persons committed to his custody, and of the offenses for which they were committed.[42]

Slaveholders might send slaves to the institution to be whipped; the lashing was administered at a fee of one shilling and sixpence. Fetters, gyves, shackles, and facilities for applying the lash were suggested as necessary equipment for the house of correction. Elementary education and industrial training in preparation for apprenticeship in some useful trade were recommended for such destitute children as might be sent to the almshouse for maintenance. In this respect the committee's attitude appears far more enlightened than that manifested in the average almshouse of a later time. And if "the westermost division of the Cellar" was chosen for the confinement of the unruly, the committee did not hesitate to say that "the upper Room at the west End of the said House should be suitably furnished for an Infirmary and for no other Use whatsoever." This infirmary gradually developed into a separate hospital, later becoming the great city institution known as Bellevue Hospital. On the basis of these modest beginnings, some historians claim for Bellevue the distinction of being the oldest public hospital in this country. The first physician appointed for the almshouse was Dr. John van Buren, who held office for thirty years at a salary of £100 yearly, out of which he paid for all needed medicines.[43]

In 1739 a separate structure was erected in order to shelter destitute victims of contagious diseases. Other additions to the combination poorhouse–workhouse–house of correction were subsequently made during the provincial period.

Following the erection of the poorhouse in New York City, similar institutions were built in other parts of the province. A provincial statute enacted in 1747, applying only to Dutchess Coun-

[42] *Ibid.*, IV, 309.

[43] New York City, Common Council, *Manual of the Corporation of the City of New York* ("Valentine's Manual") (New York, 1862), p. 658.

ty, authorized local overseers of the poor in that county to hire or erect dwellings for setting the able-bodied poor to work, and to purchase materials for that purpose. The legislature passed acts of a like nature for other counties. It is notable that all these statutes provided for the establishment of workhouses and poorhouses by individual towns and precincts. The English system of town or district unions for the maintenance of mutually controlled institutions was introduced at a relatively late date in the colonies. Massachusetts authorized town unions for the support of workhouses in 1743. With one exception, relating to the care of the insane during colonial times, the system was not introduced in New York until the nineteenth century.

CHILD WELFARE

The system of apprenticeship formed the cornerstone of child welfare in provincial times. As a part of the poor-relief policy in New York, it may be traced back to both the English poor law of 1601 and the Dutch practice which prevailed up to 1664. The records of Southampton for 1694 contain the following item illustrating the practice of binding out children in groups:

> At a meeting of ye Trustees ye 14 of June did then order that according to ye directions of ye Justices to take care of the poore and orphans within our parish, and the children of Thomas Reeves and Ben Davis deceased being both fatherless and motherless, that Isaac William and Aaron Burnatt do bond out said orphans, According on ye 15th day were five of the said orphans bound out. . . . . [44]

In the event of misfortune which temporarily prevented the support of children by their parents, the authorities might relieve the family in its home, or they might place the children in other hands until the parents were again able to care for them. In the case of a prisoner (probably a debtor) who petitioned for relief for his family, the Common Council of New York ordered, under date of February 27, 1694, "that the Overseers of the Poor doe put out the Children of the Said Petitioner in Some Good Reputable Families for their Subsistance dureing his Imprisonment."[45] In January, 1719, the Mayor's Court directed that:

[44] *Records of the Town of Southampton*, V, 67.

[45] *N.Y.C., M.C.C., 1675–1776*, I, 348.

The Church Wardens Inspect in what Condition the Widow & Children of Thomas Grisson are in at The Bowry and if they find Their Children Objects of Charity that they Relieve them at Their Discretions or putt them out Apprentice for a Term of Years.[46]

Throughout the provincial period, dependent and neglected children were commonly disposed of by apprenticeship or indentured servitude. When a boy was bound out, it was specified as a rule that his master should teach him to read, write, and cipher. Thus, when Justus Whitfield was apprenticed by order of the New York Common Council on May 24, 1720, "to Learn the Art of a Marriner," his prospective master, one Jasper Busk, was "to Provide him with Meat Drink & Apparell to learn him to Read Write and Cypher & to give him two good New Suites of Apparell at the Expiration of the Term."[47] Justus was to have thirteen years in which to learn his art, since he was apprenticed at the age of eight years. From the records of Amenia in Dutchess County we learn that boy apprentices in that town commonly received, at the end of their service, a beaver hat, "two good new suits," a new Bible, and "twenty Pounds York money in neat cattle or sheep to be appraised by Indifferent men." Girl apprentices were supplied with two suits of clothes, a new cloak and bonnet, and a Bible, and "30 Pounds of good live Geese feathers."[48]

Children might be indentured at any age up to twenty-one. A New York order for apprenticeship in 1726 names George Williams, aged four years, and an order of a year earlier designated apprenticeship as an alternative for Joseph Byng, "an Infant Aged Eighteen Months or thereabouts," the son of a feltmaker confined in the common jail.[49] Occasionally, as has been observed, a group of dependent children were offered for apprenticeship at one time. On June 11, 1750, the *New York Weekly Post-Boy* printed a notice to the effect that several children of age ten or less, available for apprenticeship, were at the almshouse.

While the indenture system offered by far the best means of disposing of dependent and neglected children, the lot of apprentices

[46] *N.Y.C., M.M.C.*, January 13, 1719. [47] *Ibid.*, May 24, 1720.

[48] *Amenia Precinct Book for the Poor, A.D., 1760–1820* (MS), pp. 3–6.

[49] *N.Y.C., M.M.C.*, December 13, 1726; July 20, 1725.

was generally a hard one, and the rights given them by law were frequently disregarded in the absence of public supervision. The records reveal, however, that the authorities occasionally put their foot down in instances of flagrant violations of such rights. On August 21, 1716, the Mayor's Court of New York ordered Peter Ament, a cooper, to appear for his examination regarding the charge that he failed to supply his apprentice with sufficient clothing. The complaint had been made by Henry Colie, father of the apprentice in question, who petitioned the Court either to cause the lad to be properly clothed or to have him released from his apprenticeship.[50]

There is some indication that the authorities kept track, in a hit-and-miss fashion, of the municipality's minor wards. A Mayor's Court order of 1735 directs the churchwardens to remove Mary Lewoll:

....a Parish Child at Nurse with Elizabeth Lowns, from the said Elizabeth Lowns, she being negligent in her Duty to the said Infant, and that they place the said Infant with Mrs. Laurier, the Wife of Michael Laurier, till further order.[51]

An interesting instance wherein preventive measures were urged against possible delinquency occurred in 1716, when Jonathan Haight of Rye informed the Westchester Court of Sessions that

one Thomas Wright, an orphan in that town, hath no certain Place of Abode there, but lives like a Vagabond and at a loose end, and will undoubtedly come to Ruine unless this Court take some speedy and effectual care for ye prevention thereof.[52]

EDUCATIONAL PROVISION FOR POOR CHILDREN

A free public-school system did not come into being in New York until late in the nineteenth century. During the provincial period free public schools were relatively few, and these were open mainly to the children of taxpayers. The majority of the poor children of the province were excluded from the benefits of school education. The first proposal for popular education in New York province was made in 1691, when a bill was introduced in the assembly providing for the appointment of "a school master for the educating and in-

[50] *Ibid.*, August 21, 1716.   [51] *Ibid.*, July 15, 1735.

[52] Charles W. Baird, *History of Rye: Chronicle of a Border Town, 1660–1870* (New York, 1871), pp. 163–64.

This Indenture Made the Sixteenth day [of]
July Anno Domini one thousand Seven Hundred
Sixty Eight Witnesseth that Conrad Winneger and [
Wright two of the Overseers of the Poor of Amenia [
in Dutchess County and Province of New York by an[d]
the Consent of Daniel Castle and Roswell Hopkins [
two of his majestys Justices of the Peace for Said Co[
by Virtue of a Law of this Colony in that Case ma[de]
Provided hath placed and Bound Isaac Osborn So[n]
John Osborn Late of Amenia Precinct aforesaid Dece[ased]
Apprentice unto Colbe Chamberlain of Said Precin[ct]
farmer with him to Dwell Continue and Serve from [the]
Date hereof until he Shall Attain the full and Comple[te]
of Twenty One years During all which Term the Sai[d]
ntice his Said Master well and faithfully Shall Serve [his]
Seents keep his Lawful Commands gladly Do and Obey [harm]
to his Said Master he Shall not Do nor willfully Suffer [to be]
Done by Others the goods of his Said Master he Shall no[t]
Imbezil or waste nor them lend without his Consen[t]
any at Cards Dice or any other unlawful Games [he Shall]
not play Taverns he Shall not frequent fornication [he Shall]
not Committ Mattrimony he Shall not Contract from [the]
Service of his Said Master he Shall not Depart at any [time]

Service of his said Master he shall not Depart at any time
to absent himself without his said Masters Leave but in
all things as a good and faithfull Apprentice shall a
will Demean and behave Himself towards his said Maste
and all his During said Term And the said Master Doth hereby
Covenant agree and Promise to find and allow unto his sai
Apprentice Sufficient Meat Drink washing and Lodging and
all other Necessaries fit and Convenient for Such an apprentic
During said Term and shall and will Learn and Instruct
said Apprentice to Read write and Cypher So as to be able t
keep Book and at the End and Expiration of said Term
shall and will find Provide and Allow and Deliver unto hi
said Apprentice two Suits of apprel good and new the one
Suit fit for the Holy Days and the other Suit fit for the
working Days and twenty Pounds york money in Cattle
to be apprayed by Indifferent men and a new Bible In
Witness whereof the Parties to thep Presents have hereunto
set their hands and Seals the Day and year first above
written
ed and Delivered
In the Presence of
   _____
Ichabod Prosper

es County ss July 16: 1768 we the
riben two of his majestys Justices of the
for said County do hereby Consent to the
y the above named poor Child apprentice
ess our Hands

FORM, 1768
the Poor, A.D. 1760–1820 (MS)

structing of youth, to read and write English, in every town in the province." This bill, evidently intended to accelerate the replacement of the prevailing Dutch culture by English, failed to pass. In October, 1702, Governor Cornbury urged "the erecting of Public Schools in proper places," and the following month the assembly responded by passing "An Act for Encouragement of a Grammar Free School in the City of New York," authorizing the city to levy fifty pounds annually for the maintenance of the school and a schoolmaster. The institution was opened in 1704, and closed five years later.[53] Not until 1732 did the provincial government renew its interest in education, when it enacted a statute to "encourage a Public School in the City of New York for teaching Latin, Greek and Mathematicks." Provision was made in this measure for free tuition to twenty students allotted among several counties. The school was abandoned after operating for six years. Here the interest of the provincial authorities in encouraging primary and secondary education at public expense came to an end. The authorities, as representatives of the Crown, regarded the common school mainly as an effective medium of propaganda for the Church of England and for royalty. The majority of provincial New Yorkers were unwilling to subject their children to such influences. This factor appears to have been largely responsible for the failure to establish and maintain province-encouraged common schools in New York.

Meanwhile, several "charity schools" were established by the Society for the Propagation of the Gospel in Foreign Parts. Significantly enough, this was an Anglican organization—and the Anglican church was definitely a royalist institution, with the king at its head, positively and without secrecy bound to carry on propaganda for the Crown as well as the faith. The Society established schools at several points in the southeastern counties. Each of these schools apparently offered primary education to the very poor without charge.[54] In 1704 it opened a school in New York City for Negro and Indian slaves, and it is claimed that through this institution

[53] William W. Kemp, *The Support of Schools in Colonial New York by the Society for the Propagation of the Gospel in Foreign Parts* (New York, 1913), p. 70.

[54] C. F. Pascoe, *Two Hundred Years of the Society for the Propagation of the Faith in Foreign Parts* (London, 1901), II, 769.

"many were raised from their miserable condition and became stead-fast Christians." Early in 1710 the Society founded a charity school in New York City for white children with forty poor boys in at-tendance. It was later taken over by Trinity Church and operated under its auspices thereafter. The custom of preaching "charity sermons" to obtain clothing and other necessities for the poor pupils was begun in 1754 and continued for many years thereafter.[55]

The authorities of New York City in 1714 made an unsuccessful attempt to raise funds to maintain "a public schoolmaster for teach-ing the poor to Read & write."[56] A later effort to encourage primary education among such poor pupils as could not be accommodated by the charity school is evidenced by the order of the Common Council, on October 14, 1731, to pay eight pounds out of public funds to the widow Sarah Huddleston

as a Gratification for the trouble and Care she and her late Son Thomas Hud-dleston deceased have taken in teaching several Poor Children of this Corpora-tion to Read and Write and Instructing them in the Principles of Religion over and above the Number allowed by the Venerable society for propagation of the Gospel in forreign parts.[57]

Among the communities in which town schools were established by people of English descent or birth were Eastchester, Rye, and White Plains. At New Rochelle the French clergy conducted a school until the mid-eighteenth century. It is unlikely that any of those schools offered tuition entirely free. The community of Johns-town established a free school in 1769.[58] At times, dependent chil-dren were relieved in kind, as shown in an action of the Mayor's Court of New York City, November 1, 1726, ordering the church-wardens to

Supply Phillip Cordus a sickly boy at the House of Anantie Delamontagne with a pair of Schoes A pair of Stockings A Blankett and some Course Linnen to make a Straw Bed, he being poor and an Object of Charity.

Children born out of wedlock who became public charges were ordinarily disposed of in the same manner as other groups of de-

[55] *New York Mercury*, October 24, 1764.

[56] *N.Y.C., M.C.C., 1675–1776*, III, 63–64.   [57] *Ibid.*, IV, 74–75.

[58] Alexander C. Flick (ed.), *History of the State o f New York* (New York, 1932–35), III, 76.

pendent children. The drain on local treasuries from this source must have proved burdensome, for in 1774, the provincial assembly enacted a law for "the Relief of Parishes and other Places from such Charges as may arise from Bastard Children born within the same." This act was derived almost word for word from an English statute of 1733 (6 Geo. II., c. 31), which in turn was based on an act passed in the eighteenth year of Queen Elizabeth's reign. Explaining in its preamble that "the laws now in being are not sufficient to provide for the securing and indemnifying Parishes and other Places, from the Great Charges frequently arising from Children begotten and born out of lawful Matrimony," the act of 1774 authorized justices of the peace in any locality to apprehend and confine in the common jail or house of correction any man charged by a single woman, under oath, with being the father of a bastard child chargeable or likely to become chargeable to the locality, upon application of the overseers of the poor or any substantial householding resident. The putative father was to be held unless he gave security to indemnify the parish or other local unit, or to appear at the next general or quarter sessions and to abide by the orders made there.[59]

Protection was afforded to the alleged father through the right of appeal against unjust detention. In cases where "the putative Fathers and lewd Mothers of Bastard Children run away out of the Parish or Place and sometimes out of the County, and leave the said Bastard Children upon the Charge of the Parish or Place where they are born," the churchwardens or overseers of the poor of the said locality were authorized to seize the property of the absconding parents against the cost of maintaining the child as a public charge.

SPECIAL RELIEF FOR THE MENTALLY AND PHYSICALLY HANDICAPPED

As a rule, public relief for the physically handicapped in New York province did not differ essentially from the forms of relief meted out to other classes of dependents. They were ordinarily supported in their own homes, boarded out with private families, or placed in the poorhouse when such an institution was available. At times, a type of vocational relief was afforded them, with the

[59] *C.L.N.Y.*, V, 689–92.

aim of rehabilitating them to a position of self-support. An instance of a more indirect method of relieving the physically disabled is contained in the minutes of the Mayor's Court in New York City for February 11, 1718, in relation to a dependent blind man:

Thomas Clifton who has lately lost his eye sight by hard Labour and sickness and Thereby rendered uncapable of getting a livelyhood for himself and his wife it is Therefore Order'd that the Church Wardens do provide for the wife of the said Thomas Clifton a Flax wheel and a pair of Wool Cards in Order for their better support they being Objects of Charity.

This practice of providing occupational tools to applicants as a means of public relief also extended to the able-bodied poor. For example, in 1733 the churchwardens of New York City were ordered to provide one Vincent Delamontagne "with a Bundle of twine for the making of a fishing Net towards his Support he being an Object of Charity."

The treatment of the insane poor constituted one of the most perplexing problems in public relief. In all ages, the care and treatment of the mentally ill naturally has reflected current attitudes toward insanity, its nature, and causes. During a large part of the provincial period mental disease was frequently regarded as a manifestation of demoniacal possession and treated accordingly. Even when insanity was recognized as something other than demoniacal possession the treatment meted out to the mentally sick was often characterized by cold brutality or else complete indifference and neglect. Consideration was seldom shown them. The major, if not the sole, concern of the public authorities in providing for the dependent insane was to protect society against violence at their hands. The needs of the insane themselves went unheeded, largely because their needs were not yet known. When their illness manifested itself in violent behavior, the insane were ordinarily incarcerated in prisons like common criminals. When their illness was of a harmless type, they were likely to be treated as common paupers. Only in rare instances was mental disease recognized as such, and its victims accorded therapeutic treatment.

An amendment of the Duke's Laws in 1665 provided for town unions when the care of "distracted Persons" who were "both very chargeable and troublesome" proved too burdensome for one town alone to bear. Advantage was taken of this provision in 1695, when the Court of Sessions of Kings County directed that "Mad James be kept by Kings County in General and that the deacons of each town within the said county doe forthwith meet together and consider about their propositions for maintenance of said James."[60] What these "propositions" were we have been unable to discover, but this incident probably represents the earliest example of county care for dependents in New York.

A special structure was ordered to be built in New York City in 1677 for the confinement of Peter Paull, a "lunatick." Pending the completion of this one-man asylum, it was directed that the said Paull "Bee confined into prison in the hold."[61] The records do not indicate whether this structure was ever completed. In later years the town jail was used for the custody of the violent insane. In 1725 the town marshal was paid two shillings sixpence by the church-wardens of New York City, "for to Subsist Robert Bullman & Madman in Prison." Usually the term of confinement was for the duration of the period of lunacy. In 1720, for example, the same town marshal was given the custody of one Henry Dove, "a Dangerous Madman, untill he shall Recover his senses."[62]

At times, the "harmless" dependent insane were provided for in their own homes or lodgings, as were other classes of dependents. On May 20, 1720, the Mayor's Court directed the churchwardens to "pay to Mr. John Moere four Shillings Weekly to be by him laid out and Applyed to the use of Mrs. Schelleux Widdow (who is non Compos Mentis) towards her Support and Maintenance She being an Object of Charity." On October 10, 1721, the Mayor's Court of New York ordered the churchwardens to "supply Susan Commonly called Mad Sew with a good pair of Shoes & Stockings & other Necessary Warm Clothing She being Very Old Poor & Non Compos Mentis." An interesting instance where relief was provided in the form of a loan is recorded in 1712, when the churchwardens in New

---

[60] Gabriel Furman, *Notes, Geographical and Historical, Relating to the Town of Brook-lyn* (Brooklyn, 1824,) p. 101.

[61] I. N. P. Stokes, *Iconography of Manhattan Island, 1498–1909* (New York, 1915–28), IV, 314.

[62] *N.Y.C., M.M.C.,* July 5, 1720.

York City were ordered "to lend Phillip Batten, butcher, thirty shillings, in order to go on with his trade (he being reduced to great poverty by reason of his wife being delirious) being an object of charity."[63]

A curious measure for preventing a possible suicide is revealed in the records of New York City for 1729:

Whereas Timothy Dally of this City Marriner is lately seized with a deep Melancholy and by intervals is perfectly distracted & non Compos Mentis so that it is feared he will lay violent hands upon himself if no Care be taken to prevent it. And he having a wife and four small children who cannot subsist without his labour it is Therefore Order'd that the Church Wardens pay to the wife of the said Timothy Dally Six Shillings p week towards subsisting The said Timothy Dally and his children during his illness they being Objects of Charity.[64]

One of the very rare instances of provision for medical care for mentally ill dependent occurred in Southampton in 1701, when the town trustees ordered Samuel Barbor to send his insane wife to "ye prison house" where she was to be maintained at town expense. At the same time, one Captain Topping was directed "to speak to Dr. Wade to come and see her [Mrs. Barbor] and to administer that which is proper for such a Person according to his skill and cunning."[65]

MEDICAL AID TO THE POOR

The first general hospital in New York province was established in 1771, and was not opened until twenty years later. Reference to hospitals appears in the records of Albany and New York in the years immediately following the close of the French and Indian War in 1763, but these were military hospitals built and maintained temporarily for sick and wounded soldiers. In 1699 the Common Council of New York ordered that "the Mayor Agree with Some person for the keeping of an hospital for the maintenance of the poor."[66] It is uncertain, however, whether a hospital for the reception of the sick poor was intended, or merely a refuge for friendless and infirm poor, as the early English usage of the term "hospital"

---

[63] Thomas F. De Voe, *The Market Book* (New York, 1862), I, 91.

[64] *N.Y.C.*, *M.M.C.*, May 13, 1729.

[65] *Records of the Town of Southampton*, V, 161–62.   [66] Stokes, *op. cit.*, IV, 418.

indicates. Most probably the latter was intended, inasmuch as the erection of a poorhouse or workhouse was being widely discussed during this period. At any rate, it is certain that neither hospital nor poorhouse was built at the time.

Practically the only means of providing medical aid to the sick poor during the provincial period was to contract with some private physician for attendance to the poor in their homes, on a salary or visit basis. At an early date the services of a salaried municipal physician were made available to the needy in New York City. Dr. Johannes Kerfyle took office in 1687 and served at least two years, the city records show. In 1713 Jacob Provost became the city physician for the poor, at a salary of eight pounds. Municipal medical care, however, was not limited to the services of the city physician. The minutes of the Mayor's Court include many items indicating that direct and indirect medical aid to needy individuals was often administered through other sources at city expense. For example:

August 23, 1715. Order'd The Church Wardens pay to Elizabeth Davis Three Pounds Current Money of New York towards paying her Doctor and defraying her Charges in the Cutting of her brest. She being an Object of Charity.[67]

In 1720 the churchwardens were directed to pay Mary Golding "for Nursing of Grace Pangborne" for three weeks. Nine years later the city treasurer was ordered to pay Dr. Jacob Moene three pounds "for Setting and Curing the broken Leg of A poor Saylor Named John who was an Object of Charity."[68]

Sick dependents were often boarded out in private homes during their illness. In 1719 the New York churchwardens were authorized to pay four pounds and eight shillings to Garrett De Bogh "for his Maintenance of Alexander Griggs a poor Sick man for Eighteen weeks." On other occasions the sick poor were sent to the dwelling hired as a poorhouse by the city. As has been noted, when the permanent poorhouse was opened in 1736, it included an infirmary intended not only for the inmates but for poor residents who fell ill.

That the city was quite generous on occasion is evidenced by the fact that on May 26, 1762, Dr. John Bard was paid seven pounds

[67] N.Y.C., M.M.C., August 23, 1715.					[68] N.Y.C., M.C.C., 1675-1776, III, 483.

for delivering an almshouse inmate of a child. On March 17, 1773, Dr. Beekman Van Bueren was paid nearly thirty-eight pounds for attending and providing medicine to prisoners in the Bridewell and the New Gaol.[69]

The custom of appointing midwives for the service of the poor seems to have been practiced in the larger towns throughout the provincial period. It is interesting to note that a New York City ordinance passed in 1731 "for regulating Midwives" contained a prescribed oath in which the following provision was included:

> You Shall swear, first that you Shall be Dilligent and faithfull and Ready to help Every Woman Labouring of Child As well the poor as the Rich; and that in time of Necessity you shall not for sake or Leave the poor Women to go to the Rich.[70]

Epidemics visited the province at frequent intervals, sometimes with disastrous results. Governor Cornbury was driven from New York City in 1702 by an epidemic of yellow fever which decimated the city. In 1731 a smallpox epidemic carried off about six hundred victims, and the churchwardens found it necessary to expend from their own purses nearly fifty pounds, in addition to contributions from private citizens amounting to a considerable sum, for the relief and burial of victims. A "contagious hospital" was added, as already noted, to the almshouse building in 1739. Yellow fever accounted for more then two hundred deaths in 1742, in a population of less than eight thousand. In 1746 Albany was visited by an epidemic (probably of yellow fever), and lost forty-five inhabitants as a result. Both New York City and Albany learned to practice stricter segregation for victims of contagious diseases as time went on. An order of April 6, 1742, consigned John Tenbrook of New York to Bedloe Island as a smallpox patient. All persons were forbidden entry to the house where he lay or to houses where other smallpox patients were domiciled, except by order of the mayor. The city authorities of Albany resolved on October 11, 1756, that all smallpox patients should be sent from the city and that a convenient place should be found for their reception.[71]

[69] *Ibid.*, VI, 289; VII, 411. [70] *Ibid.*, III, 121-22.

[71] Joel Munsell (ed.), *Collections on the History of Albany, from Its Discovery to the Present Time* (Albany, 1865-71), I, 104.

In 1771 the first general hospital in the province, and the second in the American colonies, was founded in New York City. The movement leading to its establishment began in 1769, when Dr. Samuel Bard, in a commencement address at King's College (now Columbia University), reproached the city for not having a public hospital, "one of the most useful and necessary charitable institutions that can possibly be imagined." Describing the need for a hospital, and the benefits it would bring, Dr. Bard declared:

> The labouring Poor are allowed to be the support of the Community; their Industry enables the Rich to live in Ease and Affluence, and it is from the Hands of the Manufacturer we derive, not only the Necessaries, but the Superfluities of Life; whilst the poor Pittance he earns will barely supply the Necessities of Nature, and it is literally by the sweat of his Brow, that he gains his daily Subsistance; how heavy a Calamity must Sickness be to such a Man, which putting him out of his Power to work, immediately deprives him and perhaps a helpless Family of Bread!
>
> Nor would the good Effects of an Hospital be wholly confined to the Poor; they would extend to every Rank, and greatly contribute to the Safety and Welfare of the whole Community.[72]

A campaign to raise funds for the hospital was begun and proved so successful that in 1770 Dr. Bard, together with Drs. Peter Middleton and John Jones, felt encouraged to present a petition to acting Governor Colden requesting a charter of incorporation. The charter was granted by King George III on June 13, 1771, and twenty-six governors were designated to manage the institution, which was incorporated under the name, "The Society of the Hospital in the City of New York in America." Provision for the sick poor was a primary consideration of the founders.

On September 12, 1771, the Common Council advanced municipal aid to this "usefull Undertaking, having for its object the Relief of the indigent & Diseased," in the form of a grant of land to serve as the grounds for the proposed hospital.[73] In the following year the provincial assembly voted to grant the hospital £800 annually for twenty years, the funds to be collected out of taxes on strong liquors retailed in the city. A condition of the grant was that the

---

[72] Samuel Bard, *A Discourse upon the Duties of a Physician with Some Sentiments on the Usefulness and Necessity of a Public Hospital* (New York, 1769), 18 pp., pp. 15–16.

[73] *N.Y.C., M.C.C., 1675–1776*, VII, 311.

hospital should receive and treat without charge all sick indigents resident in any county of the province.[74] The city of New York withdrew its gift of land on June 16, 1772, and substituted for it an outright donation of £1,000, thus establishing the first publicly supported institution providing medical aid to the poor in the province.

The project passed through many vicissitudes, however. Ground for the hospital was broken in 1773, but two years later, when it was completed, disaster overtook it in the form of a fire which practically destroyed the buildings. The assembly granted £4,000 toward the reconstruction of the hospital, but before the new group of buildings was ready for occupation the Revolution began and the project was halted. The hospital finally commenced operation in 1791, twenty years after its incorporation.

POOR-RELIEF ASPECTS OF SLAVERY

The number of slaves in New York province averaged about 10 per cent of the total population. Their numbers were sufficient to keep the white population in a constant state of fear in anticipation of possible insurrections, a fear reflected in the frequency and severity of the laws governing the conduct of slaves. This trepidation was particularly evident in New York City, where the so-called "slave conspiracies" of 1712 and 1741 resulted in the torture, hanging, and burning at the stake of a number of innocent Negro slaves.

It appears to have been a widespread practice for slaveowners to manumit aged or infirm slaves in order to escape responsibility for their care. The provincial authorities found it necessary, therefore, to place restriction on the practice of manumission. Records of 1750 in the Ulster County Court of Common Pleas show that Susanna Bond, conforming to the laws enacted by the Assembly, appeared in court by attorney and offered security against the possibility that four slaves, whom she desired to free, would later become public charges. Her security was rejected as insufficient.[75] In 1773 an act of the Assembly penalized with a ten-pound fine any slaveowner who allowed his slaves to beg. This act would seem to indicate that some

[74] *C.L.N.Y.*, V, 367.   [75] *Olde Ulster* (a periodical), I (1905), 11.

persons were not above letting the general populace help maintain their Negroes by charity in its commonest guise.[76]

CONCLUSION

Summarizing public welfare administration in provincial New York, we might say that its principal characteristic was the makeshift pattern and the lack of uniformity in poor relief throughout the province. Several generalizations can be made, however. The principal concern shown in poor-relief legislation was in preventing nonresident indigents from gaining settlement in the province. Measures for removing poor persons lacking settlement were very severe and were sometimes accompanied by corporal punishment, as authorized by law. In general, the poor-relief pattern was modeled closely upon that existing in the mother-country. It was based primarily on local responsibility, although here and there county care was provided for. At first public welfare administration was vested in a mixed civil and ecclesiastical authority, but with the passage of time the secular influence became predominant.

Few institutions for the care of the poor existed in the province. Relief was usually provided in the home, in cash or in kind. All classes of indigents were customarily treated alike, special provision being rare. Dependent children, however, were usually disposed of through the system of apprenticeship or indentured servitude. Free education in general fell below the standards maintained during the Dutch period. The violent insane were frequently incarcerated in prison and otherwise treated as common criminals. In the matter of providing medical care for the poor, New York City was particularly generous. The first general hospital was established toward the end of the colonial period, though it was not opened until 1791. Poor relief in the province operated, as a rule, within the framework of repression, although instances of generous provision for dependents are not wanting.

NEW YORK STATE DEPARTMENT OF SOCIAL WELFARE
ALBANY, NEW YORK

[76] *C.L.N.Y.*, V, 533.

POOR RELIEF IN A MASSACHUSETTS VILLAGE IN THE EIGHTEENTH CENTURY

ELEANOR PARKHURST

COLONIAL town records furnish valuable information regarding early methods of administering the poor laws. These scattered and fragmentary records help us to understand the local governmental procedures that have, unfortunately, survived into the twentieth century.

The town of Chelmsford, Massachusetts, from whose records most of the following extracts were taken, was settled in 1653 and incorporated in 1655. Like other colonial towns of New England, its poor relief policy was based upon English precedent—especially upon the Elizabethan statute of 1601—combined with the peculiar experimentation demanded by the New England system of complete local self-government.

For nearly one hundred years after its settlement, no demand for public poor relief was made to the authorities of Chelmsford except in the case of an elderly couple who came from another town to gain, about 1720, the doubtful distinction of being the first persons to be maintained at public expense.

July ye: 18: 1727. At a meeting of the Selectmen and overseers of the Poor, the overseers agreed that Samuel Gould should have one frie room in Zachary Emery's house to dwell in with his wife. 2dly it is agreed that in compliance with the order of the Genll Sessions that what is due to Samll Gould at three shillings pr week from the first day of January last be paid to such persons as he is now indebted for necessary provision for his subsistence. 3dly that Samll Gould shall have suitable maintenance provided for him. 4ly that Samll Gould shall be employed according to his ability in order to help forward his maintenance. 5ly that Samll Gould shall have a Horse provided for him to ride to meeting when he is capable of attending the publick worship. . . . .

This century-long dearth of "paupers" may be attributed in part, at least, to the practice of "warning out,"[1] which prevailed in Chelmsford until the passage of the Massachusetts Settlement Act

[1] J. H. Benton, *Warning Out in New England* (Boston, 1911), pp. 114 ff.

Social Service Review 11 (September 1937): 446–64
© 1937 by The University of Chicago

of 1794.[2] This Act repealed all previous laws as to town settlements and provided eight different ways in which legal settlement could be obtained. Prior to this, for example, an order of the General Court (in 1659), an article in the Articles of Confederation (1672), and an Act of 1692 had all stated that, unless persons were warned to depart from the town within three months of their arrival, they would gain a settlement there, and the town would be liable for their support if they became dependent. In 1700 the period within which a warning might be given to prevent settlement was extended to twelve months; and in 1789 a more comprehensive statute was enacted on this subject; in 1790 the period was extended to three years; in 1791 to four years; and, finally, in 1793 to five years.

The early colony laws just mentioned, as well as the Settlement Act of 1794,[3] were undoubtedly influenced by the English Law of Settlement and Removal and its various amendments, which provided, at successive periods, that persons might be removed from the town in which they were living to the place where they were legally settled if the removal took place, first, within forty days of their arrival and, later, within one year—forty days and one year being, respectively, the length of residence required to gain a settlement in England.[4] Likewise, the settlement laws of other states were very probably influenced by those of the New England colonies. For example, Ohio adopted the measure of warning out that was used by Massachusetts, New Hampshire, and Connecticut,[5] while Indiana in 1818 provided for the removal of persons who were likely to become dependent to the place of their last legal settlement unless they provided some security to the contrary.[6] Indiana, however, unlike Ohio, did not use warning out, and the provision for removal was omitted

---

[2] *Acts of 1794*, ch. 34, quoted in R. W. Kelso, *History of Public Poor Relief in Massachusetts* (Boston, 1922), p. 59.

[3] Sidney and Beatrice Webb, *English Local Government: English Poor Law History*, Part I: *The Old Poor Law* (London, 1927), p. 344, quoting from 13 & 14 Charles II, c. 12 (1662).

[4] 59 George III, c. 50 (1819), quoted in Webb, *op. cit.*, p. 345.

[5] *Ohio Laws*, 3 v p. 274, sec. 4 (1805) quoted in A. E. Kennedy, *The Ohio Poor Law*, p. 22.

[6] *Laws of Indiana*, ch. 14, p. 154 (1817–18), quoted in A. Shaffer and M. W. Keefer, *The Indiana Poor Law*, p. 31.

from the revised statutes of 1852. Ohio in 1854 omitted from the pauper act its provision for giving warning to leave the township.

Being warned out often meant a very real hardship to the persons whose presence was, for some reason, considered undesirable. During the year 1795, and within the space of fifteen days, Chelmsford warned 211 persons to leave the town. Family relations had little effect upon the exercise of warning out, for it appears that, in January, 1670, notice was given to Henery Merrifeild

to discharge the towne of his daughter Funnell which hath been at his hous about a weeke; vnless he gitt a note vnder the hands of the Select men of Melton that they will receaue her againe if need be and to looke at her as an Inhabetant of their Towne, notwithstanding her residence at her fathers hous for the p^rsent.[7]

Under date of December 8, 1671,

the wife of Henery Merrifeild appeared before the Select men, to answer for entertaining of their daughter Funnell, Contrary to towne order, whose answer was, that she was their daughter and Could not turn her out of doars this winter time but she would willingly returne to her husband as soone as a passadg p^rsents; but they were not approued in entertaining her, but the penalty of the town order the Select men would remitt and would leaue it to the County Court to determine the thing, if in Casse she be not gon before.

In 1672, there is this record:

The Select men haueing sent for John Plum and his daughter Mercy, and finding that his said daughter being marryed to Thomas Chub of Beuerlee, and being alsoe neere the time of her deliuery is not p'uided for by her said husband, nor taken home to him, but continues heer with her father, contrary to good order, and to the hazarding of a charge vpon the towne, doe therfore order and requier, that the said Mercy Chub doe speedily within Six or eight days leaue this towne, and betake herself to her said husband. And doe also warne and order the said John Plum that he noe longer entertaine his said daughter, but hasten her to her husband as aforesaid vpon the penalty by the town order in that Case p'uided, and of being complained of further to Authorety that soe the towne may be saued harmeless.

By giving some security to the town, it was possible to avoid being warned. In 1667, for example:

Richard Curtice came to the Select men, and desiered ther app'bation to Come into the Towne to liue, which was granted on Condition that he doe make ouer his house and land at Melton for the Towns Security that he be not chargable to the towne.

---

[7] Benton, *op. cit.*, p. 41.

And again:

March, 1685/6. Caleb Littlefield, living in the house formerly Thomas White's, warned to leave town, not being an inhabitant, or bring security to the selectmen.[8]

The warning-out order and its return became more or less standardized in form if not in spelling.

To mosis tiler Constable of Boxford
       thes aer to Requier you in her majesties name forth with to warn the wief of After Carey to depart out of our Towen to the place of hir former Residence the Selact men of Boxford not allowing her to Reseid in our Towen. dated the 22 of october 1703 as witness our hands the Selact men of Boxford.

October the 26 1703: in obedianc to this warent I haue warned the wief of After Carey to depart out of Boxford and not to Com in to it a gaien as an in habitant as witness my hand
                                              Mosis Tiler
                                              Constabel of Boxford[9]

As the practice of warning out increased and as the difficulty of insuring departure from the town grew, "cautions" were entered with the Court of Sessions.

Capt. Joseph Estabrook was authorized to request the Honorable Court of Sessions in June [1714] next, to enter cautions against Daniel Cutting and his wife, Sarah Cook, and Johanna Snow, that they might not be burthensome to Lexington.[10]

In some cases, the unfortunate person was actually carried out of town bodily by the constable. The story of an old man in Hanover is told, for example, who, when young, was employed by the selectmen for the purpose of removing families. "He said he left Hanover after dark, travelled all night, camped the next day in the woods, at night resumed his journey, and about midnight, reaching his destination, left the family in the street."[11] In the town treasurer's accounts in Weston such entries as these are selected at random:[12]

1757. For carreeing Thos. Partridge & family out of town.	0–4–0
1762. Carring Pacence Clark & Son to Waltham.	0–4–0
Carreeing woman & child to Newton.	0–2–8

[8] G. Nash, *Historical Sketch of Weymouth* (1885), p. 41.

[9] *Boxford Town Records, 1685–1706*, pp. 94–95.   [10] Benton, *op. cit.*, p. 60.

[11] J. Dwelley and J. F. Simmons, *History of Hanover* (Hanover, 1910), p. 23.

[12] *Town of Weston Records, 1754–1803*.

1762. Carreing woman & child to Sudbury.	0–1–4
Carreing Cox & famely to Waltham.	0–18–8
1764. Carring Moses Larkin out.	0–4–0
1766. Carreing Mary & Sary Evans to Waltham.	0–4–0
Carreing Jane Kendrick to Natick.	0–3–0
1767. Carreing Widow Beoynton to Waltham.	0–3–0

In warning out those who were considered "undesirables" (i.e., chiefly those who appeared likely to look to the town for support in the event of their dependency and by virtue of residence), the town was merely exercising a right that existed because of the theory of inhabitancy or right to live in a certain settlement, which, according to English tradition, imposed upon the inhabitants of that settlement a common responsibility for the support of any needy member. If each town were a corporation, established by free consent, it was reasoned, then each town should exercise its sovereignty by the admission or exclusion of its inhabitants. In Chelmsford, for example, it was voted that no one should own land within the town unless he had been approved and admitted as an inhabitant by a majority vote at a public town meeting.

Month: 2: Day: 1st: 1654. Wm. How, weaver, is admitted an Inhabitant and granted by the Town Twelve acres of meadow and eighteen acres of upland, promising to the Town to sett up his trade and perform the Town's work so far as he can.

Fifth Month: 1656. James Parker and Timothy Brooks admitted Inhabitants with grants from Town.

7th: ye 12 month: 1681. Joshua Sawyer at his request was admitted an Inhabitant in this Town and had Libberty granted him to purchase the Town's land as he can agree with the Committee appointed to sell Land.

John Lowell admitted as Tanner.

It was impossible to foresee all possibility of dependency, however, and, further, it was very difficult to enforce the theory of warning out even though the cause was just and the expense to the town was small.

July 20, 1738
for warning out Timothy Fletcher and fam.   0–03–0
Feb. 19, 1738
To John Davis, constable, for warning out John Buck and family
and Jane Marlin   0–4–6
For warning out Andrew Bailey and pd. to John Spaulding   0–6–0

Feb. 29, 1739
> To Capt. Chamberlain for money paid to the Clerke of the Court
> for entering a Caution against 2 persons that was warned out
> of the Town of Chelmsford   o–7–o
> To Jos. Warren for serving upon persons warrents to warn them
> out of town   o–15–6

Old residents became enfeebled and ill.

> March 21, 1733/4. To Nathaniel Harwood for paying for a coffin for Samuel
> Gould's wife: o–6–6
>
> Sept. 30, 1734. To Ebenezer Foster for digging a grave for Goody Gould:
> o–6–o
>
> Jan. 2, 1734/5. To Dr. Blazedil in part for houseroom for Samuel Gould and
> for Goody Gould's funeral: o–14–6

In 1733 the town voted that "Capt. Saml. Chamberlin be the
surety in the Room and sted of Deacon Stephen Peane who is impaired in his Reason."

The colonial wars injured some of the town's soldiers and widowed their wives. Children became orphans or half-orphans.

> Nov. 17, 1727. Voted that Elizabeth Virgin alias Elizabeth Wait's child to
> be subsusted at 3s. per week by Zachary Emery until the Town or Selectment
> shall dispose of it in a more easy maner and that the Town find sd. child cloathes
> during its abode at Zachary Emery's, and Zachary Emery consented to the
> above said vote at the meeting.

The child being voted to Mr. Emery, probably because he was an
overseer of the poor and not because he desired it, he did not hesitate to board it out. In May, 1728, Elias Foster was keeping the
child and being paid in addition for clothing and nursing it. Within
a week, however, Zachary Emery was given "6d. a week more for
keeping the child of Elizabeth Wait 16 weeks," so it is evident that
Mr. Emery was still officially interested in the case and that the care
of the child was becoming burdensome. It is not surprising, then,
to find that in January, 1728–29 certain negotiations were carried
out between the selectmen and one Josiah Tucker of Groton. It was
"Voted, that John Robins and Zachary Emery, overseers of the
poor, agree with Josiah Tucker of Groton abote the sd. Tucker's
taking and keeping the child of E. Waite's and freeing the town of
any further charges about the child." The town treasurer is then
authorized to "pay to Mr. Emery £6 to pay Josiah Tucker of Groton

for taking and keeping the child of Elizabeth Waite and securing the Town from any further charges concerning the said child." A receipt was also given:

Feb. 25, 1728. Received of John Robins and Zachary Emery, overseers of the poor, £6, the sum which the said voted me for taking as an apprentice Elizabeth Wait [?] a poor infant child and acknowledge myself hereby to clear the said town from any further charge which may arise concerning the said child.

J. Tucker (his mark)

In November, 1753, the town paid to "Mr. Wm. Parker for taking one Joanna Cory, a poor child of John Cory, deceased, and to take care of her while 18 years old: 1–4–0." Later, another member of the same family was placed out:

Jan. 26th, 1771. I, the Subscriber, promise to pay or cause to be paid unto the Selectmen of Said Town the sum of Two pound, eight Shillings and Eleven pence Lawful money, it being for the use and Benifit of Benoni Cory, a poor child of the said town, to be paid when he shall arrive at the full age of twenty-one years with Lawfull Interest for the same untill Paid as witness my hand.

Test   Aaron Chamberlin
Amos Kidder

Another case is that of Mary Lambert and her child.

February 17, 1728/9. It was putt vote whether the town would allow or disallow of a Bill of £7 signed by the Selectmen of Dotchister for Mary Lambert's lying in and nursing at Dotchister. It passed in the negative.

Voted, that there should be an answer sent to the Selectmen of Dotchister concerning the bill that they charge upon the Town for Mary Lambert's lying in at said town of Dotchister.

February 25, 1728/9. Expended aboute Mary Lambert, 0–12–0.

To Edward Foster for Jos. Barritt for keeping Mary Lambert and child, 0–10–0. To Sam. Chamberlain for 1 day aboute Mary Lambert, 0–3–0. To Sam. Chamberlain to cost of Court convicting Mary Lambert, 1–10–2. To Leut. Adams for 1 day waiting at court aboute Mary Lambert, 0–3–0. To Deacon Fletcher for going to Dunstable and getting a warrant for Mary Lambert, 0–10–0. To Josiah Fletcher for carrying Mary Lambert to the House of Correction, 0–1–6. To Josiah Scotton for keeping Mary Lambert and her child with victuals and drink and fireing in the House of Correction at Charlestown from Jan. 10, 1728/9, to the 28th of the month following, 11 weeks' allowance being made for her labour in that Time, 6–9–10. To Zachary Emery for his time and charge in bringing up Mary Lambert from Charlestown and finding her a pair of shoes, 1–7–0.

To such persons as these, the town definitely owed aid. Sickness, death, and misfortune did not wait to strike until their victims were beyond the boundaries of the town, and grim necessity overcame at one stroke the careful planning of the town fathers. Even unsettled persons—travelers, visitors, those living in town illegally (i.e., without permission, a fact that prevented the town from becoming legally responsible for their support)—had to be cared for at some time or other.

"The affair of Jane Williams," as town records term it, was doubtless that of a woman who was ill and in need of care in Chelmsford but whose place of settlement was Beverly, to which place she was returned as promptly as possible. Chelmsford was reimbursed by Beverly for its care of her.

Dec. 28, 1764. Paid for conveying Jane Williams to Beaverly, 8 shillings. For keeping Jane Williams, £3, 24 shillings. For doctor for Jane Williams, 1–1–0.

June, 1766. Received of Beaverly for Jane Williams's last sickness, £7.

July, 1766. Trip to Beaverly, 9 shillings. Letters to Beaverly about Jane Williams, 6 shillings.

The following entries are similar examples of sickness and misfortune:

For Saml. Woods, lately of this town, having lost his substance by fire—Dec. 11, 1743, was collected £16.

For Hannah Shed, in this town, though not properly as inhabitant, being sick and destitute, was collected April 12, 1744, £9.

For Daniel Raymond of Concord, whose son was wounded by a loaded sled running over his leg, and is languishing, was collected Jan. 13, 1745, £9, 11s. 2d.

In 1791, two years before the law regarding warning out was repealed, the town was still struggling to free itself of unwanted poor persons. An article in the warrant for a town meeting at the time reads:

To see if the town will take into consideration the matter respecting the maintaining Mary Brown and see if they cant be some way to free the town from that cost, as we conclude that she belongs to Billerica, or for the town to act anything thereon, as they may think proper.

Voted to choose a committee[13] to see if this town can be freed from the maintaining of Mary Brown.

Then, too, there were the Acadians, about a thousand of whom were taken to Massachusetts and supported at province expense for

---

[13] No report of this committee is found.

a long period. Their expulsion from Nova Scotia during the French and Indian Wars (1754–63) caused them to be dependent upon public support, and, while individual towns did "subsist" them, these towns were reimbursed by the Province.

Province accounts show such items as the following:

June 14, 1758. Allowed to the selectmen of Chelmsford for supporting French neutrals, £25.2.5¼.

January 17, 1759. Allowed to the selectmen of Chelmsford for supporting French neutrals, £42.2.6½.

The town rendered an account from time to time to the secretary of the Province for the support of these people, as in the case of this record of April 27, 1767:

At a meeting of the Major part of the Selectmen it was agreed upon and ordered that Oliver Fletcher, Esq., pay to Mr. Samuel Perham, Town Treasurer for the Town of Chelmsford for the year A.D. 1761, the sum of twenty-nine Pounds eight Shillings and two pence lawful money, which the sd. Oliver received of Harrison Gray, Esq., Province Treasurer, a Grant made to the Town of Chelmsford for their last account exhibited for supporting Jean Landrie and Family in this Town, which grant was made on or about the first of April current, £29–8–2.

The names of Jean Landrey and family appear most frequently in the *Town Records* from June, 1762, to December, 1764, but it is shown by the following that they came to town in 1756:

1756. Jean Landrie and a large family, being French from Nova Scotia, were thrown upon the town and maintained at the public expense, until the end of the war in 1763, at an expenditure of £200, which was reimbursed by the province, agreeable to an order of Counsel.

Chelmsford, Oct 24, 1757. In obedience & pursuant to an Order of the Great and General Court of the Province of the Massachusetts Bay, made & passed the 21st Day of January A.D. 1757.

The following is a true list of the several French Persons names in the Town of Chelmsford, the amount of their age sex & the circumstances of their Health & capacity for Labour.

The Number of French are seventeen.

Vizt. Names	Aged
Jean Landrie a man	62 yrs.
Maudlin his wife	60 weekly & unable to labour & labouring under the misfortune of a broken arm & the charges there of now.

Vizt. Names	Aged
Paul Landrie his son	22 able to Labour.
Charles Do Do	20 Sickly & not able to Labour
Simon	18 able to Labour
Asam	16 " "
Charles Trawhorn a man	29 Sickly & not able to Labour
Tithorne his wife	29 able to Labour
Mary their daughter	6½
Maudlin " "	5½
Joseph " son	4 sickly
Grigwire " "	3
Margaret " Daughter	0:7 months
Joseph Landrie a son of the sd Jean Landrie	26 years Healthy & able to Labour.
Maudlin his wife	26 " " " " "
Jean their son	2 years sickly and weakly.
Murray Maudlin their daughter	5 months.

> David Spaulding
> Daniel Proctor
> Henry Spaulding *Selectmen of Chelmsford*
> Jonas Adams
> Andrew Fletcher

The selectmen or overseers of the poor of the various towns were ordered to bind out to service all children of the Acadians for whom places could be found. Many were taken from their parents to serve under hard taskmasters. Some of these parents sent to the General Court a petition as follows, signed by Jean Landrey at Chelmsford, and by representatives at Oxford, Concord, Worcester, Andover, and Waltham:

To his Excellency the Governor General of the Province of Massachusetts Bay of New England and to the honorable Gentlemen of the Council.

We have taken the liberty of presenting you this request, as we are in sorrow on account of our children. The loss which we have suffered, of our houses, and brought here and our separations from one another is nothing compared with what we meet with at present, that of taking away our children by force before our eyes. Nature herself cannot endure that. If it were in our power to have our choice we should choose rather the taking away of our bodies and our souls than to be separated from them. Wherefore we pray in pity and to your honors that you would have the goodness to mitigate this cruelty. We have not refused from the first to work for our support of our children, provided it were permitted for our own families. Praying you in mercy to have the goodness to have regard to our Petition, thus doing you will oblige your very humble and very obedient servants.

What treatment they received may be guessed, since this petition was investigated in Council by a committee, their report being accepted April 17, 1756, ordering that "there should be no more binding out, that the Acadians were to be provided with such things as they could work up for necessary clothing, and that they were to be treated with kindness and humanity."

Various subsequent entries show payments from the town treasury for such items to the Landreys as subsistence, wood, and rent; use of cart; care of the family; and, last of all, "rent until the family moved away [December 28, 1764]."

From such records as these emerge certain conclusions as to the care of dependent persons in colonial times which are already familiar. This care was not based on any settled policy except perhaps that of the greatest economy in effort and expenditure. There was no investigation of the homes to which the poor were sent, and no investigation of the dependent's circumstances except where some aid might be drawn from their relatives or some other source.

The January, 1801, town meeting was asked "to see if the Town will appoint some suitable person or persons to make inquiry and see if there is an estate belonging to the widow Abigail Bates that can be recovered for her support, or to act anything relative thereto that the town may think proper." It was voted "to choose an agent and make inquiry to see if there is any estate belonging to the widow Abigail Bates that can be recovered for her support."

The February, 1803, warrant contained this article:

Whereas Lt. Elijah Proctor has made application to the selectmen for the support of his mother-in-law, to see if the town will appoint some suitable person or persons to see if there be any property to be found that belongs to her for her support, or to act anything thereon that the Town may think proper.

It was voted "to appoint a committee to examine and see if there is any property to be found belonging to the widow Proctor for her support."

There was no supervision after the dependent person was placed out, and no oversight or control over the living conditions of apprenticed children except, perhaps, as in the case of the Acadians, where the situation was so bad that public sympathy was aroused. The family was not considered as a unit, and little thought was given to the hardships imposed by its being broken up. With regard to the use of individual treatment for each case, however, the wheel has now turned full circle. What was then the easiest method of care has now become the most adequate when properly investigated and supervised. It must be remembered also that, granted the philosophy of local sovereignty which existed in the colonial town, the rights of inhabitancy and warning out followed naturally, and only through the agency of settlement laws and the introduction of state aid was this autonomy partially broken down in preparation for a later and more comprehensive plan of public relief.

As the number and expense of keeping dependents increased, individual disposition of their cases grew less simple and less satisfactory. Almshouse care was not common in Massachusetts until 1700 or later, although the first almshouse in Boston was built in 1660. Like the entire state, Chelmsford was slow to adopt the almshouse principle. Instead, various experiments were tried by which the responsibility of the town and the cost of support should be decreased, while the poor person was encouraged to become as self-supporting as possible by his own efforts. From being boarded out first for short periods and then for a year or more, the authorities turned to the vendue or auction, where the "paupers" were auctioned off to the lowest bidder, singly or together, for a specified period.

In 1796, there were the following entries:

To see if the Town will allow Mr. Ephraim Parkhurst 1 shilling a week for finding house room and fier wood for the widow Ruth Dutton from the last day of February last past to the first of September following, or allow it to Deacon Aaron Chamberlin for his bidding her off at the vendue and his trouble, or to act anything thereon that they may think proper.

Voted, to give Deacon Aaron Chamberlin one shilling per week for his bidding off the widow Ruth Dutton and for his trouble.

In December, 1815, the following article appeared in the warrant for a town meeting:

To see if the Town will give some directions respecting the support of the poor or act anything respecting their support that the Town may think proper.

Voted, That the overseers of the poor be directed to give contract for the support of town and state paupers which are or may be within the limits of the town of Chelmsford for the ensuing year, to commence on the first Monday in

February next, that such suitable persons as will undertake the same for the lowest sum to be ascertained at public vendue of paupers, said contract to include all expenses of every nature arising within said town for their support, clothing and nursing, doctoring, burials, etc., provided they be kept and supported to the acceptance of the Overseers of the Poor, and that the undertaker receive of the town all the money the town may receive of the state for the paupers aforesaid, and shall pay all expenses which may arise from the absconding of any pauper which may have been committed to him for support by the Overseers aforesaid, with such further conditions as the overseers may think proper.

Where all the "paupers" were taken together, a "private poor farm" might be said to have existed; and later, when "written and sealed proposals for supporting the poor" were given, this type of care was quite definitely established.

May 4, 1801. By desire of Samuel Marshall and others to see if the Town will take into consideration the propriety of John Dunn or other in his circumstances to keeping the poor of this town, or act anything thereon that the Town may think proper.

Voted, That the poor be taken from John Dunn's.

Feb. 22, 1812. To see in what way and manner the Town will support their poor the year ensuing, and act anything thereon or relative thereto that the Town may think proper.

Voted, That the poor be let out by the 6 months or the year or other ways as the Selectmen may think proper.

May, 1821. Voted, That the selectmen be directed to receive written and sealed proposals for supporting the poor of the town previous to their putting them out again and then put them out separately or together for 1 or 5 years, as they may think proper.

These methods could not have been entirely satisfactory from the point of view either of economy or of good care for the poor persons.

May 25, 1768. At request of Gershom Proctor and others, to see if the freeholders of this town will think of and come into some method to maintain the poor of this town with less cost and expense to the town than they have been for a number of years past, or act anything that they think proper thereon.

Again and again from 1732 on, the proposal to build or buy a building suitable for an almshouse or workhouse was voted down in the town meeting. In 1769 and in 1786 it was apparently decided to hire a house.

Feb., 1769. At the request of Zachary Emery and others to see what method
the town shall think proper to take with Reuben Cory and his family, or any
other poor in said town. . . . .

Voted, To build or hire an house for the poor of this town for the year ensuing:

Voted, To hire an house;

Voted, To appoint a committee to do this and report at the next meeting;

Voted, That the selectmen take some speedy and affectual meathod to put
Reuben Cory into sum business in order to maintain himself and family as far
as he is able in case he doth not improve his time for the purpose aforesaid.

1786. To see if the town will proceed to build a workhouse in said town, or
to act anything thereon that they may think proper.

Voted, not to build a workhouse.

These recommendations were not carried out, it seems, for in
1796 and 1815 the vendue was still being held. In 1822, however, a
committee appointed to investigate the problem of the poor advocated the purchase of a certain piece of property, and by 1823 the
town workhouse was opened under the direction of the overseers of
the poor. The report of the committee follows:

REPORT OF A COMMITTEE ON THE SUBJECT OF THE POOR

The maintaining the poor has become a subject of great interest and importance to many of our towns, and especially so to this town, within a few years,
and has now become so burthensome as to render it highly necessary to introduce some less expensive method of supporting them, as well as to check the increase of pauperism.

This town has generally adopted the method first introduced here, which is
to put out the poor annually to the lowest bidder at auction by the week. This
custom originated probably when the number of the poor was few and the expenses small and no doubt was at that time the best method which the town
could adopt. But inasmuch as the number and expenses of our poor have greatly increased and continue to increase, your committee are of opinion that the
time has arrived when the town ought at least to make an effort to reduce the
expenses of their poor by introducing some new system of supporting them.
As there is little prospect of the number of our poor's being less, the town probably would prefer making some lasting and permanent provision for their support. 56 persons have been either partly or wholly supported by the town during the present year, and from information received from the selectmen it is
calculated that the expense of our poor this year will not be less than $1354.00
and may amount to more of this sum. $60 is paid for house rent the present year.

What new system will best promote the interest of the town, experience must
determine; but your committee are of opinion that it is expedient for the town

to try some new method of maintaining their poor, and from the best opinion which they have obtained on the subject, they are induced to recommend to the town to purchase a farm with buildings convenient for their accommodation, so that the poor may be employed and supported on said farm, subject to such orders, rules and regulations as the town shall see fit to adopt. With this view your committee have examined several farms in this town offered for sale, and are of opinion that the farm owned by Capt. Salathiel Adams will best accommodate the town; this farm contains about 120 acres, is well supplied with wood, is capable of great improvements, may be bought for $2950, and by your committee is considered to be well worth the sum. They therefore recommend that the town purchase the farm owned by Capt. Salathiel Adams for the accommodation of the poor of this town, and that after the first Tuesday in February next the poor be supported and employed on said farm. All which is respectfully submitted by

Josiah Fletcher ⎫
B. Butterfield   ⎪
John Butterfield ⎬ *Committee*
David Perham   ⎪
Joel Adams   ⎭

Jonathan Perham, *Town Clerk*
    [November, 1822]

The rest of the story is told by the following records:

This report being accepted by the town, it was

Voted, To choose a committee to take a deed of the farm of Captain Salathiel Adams.

Voted, That said committee consist of 3 persons.

Voted, For said committee, and chose Jonathan Perham, Joel Adams, and Capt. Josiah Fletcher.

Voted & Instructed the above committee to borrow on the credit of the town the sum of $3500 for the purpose of paying for the farm of Capt. Salathiel Adams and putting the same in repair and stocking the farm for the reception of the poor.

Voted & Instructed the Overseers of the Poor to provide such help both mens and womens, as they may think proper for the care of the poor.

At the March, 1823, town meeting it was

Voted, That the house lately bought by the town of Capt. Salathiel Adams be constituted a workhouse wherein the poor of this town shall be employed.

Voted, That the Overseers of the Poor be overseers of said workhouse.

Voted, That the Overseers of the Poor be directed to prepare by-laws and orders for the government of said workhouse and report the same to the annual meeting in April next.

Voted, That the Overseers of the Poor be directed to keep an accurate account of all the expenses of supporting the poor at the said workhouse, and report the same to the town at their annual meeting in March, 1824.

The "Report of the Committee who Purchased the Farm for the Poor" follows:

REPORT OF THE COMMITTEE WHO PURCHASED THE FARM FOR THE POOR

The committee appointed to take a deed of the farm of Capt. Salathiel Adams and to make the necessary preparations for the reception of the poor have attended to that duty, as stated in the following report.

On the first day of February last your committee received a deed of the farm of Capt. Salathiel Adams to the inhabitants of Chelmsford, for which they paid $2950. They have also, agreeably to the vote of the town, borrowed the sum of $3500 on the credit of the town and have given notes for the same to the following persons, viz.:

To Capt. Abraham Prescott a note of	$1500
To Abbott and Fletcher, do.,	600
To Capt. John Butterfield, do.,	426
To Henry Adams, do.,	300
To Samuel Davis, do.,	274
To Zebulon Spaulding, do.,	200
To Oliver Parkhurst, do.,	100
To Moses Parker, do.,	100
Amounting in all to the sum of	$3500

Your committe have expended the sum of $530.72 for provisions, repairs to furniture, stock and other necessaries for the accommodations of the poor, having a balance of $19.28 unexpended. They further request the town to direct your committee to pay said balance to the Overseers of the Poor, and that your committee be discharged from further service.

All which is respectfully submitted.

Jonathan Perham
Joel Adams   } Committee
Josiah Fletcher

Joel Adams, *Town Clerk*
[Reported and accepted on March 3, 1823]

Then came the need of regulations for the workhouse, according to Article VII of the Warrant for the April town meeting, 1823:

To see if the town will accept of the regulations and by-laws made by the overseers of the workhouse for the government of the same, or act anything thereon that the town think proper.

Voted, To accept of the regulations and by-laws made by the overseers of the workhouse, and that the same be adopted by the town.

The following are by-laws and regulations made by the Overseers of the Poor and adopted and approved of by the town in legal town meeting on the 7th day of April, A.D. 1823, to wit:

At a stated monthly town meeting of the overseers of the workhouse in the town of Chelmsford the 6th day of March, 1823, the following orders and regulations were made and are now presented to the town for their approbation, viz.:

By-Laws

OR

ORDERS AND REGULATIONS FOR CHELMSFORD WORKHOUSE

1. The Overseers of the Poor shall have the inspection and government of the workhouse, with full powers to appoint a master and needful assistants, and to contract with them for their wages. Also to remove them from said trust whenever they shall deem it expedient.

2. The said Overseers shall meet at the workhouse on the first Saturday in every month at 2 of the clock, P.M., as their stated monthly meeting, to make such orders and regulations relating to such house as they shall judge necessary. One of the overseers shall visit the workhouse once a week, to ascertain if the master thereof conforms to the rules and regulations of the said workhouse.

3. Whenever any person liable to be sent to said workhouse shall be sent there by an order in writing of one or more of the said overseers or by any justice of the peace on complaint, it shall be the duty of said master to receive such person into said workhouse and there support and employ such persons agreeably to the rules and regulations thereof.

4. The master of the workhouse shall keep a book wherein shall be entered all orders and regulations made for the government of said house.

5. The master of the workhouse shall have the control and government of all persons employed therein and shall manage and employ them from time to time as the overseers shall order and direct, and shall keep a book wherein the names of all persons received into said workhouse and the time when received and dismissed shall be entered. He shall also keep an account of the expenses of said workhouse and also an account of the produce of the farm attached to the said workhouse, and also an account of the articles of produce or manufacture sold, and exhibit the same to the Overseers of the Poor whenever thereunto requested.

6. The master of the workhouse shall keep an inventory of the farming tools, household furniture, beds and bedding, and other property belonging to the town.

7. The master of the workhouse shall have power to reward the faithful and

industrious by granting favors and indulgences, but he is at the same time fully empowered and authorized to punish at his discretion the idle, stubborn, disorderly and disobedient by immediate confinement without any food other than bread and water.

8. The master of the workhouse shall cause said house and furniture to be kept clean and in good order, and shall cause habits of cleanliness, neatness and decency to be strictly observed by all persons received into said workhouse.

9. The master of the workhouse shall cause the Lord's Day to be strictly observed.

10. Every person who may be received into said workhouse or be a member thereof must obey the orders and regulations thereof and the commands of the master, and will be required by him diligently to work and labor as he shall direct, according to age, health and capacity.

11. Every person who shall absent himself from the said workhouse and the appendages thereof and farm thereunto belonging, or go without the limits thereof without leave of the master, or shall conceal him or herself from the master, shall be deemed to be an idle, stubborn and disorderly person, and punished accordingly.

12. The use of spirituous liquors is strictly prohibited except when the master, physician or overseers of the workhouse shall otherwise order; and no person shall be allowed to have or keep in their possession or bring or receive any spirituous liquors into said workhouse.

13. The regulations or bill of fare for persons received into the workhouse shall be as near as possible as follows:

For breakfast and supper, hasty pudding and milk, or molasses, bread and milk, or milk porridge, shells or chockolate; and for dinner each day in the week as follows:

Sunday, baked meats and beans and Indian pudding;
Monday, boiled salt meat and vegetables;
Tuesday, soup;
Wednesday, salt fish and potatoes.
Thursday, roast or baked meat and vegetables;
Friday, stewed beans or peas, with meat;
Saturday, salt fish and potatoes;

provided, however, that suitable food and necessaries shall at all times be provided for the sick and infirm, according to their age and condition.

> John Butterfield ⎫
> Sherebiah Spalding ⎬ *Overseers of the Poor*
> Ephraim Adams ⎭

In this period of semi-institutional and finally institutional care, there appears a stronger sense of responsibility for caring for the poor, doubtless influenced by the offer of state aid and by the im-

possibility of either preventing dependency or confining membership in the dependent group to legal inhabitants. That method of
care was apparently considered best which involved the least expenditure on the part of the town and the most effort on the part of
the person aided. So the workhouse comes into being, its inmates
unclassified as to age, sex, and "offense"; regulated by a fairly complicated set of by-laws and under supervision of the overseers of the
poor.

In turn, the mixed almshouse and the workhouse—where little
actual work was done because no authority existed to compel labor—
are being superseded. Spasmodic care is being supplanted by continuous and supervised care. No longer is a poor person required to
"resign herself into the hands of the selectmen to be taken care of
by the town," nor, once so "resigned," "to be dealt with as the other
poor persons are dealt with." No longer is the poor person forced
to face a town meeting which discusses his plight in the baldest of
terms; and no longer are the poor given over to the lowest bidder at
the vendue held at a friendly tavern. The principles and the methods
may change, but the problems remain essentially the same—relief
of the destitute; care and treatment of the aged, the crippled, the
insane, and the blind; treatment of the sick poor; care of dependent
and delinquent children; and the unmarried mother. Problems of
administration and finance remain, also, as well as those of organization and personnel and interrelationships existing between various
interested administrative units and legislative bodies, etc.

If the history of poor relief shows anything at all, it bears witness
to the painfully slow growth of public interest and knowledge concerning the problem of dependency and its causes—an interest and
knowledge that must be stimulated still further to provide a reasonable and more adequate type of care for these unfortunates.

University of Chicago

POVERTY AND ITS RELIEF IN AMERICAN THOUGHT, 1815–61

BENJAMIN J. KLEBANER

The author is a member of the faculty of the Department of Economics of the City College of the City University of New York.

THE first extensive discussions of poverty in the United States appeared in the depressed years after the Napoleonic Wars. This paper investigates the American literature on pauperism between 1815 and 1861, focusing on the explanations offered for poverty in the new Canaan and proposals for dealing with the problem, including the merits of the poor law versus private almsgiving.

As early as 1789, Benjamin Franklin wrote to a British friend that Americans had followed the example of the mother country concerning the poor laws, but we "begin now to see our error, and, I hope, shall reform it."[1] English writers, however, had already begun to see the "error" of the Elizabethan Poor Law in the seventeenth century. If the first rumblings in America against the poor law are set around 1789, the movement cannot be said to have reached sizable proportions until at least a quarter of a century later, during the period of economic distress following the second war for independence.[2] Pauperism attracted public at-

tention only when poor relief expenditures had risen to unprecedented heights in many parts of the United States. Colonial America evinced no such interest.

MORALIZING ABOUT POVERTY: THE VICES OF THE POOR

Explanations for the perturbing increase in dependence on public and private charity fall into two groups: those formulated in terms of personal failings of the pauper and those pointing to defects in the economic order. The noneconomic factors—intemperance, improvidence, and indolence—were the most frequently mentioned causes of poverty.

The majority of writers deemed the excessive use of alcoholic beverages the sovereign cause of misery and want. Agreement was almost unanimous in labeling intemperance the "cause of causes."[3] Some authorities blamed three-fourths of the poverty in the United States on intemperance.[4] An-

[1] Quoted in Howell V. Williams, "Benjamin Franklin and the Poor Laws," *Social Service Review*, XVIII (March, 1944), 82.

[2] John Bach McMaster, *History of the People of the United States* (New York, 1924), IV, 525, 532; Samuel Reznick, "The Depression of 1819–1822: A Social History," *American Historical Review*, XXIX (1933), 30; Murray N. Rothbard, *Panic of 1819* (New York, 1962), chap. i.

[3] New York Society for the Prevention of Pauperism, *Report of a Committee on the Subject of Pauperism* (New York, 1818), p. 6, and *Documents Relative to Saving Banks, Intemperance and Lotteries* (New York, 1819), p. 17. Similar views are found in Heman Humphrey, *On Doing Good to the Poor: A Sermon* . . . (Pittsfield, 1818), p. 14; *Connecticut Journal* (New Haven), September 10, 13, and 20, 1822.

[4] Samuel Austin Allibone, *A Review by a Layman of a Work Entitled "New Themes for the Protestant Clergy* . . ." (Philadelphia, 1852), p. 81;

Social Service Review 38 (December 1964): 382–99

other view had it that three-fourths was a minimum, and that perhaps as many as nine out of ten paupers could trace their need to intemperance.[5] Official bodies made similar findings.[6] The trustees of the poor of Baltimore rejected the greater ease of obtaining employment as the reason for the considerable drop in the ratio of almshouse inmates to the total population of the city during the decade 1843–53. They pointed instead to the temperance crusade, as 90 per cent of the sane persons admitted had been given to drinking. In a similar vein, the overseers of the poor of Chicopee, Massachusetts, ascribed only a part of the increase in the number of relief recipients to the shutdown of some local mills during the autumn and winter, 1850–51; in their view, the most important cause was the free use of alcohol.[7] On March 14, 1851, the *New York Daily Tribune* asserted that "if there was no rum there would be no poor houses." In short, it was hardly an overstatement to write of intemperance:

By the common consent of all who have investigated this subject [pauperism], or who

have labored to ameliorate the condition of the unfortunate, this is branded as the central source of want and woe. . . . It seems at times as if this evil were rotting the very foundations of society, eating like vitriol into the very core of the Republic.[8]

Not everyone, though, subscribed to this point of view. On one occasion Philadelphia's guardians of the poor went so far as to label "tippling Houses, and their concomitant evils" as simply one of the "incidental causes" of pauperism. The plain-spoken executives of the Female Hospitable Society blamed unemployment for most of the misery among the poor of Philadelphia during the winter of 1819–20; many cases of intemperance were the consequence of despair arising from inability to obtain the necessities of life.[9] Charleston's commissioners of the poor were unable to decide whether intemperance was the explanation of the necessitous condition of the city's poor or only "the result of their ruined fortunes."[10]

Such skepticism, however, was indeed rare. Americans, not excluding perhaps most of those who deprecated the habit in the poor, were notorious imbibers of alcohol.[11] To look afar for more abstruse and perhaps less comforting explanations of poverty was not

---

Samuel Chipman, *Report of an Examination of Poor-Houses, Jails, &c in the State of New York* . . . (Albany, 1834), p. 76.

[5] "Poor Laws: (Review of) Extracts from the Information Received by His Majesty's Commissioners, as to the Administration and Operation of the Poor Laws," *American Quarterly Review,* XIV (1833), 90 (hereinafter cited as "14 AQR"). This review is the most detailed discussion of the poor law problem to appear in the United States before 1860. Unfortunately, the name of the author is not known.

[6] Providence City Council, *Journal,* I, 382 MS in the City Hall, Providence); *Pennsylvania Archives,* Ser. 4, V, 471; Hazard's *U.S. Commercial and Statistical Register,* VI (1842), 363.

[7] Baltimore, *Ordinances,* 1854, Appendix, pp. 296, 298; Chicopee (Mass.), *Annual Reports . . . March 1, 1851* (Springfield, 1851), p. 18.

[8] Robert C. Waterston, *Address on Pauperism, Its Extent, Causes and the Best Means of Prevention* . . . (Boston, 1844), p. 23.

[9] Philadelphia Guardians for the Relief and Employment of the Poor, Minutes, VII, March 3, 1820 (MS in the Philadelphia General Hospital); Female Hospitable Society of Philadelphia, *Articles of Association . . . and Reports of the Transactions since Its Commencement* (Philadelphia, 1831), p. 23 (MS in the American Philosophical Society Library, Philadelphia).

[10] Minutes, June 4, 1829 (MS in the South Carolina Historical Society, Charleston). Among the inmates, 28 of 68 males and 15 of 52 females were reported to be intemperate.

[11] John Allen Krout, *Origins of Prohibition* (New York, 1925), p. 98.

necessary when common-sense observation pointed to one ready at hand.

The improvidence and extravagance of the lower orders, of which the large sums they spent on drink was only one example, was another often-mentioned cause of their falling into want. Many mechanics married before they could afford to support a family and, despairing of their ability to feed their wives and children, abandoned them to the mercies of the charitable in times of economic distress. Perhaps as many as one-fourth of Philadelphia's paupers fell into this category, the guardians of the poor complained in 1820.[12]

Few poor persons managed to get through the winter, when little employment was available, without some public or private assistance. They did not lay aside part of their earnings in other seasons to tide them over.[13] Lotteries were another form of foolish expenditure of the poor.[14]

The poor were often condemned for laziness. Love of sloth led depraved persons to prefer not to work but instead to enjoy a completely parasitic existence as recipients of alms. Others found it possible, because of the ample remuneration given to laborers, to work only half of each day and to spend the remainder in idleness.[15]

Intemperance, extravagance, improvidence, and indolence, singly or in combination, were thus held accountable for most cases of need. But even the most puritanic recognized that at least some poverty was the result of unforeseeable circumstances—providential events.[16] The Connecticut relieving officer was reminded that "if many [paupers] are the victims of intemperance, idleness, and vice, some at least are subjects of misfortune, sickness, and adversity."[17] Especially in large cities, the Union Benevolent Association of Philadelphia told its supporters, there were many "deserving poor"— those physically unable to labor, friendless widows, and the helpless aged. The Reverend Heman Humphrey included in the same category industrious individuals who "in the course of business; by the fluctuations of trade; by the failure or dishonesty of debtors; by the ravages of floods and fires; and by storms at sea, have been reduced with large and helpless families to extreme indigence."[18]

A distinction was made between "the honest, industrious, but unfortunate poor" and "the idle and vicious." Governor Plumer's father, a frugal, diligent farmer, of Epping, New Hamp-

[12] Philadelphia Guardians, loc. cit.

[13] "[Review of] On Doing Good to the Poor," Christian Disciple and Theological Review, N.S. I (1819), 230.

[14] N.Y. Soc. Prev. Pau., Documents Relative to Savings Banks . . . , p. 26; Charles Burroughs, A Discourse Delivered in the Chapel of the New Alms-House . . . (Portsmouth, 1835), p. 73.

[15] Virginia Poor Returns, Campbell County, 1835 (MS in Virginia State Library, Richmond; hereinafter the Virginia Poor Returns will be cited by county and date alone); see also Salem, Mass., Overseers of the Poor, "Miscellaneous, 1746–1832," letter of July 20, 1819 (MS in Essex Institute, Salem); Connecticut Journal (New Haven), September 10, 1822.

[16] Boston Society for the Prevention of Pauperism, Annual Report . . . October 1, 1852 (Boston, 1852), p. 19. One estimate suggested that less than one-tenth of the inmates of poorhouses had to resort to them because of unavoidable misfortune (Elias Cornelius, The Moral and Religious Improvements of the Poor: A Sermon . . . [Salem, 1824], p. 6 [MS in John Hay Library, Brown University]).

[17] John M. Niles, Connecticut Civil Officer . . . (Hartford, 1847), p. 307.

[18] Union Benevolent Association, Twenty-fifth Annual Report (Philadelphia, 1856), p. 8; Humphrey, op. cit., p. 9.

shire, would relieve persons in the former groups; to the latter he would give but little. Some writers advocated that the vicious be refused aid altogether, even if they became disabled as a consequence of their evil ways: "The poverty which proceeds from improvidence and vice ought to feel the consequences and penalties which God has annexed."[19]

Charitable organizations emphasized the need to avoid indiscriminate almsgiving, lest the unworthy get what was meant for the deserving poor. The societies strove, of course, to succor only the worthy. Some municipalities likewise attempted, though with indifferent success, to follow this policy.[20]

More moderate was the suggestion that no one should be left to suffer from absolute want, but those driven to seek alms as a result of an act of God should be given more comforts than those impoverished because of their folly or vice. No matter how vicious the reprobate, Christianity forbade forsaking him. A committee of the Massachusetts Legislature adduced practical considerations to show the futility of the numerous endeavors to distinguish between the two types of poor: "Absolute distress and want must be relieved, whatever causes may have produced it."[21]

Despite the practical difficulties in the way of distinguishing between the two classes of poor, the opinion of most citizens probably remained unchanged —that in the great majority of cases poverty could be traced to vice and deserved to be treated accordingly. The stigma of having to depend on charity was attached, as a rule, to creatures with deplorable personal failings—such was the prevalent conception, reflecting the dominant individualistic philosophy and Puritan theology.

ECONOMIC EXPLANATIONS OF POVERTY

Not all writers had such a simplistic outlook on the causes of poverty. A small number delved into economic factors, sometimes with considerable insight. Even those who emphasized individual responsibility usually found a place for at least some economic circumstances in making up their catalogue of the various causes of pauperism.

Surely no more assiduous defender of the poor than Mathew Carey was to be found in pre-Civil War America. The prolific Philadelphia pamphleteer took time out from his protectionist polemics to refute certain well-worn arguments. To counter the a priori speculations of the wealthy, Carey presented wage and budget estimates calculated to startle the complacent into giving alms. He argued that many classes of common labor required aid from public or private charity to survive.[22] This

[19] Memoirs of William Plumer . . . Written by Himself," p. 6 (MS in the Library of Congress); Levi Woodbury and Thomas Whipple, Report concerning the Pauper Laws of New Hampshire ("Woodbury Report," 1821), p. 11.

[20] Address of Hon. Levi Lincoln, Mayor of the City of Worcester, to the City Council, April 17, 1848, p. 13. A resolution passed by the second branch of the Baltimore City Council, which would have given "a decided preference" to the deserving poor over the vicious in the distribu-

tion of fuel by the city, was defeated in the first branch (Baltimore City Council, First Branch, Journal, January 29, 1821, p. 413 [MS in Baltimore Archives, City Hall]).

[21] Rev. Chester Dewey, in D. Budley Field, History of the County of Berkshire, Massachusetts (Pittsfield, Mass., 1829), p. 179; Massachusetts House of Representatives, Documents, 1831, No. 51, p. 3.

[22] Mathew Carey, Appeal to the Wealthy of the Land . . . on the Character, Conduct, Situation,

situation was not peculiar to Philadelphia. All the large population centers had the same problem. The New York of Philip Hone's day presented a contrast between "squalid misery and hopeless destitution" and wasteful luxury.[23]

The Owenite *Free Enquirer* triumphantly proclaimed in 1829 that at last most newspapers had acknowledged as false the hackneyed statement that any industrious person could earn a livelihood in this land of plenty. It blamed the existing wretchedness and misery on an unjust social arrangement that did not reward the producer with the product of his industry. In addition, the large population of the cities raised the cost of living while at the same time depressing wages. Similarly, Daniel Raymond, author of the first American treatise on political economy, traced pauperism to the unequal distribution of property, which led to an unequal division of the products of labor. He conceded that, if the wealthy would always employ the poor and give them the necessities of life, all pauperism except that produced by infirmity and old age would disappear; but the avaricious, seeking to accumulate for their posterity, refused to give employment to the propertyless, thereby inflicting pauperism on them.[24]

Any excess of labor resulting from overproduction at a given time had been absorbed by agriculture and released again when needed by industry. Thus far, but little pauperism could be traced to growing manufacturers. However, ran a warning issued in 1831, pauperism would increase when agriculture was no longer the predominant economic activity and industrialization reached the extent it had in England, because the factory hands would lose their efficiency as farm laborers.[25]

From another point of view it was alleged that "machinery and pauperism are marching hand in hand" in the United States. Laborsaving machinery had the effect of depriving the less intelligent of jobs.[26]

Inadequate wages, inequitable social arrangements, and industrialization were but a few of the non-personal explanations of poverty. Writers not content with moralizing about poverty frequently listed unemployment as one of the most significant causes of need. To validate the belief in personal failings as the main cause of pauperism, it was necessary to assume that work was always available for those who sought it —an assumption sufficiently plausible to be generally held. After all, there was a great and growing demand for labor in this country.

---

and *Prospects of Those Whose Sole Dependence for Subsistence is on the Labour of Their Hands* (2d ed.; Philadelphia, 1833), pp. 9–12, 15; *Plea for the Poor* . . . , pp. 6, 8; and *Letters on the Condition of the Poor . . . Containing a Vindication of Poor Laws and Benevolent Societies* . . . (3d ed.; Philadelphia, 1836), pp. 6, 19.

[23] Allan Nevins (ed.), *The Diary of Philip Hone, 1828–1851* (New York, 1927), II, 785 (January 29, 1847).

[24] Daniel Raymond, *The Elements of Political Economy* (2d ed.; Baltimore, 1823), II, 32–40, 49, 58, 59. A committee of Philadelphia guardians attributed part of the increase in the poor rates to "necessary increase of pauperism resulting from the accumulation of wealth in the hands of a few individuals" (Philadelphia Guardians, Minutes, XV, October 6, 1824).

[25] W. L. Fisher, *Pauperism and Crime* (Philadelphia, 1831), p. 31.

[26] Statement of George Henry Evans' National Reform Association, in *Working Man's Advocate*, July 6, 1844, cited in John R. Commons *et al.*, *Documentary History of American Industrial Society*, VII, 301 n. (Cleveland, 1911); New York Senate, *Documents*, 1855, III, No. 72, p. 80.

Admittedly, fluctuations occurred in foreign commerce; some artisans found their old trades no longer called for; women, children, and men no longer able to labor on the land could not always be profitably employed; in periods of depression too many were unemployed. Conceding all these factors, the New York Society for the Prevention of Pauperism still insisted:

These inconveniences are but occasional and temporary . . . wages are always high . . . labour most uniformly in demand is applied to the simplest forms of agriculture . . . no man who is temperate, frugal, and willing to work, need suffer or become a pauper for want of employment.[27]

Every able-bodied man willing to work could provide "a comfortable subsistence" for his family, it was generally believed.[28] Multitudes of laborers pleaded want of employment as the ground for their claim to relief to an incredulous audience.[29] Unemployment might sometimes be the cause of want, but not as often as pretended. Want of work, as it was said of Lowell in 1850, "has not been the usual cause of poverty with us."[30]

Thus it was that a New York legislative committee on the poor laws, finding a great increase in pauperism in the five years after 1815, an increase disproportionate to the increase of population and the cost of living, pointed to "idleness and dissipation" and the system of relieving the poor without requiring them to labor, as the causes. Boston's mayor attributed the unprecedented number of applications for relief in the autumn of 1837 to heavy unemployment, but the city council, apparently not satisfied with this explanation, appointed a committee to look into means for "preventing the increasing evils of pauperism."[31] Of the 132 Connecticut towns that answered the questions of a legislative committee in 1852 on the extent and cause of pauperism, only Union in Tolland County, with thirteen paupers, stated "want of employment" as the cause. The most frequent responses were "intemperance" and "immigration."[32] Unemployment thus frequently went unrecognized as a factor in poverty.

On the other hand, Mathew Carey gave a forthright appraisal of the problem. In a gratuitously distributed pamphlet which went through five editions, he decried the widely held notion that there was always a job waiting for the willing laborer. Actually, even in the best of times, some branches of Philadelphia industry were depressed; for seamstresses and clerks, for example, overcrowding existed. To tell such

[27] *Fifth Annual Report* (New York, 1821), pp. 25-26.

[28] George B. Arnold, *Fourth Semi-annual Report of His Service as Minister at Large in New York* (New York, 1835), p. 7.

[29] For allusions to complaints by the poor on the lack of work, see, e.g., *A Plan for the Government of the Alms-House and for Ordering the Affairs of the Poor in the City of Philadelphia* . . . (Philadelphia, 1805), p. 23.

[30] Pennsylvania Society for the Promotion of Public Economy, *Report of the Library Committee* . . . (Philadelphia, 1817), pp. 12, 19; Lowell Ministry at Large, *Sixth Annual Report* . . . (Lowell, 1850), p. 13.

[31] New York State Assembly, *Journal*, 1820, p. 615; Boston City Records, XVI, 53 (microfilm in Boston Public Library). Even persons recognizing unemployment as a cause of increased poor expenditures would sometimes deem this explanation inadequate and would inquire further into the causes of pauperism. See, e.g., New York State Assembly, *Documents*, 1856, V, No. 214, p. 7.

[32] Connecticut General Assembly, *Documents*, 1852, No. 6, p. 29; Pauper Returns, Epsom, 1827; Walpole, 1830; Bath, 1832 (MS in New Hampshire Historical Society, Concord).

workers to go to the country was use-less, as most of them were not fitted for agricultural pursuits; anyhow, they would not be needed except for a few weeks at harvest time. Moreover, dur-ing general depressions, which occurred "occasionally," Carey noted "a redun-dance of hands at almost all occupa-tions."[33]

Seasonal fluctuations in the demand for labor could be readily observed. Maritime and building trades were par-ticularly affected. Unskilled day labor-ers especially felt the brunt of such fluctuations. The leading private char-ity in Philadelphia reported that "hun-dreds of the worthy and industrious poor of our city are to be found habitu-ally suffering in the winter, for the want of employment alone." Even in a small city like Syracuse the complaint could be heard that the absence of year-round employment was "an evil whose name is 'legion.' "[34]

Cyclical unemployment was not en-tirely overlooked. Particularly in de-pression years, there were statements showing an awareness of the relation-ship between fluctuations in the volume of poor relief and business conditions. Robert Greenhow, for many years president of the overseers of the poor of Richmond, Virginia, remarked: "Everyone at all conversant with hu-man affairs, must agree, that more is required to support the poor in times of general pressure and pecuniary diffi-culty, than in times of prosperity."

Even in rural Rockingham, the over-seers of the poor perceived a connec-tion between "the deranged state of the Country in money matters" and the in-crease of pauperism between 1835 and 1837.[35] An 1817 appeal for contribu-tions from the citizens of Philadelphia stated that the number of meritorious cases among the poor had probably never been so great; many laborers of good habits could not find more than one day's work in a week.[36] The com-mon council of New York City pointed out that "the fluctuations of Commerce in a place so entirely commercial neces-sarily produce distress and render as-sistance from the public necessary to a multitude of Individuals who are desti-tute of capital to support them during a suspension of their ordinary employ-ments."[37] Correspondingly, poor relief expenditures were expected to decrease during periods of prosperity.[38]

Those who attributed most poverty to moral causes sometimes recognized unemployment as another factor.[39] In 1752 a minister had included the unem-

---

[33] M. Carey, *Essays on the Public Charities of Philadelphia* (5th ed.; Philadelphia, 1830, p. 19; *Appeal to the Wealthy* . . . , p. 8; see also *Plea for the Poor,* p. 10.

[34] Pennsylvania Society for . . . Public Econo-my, *op. cit.*, pp. 14–15, 20; Syracuse Home Asso-ciation, *Gathered Records* (Syracuse, 1874), pp. 24–25 (MS in Syracuse Public Library).

[35] *Atlas* (Boston), November 25, 1839; *Rich-mond Daily Compiler,* June 12, 1828; Rocking-ham, Virginia, 1837.

[36] Poulson's *American Daily Advertiser,* Feb-ruary 19, 1817.

[37] *Minutes of the Common Council of the City of New York,* VIII, 765 (January 13, 1817). In 1800, the council had recognized that, though wages were high and jobs were abundant in this country, instances of unemployment might occur (II, 661).

[38] New Hampshire Senate, *Journal,* November Session, 1820, pp. 205–6.

[39] Generally, unemployment would be listed, if at all, as one of several causes, and frequently in an inconspicuous part of the exposition. The Howard Benevolent Society of Boston felt called upon to point out that "it is not improvidence, or vice, or lack of foresight, which in every instance causes the want and distress which is felt in our city—but, in many cases, the absolute destitution of employment—or the utter insuffi-

ployed poor among those who might legitimately eat "the Bread of Charity." More than three-quarters of a century later, the Reverend Francis Wayland admitted the case of the unemployed as a dispensation of "the providence of God" and deserving of charity. The depressed winter of 1837–38 was one of the occasions when it was noted that the number of needy persons "not chargeable with bringing their condition upon themselves by vice" was "unusually great."[40]

Recognition that "employment cannot, even in this country, where labor is comparatively high, be always commanded by the well disposed and industrious poor" was often reluctant and grudging.[41] If it is refreshing to find a committee of the New York legislature pointing to the unusual economic paralysis, with the consequent unemployment of thousands, as the chief cause of the great increase in pauperism in the late 1830's,[42] it is because numerous tirades can be found which placed the blame for this on the viciousness of the poor. It took a severe depression to convince some skeptics that even in

this country continuous employment was not available to all laborers at all times. As business improved this fact would soon be forgotten.

REMEDIES FOR PAUPERISM

Even among those who did not recognize the role of unemployment in creating poverty, there was general agreement that employment was the best preventive or cure for pauperism. Work removed the temptations arising from a state of idleness, and earnings provided the means of support: "That charity is doubly charitable, which while it relieves, gives *employment* to the poor."[43] Those who did not go so far as to assert that the only way of preventing pauperism was to find employment for the poor envisaged a great lessening of pauperism by this means.[44]

Employment was one important cure. Other frequently proposed remedies for pauperism followed logically from the author's analysis of causes. One very significant line of attack advocated temperance, prevention of vice, and character improvement through religion and education. Agrarian reformers found a solution in free homesteads for the poor.[45] Another group believed in the efficacy of high wages.[46] Enthusiasm also ran high for savings

---

ciency of the wages, which is in many instances paid for work" (*Report . . . October 29, 1830,* p. 4).

[40] Charles Chauncy, *The Idle-Poor Secluded from the Bread of Charity by the Christian Law: A Sermon Preached before the Society for Encouraging Industry and Employing the Poor . . .* (Boston, 1752), p. 7. See Francis Wayland, *The Elements of Moral Science . . . Abridged and Adapted to the Use of Schools and Academies . . .* (Boston, 1835), p. 225. Shipwreck, fire, and flood are included in the same group as unemployment (*Journal of Commerce* [New York]), quoted in *Newark Daily Advertiser,* February 3, 1838.

[41] Union Benevolent Association, *Second Annual Report* (Philadelphia, 1833), p. 3.

[42] New York State Assembly, *Documents,* 1840, VI, No. 267, pp. 2–3.

[43] Edward D. Griffin, *Sermon Preached . . . for the Benefit of the Portsmouth Female Asylum* (Boston, 1811), p. 32.

[44] *A Warning to the Citizens of Baltimore* (Baltimore, 1821), pp. 7–8 (MS in Maryland Historical Society).

[45] *Christian Spectator,* I, 146; Jasper Adams, *Elements of Moral Philosophy* (New York, 1837), p. 135; *Young America: Organ of the National Reform Association,* N.S., II (August 2, 1845) and III (July 11, 1846).

[46] Willard Phillips, *A Manual of Political Economy* (Boston, 1828), p. 149.

banks as schools of providence for the poor.[47]

POOR LAW CONTROVERSY

However meritorious savings banks, temperance crusades, and the moral transformation of the poor might be, a number of writers argued that nothing short of the radical reformation or total abolition of the poor laws would succeed in ridding the nation of pauperism. In the United States the poor law controversy by no means produced a literature comparable in magnitude or importance to that in contemporary England, but few pre–Civil War treatises on political economy failed to make at least some reference to pauperism and the poor laws.[48]

Arguments against the poor law.—The poor law, it was commonly held, created the pauperism it sought to relieve.[49] This belief, according to Nathaniel Ware, was subscribed to by all who had thought on pauperism, and it had also been proved by experience.[50] "The more paupers you support, the more you will have to support."[51] Even-

tually, as a result of the operation of the poor laws, far more misery would have been created than it was possible for the public authorities to relieve. Such was the long-run tendency, however light poor rates might be at present.[52]

By removing the dread of want, widely held to be the prime mover of the lower orders of society, the poor laws destroyed the main incitement to industry.[53] The laws "have come in collision with the retributive justice of the deity, and frustrated, to a certain degree, his plan of reclaiming and meliorating our fallen race," proclaimed a Pennsylvania minister. Governor Thomas told the Delaware Legislature: "If the door of public commiseration is thrown too widely open the great stimulus to exertion, which providence in his wisdom, has implanted in the bosom of the community, is too apt to be weakened."[54]

Without the fear of want to goad them on, the poor became idle and improvident. Thus Philadelphia in 1824 presented the terrifying spectacle of increasing poor rates at the same time that many residents were "deliberately throwing away every thought of helping themselves."[55] Even if a man did not become a drone, his frugality and industry would deteriorate; he would

[47] N.Y. Soc. Prev. Pau., *Documents Relative to Savings Banks . . . , passim;* Portsmouth, *Extracts of Report of the Committee on the Poor (ca.* 1817), p. 16 (MS in New Hampshire Historical Society).

[48] Among the few treatises on political economy before 1861 which do not make any reference to pauperism and the poor law are Jacob N. Cardozo, *Notes on Political Economy* (Charleston, 1826), and Theodore Sedgwick, *Public and Private Economy* (New York, 1836–39).

[49] For example, see Association of Delegates from the Benevolent Societies of Boston, *First Annual Report* (Boston, 1835), p. 13; *Camden* (S.C.) *Gazette,* November 7, 1818; *New York American,* March 7, 1829; *Saturday Bulletin* (Philadelphia), quoted in Union Benevolent Association, *Historical Sketch of the First Half Century* (Philadelphia, 1881), p. 27.

[50] "A Southern Planter," in *Notes on Political Economy as Applicable to the United States* (New York, 1844), p. 194.

[51] Thomas Cooper, *A Manual of Political Economy* (Washington, D.C., 1834), p. 95.

[52] A.B., "The Operation of the Poor Laws on Agricultural Interests," *Farmer's Register,* I (1834), 110.

[53] 14 AQR 67.

[54] *The Christian Principle in Relation to Pauperism* (Philadelphia, 1826), pp. 13, 16; Delaware House of Representatives, *Journal,* 1824, p. 15.

[55] Thomas Cooper, *Lectures on the Elements of Political Economy* (Columbia, S.C., 1826), p. 251; Provident Society for the Employment of the Poor (Philadelphia), *Address and Constitution* (Philadelphia, 1824), pp. 1–2.

start buying unnecessary articles and would lose thought of the future. The poor laws offered a bounty on vicious habits, tempting men to become "degraded, dissolute, wasteful, profligate, and idle, by promising them a support if they do so."[56]

As the pauper's moral fiber atrophied, his abhorrence to entering a poorhouse because of the disgrace attached to it diminished, and he would gradually come to look upon it as a home. The evil associates with whom an almshouse inmate consorted, and his loss of self-esteem, served to further weaken his character and made him content to remain a dependent. We were thus breeding "generation after generation of hereditary paupers."[57]

Poor law relief compelled the industrious and thrifty to support the idle and improvident, thereby infringing on property rights.[58] If spent by the ratepayer, the tax for the benefit of the idle would have furnished employment to an industrious individual who needed the wages.[59]

Nathaniel Ware predicted that the poor rates in the United States would increase even faster than in England and that a greater proportion of the population would be paupers. This danger arose, according to this slave-owning protectionist who advocated a property qualification for suffrage, because the poor had the right to vote in some states and officeholders liked to distribute large funds because of the importance, patronage, and emolument this gave them. If ever America lost its freedom, a committee of the Boston

City Council warned, it would be "by the slow and insidious growth in large cities of claims for subsistence upon the public treasury."[60]

Among the noteworthy consequences of the poor laws was their baneful influence on the relations between rich and poor. Professor Cooper, of South Carolina, found the poor becoming more "careless and insolent toward their employers." Wayland saw insubordination promoted: once the obligation of the rich to support the poor was admitted, where would it stop? Dissatisfaction on the part of the poor, because they felt they should be supported better, would likely lead to "collision between the two classes."[61]

Equally galling, perhaps, was the attitude of the pauper that relief was his right and the consequent lack of gratitude to those who made it possible.[62] Compulsory charity deprived one of the pleasure of observing the supplicant's joy when his plea was granted.[63] How unnatural, therefore, was the icy poor law which superseded the tenderness of private giving! The law "eclipses half the loveliness of the character of woman, by interposing its opaque form between the shivering child of want and the sunshine of her soul."[64]

The poor laws weakened ties of family and friendship.[65] When the alms-

---

[56] 14 AQR 67, 78.

[57] 14 AQR 68. See also Cooper, *Lectures*, p. 253.

[58] 14 AQR 76.

[59] *Analectic Magazine*, X (1817), 266.

[60] Nathaniel Ware, *An Exposition of the Weakness and Inefficiency of the Government of the United States of North America* (1845), p. 191; Boston, *City Documents*, 1859, No. 27, pp. 21–22.

[61] Cooper, *Lectures*, *p.* 252; Wayland, *Political Economy*, p. 124.

[62] *Analectic Magazine*, X (1817), 265–66.

[63] Review of *Westminster Review* article on "Charitable Institutions," in *Atlantic Magazine*, II (1824), 114.

[64] Samuel Young, *A Discourse Delivered at Schenectady* . . . (Ballston Spa, 1826), p. 59.

[65] 14 AQR 68.

giver realized that the taxpayer, rather than the poor, profited from a donation he made, the stream of private benevolence would dry up. At the same time the calls on private charity would grow in number, for public funds would prove inadequate as the number of paupers multiplied.[66]

Eliminate the poor law and, according to some writers, the canker of pauperism would almost, if not entirely, disappear. There would then be comparatively few needy persons; these could obtain ample relief from private sources.[67] The care of the poor might be left with perfect confidence "to the Charitable of our good old Commonwealth, to a Christian sense of the duties which the Holy Bible teaches, and our God and Country requires of them to perform towards the poor"—so wrote the president of the overseers of Williamsburg, voicing a sentiment by no means confined to that Virginia community.[68]

Public versus private charity.—The poor law debate thus involved a consideration of the respective merits of public, compulsory charity and private, voluntary almsgiving. Religious considerations played an important role among those who preferred the latter: "Charity is heavenborn, and ceases to be a virtue, when made compulsory by a tax."[69] To substitute the arm of the state for Christian charity was fundamentally wrong. Private philanthropy turned the rich into better Christians while binding them to the poor.[70] The

belief that poor law relief did great harm to the recipient fortified the religious sanction for private almsgiving. "God has ordained that the Poor shall be always with us, as a trial of our benevolence," a citizen of Salem wrote to Josiah Quincy, "but this furnishes no apology for the exercise of the strong arm of the state in support of idleness, and lewdness."[71]

The public often distinguished sharply between the recipient of legal alms and the recipient of voluntary alms. Private charity, in fact, was a protective fence to save the individual from "falling into the gulf of public pauperism." The Union Benevolent Association of Philadelphia preferred to restrict its operations to the "unfortunate but industrious poor" who would never turn to legally provided assistance except when forced to by extreme need. Ignominy attached to the public pauper but not to the other.[72]

Joseph Tuckerman, one of the closest students of poor relief of the early nineteenth century, pointed out the perils facing the laborer who applied for public assistance in a period of unemployment. The principles by which a person strove to maintain his independence to the last deserved to be respected. The Boston minister posed a rhetorical question:

Are they respected, when under the weakness of a temporary necessity, he is aided, not

[66] Cooper, *Lectures,* p. 252; *Camden* (S.C.) *Gazette,* November 7, 1818.

[67] 14 AQR 69, 82.

[68] Robert Garrett, in Williamsburg, Va., 1844 Poor Return.

[69] Editorial in *Newark Daily Advertiser,* November 10, 1857.

[70] Massachusetts House, *Documents,* 1833, No. 6, p. 40; John McVickar, *First Lessons in Political Economy for the Use of Primary and Common Schools* (Boston, 1835), p. 82.

[71] Salem Overseers of the Poor, "Miscellaneous, 1746–1832," letter dated May 18, 1821 (MS in Essex Institute, Salem).

[72] Provident Society for the Employment of the Poor, *Second Annual Report* (Philadelphia, 1826), p. 5; Union Benevolent Association, *Tenth Annual Report* (Philadelphia, 1841), p. 4.

from private sympathy which might stir his heart, and call forth all his energies, but from funds dispensed by others than their owner, and in receiving which he is made to feel himself a pauper?[73]

The very act of applying for aid from tax-raised funds seemed to contaminate the applicant by breaking down his spirit of self-reliance. Whenever a difficulty arose henceforth, it would be easier to run to the overseer of the poor for assistance. "Once a pauper, always a pauper," noted one charitable society in 1851, "has become an axiom."[74] Private charity could seek out and aid worthy persons in genuine distress who would blush to appear on a pauper list. This was one claim that advocates of public poor relief did not contest. Helping those with a strong aversion to becoming town charges was a peculiarly fit sphere for private almsgiving.[75]

Only private benevolence was "precarious and uncertain." Further advantages of private charity in the eyes of opponents of poor laws were that it sought to stimulate self-help and did not carry with it the stamp of a right.[76]

Some students of the problem realized that charity dispensed by organizations drawing their support from voluntary contributions differed little, if at all, in its effects from tax-supported relief. Thus, prominent among the causes of pauperism listed by one author was "the injudicious multiplication of charitable societies, which are sys-

tematized and arranged, according to all the variety of human sufferings; and which are so prodigally managed, as actually to create a demand for human miseries, and to multiply them because there is such a profusion of relief."[77]

The pioneering Society for the Prevention of Pauperism in the city of New York likewise weighed the "partial and temporary good," done by the many charitable institutions in the city relieving misery and want, against the evils consequent on a reliance on gratuitous alms, and found that not even the alleviation of acute suffering could counterbalance the diminished industry and providence. Private charity no less than public relief encouraged indolence and improvidence by removing anxiety from the minds of the poor.[78] Those who subscribed to this view favored, instead of gratuitous donations, finding employment for the poor, or giving them work as a last resort, or bestowing charity personally, if indeed they were not opposed to giving of any kind.[79]

One of the points on which the dispute over the comparative merits of poor laws and private charity hinged was the equity of the two systems from the standpoint of the contributor. Under the system of voluntary giving, the rich would bear most of the burden while, under the poor laws, the poor were called on to pay. The rich would contribute much more in charity than they had paid in taxes when the poor laws were repealed, Colonel Young told

[73] Association of Delegates from the Benevolent Societies of Boston, *op. cit.*, p. 250.

[74] Prov. Soc. Emp. Poor, *Twenty-seventh Annual Report* (Philadelphia, 1851), p. 4.

[75] *Connecticut Journal* (New Haven), November 26, 1800.

[76] *Journal of Commerce* (New York), November 25, 1847.

[77] Burroughs, *op. cit.*, p. 59.

[78] N.Y. Soc. Prev. Pau., *Report on Pauperism*, pp. 8–9.

[79] On employing the needy, see Seamen's Aid Society of Boston, *First Annual Report* (Boston, 1834), *passim;* Society for the Promotion of Knowledge and Industry, *First Annual Report* (New York, 1834), pp. 8–10.

the New York Senate. James City County, where poll taxes were used, reported "barely a shadow of difference" between the poor who were taxed and the paupers of the Virginia county. In Philadelphia, too, where the funds for poor relief came from the real estate tax, it was said that those least able to bear the burden felt the tax severely.[80]

Persons favoring a tax-supported system had a ready reply to these arguments: under a system of voluntary contributions the generous bore the expense, while the avaricious, however rich they might be, escaped.[81] Besides, under a well-administered law many citizens would pay less in poor taxes than they had given to beggars whom they could not bear to see cold and hungry. Still another argument was set forth in Lowell during the severe depression of 1857: taxation was the only way the corporations could be made to pay their share for the support of the needy.[82]

Reinforcing the consideration that a tax was felt to be the most equitable mode of maintaining the poor was the view that the state was in duty bound to provide for the needy; the community as a whole was "a great friendly society."[83] A committee of the Boston City Council reasoned in 1857 that, having given to maintain the government when capable, the needy could turn to it when no longer able to support themselves. Similarly, the overseers of the poor of Rockbridge County, Virginia, viewed the poor laws as "proving that a free government does not exact from its people services in time of prosperity and then cast them off upon private charity in their hour of helpless affliction."[84] Government was obligated to participate in the relief of the poor because it was frequently responsible for poverty: a war, or a change in tariff or currency policy which disrupted the normal channels of trade, interrupted employment and impoverished the sufferers from these changes.[85]

The maintenance of persons reduced to want, then, was one of the necessary expenditures of "every humane government."[86] The highest tribunal of New Jersey recognized in 1802 that the purpose of the poor law was "to prevent the charity of individuals being oppressed and exhausted of heavy burthens."[87] Those who would rely wholly on private charity were said to have an unwarranted faith in the existing benevolence and humanity of their fellow

[80] *Daily Albany Argus,* March 18, 1835; James City County, 1836 Poor Return.

[81] Such an argument would not disturb James Arbuckle, who trusted "the adjusting courses of divine providence" to set this right (*Lecture on Pauperism* [New York, 1841], p. 13).

[82] M. Carey, in Poulson's *American Daily Advertiser,* March 24, 1838; *Lowell Daily Journal and Courier,* December 24, 1857.

[83] Alexander Hill Everett, *North American Review,* XXV (1827), 122.

[84] Boston, *City Documents,* 1857, No. 77, pp. 5-6; Rockbridge, Va., 1849 Poor Return, signed by Dr. J. McDowell Taylor. Cf. a report on the admission of a certain citizen to the poorhouse, remarking that he was "an old taxpaying citizen, and has a right to claim comfortable accommodations on public charity" (*New York Star,* quoted in Poulson's *Amercian Daily Advertiser,* February 1, 1839). An editorial hostile to poor laws deplored the popular notion that everyone had a right to live at the almshouse because of taxes paid or citizenship duty performed (*New York Journal of Commerce,* November 25, 1847).

[85] F. D. Huntington, "Treatment of Poverty and the Poor . . ." *Journal of the Society for the Prevention of Pauperism,* February, 1851, p. 6.

[86] Andrew W. Young, *Introduction to the Science of Government, with a Brief Treatise on Political Economy* (New York, 1860), p. 324.

[87] *Shreve v. Budd,* 7 N.J. 434.

men.[88] Private charity was precarious and was inadequate to meet the requirements of all the needy.[89] The poor law was needed to supply the deficiencies of private almsgiving.[90]

Proponents were impressed by the efficiency and economy of poor law charity as compared with private. Under the latter, aggressive mendicants would receive more than their due, while the modest would be unprovided for. Matthew Carey thought that the recipients of public outdoor aid in Philadelphia would probably have received three or four times as much by begging. In a public almshouse large numbers could be cared for economically under one roof. Poor law relief was efficient; casual charity on Malthus' plan was relief "bestowed in the least effectual, the least intelligent, the most wasteful manner," argued Alexander Hill Everett, a leading American critic. He insisted that "the means of subsistence being determined by the extent and character of the population, a legal provision for the infirm and aged has no effect in augmenting the number of the inhabitants any further than it may save a few individuals from a premature death."[91]

Since poor laws did not have any ill effects, Americans did not need to entertain the fears of the English Malthusians. A strong indication of the falsity of the Malthusian doctrine was the fact that it called for thwarting our nat-

ural "benevolent and social instincts" by frowning upon poor relief and early marriages.[92]

Even with the poor law, there was room for private charity. Opponents would rely exclusively on individual and organized charity; defenders of the poor law generally saw a need for the coexistence of compulsory and voluntary giving. An illustration of the pragmatic, realistic approach among friends of the poor laws is this statement by Samuel P. Newman, a professor at Bowdoin College:

> The existing arrangements in the United States for the relief of the poor, are thought to combine as many advantages, and to be as little open to objection, as any which can be devised. There is an equal distribution of the burden;—effectual relief is provided, and at the same time those moral influences are brought to bear upon the poor, which may lead to the improvement of their characters and conditions. . . . Whether in the progress of this nation, the plan now adopted shall be found insufficient or become subject to abuses, time will shew.[93]

The issue of the entire abolition of the poor laws.—Gazing on the American scene, defenders of poor laws found it satisfactory. Pointing to the English situation, opponents found its implications for the United States ominous.[94]

Only by contrast with defenders can American opponents be labeled "doctrinaire." For the most part, even

---

[88] *Springfield Town Records,* VI (May, 1824), 243–44 (MS in the City Hall, Springfield, Mass.).

[89] Mayor Colden, in N.Y. Soc. Prev. Pau., *Second Annual Report* (New York, 1820), p. 64.

[90] Laurens P. Hickok, *A System of Moral Science* (New York, 1858), pp. 261-62.

[91] Phillips, *op. cit.,* p. 146; Carey, *Appeal to the Wealthy,* p. 19; Alexander Hill Everett, *North American Review,* XXV (1827), 122–23.

[92] Everett, *North American Review,* XVII (1823), 124. Even an economist who recognized that early marriages might be encouraged by the poor laws felt that Malthus' doctrine was "too repugnant to our national sympathies, to be readily adopted" (George Tucker, *Political Economy for the People* [Philadelphia, 1857], p. 222).

[93] Newman, *op cit.,* pp. 321–22.

[94] *Farmer's Register,* I, 110; *Catskill Recorder,* reprinted in *Freeman's Journal* (Cooperstown), December 2, 1822.

Americans hostile to the poor laws did not frown upon public provision for the helpless members of the community—the aged, the infirm, and the young.[95] It was the able-bodied who were viewed with suspicion. Like Thomas Chalmers, the famous Glasgow divine, the Reverend James Arbuckle thought that an asylum for the infirm would not promote idleness and improvidence.[96] Similarly, Wayland, whose *Elements of Political Economy* was the best-selling text in the field before 1860, engaged in a diatribe against poor laws but was forced to admit the propriety of "some public provision" for those unable to provide for themselves because of age, infirmity, or sickness: cases occurred which could not be promptly enough relieved by individual giving or which would be too burdensome for the charitably disposed. Ware likewise insisted that physically fit persons must be left to shift for themselves: "Better, if it comes to the worst, let a few perish in the streets, than have one-twentieth part of mankind degraded, rendered worthless, & what is worse, eating the substance of the industrious and valuable portion of the community." Yet he too would make public provision for the sick and infirm.[97] Rarely was the extreme view expressed that no legal support should exist for any class of poor.[98]

All four widely publicized legislative investigations into the wisdom of public poor relief made during the 1820's pointed to English as well as American experience to confirm their hostility to the poor laws. Yet all were reticent when it came to the issue of the total abolition of the laws.[99] Both the report made by Josiah Quincy for Massachusetts and that by Levi Woodbury for New Hampshire—which appeared within a few months of each other in 1821 —emphasized that the system of poor laws was of long standing and generally accepted, notwithstanding the authorities and experience ranged against it. Instead of recommending the abolition of the laws, they proposed a number of improvements, including establishment of poorhouses with farms attached. Rather than place the physically and mentally ill, the aged, and the young at the mercy of precarious charity, New York Secretary of State Yates was willing to countenance public provision for them, despite the fact that abuses would occur and the industry of some be weakened. He, too, urged the establishment of poor farms. The last report, that by William Meredith, was the most irreconcilable. This young representative, soon to become a leading figure in the Philadelphia bar, informed Pennsylvania's legislature that the rapid and complete abolition of the system of public poor relief was the sole efficacious remedy for the evils attendant on the poor laws. Yet when it came to concrete resolutions the Meredith committee went

---

[95] Henry Vethake, *Principles of Political Economy* (Philadelphia, 1838), p. 355.

[96] Arbuckle, *op. cit.*, pp. 17, 23–24.

[97] Wayland, *op. cit.*, p. 417; Ware, *Notes*, pp. 196–97, *Exposition*, p. 375.

[98] Thus the minister who wrote *The Christian Principle in Relation to Pauperism* would limit relief to those "literally unable to work"; this relief was to be distributed by private charity (pp. 19–20).

[99] Phillips noted that, although many legislators in the United States, as in England, believed that the poor laws were harmful, no direct proposal for their repeal was ever made "for though, in speculation, men were well convinced of the inexpediency of those laws . . . yet any one undertaking to act practically upon it, found himself beset with innumerable difficulties" (*op. cit.*, p. 44).

no further than to suggest that the amount raised for the poor in any district in the future should never exceed the 1825 expenditure, and that the overseers of the poor should be prohibited from relieving any able-bodied persons not legally settled in the locality in which relief was required.[100] Legislators no more ventured to propose the complete elimination of all public poor relief than did the great majority of writers on the question.

To draw a hard and fast line, therefore, between supporters and opponents of the poor law is difficult and often arbitrary. It is easy to understand how the impression arose that "the soundest political economists teach that all pauper systems are wrong,"[101] but, concerning American writers, this was certainly an exaggeration. Even opponents usually conceded the propriety of supporting from tax revenues at least the infirm and the aged.[102]

According to Willard Phillips, a learned Boston lawyer, the studies and complaints concerning the heavy burden of pauperism in Great Britain had aroused the interest of Americans and led to the demand that the poor laws be repealed lest we be submerged by a flood of pauperism such as was to be found in England. Some years before, another Bostonian had complained of the American habit of reading English works on the question and then forming opinions entirely inapplicable to conditions in the United States.[103] Thus Josiah Quincy had been struck, not only by the similarity in experience of England and Massachusetts, but also by the "singularly coincident" opinions expressed in the returns of many Massachusetts overseers of the poor, compared with the utterances of English statesmen and economists. Mathew Carey was alarmed by the propagation of the ideas of the *Edinburgh Review* (favoring the total abolition of the poor laws) and their advocacy by leading citizens in America.[104]

Was this coincidence or imitation? Neither the timing of the American debate—initiated generations after the controversy broke out in England—nor the line of arguments used in the United States, was identical with the British debate.

Very few Americans used the most telling of all the British arguments against the poor laws—that overpopulation and its concomitant evils were consequences of the laws. Among them was English-born Thomas Cooper, who believed that the poor laws encouraged early marriage among the poor. Casting a forward glance, an anonymous author

---

[100] Josiah Quincy, *Report of Committee to Whom Was Referred the Pauper Laws of This Commonwealth ("Quincy Report"*; Boston, 1821), pp. 7, 9; Woodbury Report, pp. 11, 12; John Van Ness Yates, "Report on the Laws for the Relief and Settlement of the Poor," in New York State Assembly, *Journal,* 1824, pp. 386–99, and Appendix B, p. 392; William Morris Meredith, "Report of the Committee Appointed To Enquire into the Operation of the Poor Laws," Pennsylvania House of Representatives, *Journal,* 1824–25, II, 173–200. Neither proposal was enacted.

[101] *National Gazette* (Philadelphia), March 12, 1830, editorial.

[102] Cf. the statement of Governor Andrew Pickens, of South Carolina: "That the poor should be liberally provided for, by law, will not be questioned by any one; but it is of great importance that the line of distinction, between the indolent and dissipated and the poor, should be strongly marked" (Message No. 1, November 25, 1817 [MS in South Carolina Historical Commission]).

[103] Phillips, *op. cit.,* p. 143; *Miscellaneous Remarks on the Police of Boston* . . . (Boston, 1814), p. 3.

[104] *Quincy Report,* p. 2; Carey, *Appeal to the Wealthy,* p. 21.

(Cooper, perhaps?) predicted in the *American Quarterly Review* that, without the natural check to population increase, the labor market would become overstocked and wages depressed below the subsistence level. These effects, it was emphasized, were not yet felt in this country, where the demand for laborers generally exceeded the supply, but they were likely to result from our bad policy of having poor laws.[105]

Most opinion rejected the theory of Malthus, which was seldom correctly stated or understood here.[106] With a continent to conquer, it would have been grotesque to express concern over a crowded labor market consequent on the poor laws. Opponents instead contented themselves with citing the evil effects which the laws had on the working habits and economic virtues of the poor. Moreover, American critics, unlike the English Malthusians, rarely called for the entire elimination of all public provision, even for the infirm and aged.[107]

The principle of less eligibility, that the condition of a recipient of the public's bounty should not be made as good as that of the worst-paid self-supporting laborer—one of the pillars of poor law policy formulated by the Royal Commission of 1834—had its American supporters also.[108] Others, however, like the economist Francis Bowen, rejected less eligibility: the attitudes of the American laborer toward relief and the economic environment were so different from the English that it was unnecessary to render life in an American almshouse more unpleasant than it was inherently, for fear that otherwise applicants would be attracted. Secretary of State Dix even recommended that the inmates of the county farms in New York be given the comforts available to people in "ordinary circumstances."[109] Perhaps the prevailing attitude in the United States was that the situation should not be made "so comfortable as to render it desirable, and preferable to working at wages, nor so uncomfortable and irksome as to render it a place of punishment, or charitable penitentiary."[110] Once again, on the question of the kind of treatment paupers deserved, American opinion diverged from the British.

---

[105] 14 AQR 90; Cooper, *Lectures*, pp. 252–53, *Manual*, p. 13.

[106] George J. Cady, "Early American Reaction to the Theory of Malthus," *Journal of Political Economy*, XXXIX (1931), 625, 632; Joseph J. Spengler, "Population Doctrines in the United States," *Journal of Political Economy*, XLI (1933), 433, 463.

[107] Chalmers, whose writings were familiar in this country, was most often referred to as having rid his Glasgow parish of the curse of a compulsory provision for the poor. In one passage, however, he concedes the legitimacy of poor-law provision for the blind, deaf, insane, and crippled persons, as in these cases relief would not multiply the number of objects of need (Thomas Chalmers, *Christian and Civic Economy of Large Towns* [Glasgow, 1823], II, 218–19).

[108] *Report from His Majesty's Commissioners for Inquiring into the Administration and Practical Operation of the Poor Laws* (London, 1834), p. 228; Henry Vethake, "An Essay on the Moral Relations of Political Economy," in the *Annals of the Board of Education of the Presbyterian Church in the United States . . . for 1835* (Philadelphia, 1835), p. 141; Adams, *op. cit.*, pp. 244–45; Massachusetts Senate, *Documents*, 1852, No. 127, pp. 2–3; Association of Delegates . . . of Boston, *op. cit.*, p. 37; New York Association for the Improvement of the Condition of the Poor, *Fifteenth Annual Report* (New York, 1858), p. 45.

[109] Francis Bowen, "[Review of] *The Elements of Political Economy* by Francis Wayland," *Christian Examiner*, XXIV (1838), p. 51; New York State Assembly, *Documents*, 1835, III, No. 185, pp. 5–6.

[110] Phillpis, *op. cit.*, p. 147.

The consequences of the debate.— Harriet Martineau, zealous advocate of the repeal of the English poor laws, commented, on observing what seemed to her the negligible pauperism in the United States, that to Americans it was "an occasion for the exercise of their ever-ready charity." Americans indeed looked upon the poor laws as one aspect of their benevolence.[111]

Not even the vigorous analysis of the evils of almsgiving could repress the spirit of charity which pervaded the people.[112] Nevertheless, the early nineteenth century debate on the wisdom of almsgiving and the expediency of the poor laws did have certain effects. To begin with, the general public was made conscious of the problem of poverty and how best to treat it. In 1809 Governor Jeremiah Smith, of New Hampshire, could state: "That there should be legal provision for all the necessitous, it is believed will be questioned by none."[113] Just a few years later, however, this policy was subjected to critical scrutiny and attacked by many writers. Complaints were voiced about the high cost of relief, and doubts were expressed concerning the wisdom of encouraging pauperism by poor laws.

But the system of poor law relief was never overthrown. Even its enemies often conceded that the system was "so interwoven with our habits and customs" that it was probably impossible to do without it, as things stood.[114] Side by side with private efforts, public charity continued to flourish. Eloquent testimony to the utility of the poor laws is found in their continuance in the old states and their introduction in the new territories.[115] The best that opponents could hope for was a strict limitation of relief.[116]

For a time, at least, relief probably came to be administered in various localities in a more careful manner, and more attention began to be paid to the activities of the overseers of the poor.[117] Perhaps the most notable result of the discussion was the impetus it gave to the movement to institutionalize assistance, so characteristic of American relief practice for most of the nineteenth century. Organized charitable societies with fixed rules of procedure became the custom in the private sphere; in the area of public relief, in many localities the poorhouse replaced informal outdoor aid.

Received February 21, 1963

---

[111] Harriet Martineau, *Society in America* (New York, 1837), II, 289; Letter to the *South Carolina Telescope,* reprinted in *Southern Patriot* (Charleston), February 12, 1818.

[112] Cf. E. E. Ely, "Prevention of Pauperism," *Presbyterian Magazine,* II (1822), 230; Bangor, Me., *Address of the Mayor . . . March 15, 1847* (Bangor, 1847), p. 9; *American Watchman* (Wilmington), January 7, 1818 (I am indebted to Miss Gertrude Brinckle of the Historical Society of Delaware for this reference).

[113] New Hampshire House of Representatives, *Journal,* June 1809, p. 68.

[114] N.Y. Soc. Prev. Pau., *Report on Pauperism,* pp. 9–10.

[115] [Sir Francis Bond Head], "Foreign Poor Laws," *Quarterly Review,* LV (1835), 49.

[116] Artemus Simonds, *Report on Almshouses and Pauperism* (Boston, 1835) p. 44; Annual Message of Governor Thomas, in Delaware House of Representatves, *Journal,* 1824, p. 15.

[117] Phillips, *op. cit.,* pp. 143–44.

THE "BENEVOLENT FAIR": A STUDY OF CHARITABLE ORGANIZATION AMONG AMERICAN WOMEN IN THE FIRST THIRD OF THE NINETEENTH CENTURY

MARY BOSWORTH TREUDLEY

THE victorious conclusion of the Revolutionary War released an extraordinary amount of social energy among Americans. Along the eastern seaboard that energy was transformed into associations of all sorts, especially of an educational or humanitarian character. With men there were no taboos to delay the process of transferring European culture across the Atlantic by copying all the social devices that seemed worthy of imitation. But even in the greater freedom of American society, women were not accustomed to organize their activities publicly. The lag, however, could not be long since association was a primary characteristic of postwar society, while pioneer life and urban growth alike combined to free women for participation in every aspect of cultural development.

Church sewing circles, to be sure, had been formed before the Revolution, whose earliest achievement was to outfit the soldiers who marched with General Braddock to his defeat.[1] But credit for the initiation of charity organization among women is usually given to Anne Parrish, a young Quaker of Philadelphia. She visited in the homes made desolate by the yellow fever epidemic of 1793. By 1795 she had gathered her friends into what was at first called the "Friendly Circle" and, after its incorporation in 1811, the "Female Society of Philadelphia for the Relief and Employment of the Poor." It was designed to help "suffering fellow creatures, particularly widows and orphans," without "distinction of nation or colour."[2]

The statement is often made that material culture tends to be diffused more rapidly than nonmaterial. But that is not always

[1] Kate Gannett Wells, "What Women Have Done in Philanthropy," *The Second Church in Boston, 1649–1899* (Boston, 1900), p. 117.

[2] *Annual Report* (1858).

Social Service Review 14 (September 1940): 509–22
© 1940 by The University of Chicago

true. In this case, the design for women's organizations spread very rapidly. In 1797 the New York Society for the Relief of Poor Widows with Small Children was organized by Isabella Marshall Graham. In 1798 a Quaker group in New York formed a relief society with one of those mouth-filling names beloved of the eighteenth and nineteenth centuries. In 1799 the ladies of Baltimore began discussions which led to the opening of an orphanage in the following year. In 1802 in the same city, the Female Humane Society was formed to supply work to widows. The women of Savannah organized at as early a date as Baltimore. Boston, stirred by news from the South, founded the Boston Female Asylum in 1800. The Benevolent Society of Troy was started a few months sooner in that same year as was also the Female Association of Philadelphia for the Relief of Women and Children in Reduced Circumstances. Salem organized its Female Charitable Society in 1801, Providence had organized a similar society by 1801, and Charleston by 1802. Societies were at work in Newark, Newburyport, Portsmouth, and Albany by 1803.[3]

The list is probably not complete even for the decade 1793–1803, but it gives some indication of the readiness with which women filled their new leisure with philanthropy. Charity was not the only excuse for their organization. At the same time numerous Bible, tract, and missionary societies were starting to work. Women were organizing, too, to supply young men of various brands of orthodoxy with training in theology, and they were busy also in spreading free education among the children of the poor through the Sunday-school movement.

It is not quite true that organization took place first and a purpose for it was found afterward, but a particular situation of need tended to be merely the stimulus to action which might as well have taken place with some other end in view. Association was in the air. American men were not only not opposed to such organization of

[3] Thomas Alden, *A Discourse Delivered before the Members of the Portsmouth Female Asylum* (1804); Samuel Stillman, *A Discourse Delivered before the Members of the Boston Female Asylum* (1801); Eliphalet Nott, *A Discourse Delivered before the Ladies' Society for the Relief of Distressed Women and Children of Albany* (1804); William Bentley, *A Discourse Delivered at the Annual Meeting of the Salem Female Charitable Society* (1807); Irving E. Fancher, *A History of the Troy Orphan Asylum, 1833–1933* (Troy, 1933).

women's activities but in some cases were its most urgent advocates. The first suggestion that Boston women should copy Savannah and Baltimore came from a man.[4] In Newark it was the men who took the initiative in calling the first meeting for organization.[5] In practically every community men supplied funds which women, with their lesser command of income, could not have raised among themselves.

Leadership was of secondary importance once the psychological hazards of the first stage in the adoption of the new fashion had been successfully braved. Of course, the natural leaders of a community had to be at the head of any community-wide organization, but small groups were quite free to unite for some limited purpose and to seek support within their own area of influence. In the larger communities that freedom made for a wide diversity of grouping.

The only illustration of any question about the propriety of women's organizations occurred in connection with the Boston Female Asylum. Its leading spirit was Mrs. Hannah Stillman, wife of a popular Baptist clergyman, in a period when the élite of Boston were all Unitarians. In spite of that, she managed to secure a socially impressive list of contributors headed by Mrs. John Adams. But could they hold a public meeting without awakening unfavorable comment? Fortunately Mrs. Jonathan Mason, Sr., whose social status was beyond doubt, opened her home. The subscribers were secretly invited and a large number attended. No further embarrassment seems to have been felt over the public assemblying of women on their own impulse.[6]

The purposes of organization were culturally determined within definite and narrow limits. Biblical phrases, the widow and the fatherless, the sick, the hungry, Dorcas and her needle, Mary Magdalene and her sin charted the course which charity followed. But women were even more limited than men. They could relieve a family only if the father was dead or had deserted. They could pro-

[4] *An Account of the Rise, Progress, and Present State of the Boston Female Asylum* (Boston, 1803), pp. 3–4.

[5] *The History of the Newark Female Charitable Society* (1903), p. 5.

[6] Abby L. Wales, *Reminiscences of the Boston Female Asylum* (Boston, 1844), pp. 8–9.

vide for aged spinsters. They could educate young female children, and that was about the limit within which they could initiate work. As auxiliaries to men's societies they could extend their field to include prostitutes and prisoners. Convention would have permitted them to nurse the sick poor, and a few societies were organized for that purpose. But the development of that type of work was hindered, if not completely prevented, by the lack of necessary inventions of appropriate procedures. The one striking exception was Anne Parrish's society which reported in 1818 that it had, in the first twenty-three years of its existence, visited and relieved 11,977 sick poor.[7] The Female Association for the Relief of the Sick Poor, and for the Education of Such Female Children, as Do Not Belong To, or Are Not Provided For by Any Religious Society, of New York, started ambitiously to meet all unmet needs and particularly to provide for the sick, but the difficulties proved too great and they turned to the narrower field of the education of small children.[8]

The form of organization, too, was culturally determined. Most societies of any importance were incorporated so that they might hold property. They had the same elected officers and tended to choose the treasurer from among the unmarried women to avoid any legal complications arising from a husband's right to control money placed in his wife's hands. They followed the same pattern of financing. Annual dues were from one to three dollars a year, and membership depended upon their payment. There was an annual church service at which a collection was taken, and the sermon was later printed and sold. Donations were solicited or accepted from interested gentlemen who sometimes took upon themselves extensive fund raising or secured legislative grants especially to house the work of these societies. Dues were considered as income, but donations went into the capital stock which was carefully invested, as was usually part of the interest also. Only in dire emergencies, such as a yellow fever epidemic, was the capital ever touched.

Two societies were organized on a district plan similar to the one developed at Hamburg, Germany, in the late eighteenth century.

[7] *Annual Report* (1818).

[8] *Annual Report* (1814), pp. 4–5. Society organized by Quaker group in 1798.

The Female Association of Philadelphia for the Relief of Women and Children in Reduced Circumstances in 1800 divided the city and liberties into wards or districts, each with a manager in charge. It was her duty

to visit each applicant, to examine particularly into her moral character, her situation, her habits and modes of life, her wants, and the best means of affording relief, so that assistance may not be extended to the vicious and idle, when it is due only to the honest and necessitous suffering under sickness and misfortune.[9]

The Newark Female Charitable Society in 1803 followed the same plan, with six districts and a manager for each, who was responsible for seeking out the sick to be nursed and for discovering "genteel females" in need of charity for which they would not beg.[10]

The climate of opinion of the period was accepted without question by most of these societies. The poor were divided into the worthy and the unworthy, and only the former were considered deserving of aid. Large numbers of the poor were so because of their own laziness, thriftlessness, or vice. To a Scotswoman, like Mrs. Graham, who had herself experienced dire poverty, the whole class of American mechanics demanded too much in the way of luxury and had with justice to pay for their excesses during periods of depression.[11] It was an exceptional group that could attribute the misery of the hard winter of 1820–21 to the "want of *sufficient employment*" and could accept the point of view that "in many instances, the vice of intemperance was but the effect of a despairing state of mind, brought on by necessities the poor sufferer had no means to supply."[12] The Raleigh Female Benevolent Society took a revolutionary position in 1823 when it argued against necessarily giving the larger portion of its charity to the worthiest, that "the most deserving may not be the most *necessitous;* and although evil may previously have been committed, yet who shall say what has been resisted."[13]

[9] *Annual Report* (1803).

[10] *The History of the Newark Female Charitable Society*, pp. 9, 12.

[11] New York Society for the Relief of Poor Widows with Small Children, *Annual Report* (1800).

[12] Female Hospital Society of Philadelphia, *Annual Report* (1831).

[13] *Revised Constitution and By-laws of the Raleigh Female Benevolent Society, with the Reports of the Society from Its Commencement* (1823), p. 11.

The distribution of relief was usually limited to the three "charity months" January, February, and March. The New York Society for the Relief of Poor Widows with Small Children was exceptional in voting that only two-thirds of its funds should be expended in the winter. Heroically four of its managers spent the yellow fever summer of 1799 in the city, using the society's funds and the resources of their own pantries and tapping the pocket-books of their friends to enable their beneficiaries to survive its horrors. Even in ordinary summers they knew that the children of the poor, "pent up in small, confined hot rooms," almost universally suffered from the "summer complaint" and "hooping cough," as well as from scarlet fever and smallpox.[14]

Because of the feeling that the poor were but the victims of their own vices an obligation rested upon a society so to safeguard alms-giving that it would not minister to depravity. A second motive for careful discrimination was to avoid any inducement to paupers to migrate to the city either from Europe or from the surrounding countryside. Philadelphia was especially hospitable to the immigrant poor, while Boston set the first precedents for limiting assistance to established residents.

The basic procedure in administration, universally adopted in theory if not always followed in practice, was the investigation of each applicant in her own home and through her relatives and neighbors in order to establish her worthiness. For the most part there were no objective criteria of worth, and the decision rested upon the arbitrary judgment of the visitor. The field repays study, for it is around the techniques of investigation that social case work developed and it is on the basis of patterns of disciplined behavior in relief giving that professional attitudes have been formed.

The most elaborate scheme for regulating the behavior of its almoners was worked out by the New York Society for the Relief of Poor Widows with Small Children between 1797 and 1813. It is interesting, not as typical of the period, but as showing how early some of the characteristic features in the administration of relief appeared. The constitution and by-laws of 1813 crystallized sixteen years of experience. The name of the society was the first delimita-

---

[14] *Annual Report* (1800).

tion of its area of responsibility. Among poor widows, relief from the beginning was denied to the immoral and to those unwilling either to send their children to school or to apprentice them, if they had reached the proper age. By 1813 a more professional definition of its responsibility had been reached by the society. It was to care only for poor widows of "fair character" with two children under ten years of age. An aged parent or an older defective child might be considered the equivalent of a second child under ten. A fair character was deemed to be forfeited either by selling spirituous liquors or by public begging. Widows without legal residence were to be granted relief only by special vote of the board. A widow having property, the interest on which was sufficient to pay her rent, was not entitled to aid. Claims to widowhood based on the "supposed death" of a deserting husband had to be substantiated by proof that he had not been heard from for twelve months and that the probabilities were that he was dead. On the other hand, a woman with an insane husband, who had been confined for at least three months, was to be assisted as a widow.

There were no paid agents, but the distribution of relief was concentrated in the hands of the managers. Originally they met twice monthly, divided the available funds among themselves, and applied their share at their own discretion. But checks upon that discretion soon appeared. They were allowed to give relief only after a visit in the home and then only in the form of necessaries. Money grants required a special vote of the board. They were permitted to exceed their allowance of funds only in the case of illness. A committee was to be appointed by the first directress to go over the managers' books once a month and make sure "whether the distribution of the society's bounty has been judiciously made." Further, the first directress was expected to visit all the widows once a year and, in addition, to accompany individual managers to deal with "particular situations of embarassment."

The only other definite specifications related to reports. The managers were required to keep records of the name, place of abode, and circumstances of every widow relieved, the ages of her children, and the kind and amount of relief granted to each. They were also instructed, in general, to furnish suitable employment to their charges in order to create and maintain habits of industry and to find schools for the children or places in "sober virtuous families" for those ready for service.[15]

If direct relief is difficult to administer, work relief presents still more difficult problems, for which no satisfactory solution has as yet been found. Attempts to "set the poor to work" were made under public auspices in the seventeenth century and on private initiative in the eighteenth century. "Charity sewing" must have been transplanted to American shores with the first colonists, but organized effort by women to supply relief work to their own sex dates from 1795.

The main features of the orthodox program are shown in Anne Parrish's Friendly Circle. It started giving both direct and work relief, but the latter became increasingly important until in 1831 direct relief was abandoned altogether. Work at first was given to women in their own homes, but in 1798 a "house of industry" was opened, from the conviction that the beneficiaries would be better off in a well-heated workshop than in their own cold and cheerless tenements. It also permitted giving one hot meal a day to the women and to the small children whom they must bring with them. The presence of the children soon resulted, as it usually did, in the establishment of a school to keep them busy and quiet. The mothers were set to work in the beginning at spinning flax and wool and making cotton stockings for the poor, but later sewing and knitting replaced spinning. The house was kept open only during the three charity months. It was the intention to provide a small group with permanent employment during that period. The society started with ten women but soon was keeping fifty busy, and feeding, with the children, over a hundred a day.[16]

Just how many societies furnished employment for women is difficult to determine. The material for this study has been drawn from the experience of one society in Baltimore, four in Philadelphia, and two in Boston.[17] It is most nearly adequate for the discussion of two

[15] New York Society for the Relief of Poor Widows with Small Children, *Constitution* (1800, 1813).

[16] Friendly Circle, *Annual Report* (1858).

[17] The societies used with the date of founding are as follows: in Baltimore, the Female Humane Association, founded in 1802, renamed the Humane Impartial Society

types of problems facing those early societies: the market for which production was to be carried on and the wage policy.

The problems involved in production on work relief have always been stubborn though it was only through experience that that fact was realized. The early societies thought that it would be easy to set women to work and thus make them self-supporting. In Boston the Society for Employing the Female Poor, however, after struggling with the problems involved for over a decade along orthodox lines, finally suspended operations because of the impossibility of finding an acceptable solution.[18] Other societies in the same circumstances kept going, feeling that they were doing enough good to warrant continued existence. Mathew Carey, himself one of the severest critics of charitable work policies, found that it was much easier to criticize than to construct, after his own experiment in heterodoxy proved abortive. Mrs. Sarah Josepha Hale alone in this period found a thoroughly workable and satisfactory way out of the difficulties inherent in work relief. Mrs. Graham anticipated two features of the W.P.A. program by a century and a third when she paid some of her poor widows to open day schools for the children of her other beneficiaries in various parts of New York City and when she secured for one of her widows the job of managing the "soup house" established by the Humane Society.[19]

Sewing and laundry were the only two occupations, outside of domestic service, open to unskilled women, until factory doors swung wide for their employment. The needle trades were adapted first by the charitable societies to the purposes of work relief. It was apparently not until the 1820's that laundry establishments were set up. John Gallison, who wrote the prospectus for the Society for Employing the Female Poor, hoped that it might develop new

---

in 1811; in Philadelphia, the Female Hospitable Society (1808), the Provident Society for the Employing of the Poor (1824), the Union Benevolent Association (1831), and the Society for Improving the Condition and Elevating the Character of Industrious Females (1838); in Boston, the Society for Employing the Female Poor (1820) and the Boston Seamen's Aid Society (1832).

[18] *Statement of the Society for Employing the Female Poor* (1853).

[19] J. Bethune, *The Life of Mrs. Isabella Graham* (New York, 1839), pp. 54–55.

outlets for female labor or at least devise new articles and fabrics for manufacture by its seamstresses, but his hope was not realized.[20]

The question of a market for the garments that were made was consciously faced by the societies organized in the 1820's. The Provident Society for Employing the Poor, upon its organization in 1824, decided that it would not take family work because families ought to employ the poor directly. Nor would it compete with the domestic manufacturers, because that would only mean taking work from the poor whom they were employing. Instead it started with the policy of dumping its products abroad, that is, in South America, New Orleans, and the West.[21] Other societies tried the same plan. An account of these ventures in foreign trade would be interesting if it were obtainable. They all alike proved failures from the point of view of profits. The one exception came later when outfits were at a premium during the California gold rush and the migration to "Bleeding Kansas."

In the home market the orthodox opinion was that only the upper classes would prove a profitable outlet. Laundry work had, of necessity, to be limited to that brought in by customers who could pay. Sewing could be disposed of in slightly more varied fashion. Work was solicited from the well-to-do. Coarse garments were made for distribution to charitable institutions either as gifts or sales. Sometimes a shop was opened to serve the poor directly. The philanthropic were asked to buy tickets and give them to the needy to use for their purchases.

The only real market, then, was to be among the wealthy. But in the days before universal compulsory education, the women who most needed help were too ignorant to be trained for the finer grades of work which alone could be sold at a profit. The Society for Employing the Female Poor hired supervisors for both its branches and a woman to give free instruction in sewing, but it proved impossible to get satisfactory work from the very poor. The only source of skill was among the "decayed gentlewomen" and those who had "seen better days." The Boston society estimated in the 1830's that forty-three dollars out of every hundred spent on

[20] *Explanation of the Views of the Society for Employing the Poor* (Boston, 1830), p. 4.
[21] *Annual Reports* (1825, 1826, 1830).

the laundry reached its beneficiaries in the form of wages, but in sewing only twenty-five dollars out of every hundred was put in the hands of those the society was designed to help. It had never expected to be self-supporting, but the costs of work relief seemed excessive and its benefits to women at the lowest economic level negligible. For that reason the society terminated its active existence in 1837.[22]

Mrs. Hale, who is best known as "editress" of *Godey's Lady's Book* at that very time hit upon a solution that did work at least temporarily. She approached the problem from a different angle from those who were attempting to make the very poor self-supporting through service to the rich. Her plan grew in part out of her aversion to the church sewing circle, in which benevolent upper-class women came together to sew for the poor. She felt, and said so with vigor, that they had much better be engaged in their own further cultivation. For one reason, they were much better able to find "useful occupation, elegant pursuits, or improving studies" than the poor women to whom the garments were given. Sewing would keep the latter from "idle gossip, or vicious indulgences."[23]

The Boston Seamen's Aid Society was established to help Father Taylor, that lovable eccentric and powerful preacher, in his ministry to sailors. Mrs. Hale was its leading spirit during the first eight years of its existence. Starting with the idea that the poor should work for the poor, she found a natural market for the society's products among the seamen, whose demand was for cheapness and durability rather than for fine workmanship. The society was successful in serving two purposes at the same time: by employing the widows, wives, and daughters of sailors in making good and substantial articles to be sold to their own men.[24]

Mrs. Hale departed from orthodoxy with regard not only to marketing but also to training. She understood the ingratitude of poor mothers who charged that the ordinary charity school was a

[22] *Report of the Committee of Advice* (1824); *An Explanation of the Views of the Society* (1826); *Statement of the Society* (1853).

[23] Boston Seamen's Aid Society, *Annual Report* (1836), p. 6.

[24] Gilbert Haven and Thomas Russell, *Incidents and Anecdotes of Rev. Edward T. Taylor* (Boston, 1872), pp. 111–12.

device of the rich to get the daughters of the poor to work for nothing, since most of their time was spent in sewing for their benefactors. In the school that the Seamen's Aid Society opened in 1836, the thirty or forty little girls who attended either made clothes for themselves or were paid for what they did. More significantly, the society persuaded the city council to allow "plain needlework" to be taught in the public schools for one hour a day from April to November, the entering wedge for training in home economics.[25]

Mathew Carey was another vigorous critic of customary patterns of charity. He spent a good deal of his energy during the latter part of his life in trying to change the atmosphere in which the rich "considered" the poor. He disapproved with vigor of the "general censure of the poor, for extravagance and dissipation." He pointed with scorn to what seemed to him the "trickle" of charity, inadequate alike to the needs of the poor and the resources of the wealthy.[26] A steady stream of pamphlets poured from his press, which were distributed free to the leading citizens of Boston, New York, Philadelphia, and Baltimore, and aimed to increase both the tolerance and the generosity of the well-to-do. He was disturbed not only over the pittances distributed by charity but over the starvation level of wages, especially among women in the needle trades. He thought, as did Mrs. Hale, that philanthropy should not accept the iron law of orthodox wage theory but should use liberal relief as an instrument for improving the economic position of working women.

Carey's one positive contribution to the problem of women's work was through the Society for Improving the Condition and Elevating the Character of Industrious Females, established in 1838 and very short lived. He proposed to open two schools, one for sewing and one for cookery.[27] The former was designed to educate women for the better-paid branches of the needle trades such as mantua making, and actually did give such training to fifteen or twenty women

[25] *Annual Reports* (1836), p. 18; (1837), p. 9.

[26] Mathew Carey, *Essays on the Public Charities of Philadelphia* (5th ed., 1830); *Letters on the Condition of the Poor of Philadelphia* (1835); *Reflections on the System of the Union Benevolent Association* (1837).

[27] *Address to the Public* (1838); *Annual Report* (1838).

at a time for a few terms of six or eight weeks. Despite all the criticism with regard to the scarcity of good cooks, Carey could get no backing even to start his second school. His importance is as a propagandist rather than as a founder of institutions.

It was the wage policy of the charitable societies that aroused Carey's bitterest opposition, and especially of those societies that planned, not to provide for a small permanent group during the winter, but to give work to as many women as possible. For these latter societies the two questions of importance were whether they should pay market or higher than market rates and how much work they should give to each individual. The commercial rates for shirt making varied from eight to twelve and a half cents. The average seamstress could make from seven to nine shirts a week by working from sunrise to long after sunset. Minimum rent for a single room was fifty cents a week. Even the most proficient few who earned $1.25 or $1.50 a week could not make enough to live on, let alone support a child or two. Mrs. Hale figured that three dollars a week was necessary for a decent standard.[28]

The Society for Employing the Female Poor proposed to pay less than the commercial concerns in order not to tempt women from private employment. They thought of their work as preparing their beneficiaries for permanent jobs and apparently never questioned how they would live in the meantime. Some societies, like the Female Hospitable Society and the Humane Impartial Society, paid at least a half more than the sweatshops, but in good times they turned away three out of four of those who applied for work, and in depressions nine out of ten. The Provident Society for the Employment of the Poor paid twelve and a half cents and gave to most of its applicants two shirts a week and to the neediest few four. With eleven hundred women storming the door in a single day, it was difficult to resist the desire to give a little work to as many as possible.[29]

Mrs. Hale's method of wage fixing is interesting because of its

[28] Boston Seamen's Aid Society, *Annual Reports* (1834), p. 9; (1836), p. 8; Carey, *Essays on the Public Charities of Philadelphia*, p. 15, and *Female Wages and Female Oppression* (1835).

[29] Female Hospitable Society, *Annual Report* (1826); Carey, *Letters on the Condition of the Poor*, p. 10.

anticipation of later procedures. She arrived at a just price by determining first just how much a woman actually needed to be self-supporting and live decently. That figure was then divided by the number of shirts that an "industrious female" could be expected to make in a week. The rate so fixed was double that paid by many of the sweatshops. The society employed just as many women as it could keep busy at this high rate. But the influence of its practice did not stop with its own workers. One result was that private employers in the neighborhood were forced to raise their wages by a half or a third.[30]

Carey and Mrs. Hale were agreed that the charitable societies should use work relief to raise the wage scale for the most depressed groups. They, too, reached the conclusion that the government should also interfere with the market determination of wage rates by stipulating that contractors on government jobs should pay a wage sufficient to support a fair standard of living. Mrs. Hale proposed that such work should be kept for the families of soldiers and sailors and administered by the benevolent societies. Carey argued that the federal government employed about four hundred women for eight months in the year in Philadelphia and so was an important element in the labor market. Two petitions were actually sent from Philadelphia to the secretary of war, who referred them to the commissary-general of purchases because of the "extremely delicate relation to manufacturing interests and general prices for this kind of labor," from whom nothing further was heard.[31]

The early history of charitable organization is instructive not because its problems were solved but because they were defined and the lines along which they were to be attacked during the century that followed were so clearly marked out.

WELLESLEY COLLEGE

[30] Boston Seamen's Aid Society, *Annual Report* (1836), pp. 8–9, 13, 15.

[31] *Ibid.* (1837), p. 11; Carey, *Essay on the Public Charities of Philadelphia*, pp. 15–16, 41.

THE EARLY DAYS OF THE MAGDALEN SOCIETY
OF PHILADELPHIA[1]

NEGLEY K. TEETERS

ITS FOUNDING

ON MARCH 4, 1800, twenty-two citizens of Philadelphia met in the Friends Meeting House at the Corner of Fourth and Pine Streets to organize a society to give aid and succor to "that class of Unhappy Females who have Strayed from Virtue." Here is their preamble:

A number of Persons having in occasional conversation at different Times expressed their Sympathy and commiseration with that class of Females who have been unhappily seduced from the path of Innocence and Virtue and who at times feel desirous of a return thereto, met together when instances were adduced of some Females who, groaning under a humbling Sense of their deplorable Situation and anxiously longing for a deliverance therefrom but the numerous and complicated discouragements which surround them and no gleam of hope appearing, they sink further and further into Guilt and Wretchedness.

When we take a view of one of these unhappy Victims of seduction robbed in a fatal moment of her innocence and virtue, her character and reputation apparently forever lost, shun'd by her former acquaintances and discarded by her relatives and friends, lamenting her past conduct in the most bitter reproaches on her weakness, her present situation with the most poignant Sorrow and distress, looking forward with horror and amazement, she seeks below hope and sees nothing but shame and Infamy to await her, to extend a fostering hand

to those to cherish every budding of repentance, to have an Asylum provided for such to look towards where, sequestered from their miserable Associates they might by repentance and amendment of Life make an atonement to an offended Creator and become useful members of Society, are Objects we think not only desirable but highly worthy the pursuit of a christian Mind, the subject appearing of too much weight and Importance for so small a number to enter much upon, it was agreed to invite such other persons as also feel the weight of it to meet with us in order to give the subject further solid attention and endeavor to devise some plan for the relief of such Females as are in the way of ruin and wish to be rescued therefrom.

The group elected officers: Bishop William White, rector of Christ Church, president; Robert Wharton, mayor of Philadelphia, vice-president.

The first objects of the Society were to implement the purpose of its founding and to devise ways and means of raising funds. The officers assessed the members one dollar per annum; by the end of the first year the Society boasted over one hundred members. Raising money was a major problem with this infant society. They learned that "the old troop of horses posses[ses] a fund of $6,000 which could be used if a foundling hospital could be engrafted on it" but, as this was not envisaged by the organization, it could not press for such a magnificent sum.

Mayor Wharton presented a brilliant idea. He offered to contribute money received from "conviction of hucksters" and other "bench fees" received in his court. Some $300 was added to the treasury in this manner. How this could

[1] The parent organization of the present White-Williams Foundation of Philadelphia. The old society was reorganized in 1913 with a change of policy by which it pioneered in the field of school counseling. Today the agency supplies grants-in-aid to needy school children in the public schools. It took its name from Bishop William White, first president, and George Williams, one of the managers of the earlier society. Sources are the volumes of the Society's minutes and the reports of the managers.

Social Service Review 30 (June 1956): 158–67

be done is obscure. The mayor later donated "marriage fees." Boxes for the solicitation of funds were placed in the various magistrates' offices and periodically these were collected and their meager contents added to the funds of the Society.

A financial windfall accrued to the Society in January, 1801. A residue of a fund collected earlier in Philadelphia for aiding the distress of victims of some calamity in Baltimore, Providence, and Norfolk (possibly a hurricane or a plague) was to be allocated to worthy charities of the city. When this fund, which amounted to $2,050.46, was distributed, the Magdalen Society received $1,050.46.

Casting about for ideas for implementation of their humanitarian objectives, the leaders developed correspondence with the Magdalen Society of London. George Harris of that organization sent the Philadelphia group some pamphlets, which included by-laws, plans for a building, routine of the asylum under its operation, and "Psalms and Hymns" used by the London Society.

Actually, the main objective of the Philadelphia Society, that of rendering compassion and relief to the "unhappy females who have lost their virtue," was realized very slowly. A few cases that came to the attention of the group turned out, upon investigation, to be either unworthy or unsuitable for care. In the minutes of February 9, 1802, appear these plaintive words:

Little opportunity has presented of promoting the great object of the association, that of "restoring to the paths of virtue those unhappy females who in unguarded hours have been Robbed of their innocence." They, however, are not less sanguine of the utility of the Institution and of the advantages which may eventually arise from it.

That opportunities must and will occur in this large city to exercise benevolence and employ considerable funds in this way there can be no room to doubt and it is with pleasure the committee anticipate the further usefulness of the Society from its growing strength both in new members and additional funds.

An even more poignant note of despair and frustrated zeal appears in the annual report dated February 1, 1804, when, after four years, no candidate had been moved to take advantage of the Society's compassion. It reads:

The committee has to lament that not an object contemplated to be relieved by the Society has been presented—still your committee are not discouraged but entertain hopes that the period is not far distant when the spirit of all Grace shall influence the hearts of some of these unhappy females who, in an unguarded moment, have been induced by the temptations of Satan through the seductive artifices of wicked and abandoned men, to sacrifice their chastity and reputation at the shrine of sensual gratification in such a powerful manner, as to convince them of the necessity of reformation in heart and life and thus cause them to become Magdalens indeed—under such impressions and with these views (and these only) your committee look forward to the future prosperity of the Institution.

THE FIRST MAGDALENS

The first application from a "distressed female" was received December 22, 1804, when the president, Bishop White, informed the Standing Committee that an unfortunate woman desired "to become the recipient of the moral as well as the pecuniary privilege" of the Society. The committee reported on this case, known from that time forward as Magdalen No. 1, as follows:

January 14, 1805. The committee attended on the case to provide a temporary asylum for the candidate. . . . They have placed the person who on further conversation and examination [they] find a worthy object, in a religious family at boarding with a full use of a private room for herself . . . in order to [give] her full relief from her former distress they were under the Necessity of paying the amount of the debt incurred by boarding herself and child . . . and that a further sum was necessary to procure a half cord of wood, hawling, sawing and piling and a Carriage hire and for carting furniture, $41.60.

This young lady was referred to in the minutes of the Society as "Mrs. M[agdalen] O[ne]" but in the roster her name appeared as the initials "E—— O——." The men who dealt with Magdalen No. 1 were enthusiastic about her progress up the ladder of rectitude. They reported that they had paid her a visit and found her "endeavoring to procure a decent maintenance by keeping a school for the Tuition of children, and by needlework." She lived in a "respectable neighborhood and her prospects are flattering." In order to encourage her they presented her with five dollars "for the purpose of procuring benches for her scholars and to defray current expenses in living."

Nothing in subsequent records indicates a policy against giving aid to mothers but it does appear that Magdalen No. 1 was the only one possessing a child. The committee attempted to reconcile their client with her relatives but she demurred. It is interesting to note that these pioneers in "social work" worked through her rather than through her relatives. Apparently they had enough insight to ask her consent first.

The record shows that she was visited "frequently" and was found "in a religious family with whom she regularly attended divine worship and has conducted herself in an Exemplary manner cheerfully engaging in such employment as your committee has dictated."

The application of Magdalen No. 2, "L—— R——," was received by the Society on September 5, 1805:

The circumstances of a person apparently under a deep conviction of the impropriety of her former vicious course of life had been visited by the chairman . . . came under consideration. The committee inquired minutely into her character and determined the mode of procedure relative to her. [They spent $10] and found her a suitable place in a sober and religious family.

The committee was happy to report later that Magdalen No. 2 had married a respectable and religious man and that "she and her husband are both members in full Unity with a religious society."

But worthy candidates were reluctant to come forward and take advantage of the Society's largess. One Jacob Lindley of New Garden did write to the Society in "behalf of an unfortunate female" but on due consideration the committee did not feel her "a proper object of further attention of the Society."

During the year the Standing Committee, in an effort at recruitment, visited the almshouse and the local Walnut Street Jail where they hoped to locate some worthy clients. But "on conversation and strict investigation" those they saw were unfit for help. However, they distributed some Bibles and tracts for the use of the females in these establishments.

But in 1806 they finally rescued a client from the almshouse and "placed her a few miles out of town in a respectable family." It was later reported that she appeared penitent and "desirous of living agreeable to the precepts of the Gospel." She was labeled Magdalen No. 3; her initials were "J—— O——."

THE ESTABLISHMENT OF AN ASYLUM

It was considered from the beginning that a home or an asylum was of major importance if the work to which the Society was dedicated was to flourish. The Standing Committee, from time to

time, ruefully complained that many females could be aided and possibly saved
if only a suitable retreat were provided
where they could find peace and protection from the temptations of the world.

In 1807, a lot, comprising nearly an
acre, with a suitable brick building on it,
was purchased for $4,000. It lay at the
corner of what was then Schuylkill Second and Race Streets. The land was described as "under very high cultivation
and adorned with appropriate shade trees
as well as several fruit trees of different
kinds and in a known healthy situation."

After the tenants moved out, the Society advertised for a "suitable married
man to take charge as Steward and his
wife to act as Matron." David Love and
wife were employed, "both of whom are
believed to be orderly and religious persons." The Loves paid a rental for the
use of the house and were paid for boarding the Magdalens "at a reasonable
rate."

In the organization's annual report,
dated February 9, 1808, the following
quaint message was conveyed to the
members by the Standing Committee:

A temporary asylum has been provided and
fitted up for the reception and employment of
that unhappy class of the community for whose
benefit and reformation the Society was instituted; but it is lamentable to observe the in-
sensibility that generally prevails among these
deluded females, and their backwardness to
accept the charitable assistance gratuitously
offered to them, considerable pain having been
taken and labour bestowed on a number in
order to convince them of the benevolent views
of the Society which in some instances has had
the desired effect. . . . Four females . . . have
been admitted into the asylum, three of whom
now remain there, and appear to afford a comfortable prospect of their being hereafter restored with reputation to Society; the other
poor depraved creature eloped [absconded]
about three weeks after her admission. [The
Magdalens] usually come into the Asylum bare
of Cloathing and in some instances almost

naked, they are necessarily engaged some
short time in making garments for themselves
and afterwards are employed at spinning.

The Society felt more secure after it
had established the asylum. It was no
longer dependent upon private homes to
accept clients who were unprepared to
lead a potentially respectable life.

The first girl to be taken to the new
home was Magdalen No. 4. She was "not
quite twenty-one" and was taken from
the "City Prison." About a year later she
was sent to a place in the country armed
with a letter "for her use when deprived
of our verbal communications." As this
letter established a precedent of giving
discharged inmates certain advice it is
herewith included:

Asylum: April 25, 1808

S—— P——

You are now about to return to the World;
reflect on what is past—Consider how hardly
you have escaped from destruction, that the
hand that hath now relieved you can never be
extended to you again[2] and that misery is the
unavoidable consequence of sin. Think how
sharp the stings of a wounded conscience are;
Think! O think! that though death alone can
put an end to wretchedness here, it opens the
door to a scene still more dreadful for the finally
unrepentant.—But we trust what you have
experienced in life has or will lead you to true
repentance and faith in a dear Redeemer, so as
to reconcile you to God and be assured that if
you exert your utmost abilities to please him,
he will protect and assist you.

Reflect on the great advantage and comfort
of having him for your Friend who is able and
ever willing to give effectual aid to those who
strive to do his will, who will support them here,
and regard them with endless happiness hereafter—Fail not morning and evening to address
yourself to your Heavenly Father with a
humble and grateful heart, thanking him for the
blessings he has bestowed on you and that he
hath not cut you off in the midst of your sins,
and fervently implore the holy spirit to direct

[2] A girl was not given a second chance. If she
failed to make good her rehabilitation she could
not apply again.

and help you in those ways which are acceptable in his sight.

As often as you have leisure read the Scriptures, especially the New Testament. Attend divine service and omit no opportunity to improve your mind in spiritual things: Sincere sorrow for having offended the Almighty and an earnest desire for amendment are acceptable in his sight. Be chaste in your conversation and cherish not even for a moment, an improper thought. Be civil to all, but indulge not Talkitiveness; and be careful not to communicate your later situation to anyone; be diligent and industrious and as careful of the property you are entrusted with, as if it were your own.

If you wish to change your place, do not give offence that you may be discharged for good behavior is the surest way to obtain friends and reputation.—Be neat and cleanly in your dress and person; but attempt not finery or fashion. That you may follow this advice is most sincerely desired by

MEMBERS OF VISITING COMMITTEE

The early managers recognized the importance of keeping records on their clients. In March, 1807, they appointed a recorder whose duty was "to keep a private record of the real name, connections and condition of the several Magdalens who may be admitted . . . accompanied with such information relating to their conduct and behavior as may be considered to be useful and necessary; also to record such letters of the Magdalens and such as may be written to them as well as other correspondence relating to the Society as may be judged proper and useful." Here we see early censorship of letters. If such data were collected they are no longer extant. All that we have concerning these early clients are their names and a few data inscribed in the managers' records as the girls were admitted to the asylum.

ROUTINE AND PROGRAM IN THE ASYLUM
IN ITS EARLY DAYS

The routine of the home was strict and arduous, even for those early days.

Every hour of the day, from early dawn until nine in the evening, was apportioned for work, study, eating, and spiritual nourishment. Typical of the admonitions of the managers, dated March 7, 1808, shortly after the home was opened, is:

Your committee have thought it proper to recommend to the Magdalens the necessity of rising at sunrise every morning, the propriety of neatness of apparel and of cleanliness of their apartments, as well as apportioning a portion of each day to reading the Scriptures with other religious books and Tracts, also attention to religious meditation and devotion.

The inmates were clothed in "a long gown for first days [Sundays] and short gowns for the remainder of the week, of grave coloured muslin, Nankeen Petticoats, white or coloured Cotton stockings, white muslin neck handkerchiefs, muslin cap of neat modest pattern and neat leather shoes—and for the winter season the addition of linsey short gown and petticoat and woolen stockings, the stockings to be the manufacture of the Asylum as far as can be accomplished with propriety."

On November 7, 1809, the managers drew up rules governing the staff as well as the inmates. Those applying to the Magdalens include the following:

They are not to leave the Asylum on any account without permission from the Visiting Committee.

They are not to communicate with the other Magdalens any of the circumstances connected with their lives prior to their admission.

They are to avoid all kinds of levity in their conversation and conduct.

They are not to use any kind of profane or obscene language.

They are not to altercate or dispute with, nor speak evil of any person.

They are not to hinder each other in their labour.

They are not to labour on the Sabbath or first day except in works of necessity or mercy.

They are to rise in the morning with the sun, and retire to bed at nine o'clock except in cases requiring it otherwise.

They are, immediately after rising and putting on their apparel, to wash themselves, and as soon after as convenient to assemble together, when the Steward, matron, or one of the Magdalens is to read in the hearing of the rest, a portion of the Scriptures, they continuing together, and behaving with solemnity until dismissed.

The reading of the Scriptures and so forth to be observed before retiring to bed.

They are to repair to their place, and at the time appointed when and where their food is prepared for them, waiting a proper season before and after they have eaten according to the regulations that may be adopted by the Steward.

They are to occupy their time on the Sabbath or first day in the reading of the Scriptures and other religious books in meditation and pious devotion.

Many of the rules formulated at this time dealt with safeguarding the privacy of the home. No outsider, even though a visiting friend of the steward or matron, was permitted to talk to the inmates, unless such person was there on business. And even in such a case, two other persons must be present. No one manager was permitted to talk with an inmate without a colleague or the matron being present. Even the physician, who at this time served gratuitously, was never left alone with any girl who might need his professional services.

In 1809, the Society erected a three-story brick building in order to afford more room for work. The building consisted of one large room on the first floor "calculated for manufacturing," eleven "lodging rooms" on the second, and, on the third, one "large well-ventilated room." Each room for sleeping purposes had a single window and was supplied with a single bed, a small closet, and a table. The following year a board fence, eight feet high, was built around the entire lot (years later to be replaced by a brick wall) "to prevent the escape of discontented Magdalens and elude prying eyes." Long spikes were imbedded in the tops of the boards. As Anna Pratt many years later (1913) commented: "The fence seemed to prevent advancing civilization from penetrating the minds of the trustees." It was Anna Pratt who changed the function of the Society from that of caring for Magdalens to pioneering in the field of school counseling.

But despite the fence, an occasional Magdalen "eloped." Aside from moral suasion, there were no restraints used at the home. A girl could leave if she wished but, if she did, she could not return.

In 1813, the managers of the asylum made a report on the total number of Magdalens rendered assistance as well as a haven, as follows:

Whole number of Magdalens admitted.... 54
    Of whom placed at service in respectable and religious families......... 27
    Reconciled to their friends.......... 5
    Discharged at their own request..... 2
    Dismissed for improper conduct.... 3
    Removed to Alms House and not returned...................... 5
    Eloped, absconded................. 8
    Remaining in the Asylum.......... 4
                             —
                             54

From the best information to be obtained the Managers submit the following:
Of those placed at service there are deceased 4
Living at reputable service and doing well...................... 17
Married and living in good reputation 3
Unknown...................... 3
                             —
                             27

Those reconciled to friends and doing well........................... 5
Those discharged at their own request —unknown.................... 2
Of those discharged for improper con-
duct

Dead.........................	1
Unknown....................	2
Of those removed to Alms House	
Unknown	4
Removed there for medical treatment......................	1
Of those eloped	
Deceased....................	1
Unknown but feared may have resorted to their former evil course.....................	7
Those who remain in the Asylum and in a promising state..............	4
	—
	27
Total........................	54

The policy of the Society in placing out the girls who seemed to be prepared was to solicit the aid of "respectable" families or, in some instances, relatives. If a girl stayed twelve months and "conducts herself . . . as to obtain from her employer a Certificate of good conduct [she] shall be entitled to a Premium of Eight Dollars to be paid by the Visiting Committee."

On May 1, 1810, the first immigrant Magdalen was admitted to the asylum. She was Magdalen No. 26, thirty years old. Born in Amsterdam, she had arrived in this country in 1793. The record states that she had been married for ten years but had left her husband and had been living in prostitution.

In 1819, the Managers proposed that those Magdalens who were affected with syphilis should be treated in the infirmary of the home rather than to be sent, as was the custom up to that time, to the almshouse. The word "syphilis" was not used in the records until this year.

In 1822, the records state, an "impostor" had entered the house. As nothing more is stated, it is not known just what such an impostor was or why she should have wished to enter such an asylum. In 1822 also there is recorded an account of the first inmate to die in the home:

The Magdalen whose death is stated . . . we are happy in believing left the world in the faith of "him who Justifieth the ungodly"; her affliction was tedious and painful but was borne with patience and resignation and she looked with joyful anticipation to the hour of her Dissolution in a firm assurance that "to be absent from the Body was to be presented to the Lord"; all who saw her had reason to believe her end was peace. This one poor Soul, this Brand plucked from the burning is worth more than all the Labours of the Society. This Soul converted from the error of her ways and saved from death having a multitude of Sins Covered is a sight which angels beheld with delight and which but for your Asylum might never have happened.

The Society was a little tardy in asking for help from the women of the community. But in 1820 the Managers gave permission to a group to visit the Magdalens. No mention is made of their affiliation but they may have been members of the Society of Women Friends who, at the time, were active in visiting female prisoners in the city's jails.

More than ten years later (1833) a Board of Matrons, formed in the city, specifically volunteered to assist the managers in their work. The officers of this board agreed to become actively engaged under the conditions listed:

Although our number is small we consider our Board sufficiently organized to enter on duty under the following governing principles: First, let it become our constant care to cultivate harmony of spirit and unison of action in all our proceedings; Second, the prevailing object of the Board is to promote the design of the Magdalen Society in order that their noble charity shall become more extensively beneficial; Third, we propose to seek for, enquire after and hold ourselves in readiness to receive application from individuals who will be considered by the Managers of the Asylum as subjects claiming their attention; Fourth, when our applicants are thus introduced to notice, the Board of Matrons must not be expected to assume further control over their charge nor be considered responsible for their future conduct;

but to commit them to the general rules and salutary regulations of the family. To—the advice and counsel imparted by religious characters who may occasionally visit the House by permission. To—the protection of the Society—and lastly—to the preservation of a Higher Power.

In 1821 it was decided by the managers to dispense with Mr. and Mrs. Love. A Mrs. Hannah Smith, a widow and mistress of a fancy dry goods and trimming shop, was employed. She was a member of the Pine Street Presbyterian Church and "of a good reputation of piety." She proved to be an excellent selection and possessed good administrative ability. In a short historical sketch of these early days, signed only by the initials "L.M.B.," dated September 1, 1878, we find the reason why the Loves left their post. They were tobacco addicts.

Down to this period [1821] smoking of tobacco had been freely allowed the inmates, and the Steward and Matron being greatly addicted to the use of the Pipe, the Asylum building came near being destroyed by fire by their careless use of the same. This led to the following action by the Board as appears from the Minutes of February 13, 1821 which disposed of the smoking privilege and the Stewardship at the same time. . . . "Inasmuch as the family of the Steward and Matron, Mr. and Mrs. Love has become large the managers are induced to make a change in the domestic arrangements, and to employ a Matron who having no particular family of her own it is expected will be almost constantly with the Magdalens. . . ."[3]

Periodically some of the more restive Magdalens took "Scotch leave" from the home. It was always painful to report such incidents. On one occasion the girls merely found the keys to the house and

[3] The writer of this article could find nothing in the minutes of the Society that mentions tobacco or the threat of a fire in the asylum. It is not known where "L. M. B." got his information. It is possible that "L. M. B." was Mr. L. Montgomery Bond, a member of the board in 1878.

to the outer gate and walked off. The record states: "Their departure, it is feared, was promoted, in part, by desire to indulge in strong drink whereof they could not partake while part of the family." The managers were also alert to discontent among the inmates: "Some discontent and querulous disposition has been exhibited by the Magdalens but it is hoped some pretty sharp remonstrance by the committee have put an end to such unthoughtful conduct."

An atmosphere of apprehension and discontent apparently developed in the home from time to time. In 1830 (October 22) insubordination on a large scale took place. In the record for November 2 we find:

More than common attention has been paid to the Magdalens in consequence of a want of peace among themselves and much insubordination to the matron and her assistant; every effort to produce a better state in the family proved ineffectual it became necessary to discharge those that remained. . . . The committee and the matron are led to the conclusion that in future all the rules must be more rigidly enforced.

The record further states: "This paper exhibits a picture of the asylum which is without a complete parallel in the proceedings of the house, but the managers are not without hope that the course pursued will ultimately prove beneficial." But the following year there was more trouble:

Some allegations having been made that the Magdalens were not allowed sufficient space of time after being called up in the morning to permit them exercise of mental private devotion, that they were unduly restricted from walking in the garden and partaking of the fruit growing therein, and that the diet was not of a satisfactory quality.

Upon investigation the committee wrote:

Testimony furnished by one of the Magdalens the longest in the family informed your committee that from 20 to 30 minutes were allowed them after being called previous to their being expected to join the family in the duties of the day, and that they always walked in the Garden when it was suitable and partook freely of the fruit. . . . The committee also learned that the diet was of excellent quality, both in bread and in meats and that the tea and coffee were the same as would be set on the matron's table.

In 1846, the Society erected a fine four-storied brick building on its property. This building still stands in Philadelphia. It was sold in 1923 to the Philadelphia Municipal Court and is now the property of the Franklin Institute.

By 1850, after fifty years of operation, it was recorded that 925 girls had been cared for by the Magdalen Society. The record states "Restored (as we have reason to believe) to the paths of virtue, 294."

The Society carried on for yet another half century and more, hewing close to its original objective, that of saving prostitutes from the tragedy of their profession. In the annual reports, bound in pamphlet form in later years, we see a picture of the asylum under which are the following words:

To the City the seducer lures his victim. *To the City* women come to hide their shame. *The City* is the great receiver of the fallen who cannot endure to remain in the smaller towns, known to everybody. Therefore *the whole Country is responsible for the lost in the City;* and every effort to reclaim them should be supported by all Christians. Daily, numbers die; daily, numbers supply their places; and must those who might be rescued, be left unsaved for the want of means to effect it?

The managers of the Society were so close to the temptations of the city that they believed it to be solely responsible for the degradation of women. The reports are full of indictments of city life. For example we find this in 1840:

The heart sickens at the amount of guilt of this description in this city, at its increase in amount and in publicity; at the boldness of vice and at the indifference of a vicious community in regard to the prevalence of licentiousness. Our city has become more and more degraded by the prevalence of this sin. . . . Our public squares, so beautiful and which seem to be made to be trod only by the pure—are places where they are assembled in large numbers at night; and our theatres admit them—as the theatre does everyone—unblushingly within its walls. It would be doubtful whether a theatre could be sustained if this were not one part of its arrangements, so closely connected are theatrical exhibitions and licentiousness. Mere lamentation is unavailing. The managers pursue their way with unabated and increased zeal; and they would call on a virtuous and christian community to aid them in rescuing the hundreds of the guilty and abandoned in this city from vice and destruction. Let it not be forgotten that each one of the victims of vice in this city has a soul which cannot die; a soul that may be redeemed and purified by the blood of the atonement, a soul that may yet by the Grace of God become a jewel in the Saviour's Crown.

In 1848, the Society believed it necessary to employ a person to visit the brothels and areas of prostitution to persuade girls to take advantage of the charitable services of the asylum. They realized the delicacy of the situation as may be seen from the following:

To seek out a Laborer who may be deemed suitably qualified to perform this delicate and important duty, one whose years and experience of the human heart and pious devotion of Soul will give assurance under the Divine blessing of success, but whose prudent and circumspect walk will thus be an availing shield against the temptations of our common nature or the designs of unprincipled women—Should such an one be found it cannot but add to the expense of the Society.

After considerable exploration they found one Oliver Brooks whose work was "to visit the abodes of the daughters of guilt with the view of inducing them to avail themselves of the benefits of our

Asylum." Brooks was paid $100 for a three-month period. Fifty Magdalens were admitted to the asylum the following year. Whether this increase was due to the efforts of Oliver Brooks is not known. We do know, however, that he died within a few months of his employment and another worker was secured for this delicate task.

The records continue in a vein of mingled discouragement and optimism, year after year. The first half-century of the Society found it more determined than ever that the community had a responsibility to assist the weak and down-trodden female who had stumbled into the sordid realm of prostitution. It was discouraging to the managers because they saw how few actually wanted to be rescued from their blighted lives. But it was cause for rejoicing when even one woman was "snatched from the burning." Because of this occasional one the Society felt justified in continuing. And this they did for another sixty years before new concepts and new challenges changed the focus of the Society.

TEMPLE UNIVERSITY

Received February 13, 1956

The Federal Government and Social Welfare in Early Nineteenth-Century America

Walter I. Trattner
University of Wisconsin—Milwaukee

Historians and others now generally agree that, in economic matters, the "welfare state" began prior to the 1930s, some one hundred years earlier. However, it is commonly assumed that it was not until the Great Depression that active federal involvement in social welfare matters was initiated. This article, which deals with federal assistance to two charitable institutions—in 1819, to the Connecticut Asylum for the Deaf and Dumb, a private institution, and in 1826 to the Kentucky Deaf and Dumb Asylum, a public institution—suggests that the origin of the "welfare state" in this area, too, antedates the New Deal by more than a century.

For some time now, notably since publication in 1955 of Robert Lively's brilliant review essay on "the American System,"[1] historians, and others, have conceded that, in economic matters, the so-called welfare state had its start not in the 1930s but some 100 years earlier. Clearly, despite the rhetoric, which glorified limited government, the free enterprise system, and economic individualism, the history of tariff legislation, disposal of the public domain, land reclamation, creation of a banking system, canal, road and railroad construction, and other developments indicate that the role of the federal government in stimulating and aiding economic activity originated long before the New Deal.[2]

For the most part, however, it still is widely believed that in matters of social welfare, that is, in helping those in need, it was only during the Great Depression of the 1930s that the federal government began to assume an active role. Thus, for example, as one authority on the subject recently wrote, the "federal government impinged little on the every-day life of ante-bellum Americans." Indeed, the federal gov-

Social Service Review 50 (June 1976): 243–55

ernment "was remarkable for its lack of activity in relation to the 'general welfare' of its citizens," especially in matters of health and welfare, both of which have been largely twentieth century concerns: "Those who sought for reasons either pragmatic or ideological to expand national prerogatives were little moved by the needs of the blind, the sick, the impoverished. To have argued, indeed, that an essential function of a 'consolidated' government was the care of such dependent groups would have been perceived as an improbable *reductio ad absurdum* of nationalistic arguments."[3]

Or as Raymond Mohl, another student of the subject, put it: "Between the American Revolution and the Civil War, several broad patterns in public welfare emerged. In the first place, the essential ingredients of the old British poor laws," which placed responsibility for public assistance upon local government, were "written into new state legislation after the Revolution, [and] remained intact well into the nineteenth century." Thus, throughout the period, "public welfare remained a primary function of local government. Nineteenth century laissez-faire principles of government predetermined federal inaction in response to social problems such as poverty and dependency. State governments occasionally provided small annuities to private charitable agencies and institutions or made special appropriations during disasters, depressions or epidemics. But essentially the business of providing day-to-day social welfare services was a local affair handled at the municipal, town or county level."[4]

There was, of course, one notable exception, an "uncharacteristic incident," to this pattern—enactment by Congress of the famous Dorothea Dix bill, or "Act making a grant of public lands to the several states for the benefit of indigent insane persons." But only Miss Dix's "charisma and social connections," noted Charles Rosenberg, "made possible the passage of this atypical measure," a measure which was quickly vetoed by President Franklin Pierce.[5]

While, in the main, it is true that throughout the nineteenth century public welfare remained primarily a function of local government, it is also true that the federal government was not entirely dormant in matters of social welfare at this time. Indeed, the so-called Dix bill, passed in 1854, was not an isolated, novel, or "untypical" act. Rather, it was a logical measure in light of previous federal action. The federal government not only had made funds and other forms of assistance available to victims of fires, floods, cyclones, earthquakes, and other natural disasters,[6] but much more important, on at least two occasions it also had provided aid to "charitable institutions" for the deaf and dumb. A study of these two heretofore neglected incidents of federal assistance—in 1819, to the Connecticut Asylum for the Deaf and Dumb, a private institution, and in 1826 to the Kentucky

Deaf and Dumb Asylum, a public institution—suggests that the origins of the "welfare state" in this area, too, antedates the New Deal by more than a century.

For a long time, there were no serious attempts to educate the deaf and dumb. Looked upon with aversion and deemed of limited or deficient mentality, their condition, for the most part, was degraded and deplorable.[7] It was only in the second half of the eighteenth century, in Europe, that they began to receive instruction, thanks largely to the efforts of Charles Michel Abbé de l'Epée, who not only originated sign language and wrote several treatises on the subject, but also opened the first regular school for the deaf and dumb.[8] Opened in 1755 near Paris, it soon proved a success, and by the early nineteenth century similar schools were being conducted throughout western Europe.

The earliest effort to establish a training ground for the deaf and dumb in America came at around this time. In 1803, a Francis Green of Boston, who had to send his deaf son abroad (to Scotland) to be educated, called for the establishment of such a school in America. For the most part, however, little was done until 1810 when, in New York City, the Reverend John Stanford attempted to educate several deaf children he found in the city almshouse—an effort which resulted, several years later, in the founding of the New York Institution for the Instruction of the Deaf and Dumb.

In the meantime, however, America's first permanent institution for the education of the deaf and dumb was established at Hartford, Connecticut, under the leadership of Thomas Hopkins Gallaudet. A young theology student, Gallaudet had become interested in the deaf and their education after meeting Alice Cogswell, the afflicted daughter of a neighbor, whose friends had decided to establish some sort of institution for her education and the education of other deaf and dumb children throughout New England. Thus, in 1815, as a first step in carrying out their plan, they sent Gallaudet to Europe to survey schools for the deaf and dumb. There, he spent a good deal of time in France inspecting the institution founded earlier by the Abbé de l'Epée. When he returned a year later, he brought back not only much acquired knowledge but a teacher of the deaf and dumb as well, one Laurent Clerc of Paris.

Next, Gallaudet and others set out to solicit contributions for the project. After six months, about $12,000 had been raised from individuals, societies, churches, and the like, and more would follow. In May 1816, the state of Connecticut granted Gallaudet and his associates a charter and a $5,000 appropriation—perhaps the first grant of public money in America to a private school.[9] In any event, the institution opened its doors on April 15, 1817, under the name of the

Connecticut Asylum for the Education and Instruction of Deaf and Dumb Persons.[10] Thus began the history of American schools for the deaf and dumb.

Although founded as a private "charitable institution" for the "relief" of the deaf and dumb, the asylum's main aim was to educate its students—to instruct children denied hearing and speech so that they could be restored to society as useful, self-supporting citizens. A residential institution in which the students lived during the school year, indigents were accepted free while those who could afford to pay were charged tuition. Despite the tuition, or "membership fees," as they were called, other private donations, and the legislative grant, the institution quickly ran into financial straits as the student body increased rapidly. Opening its doors with only seven students, by the end of the first year the number had climbed to thirty-three, and before long reached fifty as applicants from throughout New England, and elsewhere, sought admission. It was at this point that the institution's Board of Directors decided to turn to the federal government for aid.

At a meeting held at the asylum on January 25, 1819, the Board voted to "present a Petition to the Congress of the United States . . . praying for a grant of money or land for the benefit . . . [of the] Institution" which, in part, read:

The Asylum [which now had more than fifty pupils] has hitherto depended for its support chiefly on the contributions of charitable Individuals, but it cannot be expected that supplies can be drawn from this source in [the] future, equal to the wants of the Institution. In consequence of the great increase of the number of Pupils it has been found difficult to hire suitable buildings for their accommodation, and it has become necessary to erect new ones for that purpose; but the Petitioners are in want of funds to defray the expense of erecting such buildings, as well as other unavoidable expenses of the school. Considering this Institution to be of the most benevolent and useful character, and that its utility is not confined to the State in which the school is located, but is calculated to be general and extensive, not only by affording instruction to great numbers of this unfortunate description of persons, in all parts of the Union, but by furnishing Instructors for other schools of the like kind, which may hereafter be established, your Petitioners are emboldened to ask the Honorable Congress to grant to them for the uses aforesaid either in money, or in unlocated lands of the United States, something out of that abundance with which Providence has blessed our Country. . . .[11]

The petition for federal aid was introduced in the U.S. House of Representatives on February 18, 1819 and immediately referred, for consideration, to a select committee headed by Congressman Nathaniel Terry of Connecticut. Four days later, the committee reported back favorably, stating that the institution, designed to educate and rescue the deaf "as far as practicable from their state of ignorance and degradation, and to fit them for social intercourse and happiness," had more than fifty students from throughout the United States. Its funds, however, which "have arisen almost entirely from voluntary contributions, are too small to admit of its becoming excessively useful." All things considered, especially "that it is the first attempt of the kind in the United States, and that it has been raised to its present condition, by the care, and at the expense of charitable individuals, most of whom had no particular interest in its success, the committee are of the opinion, that it is worthy of the patronage of Congress, and that the prayer of the petition ought to be granted, and for that purpose they report a bill."[12]

The bill, designed to grant the Connecticut institution six sections—or a township—of the public lands, was then introduced, read twice, and ordered to lie on the table. When, on March 1, 1819, Congressman Terry sought to bring up the proposed measure for debate and a vote, Speaker of the House Henry Clay, architect of the "American System" and a proponent of national planning who displayed a particular interest, or concern, in the undertaking, cast the deciding vote in favor of doing so.[13]

Terry began the debate by adverting to the humane object of the institution and the need for additional funds to sustain it. Support for the measure came from William Henry Harrison of Ohio, Timothy Pitkin of Connecticut, Charles Mercer of Virginia, and others, but opposition surfaced and a heated debate ensued. Led by George Poindexter of Mississippi and Burwell Bassett of Virginia, who argued that the institution was a local one and hence "not deserving, more than any other local object, the expenditure of national funds on it." Furthermore, in Bassett's opinion, it would establish a "precedent which might hereafter be regretted when too late."[14] An attempt to commit the bill and postpone it indefinitely failed, however, and the measure was read a third time and passed by a vote of fifty-seven to forty-five.[15] Two days later, on March 3, 1819, the bill—"An Act in Behalf of the Connecticut Asylum for Teaching the Deaf and Dumb" —went through the Senate, either without debate or without any that was recorded, and was signed into law by President James Monroe.[16]

So it was that Congress bestowed upon the private asylum, located in Hartford, Connecticut, some 23,000 acres of public land which, in time, netted the institution almost $300,000, enough to sustain it for many years to come. Thus, at a time when the federal government sought to create a strong economy and bolster national unity through protective tariffs, the building of roads and canals, the establishment of a national bank, and the like, it also recognized the necessity, or desirability, of federal participation in matters of social welfare—or at least the education of the deaf and dumb.

In the meantime, other such institutions were founded. When the

Connecticut Asylum came into being, it was felt that one facility would suffice for the entire country. It soon was found, however, that deaf mutes were more numerous than had been supposed; thus, on May 20, 1818, the nation's second asylum, the New York Institution for the Instruction of the Deaf and Dumb, opened its doors.

Like its predecessor, the New York asylum was a private institution that on occasion received some public support, first by the city of New York and then the State. In addition, it also was largely a residential institution with some students paying their way and others attending free of charge. And, as might be expected in light of the Connecticut experience, it, too, ran into financial difficulty and asked Congress for a "donation of land."[17]

Introduced in the House on December 9, 1819, the request was referred to a select committee, headed this time by Representative Henry Meigs of New York. Nearly three weeks later, the committee reported back favorably and proposed a bill "granting one township of land to said institution," which was read twice and then committed.[18] When, however, on January 7, 1820, the measure came up for debate and a vote, it ran into far more opposition than its predecessor. Indeed, only Congressman Meigs and Ezra Gross, another New Yorker, openly supported the bill in the lengthy discussion that ensued, extolling the institution and its success (mainly as an educational enterprise), rebutting critics of the measure, and calling their colleagues' attention "to the case of the Asylum at Hartford, which received last year from the national munificence a grant precisely similar to the one contained in the present bill."[19]

Opposition to the measure was to be expected; its intensity, and sources, however, must have been surprising. Congressman Samuel Foote, for example, a newly elected Representative from Connecticut and a member of the select committee that studied the memorial, vigorously opposed the bill, particularly the plea that precedent dictated its passage: "Whenever we shall be governed by" precedents, he bellowed, "we shall be in the fair road to despotism." Even on the principle of precedent, however, the New York institution could not be compared to the Connecticut one, said Foote, for the latter was the first of its kind in America, one which paved the way for others and whose benefits embraced the afflicted of many other states; thus, "it had peculiar claims to the aid of the Government."[20]

Perhaps even more surprising, however, was the opposition of Henry Clay of Kentucky, champion of the Connecticut grant who, as he put it, regretted having to oppose the measure, "especially as it was a bill with such a benevolent object." Clay spoke against the measure on several grounds. First, he argued that Congress had to retain control of the sale of public lands, (especially with an "empty exchequer,") because it could better regulate the manner in which they were placed on the market and thus "could count with more certainty upon the produce of the revenue from that source." Then he went on to argue that the Connecticut Asylum could handle the problem and that another deaf and dumb institution in America was unnecessary. Finally, even supposing that another institution was necessary, was it proper, Clay asked, "that it should be fixed at New York, which was not more than one hundred miles from the asylum at Hartford; and least of all would it be proper to locate it in a place so expensive as New York?" If another institution was to be encouraged, let it go into the interior, he declared, where people with "frugal, regular, and industrious habits, and simplicity of character" resided, not, he repeated, "in a large city remarkable for its expensive and luxurious habits,"[21] a comment especially poignant in light of New York's present financial problems. In any event, after a great deal more give and take, the measure was defeated.[22]

Shortly thereafter, however, other institutions for the deaf and dumb were founded. Pennsylvania was next in line when, in 1821, it established one at Philadelphia.[23] While these three institutions—at Hartford, New York, and Philadelphia—were the pioneers, efforts to educate the deaf and dumb quickly spread to other parts of the United States, including the south. Thus the nation's fourth such institution, which opened its doors in April 1823, was established at Danville, Kentucky. More important than its location outside the northeast and away from the Atlantic seaboard, however, was the fact that the Kentucky Institution for the Tuition of the Deaf and Dumb, as it was called, was the nation's first such public institution, from the outset being state owned and operated (although at the beginning it received some private contributions, including a number from outside the state).[24]

When incorporated (on December 7, 1822), the state legislature appropriated $3,000 to establish the institution plus an additional $100 a year per pupil for board and tuition, limited in number to twenty-five, all of whom had to be residents of the state. Early in 1824, however, the legislature increased the per capita allocation for state pupils to $140 a year and authorized the admission of private, or "pay" pupils, from other states, so that students quickly were attracted to the institution from all over the south.[25]

Meanwhile, at the request of the institution's trustees, who sought additional funds both from the state and the federal government, a joint committee of the state legislature (consisting of two members of the Senate and four of the House) had been appointed to visit and examine the institution. After having spent two days on its grounds, it reported back that it was "greatly gratified" with the asylum's operation, and recommended "the continued and extended patronage of the legislature." Committee members also noted, however, that there were far more persons within the state who could use the institution's services, and a great many others from adjoining states who would do so as well. As a result, they urged, and the state legislature passed, the following resolution: "That a respectful memorial from the legislature be transmitted to the Congress of the United States, on behalf of the Kentucky Institution for the Tuition of the Deaf and Dumb; soliciting their attention to the petition of the Trustees of said institution, for the aid of the National Legislature."[26]

That memorial, actually drawn up by the institution's trustees and dated March 15, 1824, indicated that the "petitioners were gratified to find, that a former Congress gave, with a liberal hand, aid to the Hartford Institution, located in a convenient place to supply the Northeastern section of the Union; and we hope," it went on to state, "that the national bounty will be extended to our Institution, similarly located in the West."[27]

The petition was presented to Congress on April 5, 1824, by Representative Thomas P. Moore of Kentucky, in whose district the institution was located. As usual, it was referred to a select committee, headed by Congressman Moore.

One month later that committee reported back to the House that it had "entered upon the investigation of the subject referred to, . . . [that it was] deeply impressed with the conviction that the great object of human legislation is to promote the happiness, as well as the security of the species," and that the "legitimate sphere" of federal legislation, therefore, extends to "those domestic institutions, which are formed to alleviate the ills which originate in the infirmity of our nature. . . ." The Kentucky institution thus had a strong claim to the protecting benevolence of Congress, especially since it was "the only institution of the kind existing in all that vast and fertile range of country which lies west of the Allegheny" mountains. Moreover, since the "principle and policy of extending relief to institutions of this character, have been recognized by the Congress of the United States, in a grant made to the Connecticut Asylum, . . . [the Committee] therefore beg[ged] leave to report a bill."[28]

What happened between that date, May 4, 1824, when the "bill for the benefit of the said institution," was read twice and committed, and April 1826, is quite confusing. Apparently, that session of Congress (the first session of the eighteenth Congress) came to an end before any action on the measure was taken. Then, shortly after the new session began, the bill was re-introduced and referred to another select committee, accompanied this time, however, by a similar measure aimed at benefiting the deaf and dumb institutions at New York,

Philadelphia, and a newly created one at Detroit (in the Michigan Territory). On January 19, 1825, that committee reported back favorably and introduced a new bill to aid all four institutions.[29] Again, however, Congress adjourned without acting on the measure.

Somehow, on March 10, 1826, in the middle of the first session of the new Congress—the nineteenth—a bill "for the benefit of the Asylum for teaching the Deaf and Dumb of Kentucky," was brought up for discussion.[30] How it emerged and how the Danville institution was separated from its northern counterparts in the proposed legislation, remains a mystery. Nevertheless, after a lengthy Committee of the Whole discussion in which most speakers supported the measure, including James Buchanan of Pennsylvania and Churchill Cambreling of New York, who indicated they soon would introduce a similar bill to aid the institutions of their states, it was decided to bring the measure to a vote the next day.[31]

The next day, only Representative William McCoy of Virginia, who the day before had reminded his colleagues that only a short while earlier the House had defeated a similar request from the New York institution, voiced opposition to the measure, because, in his words, "the House has no power to pass such a bill." Grant "such land to Kentucky," he declared, and "you will have to do the same to other states." Despite McCoy's objections, the bill passed—again, however, by an unrecorded vote.[32]

Two weeks later, when the Senate took up the measure, a lengthy debate ensued. The bulk of that debate, however, dealt not with the merits—or demerits—of the bill but with its specific details, particularly its land provisions.[33] But after several unsuccessful attempts to kill the measure, chiefly by adding amendments to it, including one that would have granted similar benefits to a recently created New Jersey institution, the "Act for the benefit of the incorporated Kentucky Asylum for Teaching the Deaf and Dumb" was passed by a vote of twenty-seven to six and was signed into law by President John Quincy Adams.[34]

Thus it was that within seven years, in 1819 and again in 1826, the U.S. Congress granted—and Presidents James Monroe and John Quincy Adams approved those grants—townships of public land to two social welfare institutions, a private one in Connecticut and a public one in Kentucky. The latter institution, however, was not as fortunate as the former. Due to a series of misunderstandings and hassles over selection of that land, located in Florida and Arkansas, and the untimely death of the agent hired by the institution to sell it, only about $60,000 was ultimately realized.[35]

Although no other institution for the deaf and dumb received a congressional grant at this time,[36] turning to Washington for funds was a natural thing to do in 1848 when Dorothea Dix began her crusade for federal aid to the mentally ill. More than 135 million acres of the public domain already had been ceded to the various states, numerous individuals, and a number of institutions of one kind or another; why not grant a small portion of the vast remaining area for the indigent insane who, in Miss Dix's words, "through the Providence of God, are the wards of the nation"? A government which provided schools, homesteads, and highways for its sane and healthy population, canals, loans, tariffs, and other subsidies of one kind or another to its businessmen, land grants to public and private "charitable institutions" for the instruction of the deaf and dumb, surely owed to its destitute and mentally defective citizens at least shelter and humane treatment, as she pointed out in her memorial to Congress.[37]

Congress, of course, eventually agreed, and in 1854 passed the so-called Dix bill, which allotted ten million acres of public land to the states, the proceeds of which were to be used for the care of the indigent insane.[38] The promise of a continued, and perhaps an expanded, social welfare program stimulated by federal funds was shattered, however, by the veto from the pen of President Franklin Pierce. While expressing "the deep sympathies in [his] . . . heart" for "the humane purposes sought to be accomplished by the bill," Pierce felt compelled to veto it, he said, because it was illegal: "If Congress has the power to make provision for the indigent insane . . . it has the same power for the indigent who are not insane," and thus all the nation's needy and, he continued, "I cannot find any authority in the Constitution for making the Federal Government the great almoner of public charity throughout the United States." To do so, in his judgment, "would be contrary to the letter and spirit of the Constitution, and subversive of the whole theory upon which the union of these states is founded." As for previous acts of Congress which furnished precedents for the bill, particularly the land grants to the Connecticut and Kentucky institutions, Congress, in his opinion, simply had erred—it had transcended its power. Those examples, he declared, should "serve . . . as a warning [rather] than as an inducement to tread in the same path."[39]

For the most part, the President's reasoning was followed; the veto was upheld and federal involvement in social welfare was curtailed for years to come[40]—setting back both the concept of an expanding role for government and the American social welfare system.

Exactly why Pierce vetoed the measure,[41] why, in light of its previous actions, Congress did not override the veto, and precisely what its impact was, are all important questions that have not yet been adequately answered. What is clear, however, is that federal involvement in the nation's social welfare system is not a relatively recent development; it goes back much further than has been generally assumed.

Notes

The author wishes to thank the University of Wisconsin—Milwaukee Graduate School for the financial assistance which enabled him to conduct the research for this article.

1. Robert Lively, "The American System: A Review Article," *Business History Review* 29 (March 1955): 81–96.

2. For a good review of these developments, see Frank Annunziata, "The Welfare State in America: A Theme for Interpreting 20th Century History," *Social Studies* 65 (February 1974): 51–58.

3. Charles Rosenberg, introduction to the *New American State Papers: Social Policy,* ed. Thomas C. Cochran, 5 vols. (Wilmington, Del.: Scholarly Resources, Inc., 1972), 1:13 (hereafter cited as *NASP*). Rosenberg, however, does point out that the federal government did take some steps in this direction. In 1790 it authorized the establishment of pensions for disabled veterans of the Revolutionary War. Eight years later Congress instituted a system of marine hospitals. It also undertook investigations of patent medicine frauds and of steps necessary to control epidemics. Most important, however, was federal involvement in the area of education. Under the provisions of the Northwest Ordinance of 1787, each new state in the Union was to be given one section of the public domain, the proceeds from the sale of which were to be used for public education. Then, of course, there was the Morrill Act of 1862, which provided the foundation for most of the present state universities.

4. Raymond Mohl, "Three Centuries of American Public Welfare: 1600–1932," *Current History* 65 (July 1973): 7, 8. For examples of other historians who assert, or strongly imply, that federal activity in the social welfare system was a twentieth century, especially New Deal phenomenon, see Roy Lubove, ed., *Poverty and Social Welfare in the United States* (New York: Holt, Rinehart & Winston, 1972), p. 4, and Roy Lubove, *The Struggle for Social Security* (Cambridge, Mass.: Harvard University Press, 1968), p. 179; David J. Rothman and Sheila M. Rothman, *On Their Own: The Poor in Modern America* (Reading, Mass.: Addison-Wesley Publishing Co., 1972), p. xix; and Ralph Pumphrey and Muriel Pumphrey, *The Heritage of American Social Work* (New York: Columbia University Press, 1964), p. 432.

5. Rosenberg, 1:14–15.

6. The *Annals of Congress,* the *Congressional Debates,* and the *Congressional Globe* are replete with examples of these; however, Senator Solomon Foot of Vermont, in a speech in 1854 in support of the Dix bill, alluded to many such examples. See *Congressional Globe,* 33d Cong., 1st sess., 1854, 28, pt. 1: 455–56 (also see ibid., 1854, 31, N.S., Appendix, pp. 550–52).

7. Harry Best, *Deafness and the Deaf in the United States* (New York: Macmillan Co., 1943), pp. 371–80. Their affliction often was looked upon as the divine origin and they were considered little better than small children intellectually—or indeed, at times, as little better than imbeciles.

8. The Abbé de l'Epée, who devoted his entire life to the cause, was not the first instructor of the deaf; however, his zeal, his writings, and his example of disinterested benevolence awakened a real interest in their fate and led the way to the establishment of institutions for their instruction.

9. Best, p. 391.

10. In May 1819, the institution changed its name to the American Asylum at Hartford for the Education and Instruction of the Deaf and Dumb because, as stated in the act that implemented the name change, "the said institution, although styled the Connecticut Asylum, was originally founded for the relief of the Deaf and Dumb wherever situated, and that no preference has ever been given to applicants for admission on account of their residence" (see the Act to Alter the Name of the Asylum, reprinted in Edward Allen Fay, ed., *Histories of American Schools for the Deaf, 1817–1893,* 3 vols. [Washington, D.C.: Volta Bureau, 1893], 1:30).

11. Petition of the president and director of the Connecticut Asylum, January 18, 1819, HR 15A-G.17.3, National Archives and Records Service, Washington, D.C. Under the provisions of the Ordinances of 1785 and 1787 and the United States Constitution, the U.S. Congress had the power "to make all needful rules and regula-

tions respecting the territory of the United States," including the right to "dispose of " the public lands, something Congress already had been doing from some time. See Roy M. Robbins, *Our Landed Heritage: The Public Domain, 1776–1936* (Lincoln: University of Nebraska Press, 1962).

12. *Annals of Congress,* 15th Cong., 2d sess., 1819, 2:1329–30. The House committee report, dated February 22, 1819, is reprinted in the *NASP,* 1:311–12.

13. *Annals of Congress,* 15th Cong., 2d sess., 1819, 2:1427–28.

14. Ibid.

15. Ibid., p. 1431. The author examined closely this and all subsequent recorded votes on this matter and could find no political or regional splits on the issue.

16. *Annals of Congress,* 15th cong., 2d sess., 1818–19, 1:279, 280, 282. The measure stated: "That there be granted to the Connecticut Asylum for the education of deaf and dumb persons, a township of land, or a tract of land equal thereto, to be located . . . in tracts of not less than four entire sections each, in any of the unlocated lands of the United States to which the Indian title has been extinguished. . . ." See ibid., 1819, 2:2513.

17. For a brief history of the New York institution, see *A History of the New York Institution for the Instruction of the Deaf and Dumb* (New York, 1893), reprinted in Fay, or in Best, pp. 393–94.

18. *Annals of Congress,* 16th Cong., 1st sess., 1819–20, 1:885.

19. Ibid., pp. 883, 887–88, 890–91.

20. Ibid., p. 885. Others also repudiated the precedent argument. Thus, e. g., Congressman Henry Warfield of Maryland stated that the Connecticut grant "was no reason for going on and bestowing the property of the nation on all who asked [for] it." And John Randolph of Virginia argued that if "we go on by precedents, we shall lose sight of the Constitution instead of looking to it—looking to it as a constitution of delegated powers—a jealous, guarded delegation of authority." "As to being ashamed to refuse this grant, after passing others which Mr. Meigs had referred to," he declared, "let the galled jade wince" (ibid., pp. 885, 884, 886).

21. Ibid., pp. 883–84, 889.

22. The vote was not recorded in the *Annals of Congress;* it merely stated that the "bill was rejected."

23. Best, pp. 394–95.

24. Ibid., p. 395. Also see Charles P. Fosdick, *A Short History of the Kentucky School for the Deaf* (Danville, Ky., n.d.), reprinted in Fay.

25. Thus, within a month, by February 1824, nine of the institution's nineteen students were out-of-state residents.

26. "Report of the Superintending Committee of the Kentucky Institution for the Tuition of the Deaf and Dumb, November 3, 1823," *NASP,* 1:317–20.

27. "Petition of the Trustees of the Kentucky Institution for the Tuition of the Deaf and Dumb, March 15, 1824," *NASP,* 1:316–17.

28. *Annals of Congress,* 18th Cong., 1st sess., 1824, 2:2542–43. The Committee Report is reprinted in *NASP,* 1:313–15.

29. *NASP,* 1:326–27.

30. *Congressional Debates,* 19th Cong., 1st sess., 1825–26, 2:1600.

31. Ibid., pp. 1600–1604.

32. Ibid., p. 1609.

33. Only Senator Thomas W. Cobb of Georgia objected to the bill as a matter of principle, calling it an unconstitutional grant of common property for a local purpose (see *Congressional Debates,* 19th Cong., 1st sess., 1825–26, 2:371).

34. Ibid., pp. 371–72 (also see ibid., 1826, 2, pt. 2:1913–14). Voting against the measure were John Branch of North Carolina, John Chandler of Maine, Dudley Chase of Vermont, Thomas Cobb of Georgia, and William Harper and Robert Hayne of South Carolina.

35. Basically, there were two problems: (1) whether or not the land chosen by the institution complied with the instructions Congress gave it for making that choice, and (2) whether or not it interfered with the claims of individuals under legislation enacted by Congress regarding pre-emption rights. For a history of the squabble and wha

happened to the institution's lands, see *Congressional Debates*, 21st Cong., 1st sess., 1830, 6, pt. 2:757–60, and *NASP*, 1:340–65 (also see Best, p. 395, and Fosdick).

36. A number of other institutions for the deaf and dumb were established in the following years: in Ohio in 1829, in Virginia in 1839, in Indiana in 1841, in Georgia in 1842, in Tennessee and North Carolina in 1845, in Illinois in 1846, and in South Carolina in 1849. Thus, by the middle of the nineteenth century, or thirty-two years after the founding of the first one, there were a dozen institutions for the deaf and dumb in America. Each of the new ones, along with the older New York and Pennsylvania institutions, tried unsuccessfully on various occasions throughout this period to secure federal aid (although on two occasions bills providing for federal endowment of all the then-existing schools for the deaf and dumb apparently came close to being enacted) (see Best, pp. 396–98, 423–24).

37. The "Memorial of D. L. Dix Praying [for] a grant for the relief and support of the indigent curable and incurable insane in the United States" can be found in the *NASP*, 1:385–416 (also see *Congressional Globe*, 30th Cong., 1st sess., 1848, 17 [n.s.]:875). When the bill was introduced in Congress for the first time (1848), it called for the granting of five million acres of public land for the insane; when it was re-introduced at a later date, it called for the allotment of 12.25 million acres of land, ten million for the insane and the remainder for the blind and the deaf and dumb. When finally passed in 1854, however, the measure called for the appropriating of ten million acres of land for the insane (also see Helen Marshall, *Dorothea Dix: Forgotten Samaritan* [New York: Russell & Russell, 1937], pp. 129–54).

38. The measure passed the Senate on March 8, 1854, by a vote of twenty-five to twelve, and the House on April 19, 1854, by a vote of eighty-one to fifty-three.

39. For Pierce's veto message, see *Congressional Globe*, 33d Cong., 1854, 28, pt. 2:1061–63, or *NASP*, 1:417–25.

40. For congressional debate on the veto, see *Congressional Globe*, 33d Cong., 1st sess., 1854, 28, pt. 2:1063 ff. (also see ibid., 1854, 31, N.S. appendix, pp. 550–52, 642, 798–99, 804–7, 969–71, 979–85, 1068–69). Aside from creation of the so-called Freedmen's Bureau (1865–72) and revision of the immigration statutes (in the late nineteenth century) to deal with the mentally ill, federal involvement in social welfare seems to have begun again in 1909 with the calling of the White House Conference on Dependent Children, and in 1912 with the establishment of the U.S. Children's Bureau.

41. Generally, it is assumed that Pierce, a "strict constructionist" and a wily northern politician, vetoed the measure in an effort to court southern favor in the midst of the states' rights controversy raging at the time (see, e.g., Marshall, pp. 151–52).

THE TRAGEDY OF THE TEN-MILLION-ACRE BILL

SEATON W. MANNING

The author is a member of the faculty of San Francisco State College

THE protracted but unsuccessful effort of Dorothea Lynde Dix to secure federal assistance for the mentally ill in the United States has come to be regarded as a significant bench mark in the history of social welfare in this country. It serves in the first place to demonstrate, if further demonstration were needed, the perseverance and dedication of this remarkable, untiring woman who, by the time she first memorialized Congress in 1848, had successfully induced the legislatures of several states to provide at least a minimum of humane care for the institutionalized insane. Because of her work as legislative advocate for a helpless and outcast group, her name had become a byword in households throughout the country.[1] The failure of her effort, although personally disappointing, did not diminish her zeal or effectiveness as a reformer or the esteem in which she was generally held.

However, the real significance of Miss Dix's thwarted attempts to secure federal assistance for the mentally ill was its effect on subsequent social welfare development. Writers who have surveyed the history of social welfare in this country are in unanimous agreement that President Pierce's veto of the Dix proposals established the principle and pattern of federal non-participation in social welfare matters until the fed-

eral emergency relief measures of the 1930's and the passage of the Social Security Act in 1935. The effect of the presidential veto, it is believed, was to turn back the growing tide of expectation of congressional aid for specific categories of needy persons.

The story of the legislative vicissitudes of the Dix proposal to Congress is fairly well known. However, we shall review them here in order to point out some of the influences and conflicting interests which delayed its passage by Congress and which may have affected President Pierce's decision to veto the bill.

I

On June 23, 1848, Dorothea Dix memorialized Congress for a grant of five million acres of public lands which were to be sold and the proceeds used "as a perpetual fund for the care of the indigent insane." For many years Miss Dix had labored with the several states and had discovered that some of them were unable and others unwilling to bear the cost of providing adequate institutions for the mentally ill. She therefore turned to the national government to provide aid for this category of indigent persons. Since the national government had given land grants for educational purposes, for the building of roads, and for other internal improvements, she believed that Congress might also provide in the same way for the relief and institutionalization of the indigent insane. There were already precedents for congressional help to local communities for meeting a special category of need. In 1819 a township of land had been given to Connecticut to

---

[1] The story of Dorothea Dix is so well known that it will not be reviewed here. The reader is doubtless familiar with the following: Francis Tiffany, *Life of Dorothea Lynde Dix* (New York: Houghton, Mifflin Co., 1890); Albert Deutsch, *The Mentally Ill in America* (New York: Columbia University Press, 1949); and Helen E. Marshall, *Dorothea Dix, Forgotten Samaritan* (Chapel Hill: University of North Carolina Press, 1927).

Social Service Review 36 (March 1962): 44–50

support an asylum for the deaf and dumb and in 1822 Kentucky had been granted federal land for a similar purpose.[2]

Despite these favorable past actions of Congress, Miss Dix was not overly optimistic about the outcome of her proposal. The agitation for free homesteads was gaining momentum in the northern states, accompanied by a growing aversion to further land grants and reserved sales. According to Tiffany, this agrarian movement "had carried consternation into the ranks of the Democratic party."[3] Consequently, and as Miss Dix had anticipated, no action was taken on the proposal. Debate on the measure was deferred, and it was finally allowed to lapse.

At the beginning of the 1850 congressional session Miss Dix again memorialized Congress on behalf of the mentally ill. This time, however, she asked for ten million acres for the insane and two and one-quarter million acres for the support of the indigent deaf and dumb. The proposal received more favorable legislative treatment than the bill of 1848. A bill containing the essential features of the new proposal was passed in the Senate in the winter session of 1851 but was again deferred in the House.

The Senate debate on the Ten-Million-Acre Bill (as the Dix proposal was referred to in Congress) during the winter session of 1851 reflected the conflicting views held by people throughout the country about the disposition of federal public lands and indicated, further, that the federal government itself had no settled and consistent policy. Some wanted the public lands dis-

tributed without cost to those who would settle on them. This was the intent of the various homestead bills which were introduced in Congress over a span of a dozen years and which finally became law in 1862. Others thought that the public lands should be held as a source of revenue for the federal government. Still others believed that title to the public lands should be surrendered to the states in which the lands were located. Certain industrial interests and their political spokesmen in the eastern states, alarmed at the movement of population to the new states of the West, advocated postponing the distribution of public lands.[4] Finally, there was the position of the slaveholding South. Quick to sense and oppose any movement that would extend free-soil territory and influence, it opposed the free distribution of land to settlers as advocated by the homestead "agitators" of the North and West.

The measure for a grant of public lands for the care of the mentally ill was therefore supported or opposed by the legislators depending upon which of these several points of views they found congenial or politically expedient. In general, the representatives from the new states of the West, where most of the land was located, opposed the Ten-Million-Acre Bill on the grounds that "the states which have no federal lands within their borders would, under the terms of the Act, acquire such lands in the states which have." They feared that the states would then "become taxpayers to each other and the land exhausted by the taxation which the states might impose on each other."[5] They argued,

---

[2] *Congressional Globe* (31st Cong., 2d sess.), February 11, 1851, p. 509, remarks by Senator Pearce.

[3] Tiffany, *op. cit.,* p. 179.

[4] Carl Brent Swisher, *American Constitutional Development* (New York: Houghton Mifflin Co., 1943), p. 370.

[5] *Congressional Globe*, February 11, 1851, p. 507.

further, that the land made available under this bill would compete with lands already set aside for schools, universities, and public works and that this competition would decrease the value of lands held by the states.

Support for the measure, on the other hand, came from those who advocated the surrender by the federal government of title to the public lands. Senator Burland of Arkansas was the principal spokesman for this viewpoint. He favored the Ten-Million-Acre Bill because it would help to divest the United States of title to the public lands and place it in private hands from which the states could derive taxes.[6] The needs of the mentally ill and the emergent nature of the problem of their care were almost overlooked in the conflict of views over the larger issue of determining a policy for the disposition of the federally owned lands. It remained for Senator Dawson of Georgia to make a plea for the bill on the basis of its humanitarian intent. "We cannot do a more charitable act," he said, "than that which is proposed by this bill." He pointed out that land had been appropriated for a variety of purposes, but when it comes to the "poor, unfortunate, dependent lunatic, not an acre must be appropriated to relieve him from the distresses which the God of Nature may have inflicted upon him."[7]

Among the more impassioned objectors in the Senate was Jefferson Davis of Mississippi, who was later to become a member of President Pierce's Cabinet and to hold the post of Secretary of War when Pierce, in 1854, vetoed the bill containing the Dix proposal. In language remarkably similar to that later used by Pierce, he condemned the bill

as unconstitutional. The United States government, he said, "was not founded for great eleemosynary purposes." He continued:

This government was established as the agent of the States in their foreign relations, and as an umpire between the States in their relations one to another, not to dispense charities to the indigent, nor to establish workhouses or houses of correction for the vicious within the States. These objectives are all left to the Sovereign States in which they resided before the Union was formed. . . . If we have the power to grant charities to one class of the community who may be suffering, why not to another? If to the lunatic, why not to the blind . . . the deaf and dumb, and to the whole range of paupers whose provision is now confined to the communities to which they belong?[8]

He argued that Congress should watch over the public land as "a great proprietor." Grants of public lands should therefore be limited to those cases in which the grant would benefit the treasury of the United States—the kind of profitable action which "a great proprietor" might reasonably take. As a southern gentleman, he paid his compliments to Miss Dix: "Too much credit cannot be given to the lady at whose solicitation this bill was introduced. But we should remember that we are here under delegated powers, to dispense justice and not to answer to our feelings."[9]

In spite of the opposition of Senator Davis and the western bloc, the bill passed the Senate but, as noted before, was deferred in the House. In the session of 1852 Miss Dix again appealed to the Congress but no action was taken by either House. At the beginning of the 1854 session the occasion seemed more favorable for the resumption of the campaign. According to Tif-

[6] *Ibid.*, p. 508.

[7] *Ibid.*, p. 507.

[8] *Ibid.*, p. 508.

[9] *Ibid.*

fany, "The first fierce excitement in the Democratic Party over the land issue had in a measure subsided while the unexampled series of triumphs she herself had achieved in so many States had steadily increased in Congress the moral ascendancy of her name."[10] She again memorialized Congress, with favorable responses from both Houses. The bill passed the Senate March 8, 1854, by a vote of 25 to 12. It passed the House in April and was sent to the President.

That the issue had been a divisive one for the Democrats is reflected in the Senate vote. Of the 25 "aye" votes, 8 were cast by Democrats, while all 12 "nay" votes came from the Democratic ranks. The Whigs, on the other hand, voted solidly for the measure. Whig support was not surprising. As politicians, Whigs were to be expected to espouse measures which they knew would create embarrassment and division among their Democrats opponents. However, their support was not simply and entirely an expression of the usual political motive. The Whig philosophy as to the function of government, particularly on the national level, was considerably more liberal than that of the Democrats. Whigs tended to regard government as "an instrument for the promotion of the general welfare."[11] There were at this time in the Senate 36 Democrats, 20 Whigs, and 2 Free Soilers. Four seats were vacant. When the question came to vote whether to pass the bill over the President's veto, Democratic ranks closed and the veto was sustained by a vote of 26 to 21, largely along party lines.

[10] Tiffany, *op. cit.*, pp. 187–88.

[11] Glydon G. Van Deusen, "Some Aspects of Whig Thought and Theory in the Jacksonian Period," *American Historical Review,* LXIII (January, 1958), 305–22.

II

In the drama of the Ten-Million-Acre Bill President Pierce emerges as the villain whose unexpected veto placed a strait jacket on social welfare development which was not, and presumably could not be, removed for over eighty years. While there is some recognition of the fact that the Dix proposal was inextricably bound to the complex and controversial issue of the disposition of public lands as well as to the even more emotionally charged slavery question, Pierce is held personally to blame, and his veto is regarded as an act of deliberate callousness, if not downright villainy. Francis Tiffany charged that the President, actuated by hatred of "sentimental legislation," was a man who panicked "at the slightest intrusion of humane sentiment into politics."[12] He branded the President's veto arguments as "weak and vacillating" and found it hard "to account for his action on any other ground than that of personal idiosyncracies of character and opinion."[13] Tiffany's final judgment was that the veto was "the veto more of an individual than of a great public official." In his biography of Pierce, Roy Franklin Nichols describes the President as a man who "would administer government by strict adherence to precedent rather than by creative statesmanship," and states that "Creative statesmanship was unknown to him except as a dangerous violation of tried doctrines advocated by men both unstable and unprincipled or by dangerous fanatics."[14]

[12] Tiffany, *op. cit.*, p. 199.

[13] *Ibid.*

[14] Roy Franklin Nichols, *Franklin Pierce* (Philadelphia: University of Pennsylvania Press, 1958), p. 289.

Franklin Pierce, the undistinguished Democratic politician from New Hampshire, may have had all of the shortcomings attributed to him by Tiffany and Nichols. His narrow conception of constitutional authority may indeed have nipped the expanding aspirations of social welfare and closed the door to federal participation in providing some of the means for meeting social welfare needs. But need that door have remained closed for two generations? Franklin Pierce was, after all, president for only four years. What efforts were undertaken in the years following his administration to overturn the principle of federal non-intervention established by his veto of the Ten-Million-Acre Bill? Where were the social reformers and welfare workers? Why did they not organize to continue the struggle begun by Dorothea Dix, seeking to take advantage of social and political changes which, if properly exploited, might have enabled them to achieve the objective which Miss Dix sought but could not reach?

The answers to these questions are speculative rather than factual. Albert Deutsch and Campbell Murphy suggest that the essential weakness of Miss Dix —a weakness which may have contributed to the failure of her effort—was lack of organizational skills. Murphy compares her methods with those used a century later to secure the passage of the National Mental Health Act.[15]

Deutsch took a somewhat similar point of view but saw the lack of organizational skill as endemic to the times as well as a unique peculiarity of Miss Dix's temperament:

Miss Dix had throughout her career played the role of the lone eagle, partly because the stage of humanitarian reform in her time gave rise to the individual crusader of the type she represented, partly through the dictates of her peculiar temperament. By the sheer force of her personality she had awakened public opinion to the sufferings and needs of the mentally ill to a degree unparalleled by any other individual before her time or for many years after. She had succeeded in forcing on recalcitrant public authorities the acceptance of definite standards of care and treatment. However, to *organize* that enlightened opinion on a permanent basis so as to safeguard adequate standards, in addition to obtaining immediate gains, was beyond the capacity of any individual at that time, even of such a rare person as she was.[16]

It is perhaps unfortunate that Dorothea Dix did not possess, or exercise, the talents necessary to involve others deeply in her cause and to create a permanent organization to work for the fulfillment of her goals. In this sense the real tragedy of the Ten-Million-Acre Bill was not in Pierce's veto, as discouraging and disappointing as it was. Given the President's narrow conception of what was constitutional and the pressures exerted on the Democratic party (which he headed) to call a halt to the lavish distribution of the public lands, the veto was inevitable. The tragedy lay in the fact that the effort which the bill represented collapsed with the veto and with Miss Dix's involvement in other matters. No person or organization came forward to carry on the campaign for federal participation and assistance in meeting welfare needs. Thus, eight years later, when the political climate had changed to such a degree as to make possible the provision of federal land grants for assistance to other worthy causes, the mentally ill and other pressing social welfare problems had no organized voice in the land or champion in Congress.

Deutsch's assertion that organizing

[15] Campbell G. Murphy, *Community Organization Practice* (New York: Houghton Mifflin Co., 1954), pp. 83–85.

[16] *Op. cit.*, pp. 183–84.

on a permanent basis was "beyond the capacity of any individual at that time" is difficult to accept in the light of the recognized talents which constituted in part the social reform movements of the period—Neal Dow, Elizabeth Cady Stanton, Robert Rantoul, Horace Mann, Charles Loring Brace, Horace Greeley, Theodore Parker, James G. Birney—to mention some of the great figures who were artfully pricking the moral conscience of America. It is probably more accurate to say that these and other reform leaders had committed themselves to other issues and other struggles and that general interest in the cause of obtaining federal aid for the mentally ill or any other category of needy persons was no longer of paramount importance once the commanding personality of Dorothea Dix was removed.

The rise of the Republican party in the 1850's and its ascension to power in the election of 1860 provided the means whereby the principle of federal non-intervention in social welfare, established by the Pierce veto, might have been successfully challenged. This new political party, composed of many diverse groups, was, in its early years at least, a party of reform. It attracted crusaders of various and sometimes conflicting stripes—abolitionists, prohibitionists, free soilers, nativists, feminists, homesteaders—as well as many of more conservative hue. To a considerable degree the new Republicanism was all things to almost all men, and its early doctrines reflected the diversity of beliefs of the motley groups which composed it. From its substantial Whig element it inherited the idea of the liberal use of government powers to promote the general welfare, a certain degree of economic liberalism, and advocacy of internal improvements as

well as the more conservative views of the old-line Whigs who wanted protective tariffs and a "hands-off-business" policy on the part of the federal government.[17] The abolitionists and free soilers gave to the party its strong antislavery bent, the one advocating total abolition of slavery and the other striving primarily to prevent its extension to the territories. The party also embraced the idea of free homesteads to those who would settle the land—a radical idea which after a decade of political juggling had become increasingly popular, particularly in the West, and which now profited from the support of Horace Greeley, the crusading founder-editor of the *New York Tribune* and the new party's most effective propagandist. The Republican party platforms of 1856 and 1860 gave official voice to those ideologies, and the party achieved victory in 1860 committed, among other things, to a free homestead law, a railroad to the Pacific Ocean aided by federal land grants, and a protective tariff.

In the light of the Republican party's composition and its official advocacy of liberal use of federal lands for homesteads and railroad construction, it is not at all improbable that it might have espoused also the cause of federal aid to specific categories of needy persons. In the years between its organization and its first national victory in 1860, the party had maintained an open-door policy with respect to people and issues. It was "on the make," striving for power, and it could ill afford to ignore any group which sought entry into the party or any idea which might have appeal, however limited. The time was propitious for raising again the great concern

[17] Malcolm Moos, *The Republicans: A History of Their Party* (New York: Random House, 1952), p. 30.

for which Dorothea Dix had struggled and had suffered defeat—this time in a political climate that was much more congenial than the Democratic atmosphere of the period 1848–54. There is, however, no indication that this issue was ever presented for party consideration and indorsement. Among the many voices heard in the determination of Republican doctrine, none spoke on behalf of the idea of federal responsibility for meeting the needs of the mentally ill or any other group of needy persons. The social reformers, many of whom held membership in the party, were silent on this question. An opportunity was thus lost, or perhaps never originally perceived.

Even without specific Republican party indorsement, it still might have been possible, again because of prevailing Republican sentiments, to secure passage of legislation favorable to federal assistance in the welfare field if interest, organization, and leadership had been available. The history of the movement to obtain federal land grants for the establishment of agricultural and industrial colleges in each of the states illustrates what could be done by a well organized and determined group to exploit successfully the changed political situation. When the issue of the land-grant colleges was thrown into the political arena in 1857, the westerners, who originally sponsored the movement, persuaded Representative Justin S. Morrill to introduce the measure in the House of Representatives in order to avoid the sectional ill-will of the eastern bloc. The bill passed both houses of Congress but was vetoed by President Buchanan, who used essentially the same arguments which Pierce had applied to the proposal of Dorothea Dix

in the Ten-Million-Acre Bill.[18] The bill's supporters, taking advantage of the change in administration and the encouraging fact that the Republican party had indorsed the homestead proposal and had made it one of the planks in the party platform, reintroduced the measure for agricultural and industrial colleges in the 37th Congress. It was passed during the second session and signed by President Lincoln. The act (known as the Morrill Act) gave each state the income from 30,000 acres of land for each member of Congress, with the provision that the funds should be used for mechanical and agricultural colleges, with provisions for military training. In passing, it is of interest that during this same session the Homestead Act was also passed, as well as an act creating a Department of Agriculture within the federal establishment.

The movement for the land-grant colleges could very well have served as a model for the forces of social welfare reform. But, as indicated above, organization and leadership, and perhaps even interest, were lacking. The narrow construction of federal authority in the welfare field as set forth in the Pierce veto remained unchallenged. The result was that the traditional patterns of exclusive local and state responsibility for social welfare matters continued unchanged until the ravages of the Great Depression, producing bankrupt local governments and overburdened voluntary agencies, forced significant modifications of the old traditions.

SAN FRANCISCO STATE COLLEGE

Received November 9, 1961

[18] *Congressional Globe* (35th Cong., 1st sess.), 1857–58, pp. 1412–13.

PART III

Late Nineteenth-Century Reform and Early Twentieth-Century Social Welfare Progress: Introduction

The American system of social welfare, which had evolved piecemeal since colonial times, underwent far-reaching transformations in the half-century following the Civil War. Antebellum Americans had relied upon private and religious charitable institutions and limited local expenditures to care for those in need; the federal role in social welfare remained practically nonexistent. On the surface, little had changed by the end of the nineteenth century. Voluntary social welfare agencies had increased in number and function, and state governments had expanded their activities somewhat, but the federal role in welfare had not been altered. Yet, by 1900, fundamental economic and social transformations in American life were well underway, and the nature of both private and state social welfare activities soon reflected this.

Forty years later, the American system of social welfare hardly resembled that of the turn of the century. Voluntary charitable activities had become ancillary to government-financed programs, the range of government social welfare concerns had expanded enormously, and, most important, the federal government had assumed primary responsibility for social welfare policy. Furthermore, a well-organized corps of paid professional social workers had arisen to administer welfare programs and to care for those in need. In short, by the time America entered World War II, the major elements of our modern social welfare system were in place. The articles in this section help to explain how this transformation occurred.

The Civil War and its immediate aftermath resulted in significant changes in social welfare services, particularly in the states of the defeated Confederacy. As John Hope Franklin demonstrates in

"Public Welfare in the South during the Reconstruction Era, 1865–80," prior to the war southern states had lagged far behind the rest of the nation in providing for those in need. In the years of Reconstruction, significant increases in state-funded social welfare programs occurred in most southern states, partly as a result of the grave needs created by the war's devastation, and partly because of changes in southern state governments under Reconstruction. Franklin shows also that progress in provision of adequate social welfare services was severely hampered by the white south's continuing obsession with racial segregation and that black people were generally served much less well than whites by the new state social welfare institutions. After the war, the federal government for the first time administered social welfare services directly through its Bureau of Refugees, Freedmen and Abandoned Lands, commonly called the Freedmen's Bureau. The bureau, which assisted both blacks and whites, disbanded in 1872.

American social welfare policy transformed in these years more as a result of industrialization and urbanization, however, than from the political repercussions of the Civil War. Between 1850 and 1910, the percentage of the total United States population living in incorporated municipalities of 2,500 or more increased from 20 percent to 46 percent. Large industrial enterprises, employing thousands of workers at long hours, low pay, and under dangerous conditions, sprang up throughout the country. Much of the labor for the new factories consisted of foreign immigrants. Between 1865 and 1885, approximately ten million immigrants entered the United States; approximately fifteen million came in the years between 1885 and the end of World War I.

The consequences of this emergence of a large, urban industrial proletariat were readily apparent in nearly any large American city. Poverty and deprivation were highly visible in the slums which housed workers and their families. Large-scale violence erupted on numerous occasions when workers sought to unionize and demanded higher wages. Even in times of prosperity, conditions were bad, but cyclical depressions, like those that began in 1873 and 1893, made economic security for workers seem especially tenuous.

These changes affecting the lower level of the American social structure occurred simultaneously with other less dramatic but equally profound developments within the middle class. A new faith in science gripped American thought in the late nineteenth century. The modern university began with its division of academic labor into specialized disciplines and its commitment to the expansion of all kinds of knowledge. Faith in specialized expertise grew, and with it the number of new, expert professions. Middle-class women started attending college in significant numbers, although career opportunities for these women in the new, specialized professions were generally restricted.

Two social movements of profound importance for the development of modern social welfare institutions—the scientific charity movement and the social settlement movement—illuminate how these latter developments in middle-class America affected the world of the urban proletariat. Leaders in government and private charitable work in the 1870s, convinced that poverty was reaching crisis proportions and that scientific knowledge could be harnessed to reverse the trend, began urging that relief be dispensed in a more systematic and "scientific" manner. The scientific charity movement urged that all charitable resources in a city be coordinated by a single agency, that all requests for aid be handled by that agency (which would send an agent to investigate the request and determine the extent of genuine need), and that indiscriminate almsgiving to the poor be discouraged as harmful and wasteful. Robert H. Bremner describes this movement in " 'Scientific Philanthropy,' 1873–93." The new Charity Organization Society soon developed into our modern private social agencies, and professional social caseworkers eventually replaced the friendly visitors.

In the late 1880s and early 1890s, the earliest founders of social settlements in the slums of American cities took a rather different approach to the problems of the poor. Settlement works moved into the poorest city neighborhoods in order to provide services to those around them and to learn firsthand about the problems of the poor. Many of these settlement residents were women who, having completed college, were looking for useful work; many others were Protestant ministers seeking to apply the Christian spirit to the urgent social problems of their day.

The movement spread rapidly, and settlement workers soon established a wide variety of classes, clubs, and services to community residents. More important, however, settlement residents gathered extensive data about the nature of the slum environment and its effect upon people. They then undertook vigorous crusades to remedy the social ills they had discovered. As such, they became translators of the experiences of the urban poor to the rest of society and leaders in the struggle to improve the quality of life for the poor through voluntary, and later governmental, means. Allen F. Davis illustrates the role settlement residents played in municipal reform in his study of "Raymond Robins: The Settlement Worker as Municipal Reformer."

Most of the settlement houses were located in areas of the city inhabited largely by immigrants and their children, and settlement-house residents quickly developed an appreciation of immigrant cultures and a deep interest in easing their transplantation from foreign to American urban soil. George Cary White, in "Social Settlements and Immigrant Neighbors, 1886–1914," analyzes the settlement residents' encounter with and appreciation for immigrant culture. In "Chicago Social Workers and Blacks in the Progressive Era," Steven J. Diner shows that settlement workers at the same time became interested in the culture of the relatively small black communities in industrial cities like Chicago. Diner argues that Chicago social workers not only were among the first people in American society to see the similarities between immigrant and black cultures but they also noted the unique handicaps imposed upon southern black migrants to northern industrial cities.

By the beginning of the twentieth century, settlement workers—allied with university professors, club women, lawyers, physicians, businessmen, and many other middle-class people—initiated a series of wide-ranging and diverse reform movements to improve the quality of urban life. Not all of the reform movements were successful, and not all of them were supported by the exact same coalition. All of them, however, proposed to expand the role of government to protect poor and working-class city dwellers and to decrease economic dependency. These movements formed the foundation upon which our modern welfare state rests.

The remaining articles in this section consider a few of the urban social reform movements of this period—their leaders, programs, assumptions, successes, and failures.

The movement to provide state-funded "pensions" for single mothers with young children was a major successful crusade of this period. First enacted in 1911 in Illinois, the concept spread rapidly to other states. Mark H. Leff, in "Consensus for Reform: The Mothers'-Pension Movement in the Progressive Era," explains how a broad-based consensus for this new form of government intervention in the social welfare needs of the poor emerged, and shows why this program was enacted so broadly at this time.

Another highly successful reform of the Progressive Era was the enactment of workmen's compensation legislation providing insurance for workers who were injured in industrial accidents. In "Prelude to Welfare Capitalism: The Role of Business in the Enactment of Workmen's Compensation Legislation in Illinois, 1905–12," Joseph L. Castrovinci demonstrates that businessmen supported this new incursion of government into economic life because it was in their interest to do so. This helps explain the wide acceptance of workmen's compensation by the state legislature.

Workmen's compensation was the only major form of social insurance to win widespread acceptance during the first two decades of the twentieth century. Many social welfare reformers of the period advocated a broad program of social insurance which would include old age, health, and unemployment benefits for workers. J. Lee

Kreader describes the career of one of the leading pioneers in this struggle for social insurance. In "Isaac Max Rubinow: Pioneering Specialist in Social Insurance," Kreader details Rubinow's efforts on behalf of the kinds of government programs eventually embodied in the Society Security Act of 1935, as well as some others.

No group won so much sympathy from reformers in these years as children, and a series of laws were passed to protect the health and welfare of the young. A special Juvenile Court was established in Illinois in 1899, an innovation copied by numerous states in succeeding years. The federal government, foreshadowing the large role in social welfare it would play later on, established the United States Children's Bureau in 1912. The concluding articles deal with two of the major manifestations of this child welfare movement. Lynn Gordon, in "Women and the Anti-Child Labor Movement in Illinois, 1890–1920," traces the effort of reformers, particularly women, to prohibit the employment of children in industrial occupations. Benjamin McArthur in "The Chicago Playground Movement: A Neglected Feature of Social Justice" shows how reformers sought to improve the quality of life for children in crowded city neighborhoods by constructing playgrounds, and he examines the reformers' assumptions and methods.

Not all of the proposals of reformers in these years won legislative approval. Proposals for state-sponsored old age, unemployment, and health insurance, for example, failed to win acceptance. Yet, taken together, the developments in the years between the end of the Civil War and the beginning of American entry into World War I moved the country far along the path to a system of social welfare that differed markedly from that of antebellum America. By 1917, most states had expanded greatly the range of human social needs that were deemed the proper concern of government. Some of these programs remain state responsibilities today, like workers' compensation. The federal government, which today dominates social welfare policy, did not substantially enter the social welfare field until the Depression of the 1930s and the resulting political changes of the New Deal. When it did enter, however, it had considerable state experience on which to draw. Mothers' pensions, for example, which most states had enacted by that time, became part of the Social Security Act of 1936. Today's program of Aid to Families with Dependent Children is a direct outgrowth of the mothers' pension laws enacted by the state. The Social Security Act also contained various proposals articulated during the Progressive Period that had failed to win state enactment (e.g., old age pensions).

By the end of the New Deal, the major features of our modern system of social welfare were fully established. Social welfare had become primarily a government responsibility, and the federal government had replaced state and local governments and voluntary associations as the major agency responsible for administering programs. Furthermore, the social welfare profession, which had begun with the scientific charity movement of the 1870s, had become an indispensable agent in the delivery of social welfare services. Voluntary charitable institutions, staffed also by professional social workers, were more numerous and specialized than they had been seventy years earlier; but their role had become supplementary to that of government.

PUBLIC WELFARE IN THE SOUTH DURING
THE RECONSTRUCTION ERA, 1865–80

JOHN HOPE FRANKLIN

University of Chicago

During the Reconstruction era the Southern states, for the first time, gave attention to the matter of providing public welfare services on a large scale. Before the Civil War a few Southern states had established public schools, and some had attempted to cope with the problems of intemperance and insanity. During the decade and a half following the war, the states, with varying degrees of effectiveness, established public policies and programs covering a wide range of problems, including health, education, the care of orphans and widows, the poor, the insane, the deaf, dumb, and blind. Throughout the period, however, most of the energies and resources of the former Confederate states were expended in the effort to establish and maintain separate public institutions for the two races, which inevitably meant inferior facilities for the former slaves.

The journey of the states of the American South toward the achievement of a full-scale, wide-ranging program of public welfare was long and tortuous. It began in the antebellum days with the struggle to do something about such problems as the insane and the drunkards, and it would not end even in the last quarter of the twentieth century as the task of providing unsegregated public education for the children of the South and of relieving the destitute victims of the new agricultural and industrial technology confounded and tor-

This paper was prepared for presentation as a Sidney A. and Julia Teller Lecture at the School of Social Service Administration of the University of Chicago on February 25, 1970.

mented the more sensitive of those who lived in the region. For welfare, especially public welfare, is a concept of human compassion and responsibility that has always had problems of acceptance in the states that made up the former Confederacy.

In the years before the Civil War Dorothea Dix made some headway in the South, as she persuaded one public leader after another that the insane were not criminals and should not be treated as such. By 1860, due largely to her tireless efforts, all states in the South, except Florida and Arkansas, had asylums for the care of the mentally ill (19:79–81, 113–21, 197). The

Social Service Review 44 (December 1970): 379–9̃
© 1970 by The University of Chicago

movement to control or eliminate the consumption of alcoholic beverages was not so successful. Southerners believed too much in personal liberty to follow Maine and some other Northern states in the 1850s in the enactment of state prohibition laws. Such restrictive legislation was merely another of the Northern "isms" that they must avoid at all costs. They placed such legislation in the category with restrictions against the holding of slaves, and once the barrier was down, they feared, it would be impossible to make the kind of distinction that would assure the preservation of their cherished institutions, especially slavery. Pledges of total abstinence, the imposition of high license fees on stores that sold liquor, and the zoning of churches and schools outside the area of the grog shops—that was as far as the Southern states were willing to go (11:436–37).

The problem of education for the masses was, in a very real sense, a problem of public welfare, for the view was widely accepted that if one could not afford an education he was not entitled to it. It was quite all right if private academies for the sons and even the daughters of planters flourished, but if they could not sustain themselves on the basis of tuition and contributions from the affluent they should close their doors.[1]

Before the Civil War North Carolina and Kentucky had something resembling systems of public education, thanks to the efforts of two remarkable prophets of public education, Calvin H. Wiley and Robert J. Breckinridge. Elsewhere the common schools were, in fact, charity schools for poor children

[1] The difficulties of achieving the principle of free public education in the South are discussed in Knight (18:160–267). See also Dabney (9:32–88, 164–73).

and orphans. The support for such institutions was so slight and so begrudging that it may fairly be said that they did little even to lower the rate of illiteracy among their students (10:68–69).

The South lagged behind the rest of the country in social reform generally because of its obsession with defending slavery and engaging in the struggle for power in national politics. There was no need for social reform, said George Fitzhugh—perhaps the shrewdest of all professional Southerners—because slavery provided the proper safeguards against the evils of a free society—such as unemployment and all the problems related to it—to which social reform addressed itself. If slavery was more widely accepted, Fitzhugh said, man would not need to resort to such unnatural remedies as women's rights, limited marriages, child welfare, communism, and the like (13:250–56). And if most of the energy of its ablest thinkers was deflected from human welfare by their concern over the preservation of slavery, virtually all of the time and attention of its politicians was focused on fighting the battle for slavery in the national arena. "What might not South Carolina now be," Benjamin F. Perry observed in 1853, "if her Calhouns, Haynes, McDuffies, Hamiltons, and Prestons had devoted their great talents and energies in the commercial and internal improvement of the state, instead of frittering them away in political squabbles, which ended in nothing?" (17:302). The general neglect of social problems was as great as the neglect of industry and commerce. South Carolina and the entire South would have been much different if they had given even a small amount of attention to the general welfare of their people during the antebellum period.

The Civil War forced Southerners to look at some areas of life that they had studiously neglected in previous years. The magnitude of the military undertaking created conditions in which the intrusion of the government into the lives of the people was as natural as it was inevitable. The conscription of whites for military service and the sequestering of blacks for menial and manual work were indications that all-out war touched the lives of most Southerners. Under the circumstances it was necessary to provide some public services in order to ameliorate the suffering that resulted. In the beginning, the relief for widows, orphans, wounded soldiers, and refugees was undertaken by individuals, private associations, and religious groups.[2] However generous such relief was, it was quite inadequate, as suffering and privation increased. Inevitably, state and local governments were forced to intervene. In North Carolina the state and local governments appropriated some $26 million for relief during the war. Louisiana established a pension fund from which soldiers' dependents received a fixed amount each month. By 1862 Virginia was appropriating $400,000 per year for relief and medical care. Other states and local communities set up similar relief programs for the destitute and the wounded (8:426–27; 22:61–68).

Some observers have suggested that these public and private actions were not motivated by humanitarian considerations, but merely by the struggle for survival. The complaint, too frequently heard during the war, that the conflict was "a rich man's war and a poor man's fight" was disquieting, to say the least. If it persisted, it could

lead to a new order, perhaps a real revolution, once the war was over. When petitions asking for relief for poor people began to flow into the Confederate Congress and the state legislatures, it was time to act. Relief and welfare measures were the result. But the war also changed the views and attitudes of some Southerners. Even as they clung tenaciously to the past, they recognized that some compromises were necessary in order to salvage at least something of the old order. One thing they could not afford to have was division among the whites, and one of the first steps the leaders took in the postwar years was to provide opportunities for relief and rehabilitation among the whites, undoubtedly for the sake of unity as much as for the sake of humanity.

It is well to remember that, for the first two years following the close of the war, the government of the former Confederate states was largely in the hands of former Confederates.[3] Under the Lincoln and Johnson plans of reconstruction, persons who would swear allegiance to the United States were restored to full citizenship; and when one-tenth of the number that had voted in the election of 1860 had taken the oath of allegiance to the United States the state government could begin to function. No Negroes, of course, could vote or hold office under this arrangement. The leaders were, for the most part, committed to Confederate sentiments, and the welfare programs they instituted reflected those sentiments. One of the first things the new governments did was to institute relief and welfare programs for the Confederate veterans and their dependents. In 1866 Mississippi spent one-fifth of its revenue on artifi-

---

[2] For discussions of the evolution of policies and practices of wartime relief see Coddington (7), Simkins and Patton (25), and Zornow (30).

[3] For a discussion of Confederate influence during the early years of Reconstruction see Franklin (15: 32–53).

cial arms and legs for Confederate veterans, while South Carolina appropriated $20,000 for that purpose the same year (16:123; 26:47).[4] Some states, moreover, attempted to provide direct relief for the suffering population. In 1866 the South Carolina legislature provided for the issuance of $300,000 in bonds to purchase 300,000 bushels of corn, but the bonds could not be sold at par and the corn could not be purchased for one dollar per bushel (26:45). In Mississippi, county boards of police were authorized to compile a list of people who qualified for aid. Such lists were to serve as a basis for a pro rata distribution of the indigent fund.[5]

In the area of public education the white rulers of Confederate reconstruction were as determined to erect a system exclusively for whites as they had been in other areas of public welfare. In July 1865, the editor of the Charleston *Courier* put it quite bluntly, if somewhat inelegantly, when he said: "The sole aim should be to educate every white child in the Commonwealth" (6). A member of the Louisiana legislature said that he was "not in favor of positively imposing upon any legislature the unqualified and imperative duty of educating any but the superior race of man —the White race" (39:159–61). Thus, the former Confederate states either ignored the question of Negro education or specifically excluded Negroes from public education. In 1866 the Georgia legislature enacted laws providing for a "thoroughgoing" system of free public education for any white inhabitant be-

tween the ages of six and twenty-one (36:58–64). The Texas constitution of 1866 declared that the public school fund would be "exclusively for the education of all white scholastics" of the state (50:28–29). In 1867 Arkansas established a system of free public education limited to whites (32:98–100). By that time all the former Confederate states had established public school systems that were restricted to whites.

One of the ironies of Confederate reconstruction is that those in the South who inveighed most bitterly against the federal government and its agencies were the beneficiaries of their largesse. Between 1865 and 1869 no Southern state provided as much public welfare in so many different areas as the federal government. In March 1865, Congress created the Bureau of Refugees, Freedmen, and Abandoned Lands. Commonly referred to as the Freedmen's Bureau, this federal agency, as its official name suggests, was authorized to assist in the relief and rehabilitation of all destitute persons, of whatever race. In the first three years of its existence, the Bureau issued some 18,300,000 rations, with approximately 5,230,000 going to whites. By 1867 there were forty-six Bureau hospitals serving whites as well as blacks and adequately staffed with physicians, surgeons, and nurses. It also maintained orphanages for Negro children in many parts of the South. A rather poignant note is that the Bureau sought relief for Negro veterans of the Union cause in much the same way that organizations in the Southern states were seeking relief for their white veterans of the Confederate cause.[6]

The Bureau achieved its greatest suc-

---

[4] Georgia's Constitution of 1865 also provided for the relief of indigent widows and orphans of soldiers (38:231).

[5] The act also provided that indigent children of deceased or disabled veterans or maimed veterans themselves were entitled to free education at any state institution of learning (42:149–52).

[6] The best general study of the agency is by Bentley (2). For the relief, medical, and educational work of the Bureau see especially chapters 5 and 6.

cess in education. It set up or supervised schools of every description: day, night, Sunday, and industrial schools, as well as colleges and universities. It worked closely with philanthropic and religious organizations in the North in the establishment of many institutions. Among the institutions founded by or that received aid from the Bureau were Howard University, Hampton Institute, Atlanta University, Fisk University, and Talladega College. The Bureau promoted education so vigorously that by 1867 it had set up schools "in the remotest counties of each of the confederate states." When its educational work came to an end in 1870, there were 247,333 pupils in 4,329 schools. Most of them were black, but that is because the whites preferred not to attend school with the freedmen. Indeed, they justified the exclusion of blacks from the public schools on the ground that the Bureau was attending to their educational needs. The Bureau, however, never excluded whites from its schools, and the children of many white teachers attended the Bureau schools, for in the South at the time these were the only educational institutions that they could safely attend (2:169–84).

In many ways the program of reconstruction that was inaugurated by Congress in March 1867 was not radical, despite the persistent reference to it as radical. One may concede that the enfranchisement of blacks and their participation in the affairs of government was a radical departure from anything that had ever happened in the South. This, however, was not a development that was substantially radical. The mere presence of Negroes did not guarantee that the legislative councils in which they sat would inevitably take a radical turn. Their participation, moreover, was

on a very limited scale. They controlled no state government, and they constituted the majority, for a part of the period, of only one state legislature— South Carolina. What was somewhat radical was the new conception of the role of government with its significantly enlarged sphere of activity. What government achieved under this new conception of its role was the work of the new residents of the South, called opprobriously "carpetbaggers," their Negro associates, and a surprisingly large number of Southern whites, castigated by their bitterly jealous Southern white critics as "scalawags" (15:85–103).

The new governments of the South undertook, first of all, to introduce the principle that government was instituted to serve all the people. There could be no public services designed for the exclusive benefit of one racial group of the population. Second, the new governments perceived their role to be one that, indeed, promoted the general welfare. If this meant enlarging existing agencies or creating entirely new agencies, they would do so, despite the objections of some members of the government who did not share that point of view. Finally, the new governments, under great pressure from various interest groups, sought to guard against the real possibility of becoming the tools of such groups and to escape the pitfalls of waste and corruption virtually inherent in what may be called "big" and "innovative" government. They did not always succeed; and if they erred they gallantly sought to expiate their guilt by compensatory legislation to redress the balance.

The new approaches and principles were so important that the agencies designed to implement them were frequently written into the new constitutions. The years 1867 and 1868 were the time of constitution-making in the South. Since the former Confederate states could not re-enter the Union if they did not have constitutions embodying the principle of political equality and guarantees against crippling racial distinctions, the states wrote new constitutions. Some of the most significant discussions ever to take place in the South regarding human rights and human welfare occurred in those constitutional conventions. In South Carolina there was a lengthy debate regarding the role of the state in providing relief and welfare (47). In North Carolina there was a full-dress debate over the question of orphanages and charities (44, 20). In Mississippi the convention devoted considerable time and attention to the question of "adequate relief and protection of the state and the citizens thereof." Many argued with great cogency that it was the responsibility of the state to establish permanent agencies to deal with the destitution that prevailed in most parts of the state (41: 157, 180–81, 402–504).

One of the first tangible things that the new governments did was to establish systems of public education for all the people. While many whites had the most serious reservations about educating blacks, no state seriously considered the possibility of excluding them from public education altogether. Even if the whites were inclined to do so, they feared that the Fourteenth Amendment forced them, in this regard, to provide "equal protection of the laws." Most states merely provided for the education of all children.[7] Some added, significantly, such phrases as "for the equal benefit of all the people" (e.g., 49:137). This did not mean racially

mixed schools, however. Native white members of the constitutional conventions were generally opposed to the education of blacks and whites together. In Alabama native whites were rewarded for their efforts by a move on the part of the state board of education, which had legislative powers. In what may be regarded as a precursor of the present-day pupil-placement laws, the board declared that racial mixing in the schools would be permitted only on the unanimous consent of the parents or guardians of the children involved (3: 93–94). Only in South Carolina and Louisiana did the constitutions unequivocally provide for racially mixed schools.

Of the many matters that the new governments took up, none was more critical than the question of land. It was discussed in the constitutional conventions and in subsequent legislative sessions. Many observers, North and South, watched the disposition of this matter with great interest. The destitution of the freedmen was acute, and nothing would provide immediate relief like the redistribution of land. Would Negroes use their new political power to attempt to take their forty acres by expropriation, even if there were not enough mules to go around? Many were relieved when no program materialized for the confiscation and redistribution of land. South Carolina Negroes hoped that the federal government would lend them money with which to purchase land. When they concluded, on the basis of reports from Washington, that such an eventuality was unlikely, the constitutional convention created a commis-

[7] The Constitution of Arkansas, for example, provided that the General Assembly "shall establish and maintain a system of free schools, for the gratuitous instruction of all persons in this State between the ages of five and twenty-one" (33:31).

sion to purchase land and resell it to Negroes. In 1869 a land commissioner was appointed who was to receive from the state treasurer bonds in the amount of $200,000 bearing 6 percent interest, payable in twenty years. Lands bought with the money were to be sold to actual settlers on terms at 6 percent interest. An additional $500,000 was made available in 1870 (47: 424–34; 26:438–39). No other state went this far in providing public financing for the purchase of land. A more generally practiced form of public assistance was afforded through tax exemptions on real and personal property. Of course, if the freedmen had no real or personal property, tax exemptions were meaningless.

Closely allied with the desire to obtain land was the desire to provide a constitutional basis for a wide range of other public welfare programs. The Florida constitution of 1868 authorized the counties of the state to provide for those inhabitants "who by reason of age, infirmity or misfortune, may have claims upon the aid and sympathy of society" (35:209). The North Carolina constitution of 1868 provided that the General Assembly should appoint and define the duties of a board of public charities, to whom "shall be entrusted the supervision of all charitable and penal state institutions and who shall annually report to the governor upon their condition, with suggestions for their improvement" (43: Art. II § 7). In the next General Assembly the Board of Public Charities was created, and it undertook immediately to investigate the conditions of the poor and the institutions attending to their welfare. It was a sobering experience for the Board to discover that there was no widespread public interest in the well-being of the disadvantaged and that many of the

most influential people of the state were opposed to the Board's very existence because it had been created by a so-called Radical Reconstruction legislature. The hostility increased by the month, and the unwillingness of the more affluent taxpayers to support its program literally drove the Board into inactivity in 1872. It remained moribund until 1888, by which time a "redeemed" government, as well as the urgent problems of poverty and other disabilities, forced a new consideration of the general problem of public welfare (23:11).

Few states went as far as Florida and North Carolina in establishing centralized systems of public welfare. There was, in most of the South, a rather strong antipathy toward the kind of centralization represented by a state board of charities. Much of the antebellum and wartime sentiment against state-controlled institutions survived the war. And even when state governments were inclined toward centralization, fierce opposition frequently prevented its accomplishment. There was the strong conviction, moreover, that the objects of public assistance could best be served, if they were to be served at all, by local agencies familiar with the circumstances. Even policy matters could most successfully be determined at the local level. How else, many Southerners asked, could they be certain that the taxpayers' contributions were not squandered by some scheming politican who had no interest in the sick, the indigent, or, say, the deaf-mutes?

There were a few areas, nevertheless, in which state-wide public assistance—or, at least, the policy out of which programs could be developed—seemed both desirable and feasible. One of these areas was child welfare. The problem of what to do about orphans or children whose parents could not or would not support them was as old as the South itself. Before the Civil War the county courts apprenticed orphans and illegitimate children to farmers or artisans until they reached the age of eighteen, if girls, or twenty-one, if boys. Some orphans were cared for in orphanages founded by churches or benevolent societies or by philanthropists. In the years immediately following the war, the problem of child welfare was greatly complicated by the necessity for establishing a policy regarding the children of freedmen. In 1865 and 1866, however, much attention was given to the welfare of orphans of Confederate soldiers.[8] Where orphanages were not established or where the facilities were inadequate, legislation provided for the apprenticing of such children to individuals. It may be argued that such arrangements for the care of children were never designed for the benefit of the children, but rather for the benefit of the guardian. There were, however, certain guarantees that were written into the indentures that dealt with matters of food, clothing, training, and the like. Many whites in 1865 took the position that these guarantees were not necessary where Negro children were concerned. The task of white guardians of black children was to solve the problem of labor and, at the same time, to establish those means of social control that would contribute to the maintenance of peace in the community.

One obvious way of solving the problem was to make as many black children as possible available as workers in the fields, shops, and kitchens of the whites and to give the white guardians virtually complete control over the lives of their young wards. This could best be handled at the state level, and most states enacted laws dealing with it. In 1865 Mississippi, for example, declared that all freedmen and free Negroes under the age of eighteen who were orphans or whose parents did not have the means to support their children should be apprenticed to some competent and suitable person, *"Provided,* that the former owner of said minor shall have the preference when, in the opinion of the court, he or she shall be a suitable person for that purpose" (14: I, 282).

The language of these postwar apprentice laws was similar to those of the antebellum period, with the addition of the clause giving preference to former masters. Many observers regarded this arrangement as merely a continuation of the system of slavery.[9] If preference was given to the former master, it would be easy for him to maintain complete control, and it would be difficult for the former slave child to make any meaningful distinction between his new status and his former status. While the policy was enunciated by the state, it was the local judge or magistrate who carried it out. This seemed to facilitate the "re-employment" of the child by the former master. Some Negro parents objected to the apprenticing of their children without their consent. In Mississippi several such parents appealed the matter to the higher courts in 1866, won their cases, and regained their children. Their main argument was that under such circumstances the apprenticing of their children was tantamount

---

[8] See, for example, the message of Governor Isaac Murphy to the Arkansas General Assembly, April 17, 1865 (34:30–31).

[9] For a discussion of local criticism of the Mississippi Apprentice Law see Wharton (28:84–85).

to their re-enslavement. The courts seemed to agree (28:91–92). Small wonder that Northern unionists strenuously objected to the apprenticeship laws. Small wonder that the new governments in 1868 hastily modified or repealed the legislation. Most states wrote into their new constitutions provisions such as those of Louisiana, which declared that "all contracts by which children were bound out without the knowledge or consent of their parents are null and void" (40:306).

The experience of Southerners with the scourges of cholera, yellow fever, smallpox, and other contagious diseases extended back into the prewar years. Despite the fact that thousands died annually from such diseases—especially cholera and yellow fever—the states of the South did little to deal with the problem. In 1853, for example, some forty thousand people in New Orleans contracted yellow fever, of whom some eight thousand died (12:70–71; 24: 53). There were days of mourning, and there was much effort to provide relief for the decimated families, but the physicians seemed helpless in confronting the disease. Perhaps it was because the most eminent among them—Dr. Josiah C. Nott and Dr. S. C. Cartwright—were preoccupied with making the argument and writing learned treatises to prove that slavery should be maintained because of the physiological inferiority of Negroes. Meanwhile, localities such as Charleston, Pensacola, Mobile, New Orleans, and Richmond undertook to deal with what they regarded as local problems. Northern states, where there were greater concentrations of population, had begun to address themselves to health problems at the state level in the 1840s and 1850s, but even in those areas effective state approaches to

health problems did not come until after the Civil War.[10]

During the Reconstruction era, the outbreak of epidemics of yellow fever and cholera in several Southern states stimulated numerous groups to demand that the problem be attacked more systematically than before. There was a severe cholera epidemic in Tennessee in 1866, and there were yellow fever epidemics in Virginia, Alabama, and Louisiana early in the following decade. It was not merely the increased prevalence of disease that prompted citizens to do something about it. There had occurred a change in attitude toward the role of government in society that helped to bring about some action. Communities that had come to regard education and the treatment of the insane as public responsibilities could also be disposed to regard health care as a public responsibility. But it was physicians rather than the general public that began to press for overall health programs and policies during the Reconstruction era (1:10–25).

Although there were epidemics in 1865 and 1866, the movement to involve the state in problems of health did not occur at that time. Perhaps the governments, under the control of the former Confederates, were too preoccupied with what they regarded as more urgent problems, such as formulating codes of conduct for the former slaves. Perhaps it was also because the federal government, through its Freedmen's Bureau, was ministering to the health of Southerners, black and white (2:76). There was much sickness and destitution among the former slaves, but the Southern whites were unconcerned. Many subscribed to the view of the eminent

[10] For a discussion of early efforts to control disease through public action see Allen (1).

Southern educator, Dr. C. K. Marshall, who confidently predicted that by January 1, 1920, the Negro population would have disappeared. There was nothing that could be done about it, said the Natchez *Democrat,* adding that "the child is already born who will behold the last Negro in the state of Mississippi."

Once the so-called radical governments completed the business of undoing the work of earlier Reconstruction governments, and once they sensed the inherent dangers arising from the spread of dread diseases, they used the powers of the state to deal with the problems of health. In 1872 Virginia established a state board of health composed of seven physicians appointed by the governor. In 1875, Alabama, staggering from the blow of a yellow fever epidemic in the vicinity of Mobile, established a board of health under the auspices of the state medical association. It charged the board to "investigate the causes and means of prevention of endemic and epidemic diseases," to "investigate the influences of localities and employment upon the public health," and "from time to time make to the General Assembly such suggestions as to legislative action as, in their judgment, may seem advisable," and to be, "in all ways, the medical advisers of the State." It was as yet too early to charge such boards with active control of disease, and the legislatures did not appropriate adequate funds for the use of the boards. In the post-Reconstruction years, the legislatures would be more generous both in the appropriation of funds and in conferring greater powers on the boards for the care of health and the control of disease.[11]

[11] Allen (1:30 ff.) gives an account of the establishment of each state board of health in the South.

During the Reconstruction era the Southern states continued their care for the mentally ill that had been stimulated by Dorothea Dix during the antebellum years. Florida and Arkansas, which had not been a part of the earlier reform movement, joined the ranks and established institutions for the insane. In no other area of public welfare were the Southern states more willing to join in a nation-wide reform movement.[12] But there was a new problem for those who administered institutions for the insane, and that was the question of what to do about those insane persons who happened to be black. Before the war they had been generally ignored, and masters had been expected to do whatever was necessary for their slaves with mental problems. One is tempted to speculate that most masters were of the opinion that their slaves did not have mental problems and diagnosed such disorders as one more example of their devious efforts to avoid hard work (5:64–69). After the war, however, such persons were a public responsibility. Although it perhaps made no difference to the patients, the states felt obliged to separate them by race.[13] In 1865 the Tennessee legislature appropriated funds

[12] In appealing to the governor of Alabama for more support for the insane asylum, the superintendent said: "In every state of the Union, even where the desolations of war are most apparent, the piteous appeals of this unfortunate class have been most sacredly considered, and regarded paramount to all others" (4). See also Title VII, Article 143, of the 1868 Louisiana Constitution.

[13] In his report for 1865, the superintendent of the North Carolina Insane Asylum pointed out that the institution had received eight "colored patients," and he asserted that there was a problem regarding the accommodation of them in the same apartments "in common with the whites." To the extent, he said, that the apartments be applied to the use of the colored insane, they will "deprive the citizens, for whose benefit they were built." He then asked that the legislature make special provisions for the "colored insane" (46:8).

for the erection of a hospital for the "colored insane" (48:5–6). In 1868 South Carolina—as a part of its new public welfare program—repaired its lunatic asylum, placed it under a more efficient management, and made provision for the reception of colored patients (26:47). In North Carolina the Negro patients of Dix Hill, the state hospital for the insane, were transferred to a new state facility, exclusively for blacks, in Goldsboro.[14]

The question of the care of the poor has always been a source of dispute in the United States. In the nineteenth century there were many citizens who believed that almshouses and other centers for the relief of the destitute had no place in a country in which opportunities were regarded as unlimited and in which labor was generally in short supply. The Southern states were no exception, although there are early examples of public poor relief in the South as well as in the North. There was, however, no general program or policy for the care of the poor during Reconstruction. It was a question that was widely discussed in conventions, legislatures, and public gatherings, for privation was evident, and suffering transcended racial lines. "In many counties," the committee on relief of the Arkansas constitutional convention reported, "where the crop of the last season consisted chiefly of cotton, startling destitution prevails. Gaunt Famine stalks abroad: the people are crying out for bread." Even so, after much debate the legislature decided against providing state aid for the poor (27:233).

In 1870 the Louisiana legislature rejected a bill for the relief of the poor. Such a state-wide program, the reporting committee argued, was "calculated to encourage laziness and make the state of Louisiana a receptacle for the poor of other states." Instead, the state of Louisiana, as did other Southern states, encouraged local communities to do whatever they deemed necessary to provide relief to the poor (29:29).

Some states took a more definitive stand on relieving the poor. The Alabama Constitutional Convention of 1867 passed a resolution incorporating into the education section of the new constitution a provision for a poorhouse in each county with "no less than eighty acres of land attached" (31:24). Texas required each county to provide a "manual labor poor house, for taking care of, managing, employing, and supplying the wants of its indigent and poor inhabitants, under such regulations as the Legislature may direct" (51:38).

Southerners seemed much more disposed to offer public assistance to those physically handicapped than to those who were the victims of economic or social misfortune. In 1865 North Carolina already had a "deaf, dumb, and blind" institution—for whites only, to be sure—with a budget of more than $20,000 in United States currency (45). Georgia by 1866 had an Academy for the Deaf and Dumb, which Governor Charles J. Jenkins described as "another of those great humanitarian enterprises" (37:23). By that time, moreover, the state had a separate institution for the education of the blind (37: 22).[15] There is no reason to believe, in any of these cases, even after 1868, that

[14] The *Raleigh News and Observer* (21) gives a history of the Goldsboro facility. North Carolina asserted that it was the first state to set up a hospital exclusively for "colored insane," but Tennessee had authorized the erection of one "separate and apart from white patients" in 1865.

[15] Mississippi's Constitution of 1868 provided for schools for the deaf, dumb, and blind as well as for "houses of refuge for the correction and the reformation of juvenile offenders (41:740).

the institutions were not racially segregated.

The Southern states, saddled with the task of bringing order out of the chaos of the Civil War, only gradually evolved programs of public welfare that reflected a systematic approach to the problem. Even in the makeshift programs of the early postwar years, public welfare efforts all too frequently addressed themselves exclusively to the needs of the whites. This could be done in such areas as poor relief and education, but it was scarcely practical in the area of health. Even in the later years of Reconstruction, when there was a larger view of the importance of public welfare, the factor of race was ever present, and it dictated public policy even when it was not only an expensive but an absurd basis for public policy. What is frequently overlooked is that even after 1868, when the governments of the South were allegedly "radical," there was a sizable component of native white Southerners in government—indeed, a majority in several of the states—who were as opposed to equal treatment of the races as any Confederate had been. Add to that the indifference or even the downright opposition to racial equality on the part of many of the so-called carpetbaggers, and the setting was ideal for the introduction of racial segregation and even discrimination in public welfare programs.

The record of the Southern states in the area of public welfare is not a remarkable one. Given the antebellum approach to social problems, the chaos brought on by civil war, and the inordinate preoccupation with matters of race, it could hardly have been remarkable. But it was better than many historians have led us to believe. Historians of the Reconstruction era have been so preoccupied with politics, so anxious to condemn radicalism, and so determined to expose waste and corruption that they have not given adequate attention to many fundamental social problems or to the effort that was made to solve them. The states did establish for the first time in the South universal public education. They did give attention to the problem of children—with an oppressive program at first and then, later, a more enlightened one. They did attempt to set up agencies for the improvement of health conditions. They did attempt programs of poor relief, at the local level more than at the state level. And they were considering other programs—for the blind and deaf-mute, for example. The verdict they received from historians was that they were irresponsible, extravagant, profligate, and politically motivated. It must be said now that, with all their mistakes, shortsightedness, and prejudice, they made a start, albeit a halting one, toward the public assumption of responsibility for the less fortunate among them. Even if some of the things they did were open to serious question, they laid the foundation on which the future could build.

Received February 25, 1970

REFERENCES

BOOKS

1. Allen, Francis R. "Public Health Work in the Southeast, 1872–1941." Ph.D. dissertation, University of North Carolina, 1946.
2. Bentley, George R. *A History of the* *Freedmen's Bureau.* Philadelphia: University of Pennsylvania Press, 1955.
3. Bond, Horace Mann. *Negro Education in Alabama: A Study in Cotton and Steel.* Washington, D.C.: Associated Publishers, 1939.

4. Bryce, P., to Patton, Robert, December 14, 1867. Patton Papers. State Department of Archives and History. Montgomery, Alabama.

5. Cartwright, Samuel A. "Diseases and Peculiarities of the Negro Race." *De Bow's Review* 11 (July 1851): 64–69.

6. *Charleston Daily Courier,* July 4, 1865.

7. Coddington, Edwin B. "Soldiers' Relief in the Seaboard States of the Confederacy." *Mississippi Valley Historical Review* 37 (June 1950): 17–38.

8. Coulter, E. Merton. *The Confederate States of America, 1861–65.* Baton Rouge: Louisiana State University Press, 1950.

9. Dabney, Charles W. *Universal Education in the South.* Vol. 1. Chapel Hill: University of North Carolina Press, 1936.

10. Eaton, Clement. *Freedom of Thought in the Old South.* Durham, N.C.: Duke University Press, 1940.

11. ———. *A History of the Old South.* 2d ed. New York: Macmillan Co., 1966.

12. Fenner, E. D. *History of the Epidemic Yellow Fever at New Orleans, La., in 1853.* New York: Hall, Clayton & Co., 1854.

13. Fitzhugh, George. *Cannibals All! Or, Slaves without Masters,* edited by C. Vann Woodward. Cambridge: Harvard University Press, 1960.

14. Fleming, Walter L., ed. *Documentary History of Reconstruction.* Vol. 1. New York: McGraw-Hill Book Co., 1966.

15. Franklin, John Hope. *Reconstruction after the Civil War.* Chicago: University of Chicago Press, 1961.

16. Garner, James Wilford. *Reconstruction in Mississippi.* Gloucester, Mass.: Peter Smith, 1964.

17. Kibler, Lillian A. *Benjamin F. Perry, South Carolina Unionist.* Durham, N.C.: Duke University Press, 1946.

18. Knight, Edgar W. *Public Education in the South.* Boston: Ginn & Co., 1922.

19. Marshall, Helen E. *Dorothea Dix, Forgotten Samaritan.* Chapel Hill: University of North Carolina Press, 1937.

20. *North Carolina Standard,* March and April 1868.

21. *Raleigh News and Observer,* September 8, 1929.

22. Ramsdell, Charles W. *Behind the Lines in the Southern Confederacy.* Baton Rouge: Louisiana State University Press, 1944.

23. Shivers, Lyda Gordon. "The Social Welfare Movement in the South: A Study in Regional Culture and Social Organization." Ph.D. dissertation, University of North Carolina, 1935.

24. Shugg, Roger W. *Origins of Class Struggle in Louisiana.* University, La.: Louisiana State University Press, 1939.

25. Simkins, Francis B., and Patton, James W. *The Women of the Confederacy.* Richmond and New York: Garrett & Massie, 1936.

26. Simkins, Francis B., and Woody, Robert H. *South Carolina during Reconstruction.* Chapel Hill: University of North Carolina Press, 1932.

27. Staples, Thomas S. *Reconstruction in Arkansas, 1862–74.* New York, 1923.

28. Wharton, Vernon L. *The Negro in Mississippi, 1865–1890.* New York: Harper & Row, 1965.

29. Wisner, Elizabeth. *Public Welfare Administration in Louisiana.* Social Service Monographs, No. 11. Chicago: University of Chicago Press, 1930.

30. Zornow, William F. "State Aid for Indigent Soldiers and Their Families in Louisiana, 1861–1865." *Louisiana Historical Quarterly* 39 (July 1956): 375–80.

STATE DOCUMENTS

31. Alabama. *Official Journal of the Constitutional Convention of the State of Alabama.* Montgomery, 1868.

32. Arkansas. *Acts of the General Assembly of the State of Arkansas.* Little Rock, 1867.

33. ———. *The Constitution of the State of Arkansas, 1868.* Little Rock, 1869.

34. ———. *Journals of the House of Representatives for 1864–1865.* Little Rock, 1870.

35. Florida. *Acts and Resolutions Adopted by the Legislature of Florida at the First Session (1868).* Tallahassee, 1868.

36. Georgia. *Acts of the General Assembly of the State of Georgia, 1866.* Macon, 1867.

37. ———. *Journal of the House of Representatives of the State of Georgia.* Macon, 1866.

38. ———. *Journal of the Proceedings of the Convention of the People of Georgia.* Milledgeville, 1865.

39. Louisiana. *Debates in the Convention for the Revision and Amendment of the Constitution of the State of Louisiana.* New Orleans, 1864.

40. Louisiana. *Official Journal of the Proceedings of the Convention for Framing a Constitution for the State of Louisiana.* New Orleans, 1868.

41. Mississippi. *Journal of the Proceedings in the Mississippi Constitutional Convention, 1868.* Jackson, 1871.

42. ———. *Laws of the State of Mississippi, Passed at a Regular Session of the Mississippi Legislature, Held in the City of Jackson, October, November, and December, 1865.* Jackson, 1866.

43. North Carolina. *The Constitution of the State of North Carolina.* Raleigh, 1868.

44. ———. *Journal of the Constitutional Convention of the State of North Carolina at Its Session 1868.* Raleigh, 1868.

45. ———. *Report of the North Carolina Institution for the Deaf and Dumb and the Blind.* Raleigh, 1865.

46. ———. *Report of the Superintendent of Insane Asylum, Ending 30th of September, 1865.* Raleigh, 1865.

47. South Carolina. *Proceedings of the Constitutional Convention of South Carolina, Charleston, January 14 to March 17, 1868.* Charleston, 1868.

48. Tennessee. *Acts of the State of Tennessee, Second Session of the 34th General Assembly, 1865–66.* Nashville, 1866.

49. ———. *Journal of the Proceedings of the Convention of Delegates Elected by the People of Tennessee to Amend, Revise or Form a New Constitution.* Nashville, 1870.

50. Texas. *The Constitution as Amended and Ordinances of the Convention of 1866 for the State of Texas.* Austin, 1866.

51. ———. *Constitution of the State of Texas, Adopted at the Constitutional Convention Convened under the Reconstruction Acts of Congress.* Austin, 1869.

"SCIENTIFIC PHILANTHROPY," 1873–93

ROBERT H. BREMNER

"What shall it profit a beggar if he gain the whole world and lose his own soul?". . . . What would be thought of a man who should give medicines at random to every applicant, without troubling himself as to their effect, on the plea that he had not time to investigate the case, and that if he did not give, some poor sick creature might die for want of a remedy?[1]

IN THE bestowal of charity and in the prevention of misery, the world has reached a new epoch."[2] The speaker was Daniel Coit Gilman, president of Johns Hopkins University, and the time was 1893. Gilman's optimistic pronouncement reflected the views of those militant reformers who deemed pauperism to be the major danger confronting the nation and who thought the best way to attack the problem was to reform philanthropy. Throughout the earlier part of the nineteenth century there had been numerous attempts to suppress pauperism by inducing the rich to exercise greater care in the bestowal of charity. After the Civil War the crusade against pauperism was continued by a sizable group of men and women who addressed themselves with utmost seriousness to the task of applying rigorously systematic principles to charitable work. Their objective, in keeping with the spirit of the time, was to make philanthropy a science—the science of social therapeutics.[3] In this paper we shall examine the methods by which they sought to demonstrate that true charity was a matter of the head as well as the heart, and we shall consider some of the ways in which their efforts have influenced later developments in welfare and social reform.[4]

The scientific philanthropy movement began as a protest against the unsatisfactory operation of public and private relief agencies during the depression of 1873–78. Critics of prevailing methods of caring for the needy pointed out that at least half of the money raised for the victims of the depression was wasted on impostors, and that the portion actually received by the deserving poor tended to degrade rather than to elevate them. The charity reformers were particularly alarmed about mounting expenditures and taxation for public relief. Drawing upon American experience and English theory, they argued that "official assistance" was often corrupt and usually ineffectual. The burden of their complaint, however, was that public outdoor relief— that is, aid furnished outside of institutions—was unnecessary; private benevolence could and should assume entire

---

[1] Oliver Dyer, "The Condition of the Destitute and Outcast Children of the City of New York," in *Fourteenth Annual Report of the Superintendent of Public Instruction* (Albany, 1868), pp. 141–42.

[2] Daniel Coit Gilman, "A Panorama of Charitable Work in Many Lands," in Gilman, ed., *The Organization of Charities* (Baltimore: Johns Hopkins Press, 1894), p. xvii.

[3] D. O. Kellogg, "The Objects, Principles and Advantages of Association in Charities," *Journal of Social Science*, XII (1880), 86; and Amos G. Warner, *American Charities: A Study in Philanthropy and Economics* (New York and Boston: Thomas Y. Crowell & Co., 1894), pp. 399–402.

[4] This topic is dealt with in more detailed fashion in Robert H. Bremner, *From the Depths: The Discovery of Poverty in the United States* (New York: New York University Press, 1956), chaps iii and iv.

Social Service Review 30 (June 1956): 168–73
© 1956 by The University of Chicago

responsibility for noninstitutional relief.[5]

Unfortunately, experience during the depression had revealed private charity to be as lax in method and as baneful in effect as public relief. The reformers thought that kindly but mistaken philanthropic ventures had attracted hordes of vagrants into the cities with a resultant increase in crime, intoxication, and disease. They maintained that this indiscriminate, soup-kitchen charity was as incapable of aiding the truly deserving as it was powerless to cope with "the forces of experienced and crafty pauperism." It was "dispersed in tantalizing doles miserably inadequate for effectual succor where the need was genuine, and dealt out broadcast among the clamorous and impudent."[6] Even worse, the abundance of private relief agencies allegedly tempted workmen to forsake habits of industry and to become social parasites. A scandalized observer reported that charity was in effect siding with labor against capital: the unemployed, fed and lodged by unthinking philanthropists, refused to work except at exorbitant wages, and spent their savings on union dues and strike benefits.[7]

The well-publicized work of the London Charity Organization Society, founded in 1869, suggested a method of bringing order out of the chaos of private charity. During the late 1870's organizations patterned after the London Society were set up in a number of American communities, usually as a result of the efforts of the same individuals and groups active in the campaign to abolish public outdoor relief. The first fully developed charity organization society in the United States was established in Buffalo in 1877 by the Reverend S. H. Gurteen, an Episcopal clergyman who had formerly worked with the parent society in London. By 1883 similar organizations had been formed in twenty-five cities, including Boston and New York; and by a decade later nearly one hundred of them were functioning in cities and towns throughout the nation.[8]

The immediate purpose of the charity organization societies was to promote co-operation and higher standards of efficiency among the numerous groups already engaged in dispensing relief. Their method of operation was to secure registration of all applicants for public or private assistance, to investigate the need and worthiness of all persons seeking aid, and to encourage friendly visiting of the poor by volunteer workers drawn from the higher walks of life. The ultimate goal of the societies was to husband the charitable resources of each community so that money or other aid, instead of being dissipated on persons who did not really need material help, would be available in sufficient quantity to provide adequate assistance for all deserving cases.

Some of the techniques of charity organization had been accepted in principle, if not always observed in practice, long before the 1870's. What was unique about the new societies was that they

[5] S. H. Gurteen, "Beginning of Charity Organization in America," *Lend a Hand*, XIII (1894), 355–56; Charles D. Kellogg, "Charity Organization in the United States," *Proceedings of the National Conference of Charities and Correction, 1893* (Boston, 1893), pp. 68–69; and Seth Low, "The Problem of Pauperism in the Cities of Brooklyn and New York," *Proceedings of the Conference of Charities, 1879* (Boston, 1879), pp. 202–4.

[6] Henry E. Pellew, "Out-Door Relief Administration in New York City, 1878," *Proceedings of the Conference of Charities, 1878* (Boston, 1878), p. 72; and Charles D. Kellogg, "Charity Organization in the United States," *op. cit.*, p. 54.

[7] R. T. Davis, "Pauperism in the City of New York," *Proceedings of the Conference of Charities, 1874* (Boston, 1874), pp. 21–23.

[8] Frank Dekker Watson, *The Charity Organization Movement in the United States: A Study in American Philanthropy* (New York: Macmillan Co., 1922).

were not intended to function as relief associations. "Not alms but a friend" was their motto. Theoretically, they furnished no material aid to the poor from their own funds, but acted simply as bureaus of information, registration, and investigation, referring "helpable" applicants to the appropriate relief-dispensing agency. NO RELIEF GIVEN HERE, announced signs posted on both sides of the entrance to the Buffalo COS.[9] When prospective contributors to the New York Society asked its founder, Josephine Shaw Lowell, how much of their donations would go to the poor, Mrs. Lowell always replied: "Not one cent."[10]

The pioneers of the movement not only intended to furnish no alms from the funds of their societies, but sought to discourage the entire practice of almsgiving. Having already decided that outdoor relief should be provided by voluntary rather than tax-supported agencies, they now demanded that restraints be imposed on private benevolence. They recognized that it was sometimes necessary and proper to aid the poor in material ways, but they insisted that *in the interest of the recipients* such assistance should be granted with the utmost caution. "We must all remember that it is very easy to make our well-meant charity a curse to our fellow-men," warned one writer.[11] "Alms are like drugs, and are as dangerous," declared another; very often "they create an appetite which is more harmful than the pain which they relieve."[12]

The reformers' hostility to almsgiving was based on an individualistic interpretation of poverty and a pessimistic view of human nature. Mrs. Lowell, in many respects one of the most enlightened of the charity reformers, held as firmly as any of them to the conviction that "the usual cause of poverty is to be found in some deficiency—moral, mental, or physical—in the person who suffers." She took it for granted that no one would work if he did not have to, and that whenever the pressure of necessity was relaxed, workers inevitably tended to become idlers.[13]

From the reformers' point of view, the villains of the piece were the thoughtless philanthropists whose cruel kindness, by producing and perpetuating pauperism, wrought as much misery as war, famine, or pestilence. "We must reform those mild, well-meaning, tender-hearted, sweet-voiced criminals who insist upon indulging in indiscriminate charity," cried the Reverend H. L. Wayland, founder of the New Haven COS.[14] According to Gilman the most necessary step in the reform of these dangerous do-gooders was to make them aware that "they are not the most devoted to the poor who drop a quarter or a nickel in the hand of every beggar."[15] Almsgiving was counterfeit philanthropy; true charity required something much more demanding —"personal interest in persons."[16] Robert Treat Paine, who coined the slogan "Not alms but a friend," counseled friendly visitors of the Boston Associated Chari-

[9] Gurteen, *op. cit.*, p. 354.

[10] Community Service Society of New York, *Frontiers in Human Welfare: The Story of a Hundred Years of Service to the Community of New York, 1848–1948* (New York: The Society, 1948), p. 35.

[11] Joseph Henry Crooker, *Problems in American Society* (Boston: George H. Ellis, 1889), p. 112.

[12] Frederic Almy, "The Problem of Charity from Another Point of View," *Charities Review*, IV (1894–95), 170. For a similar expression of opinion, see Warner, *op. cit.*, p. 38.

[13] Josephine Shaw Lowell, "The True Aim of Charity Organization Societies," *The Forum*, XXI (1896), 495–96.

[14] H. L. Wayland, "A Scientific Basis of Charity," *Charities Review*, III (1893–94), 268, 273.

[15] Gilman, *op. cit.*, p. xvii.

[16] William Rhinelander Stewart, *The Philanthropic Work of Josephine Shaw Lowell* (New York: Macmillan Co., 1911), p. 82.

ties: "You are to give—what is far more precious than gold or silver—your own sympathy, and thought, and time, and labor." Doles of food and clothing and coal and stray coins seemed petty indeed, when one could give the poor what they really needed—"self-respect, hope, ambition, courage, character."[17] It was in this spirit that Washington Gladden advised delegates to the National Conference of Charities and Correction that Christians fulfilled the perfect law of charity, not by attempting to remove the entire burden of suffering from an unfortunate neighbor's shoulders, but by putting strength into the sufferer, so that he would be willing and proud to bear his burden.[18]

Despite these ethical considerations, the constant aim of charity organization was to separate philanthropy from religion and bring it into harmony with the principles of political economy. No one was more insistent on this point than the clergymen active in the movement. "There must be no attempt at proselytism on the part of agents or others employed by the organization" decreed the Reverend Gurteen. Furthermore, "There must be no sentiment in the matter. It must be treated as a business scheme."[19]

In striving to be businesslike the charity reformers at first tended to emphasize the detective and repressive aspects of their work. They regarded the apprehension of impostors as the principal object of the investigations conducted by COS

agents; and they deemed the files of family histories maintained in each society useful mainly as means of exposing cases of fraud and duplication. By the late 1880's, however, workers in the movement had begun to lay more stress upon the constructive purposes of charity organization. They now presented detection and repression as incidental to the positive benefits of scientific philanthropy, and described investigations as the necessary prerequisite to intelligent treatment of distress. "It is essential that the physician should know what ails his patient before he prescribes, and not give a splint to the consumptive and cod-liver oil to the man with broken bones," commented one student.[20] Just so, according to an analogy frequently drawn, the charity agent must ascertain the immediate and underlying causes of an applicant's need before attempting to treat the case. As another worker put it: "The possibility of imposture is not so much to be guarded against as the constant danger of mistakes. . . . Two-thirds of the errors in charity work arise from misinformation or lack of information."[21]

The shift in emphasis within charity organization developed in part in response to criticism directed at the movement from several quarters. Charity agents were well aware of the popular feeling that their efforts were designed mainly to protect the pocketbooks of the rich. They knew that it was often said that the motto of the charity organization societies should be "Neither alms nor a friend."[22] One of the leaders of the movement, critical of some of its tenden-

[17] Robert Treat Paine, "The Work of Volunteer Visitors of the Associated Charities among the Poor," *Journal of Social Science*, XII (1880), 103, 113.

[18] Washington Gladden, "The Perfect Law of Charity," *Proceedings of the National Conference of Charities and Correction, 1893* (Boston, 1893), pp. 277–78.

[19] S. H. Gurteen, "Charity Organizations," *Thirteenth Annual Report of the New York State Board of Charities* (Albany, 1880), p. 199.

[20] C. D. Kellogg, *op. cit.*, p. 73.

[21] Zilpha D. Smith, "Report of the Committee on Organization of Charities," *Proceedings of the National Conference of Charities and Correction, 1888* (Boston, 1888), pp. 126–27.

[22] Watson, *op. cit.*, p. 226, fn. 1.

cies, quoted with reluctant approval John Boyle O'Reilly's bitter lines:

The organized charity, scrimped and iced
In the name of a cautious, statistical Christ.[23]

No matter how dedicated to the principles of scientific philanthropy, charity workers could not be indifferent to repeated accusations that they gave the poor only good advice—and for that probably sent in a bill to the Almighty; that they assumed poverty to be the natural lot of the masses; and that their program sought merely to palliate rather than to correct social injustice.[24] A member of the New York COS pointed out the dilemma of scientific philanthropy when he plaintively remarked that the Society was on sure ground until it found a deserving case, and then it was all at sea.[25] But the charity organizations were no more at sea about the proper measures to be taken to help the deserving poor than was American society as a whole. The important thing was that charity workers came into daily contact with the problem and were constantly seeking answers to it. Considered as an agency of social reform, scientific philanthropy had obvious limitations—so many, in fact, that critics have argued that it actually impeded the correction of some outstanding abuses.[26] In the long

run, however, its effect on reform was more positive than negative; for despite the limited objectives and narrow sympathies of the founders of the movement, and often in ways that they did not anticipate, scientific philanthropy made valuable contributions to our understanding and handling of social problems.

In the first place, the individualistic orientation of the movement, which so many critics have deplored, fostered the development of a factual, undogmatic approach to social questions. The case method used by the charity organization societies required that each family or individual seeking assistance be treated as a unique problem. This necessitated the abandonment of preconceived notions about "the poor," "the oppressed," or "the depraved" and the substitution for these stereotypes of efforts to discover pertinent data about particular family histories.

In addition to introducing a more objective attitude into the study of social welfare, scientific philanthropy accumulated and organized a fund of detailed knowledge throwing needed light on the living standards of low-income families. As already noted, the basic task of the charity agents was to get the facts about the families they tried to help. In practice this meant obtaining information not only about personal character and habits, but also about earnings, expenditures, housing, health, and education. The thousands of case records in the files of charity organization societies provided more comprehensive, reliable, and specific data on the actual condition of the poor than had ever before been available to American students. Beginning in the

[23] J. O. S. Huntington, "Philanthropy—Its Success and Failure," in Jane Addams *et al.*, *Philanthropy and Social Progress* (New York and Boston: Thomas Y. Crowell & Co., 1893), p. 135. The quotation was from John Boyle O'Reilly, "In Bohemia" (1886).

[24] For some typical criticisms of the charity organization movement see James G. Schonfarber, "Charity from the Standpoint of the Knights of Labor," *Proceedings of the National Conference of Charities and Correction, 1890* (Boston, 1890), pp. 58–62; William Dean Howells, "Tribulations of a Cheerful Giver," in *Impressions and Experiences* (New York: Harper & Bros., 1896), pp. 150–88; and Jeffrey R. Brackett, "Charity Organization," *Charities Review*, VII (1898–99), 182.

[25] Quoted in Huntington, *op. cit.*, p. 118.

[26] On this point, see Florence Kelley, "Labor Legislation and Philanthropy in Illinois," *Charities Review*, X (1900–1901), 287–88; and J. O. S. Huntington, "Philanthropy and Morality," in Addams *et al.*, *op. cit.*, p. 176.

1880's, and increasingly thereafter, these records were utilized in social research.[27]

The most important result of scientific philanthropy was to make later students think in terms of preventing rather than of relieving distress. From the start the movement was committed to the idea of restraining the charitable impulse. Its leaders, believing that people ought to be self-supporting, resented the very necessity for charity. Workers in the movement applauded statements such as, "The true charity is that which removes the need for charity" and "The first duty of a community . . . is not to feed the hungry and clothe the naked, but to prevent people from being hungry and naked."[28] Very often, it is true, advocates of scientific philanthropy thought that "preventing pauperism" involved only the withholding of alms, and that "uprooting the sources of poverty" meant reforming individual character. By logical extention, however, "prevention" could be interpreted to mean the removal of the economic and environmental causes of distress, and in the 1890's it was already being used in this sense by experienced charity workers.[29]

A widely quoted observation of Professor Francis G. Peabody of Harvard is perhaps still the best summary of the achievement of scientific philanthropy: "The old charity had but one way of expression; the new charity has a thousand channels."[30] These channels did not always follow the old paths or run in the old direction. Scientific philanthropy had always recognized that the treatment of poverty required more fundamental remedies than an increase in generosity on the part of the rich. But the fundamental remedies, originally thought of as purges to be administered exclusively to the poor, eventually came to be regarded as correctives for the maladjustments of society. During the 1890's charity workers acknowledged that not only pauperism and poor relief, but poverty, too, impinged on all the other issues affecting the living conditions of the masses — issues such as wages, working conditions, housing, industrial accidents, illness, and unemployment. Before the decade had closed practicing philanthropists were expressing the opinion that pauperism and poverty should no longer be treated as isolated phenomena, but rather as "part of the study of the economic life of the people as a whole." Solutions for these problems, it was now believed, could be achieved only through an uplifting of the general conditions of life of all the people of the nation.[31]

Two decades of experience and study had preceded the emergence of this point of view. With its gradual acceptance around the turn of the century scientific philanthropy evolved into the newer movement of preventive social work, a movement destined to exert a strong influence on the social reforms of the Progressive era.

DEPARTMENT OF HISTORY
OHIO STATE UNIVERSITY

Received January 10, 1956

[27] There are observations on this aspect of charity organization in John R. Commons, *Myself* (New York: Macmillan Co., 1934), p. 43; and Edward T. Devine, *When Social Work Was Young* (New York: Macmillan Co., 1939), pp. 34–35, 69–70.

[28] Wayland, *op. cit.*, p. 273; and Davis, *op. cit.*, p. 24.

[29] See, for example, Warner, *op. cit.*, p. 399.

[30] Francis G. Peabody, "The Problem of Charity," in Gilman, ed., *The Organization of Charities*, p. xxii.

[31] Robert Treat Paine, "Pauperism in Great Cities: Its Four Chief Causes," in John H. Finley, ed., *The Public Treatment of Pauperism* (Baltimore: Johns Hopkins Press, 1894), pp. 25–54; and James Mavor, "The Relation of Economic Study to Public and Private Charity," *Annals of the American Academy of Political and Social Science*, IV (1893–94), 39–40.

RAYMOND ROBINS: THE SETTLEMENT WORKER
AS MUNICIPAL REFORMER

ALLEN F. DAVIS

THE modern social worker has been criticized for being more a bureaucrat than a reformer, more concerned with holding conferences than with improving social welfare. In a recent article, Marion K. Sanders charges that the social worker has gained professional status only at the expense of his sense of mission. She suggests that perhaps the modern social worker should strive to recapture some of the dedication and idealism that inspired the early settlement workers.[1]

The early settlement workers were idealistic, but their idealism was often tempered by the reality of living in a slum neighborhood. Many settlements had little impact outside their local areas, but settlements like South End House in Boston, Henry Street and University Settlements in New York, Chicago Commons and Hull-House in Chicago became centers of investigation and discussion, as well as points of agitation, in the movement to make the city a better place in which to live. Settlement workers participated in, and sometimes led, the fight for better housing laws, shorter work hours, and better working conditions, and their surveys and reports provided the basis for some of the legislation that improved urban living in the Progressive era. Some historians have recognized the important role played by the settlement worker in municipal reform, but no one has treated

their contribution in detail, and other historians still emphasize the local and impractical aspects of the early settlement movement.[2] The modern social worker, on his part, studies only that aspect of the early settlement movement that aided in the development of professional social work.[3] The typical settlement worker was probably an unmarried woman, but few people better combined a sense of mission with a practical approach to reform than did Raymond Robins. Robins, who led the Red Cross expedition to Russia in 1917, is usually thought of in connection with Russian-American relations.[4] His importance as a social worker and progressive reformer has been overlooked.

[1] "Social Work: A Profession Chasing Its Tail," *Harper's Magazine*, CCXIV (March, 1957), 56–62.

[2] For brief, but favorable, accounts of the reform aspects of the settlement movement, see Charles A. and Mary R. Beard, *The American Spirit: A Study of the Idea of Civilization* (New York: Macmillan Co., 1942), pp. 477–79; Robert H. Bremner, *From the Depths: The Discovery of Poverty in the United States* (New York: New York University Press, 1956), pp. 60–66. For a less favorable view of the settlement movement, see Oscar Handlin, *The Uprooted* (Boston: Little, Brown & Co., 1951), pp. 283–84; Arthur M. Schlesinger, *The Rise of the City, 1878–1898* (New York: Macmillan Co., 1933), pp. 351–53.

[3] See, e.g., Frank J. Bruno, *Trends in Social Work* (New York: Columbia University Press, 1948), pp. 112–19; Lois Corke De Santis, "Settlements and Neighborhood Centers," *Social Work Year Book, 1957*, pp. 512–17.

[4] See George Kennan, *Soviet-American Relations, 1917–1920*, Vol. I: *Russia Leaves the War*, and Vol. II: *The Decision To Intervene* (Princeton: Princeton University Press, 1956–57); William A. Williams, *American-Russian Relations, 1781–1947* (New York: Rinehart & Co., 1952).

Social Service Review 33 (June 1959): 131–41
© 1959 by The University of Chicago

The early life of Raymond Robins reads like an adventure story. While most settlement workers came directly from college to life in the slums, Robins had an incredible series of experiences before he become a settlement worker at the age of twenty-seven. His early contacts and experiences went a long way toward making him realistic in his approach to reform. Brought up by an uncle in Florida, Robins at fifteen was in business for himself raising fruit. At seventeen, without finishing high school, he left his fruit-growing venture and his uncle's home to become, in quick succession, a phosphate miner, a day laborer, and a storekeeper. Then in 1891 the report of a dollar a day lured him to Tennessee to the dangerous, back-breaking work of a coal miner. Thrown in with older, more experienced men, Robins learned about strikes and labor unions. He helped provoke a strike himself, and then drifted to Colorado where he worked in a silver mine and attended night school. He also joined a union, and, for the first time, heard about Henry George and the single tax. Like Tom Johnson, Clarence Darrow, and many other reformers, Robins was greatly influenced by *Progress and Poverty*.[5]

Before he was twenty-one, Robins had drifted across the country three times. He made a considerable amount of money prospecting for kaolin in Florida and for gold in New Mexico. He associated with all kinds of men, from tramps to Wall Street bankers, and was impressed with the contrast he found in American life. He was struck by the extreme poverty and the political corruption in the cities, from San Francisco to New York, and he vowed that some day he would help do something about it.[6]

In order to prepare himself for his reform role, he decided to study law. Reversing the usual procedure, Robins read law in a Florida law office, passed the bar examination in 1895, and then entered law school. In one year he finished a three-year course at Columbia Law School in Washington, D.C., and also found time to take a special course for orators. On the move once again, he headed for San Francisco in June, 1896. Stopping long enough in Chicago to hear Bryan's "Cross of Gold" speech, he became converted to Bryan's cause. In San Francisco, Robins was an immediate success as a lawyer and as a political campaigner for Bryan. But success came easily for Raymond Robins. In July, 1897, he gave up his position and headed for the Klondike gold fields.[7]

THE LURE OF GOLD
AND RELIGION

The story of Robins' Alaskan adventures is even more unbelievable than are his earlier wanderings. He discovered gold in Alaska, but that was not all he discovered. An agnostic during most of his adult life, suddenly in Alaska he became converted to Christianity. He applied for and received licenses to preach from both the Methodist and the Congregational church; then in 1899 he went, as a Christian minister, to the law-

[5] Raymond Robins to Frank Bodine, December 22, 1895, Robins' MSS, State Historical Society of Wisconsin (all subsequent items not otherwise identified are from this collection); Elizabeth Robins, *Raymond and I* (New York: Macmillan Co., 1956), pp. 15 ff.; William A. Williams, "Raymond Robins and Russian-American Relations, 1917–1938" (unpublished Ph.D. dissertation, University of Wisconsin, 1950), pp. 5–6.

[6] Robins to Bodine, December 22, 1895; E. Robins, *op. cit.*, pp. 18–20.

[7] Robins to Bodine, December 22, 1895; "Raymond Robins," *Public*, X (September 12, 1907), 582; E. Robins, *op. cit.*, pp. 26–31.

less boom town of Nome. There for a year and a half he preached the gospel. He also organized a hospital, a school, and a literary club and helped to clear up some of the vice and corruption in the gold-mining town.[8]

Raymond Robins, however, was not content to remain in Nome. He was thinking of reform on a much larger scale. Alaskan gold and his earlier ventures made him financially independent. Religious conversion gave purpose to his vague thoughts of reform. Before he left Alaska he made a vow to dedicate his money and his time for the rest of his life to bettering the economic conditions of the laboring man, to improving the character of government, and to developing and strengthening the moral sanctions in society.[9] One of his friends in Alaska told him about the work that social settlement leaders were trying to do. To Raymond Robins a social settlement seemed like a practical place to begin his work for reform. In February, 1901, he wandered into Chicago Commons and asked Graham Taylor's permission to work full time at his own expense.[10]

Chicago in 1901 was a city of stockyards and railroads, a city of crowded tenement districts that were becoming more crowded every day as Italians, Slavs, and Poles in increasing numbers added new elements, or at least new emphasis, to the city's problems. It was a city that Lincoln Steffens described as "first in violence, deepest in dirt, loud, lawless, unlovely, ill-smelling, irreverent, new; an overgrown gawk of a village, the tough among cities, a spectacle for the nation." But Chicago was not all bad; even Steffens was impressed by the relatively good municipal government. The bosses still ruled in most of the wards, he decided, but "politically and morally speaking Chicago should be celebrated among American cities for reform."[11]

Much of this reform was the result of the efforts of a small number of civic leaders who had organized the Civic Federation (which in the late nineties pushed through a new civil-service law, fought political graft, dirty streets, and gambling houses) and the Municipal Voters' League (which tried to select good candidates for city offices). Much of the impetus for the Civic Federation, the Municipal Voters' League, and other reform organizations came from a remarkable group of young men and women who centered their activities at the social settlements. Most famous were Jane Addams at Hull-House, Mary McDowell at the University of Chicago Settlement, and Graham Taylor at Chicago Commons.[12]

CHICAGO COMMONS AND BEYOND

Chicago Commons had been founded in 1894 in "the most crowded river ward in Chicago." Located on the West Side, the Seventeenth Ward was predominantly Italian, Polish, and German, but it was a ward in which two-party rivalry was still real. From the beginning Chicago Commons, through the Seven-

[8] E. M. Rininger to L. S. Dickey, July 24, 1908; E. Robins, op. cit., passim; Albert J. Nock, "Raymond Robins," American Magazine, VII (November, 1910), 41.

[9] Mary E. Dreier, Margaret Dreier Robins: Her Life, Letters, and Work (New York: Island Press Cooperative, 1950), p. 24.

[10] Graham Taylor, Chicago Commons through Forty Years (Chicago: Chicago Commons Assoc., 1936), p. 260.

[11] Lincoln Steffens, The Shame of the Cities (New York: McClure, Phillips & Co., 1905), pp. 234–35.

[12] Harvey Wish, "Altgeld and the Progressive Tradition," American Historical Review, XLVI (July, 1941), 813–31.

teenth Ward Community Club, exerted a strong influence on ward politics. In 1896, the settlement club had nominated and elected an independent candidate for alderman. The *Commons,* its monthly publication containing comments on all phases of social work as well as on the political and industrial situation, gradually gained a nation-wide circulation. Locally, its weekly "free-floor discussion," attended by anarchists and labor leaders as well as university professors, acted as a "safety valve for the neighborhood."[13]

Raymond Robins quickly began to take part in the various activities of the settlement. He became moderator of the "free-floor discussion," and when Graham Taylor was away he filled in as editor of the *Commons.* His most effective work, however, was with the Seventeenth Ward Community Club (made up of young men who tried by various means to make the ward a better place in which to live). He organized a group of volunteer street inspectors (probably borrowing this idea from Hull-House) and, with Robert Hunter, began work for a series of parks and playgrounds.[14] He became a member of the Municipal Voters' League and worked through its organization to get the best possible candidates to run for political offices in the ward. In 1902, Robins helped to persuade William Dever, a young Irishman who had studied law at night while working in a tannery during the day, to run on the Democratic ticket for alderman.

With the enthusiastic backing of Robins and the Community Club, Dever was able to win the election. He served for five terms in the City Council and cooperated closely with Robins on many reform projects.[15]

Graham Taylor and several other prominent Chicago citizens urged Robins to run for the state senate in an attempt to defeat two especially corrupt candidates, but Robins preferred to remain in the background. Instead, John J. McManaman was nominated on an independent ticket. Thanks primarily to the active campaigning of Robins and Clarence Darrow and to the energetic support of the Seventeenth Ward Community Club and the labor unions, McManaman was able to defeat both regular party candidates in a district in which an independent had never won before. In his first few months at Chicago Commons, Raymond Robins demonstrated to Graham Taylor that he was a "past master of ward politics." He did not, however, confine his activities to one ward. The settlement, to Raymond Robins, was more than an instrument for neighborhood improvement.[16]

Not many months after Robins arrived in Chicago, the nation was shocked by the assassination of President McKinley by an anarchist in Buffalo, New York. In Chicago, where the memory of the Haymarket Affair was still vivid, a police dragnet arrested hundreds of people, most of them immigrants suspected of holding radical views. One of those arrested was Abraham Isaacs, a Russian immigrant and the leader of a society of

---

[13] Graham R. Taylor, "Chicago Settlements in Ward Politics," *Charities and the Commons,* XVI (May, 1906), 183–85; Robert Woods and Albert Kennedy, *The Settlement Horizon: A National Estimate* (New York: Russell Sage Foundation, 1922), p. 224.

[14] Taylor, *Chicago Commons,* pp. 259–60; Joliet Freeclosko to Robins, May 31, 1901, December 31, 1901.

[15] Taylor, *Chicago Commons,* p. 71; Graham Taylor to Robins, December 20, 1902. Dever later became judge of the Superior Court of Cook County and then Mayor of Chicago.

[16] Taylor, *Chicago Commons,* pp. 133–44, 259; *Chicago Tribune,* September 10, 1901.

philosophical anarchists. Isaacs was a thoughtful, sensitive, well-educated man in his mid-fifties. He was married and had a sixteen-year-old daughter and a twenty-two-year-old son. He edited a paper called *Free Society,* and regularly attended the free-floor discussions at the Commons, where he was always a vigorous opponent of the socialists. On the night of the President's assassination, officers of the Detective Bureau entered the Isaacs' tenement dwelling and arrested Isaacs along with his wife and two children. They destroyed his presses and confiscated his books (including his volumes of Shakespeare) on the grounds that they were incendiary literature. Raymond Robins and Jane Addams immediately rushed to his defense. They believed that free discussion at the settlements as well as the right of free speech and ordinary justice were at stake. They attempted to get the prisoners released on bail, but when that failed they went directly to the Mayor to protest against his use of the police power. Because of their intervention the Isaacs family was released and the damaged property replaced. Windows were broken at both Hull-House and Chicago Commons by those who disagreed with the action of the two settlement leaders, but with this case as a precedent all those arrested because of radical views were quickly released.[17]

"THE ORACLE OF THE SETTLEMENTS"

Chicago soon heard more about Raymond Robins. Various groups discovered that he loved to make speeches. More important, he had something to say and said it entertainingly. He soon became known as "the oracle of the set-

[17] Robins to Medill McCormick, September 5, 1914; Taylor, *Chicago Commons,* pp. 133–34.

tlements," and was considered by many second only to William Jennings Bryan as an orator. Robins spoke before women's clubs, settlement houses, church organizations, young peoples' groups, labor unions, high-school commencements, businessmen's lunches, single-tax clubs, and socialist organizations. He told of his Alaskan experiences. He talked of the "social spirit," of the need for labor to organize and for the churches to become more concerned with the "Industrial Situation." He talked about municipal problems, school problems, the problem of the immigrant, and always about the need for reform. He spoke deliberately and carefully from notes, making only a few major points in each speech but vividly illustrating each point with his own personal experiences. The urgency of his appeal was especially effective. "The dollar must give way to the home," he anounced on one occasion, "dividends must be second to childhood and womanhood; all industry must conform to this standard, both the state and the church must sit in judgment; unfair working conditions, dishonest competition must be condemned and outlawed."[18]

Statements of this kind and his old union card quickly won him friends in organized labor in Chicago. He met John Fitzpatrick, a horseshoer by trade but president of the Chicago Federation of Labor, and Margaret Haley, the fiery little Irishwoman who was president of the Chicago Teachers' Federation. He also met John Mitchell, president of the United Mine Workers. Robins so impressed Mitchell that in October, 1903, during the crisis of the anthracite coal miners' strike, he was asked to attend

[18] "Raymond Robins," *Public,* X (September 12, 1907), 585. See also outline notes for speeches 1901–5, Robins MSS; Nock, *op. cit.,* p. 41.

the mediation conferences and was chosen to speak for the delegation that visited President Theodore Roosevelt to demand arbitration. This was his first contact with Roosevelt. (Later the two would become good friends.) Although impressed with Roosevelt's handling of the strike, Robins remained a Bryan Democrat.[19]

Robins' open support of organized labor, plus his tendency to offer the single tax on land as the eventual solution of the nation's social problems, marked him in the minds of many people as a radical. On several occasions Graham Taylor thought it necessary to caution him about emphasizing tax reform, especially when he was addressing business and church groups. In spite of warnings, Robins joined the Chicago Henry George Association, made frequent speeches at single-tax gatherings, and became the close friend of Louis Post, the editor of the *Public* (probably the country's major single-tax journal). His single-tax friends looked upon his settlement work as next to useless. Robins annoyed them by refusing to devote his full time to the single tax. Raymond Robins, a practical politician, knew that immediate adoption of the single tax was impossible. While he continued to support single-tax schemes, he devoted most of his time to other methods of reform.[20]

In March, 1902, he was appointed to the position of superintendent of the Municipal Lodging House. He succeeded Robert Hunter, another settlement worker and, later, author of a book called *Poverty*. The Municipal Lodging House, which had been founded in 1900 at the insistence of the City Homes Association (whose membership included Jane Addams, Mrs. Cyrus McCormick, and Mrs. Emmons Blaine), represented something of a new departure in the control of the tramp problem in a large city. At the Municipal Lodging House any man in need could receive, free of charge, two meals, a bath, and a bed for one night. Under Robins' direction, the Lodging House made an attempt to separate the sick from the well and the drifters from those who wanted work. An employment bureau was set up to get the employable men permanent jobs, replacing, in part, the indiscriminate "work test" used by so many charity organizations. Most of the men who visited the Lodging House were native-born, but Robins and his assistant, James Mullenbach (also of Chicago Commons), helped many disillusioned immigrants to return to their native lands.[21]

Robins' experiences with all kinds of men, in mining camps, on freight trains, and in Alaska, helped him to look upon these "down and outers" with a sympathy and understanding impossible for many social workers. He was convinced that in most cases it was not their fault but the fault of American society that made them tramps and bums and alcoholics. Three years as head of the Municipal Lodging House made Raymond Robins more convinced that something was wrong in America, more sure that he must do something about it.[22]

[19] Memo, n.d., Robins' MSS. See also Williams, "Raymond Robins and Russian-American Relations," p. 17.

[20] Taylor to Robins, September 1, 1902; Robins to F. B. Fillebone, February 12, 1901; Joseph Leggett to Robins, May 1, 1901; "News Notes," *Public*, VI (September 12, 1903), 362.

[21] "The Month at Chicago Commons," *Commons*, VII (April, 1902), 20; Raymond Robins, "The Tramp Problem and Municipal Correction," *Commons*, VI (September, 1902), 1–9; Robins to Benjamin March, January, 1904.

[22] R. Robins to E. Robins, July 5, 1914.

POLITICS AND ROMANCE

Robins continued to live at Chicago Commons and to take an active part in the settlement's activities until July, 1903, when he was appointed head resident of Northwestern University Settlement. Northwestern Settlement, founded by Charles Zueblin in 1891, was located only a mile from Chicago Commons on the opposite side of the Seventeenth Ward. Here Robins organized a Civic Club very similar to the Community Club at the Commons. Through the co-operation of Northwestern Settlement and Chicago Commons, an independent political organization grew up that managed to control the votes in the ward. Usually the best possible regular party nominee was supported, but, if necessary, an independent candidate was nominated.[23] Three weeks before the election in 1906, William Dever, alderman from the Seventeenth Ward, voted for an ordinance that raised the license fee for saloons. In a ward in which there were over four hundred saloons, this was considered political suicide. The Civic Club and the Community Club rallied to Dever's support. They worked long and hard at a campaign that caused more excitement than a mayoralty election. The result again showed the power of independent organization. The Italian vote in the ward refused to be "delivered" as the bosses directed, and Dever was re-elected by a large majority. In one ward, at least, the social settlement was an effective antidote to boss rule in local politics.[24]

While Graham Taylor was content to confine the settlement's political influence to the ward, Raymond Robins felt

that one honest alderman, one clean ward, did very little to aid the larger reform picture that was always in his mind.[25] Robins began to think of reform in terms of the whole city. He toured the city wards, urging interested groups to take part in "practical politics" in order to defeat the bosses at their own game. He encouraged a careful study of the precinct vote, a knowledge of the local situation, friendship with the local voters, and then co-operation with the politicians in order to elect the best candidate or, at least, a reasonably good one. Above all, he urged people to get interested in politics, for this was the only way reform could be accomplished.[26]

Quite suddenly in April, 1905, Robins became interested in something besides reform. While in New York on a speaking engagement he was introduced to Margaret Dreier, a young social worker who came from a wealthy and socially prominent New York family. They found more in common than their mutual concern for the problems of the working class, though this was the beginning. Two months later they were married.[27] Returning to Chicago, they moved into a third-floor tenement apartment located midway between Chicago Commons and Northwestern Settlement. This little cold-water flat at 1437 Ohio Street became the base from which Raymond and Margaret Robins launched their various reform ventures for nearly twenty years. It was also "home" where they enter-

---

[23] Woods and Kennedy, op. cit., p. 225.

[24] Taylor, "Chicago Settlements in Ward Politics," loc. cit.

[25] Taylor to Robins, December 20, 1902. Taylor personally took part in many city-wide reform schemes and occasionally in city politics, but he refused to support one party or to involve the settlement politically outside the ward.

[26] "Outline of Plan To Function Independent Citizens in Practical Politics," n.d., Robins' MSS; Public, VII (May 28, 1904), 113.

[27] Dreier, op. cit., pp. 24–25; Robins to Margaret Dreier, May 8, 1905.

tained immigrants and college professors, labor leaders and ministers. There were never quite enough chairs to seat all the people who gathered there to discuss the nation's problems, but that did not seem to matter. The milk bill was out of all proportion to their needs, because Mr. and Mrs. Robins provided milk for most of the children in the neighborhood. Their little flat was hot in summer, cold in winter, and without water most of the time; yet they never talked of moving. Margaret Robins was especially active in the Women's Trade Union League, but she supported her husband in his schemes for a better Chicago. Their decision to live midway between two of the oldest settlements in Chicago was no accident, for Robins had learned, in more than four years of settlement work, that a great part of the spirit of reform in Chicago emanated from the settlements.[28]

In 1905, Robins and Allen T. Burns, another young settlement worker, actively supported Republican John Harlan in the mayoralty campaign.[29] Robins, normally a Democrat, had known Harlan (the son of his law-school teacher) for several years. The principal issue of the campaign was municipal ownership of street railways. During the campaign, the Democratic candidate, Judge Edward Dunne, supported municipal ownership a little more vigorously than did Harlan, and it was Dunne who was elected. Robins made several speeches for Harlan, and, in the process, met a young man not yet out of law school, Harold Ickes, who was managing Harlan's campaign. Robins and Ickes became good friends, and remained political partners for many years.[30]

"AGGRESSIVE, POLITICAL-MINDED SOCIAL WORKER"

When it became quite apparent, after the election of 1905, that Edward Dunne was doing his best to give Chicago a good administration, Robins, in an open letter, pledged his support to the new mayor. Dunne took him at his word and quickly began to utilize this "aggressive, political-minded social worker."[31] Robins was appointed to the advisory committee of the Municipal Ownership League and was made a member of the school board. He also was made chairman of the Mayor's nominating committee, charged with investigating the records and qualifications of all Democratic candidates for alderman in the city.[32] In conducting this investigation, Robins was able to use information and techniques that he had developed at Northwestern Settlement and at Chicago Commons. A few days after he filed his final report with the Mayor, he was attacked and severely beaten by three men. The *Chicago Tribune* was outraged at this open attack on a well-known "settlement worker and city reformer." Both the *Tribune* and the *Record-Herald* blamed the attack on "Ed" Carrol, a gangster and former labor leader who had been denounced as "utterly unfit" in Robins' report ("in a ward where such a report practically meant his defeat at the primaries"). Robins was not seriously injured, but the incident demonstrated to him how one element in Chicago felt

---

[28] Dreier, *op. cit.*, pp. 26–27, 48–49.

[29] Allen T. Burns to Robins, March 18, 1905.

[30] Harold L. Ickes, *The Autobiography of a Curmudgeon* (New York: Reynal & Hitchcock, 1943), p. 107.

[31] Robins to Edward F. Dunne, May 8, 1909; Ickes, *loc. cit.*

[32] George Schilling to Robins, December 29, 1905.

about the importance of his work.[33]

Together with Harold Ickes and Charles Merriam (professor of political science at the University of Chicago), Robins led a fight in 1906 and 1907 for a revision of the city charter. He advocated the inclusion of a corrupt-practices act (forcing publication of campaign expenses) and a direct primary provision. The charter convention, however, threw out both proposals, added provisions that reorganized the wards, made the school board responsible to the mayor, and increased the terms of the aldermen. Both Ickes and Robins opposed the passage of this charter. With the co-operation of the Community Club, the Civic Club, and the Municipal Voters' League, they were, at least in part, responsible for its defeat.[34]

Robins joined a great variety of reform organizations in the city and state, but, like many other reformers in American cities, he devoted much of his time and effort to supporting the fight for municipal ownership of street railways. In Chicago, Charles T. Yerkes, among others, had built a huge commercial empire out of the city's transportation system. Here a large portion of the corruption in Chicago was centered. Edward Dunne, after his election as mayor in 1905, declared war on the "traction interests." Raymond Robins was his chief strategist in the fight that followed. Robins made speeches, helped to win the support of the labor unions, and spent a great deal of his own money in preparing and circulating petitions. A referendum showed that the majority of the voters favored municipal ownership, but the powerful traction group was able to checkmate the reformers in the City Council. The battle for municipal ownership was lost, at least for the time.[35] Robins, however, was no stranger to lost causes. He turned his attention to reform in another area.

THE SCHOOL BOARD AND THE
RISKS OF REFORM

The social settlements in Chicago had a close relationship with the public schools in the city. Classes in English and history as well as the more "practical" subjects were taught at most settlements, usually in co-operation with the schools in the neighborhood. The settlements were often pioneers in the field of adult education and in introducing new teaching techniques.[36] It is not surprising then that Raymond Robins was concerned about the public school situation in Chicago. School affairs in Chicago had long been tied to politics, and most school boards (appointed by the mayor) had little interest in, and less knowledge about, the conditions of education in the city. Mayor Dunne, however, "owing largely to the influence of Robins," appointed "the best board of education Chicago ever had." The board included Jane Addams, Mrs. Emmons Blaine, Louis Post, Dr. Cornelia DeBey, John Sonesteby, and Robins himself.[37]

The new school board, with the close

[33] *Chicago Tribune*, February 18 and 20, 1906; *Chicago Record-Herald*, February 18, 1906.

[34] Raymond Robins, "The Charter Situation: What Next?" *City Club Bulletin* [Chicago], I (October 23, 1907), 217–20; Merriot Hoover to Robins, September 7, 1907.

[35] Margaret Haley to Robins, December 11, 1905; Ickes, *op. cit.*, pp. 107–8; Edward F. Dunne, "Our Fight for Municipal Ownership," *Independent*, LXI (October 18, 1906), 927–30.

[36] See Lawrence A. Cremin, "The Progressive Movement in American Education: A Perspective," *Harvard Educational Review*, XXVII (Fall, 1957), 257–62.

[37] Ickes, *op. cit.*, p. 107; "Raymond Robins," *Public*, X (September 21, 1907), 584.

co-operation of Margaret Haley of the Chicago Teachers' Federation, immediately launched an attack on education in Chicago. During the next two years the new board reduced the number of pupils per room from fifty-four to forty; it abolished promotional examinations and the secret marking system for teachers. It increased teachers' salaries and showed clearly that book and coal contracts had been given out without competition. The most controversial thing the new school board did was to conduct an investigation of land leased from Chicago schools by several businesses, including the *Chicago Tribune* and the *Chicago Daily News*. The investigation revealed that the *Tribune*, especially, had been influential in getting a land re-evaluation clause struck out of the agreement so that it was paying thousands of dollars less in rent than the land was worth.[38]

It was not long before the newspapers of Chicago, led by the *Tribune*, were vigorously attacking the Dunne school board, calling the members "radicals," "socialists," "tools of labor," and "subservient to Roman Catholic interests." The attack reached its height on October 19, 1906, when the *Tribune* referred to the members of the board as "freaks, cranks, monomaniacs, and boodlers."[39]

In the spring of 1907, Dunne was defeated for re-election by Fred Busse. The first thing Busse did upon taking office was to demand the resignation of twelve of the twenty-one members of the school board. Raymond Robins, Louis

Post, and Cornelia DeBey led the group of seven members who refused to resign on the ground that the Mayor did not have the power to remove them. Led by the *Tribune*, the Chicago newspapers (with the exception of the *Public*, the *Union Labor Advocate*, and the *Daily Socialist*) supported Mayor Busse's action.[40]

Jane Addams was one of the few members of the board who were not asked to resign. Robins and Post expected her to take a definite stand in their favor, but "Saint Jane" (as she was called by Robins, with something less than reverence) refused to take a position either for or against the expelled members. Earlier Margaret Robins had offered to replace up to $20,000 any support withdrawn from Hull-House because of her position on the school board. Even this offer, however, did not move Jane Addams from her cautious position.[41]

The settlement worker who played an active role in city affairs risked the reputation and the financial support of his

[38] Dreier, *op. cit.*, pp. 30–31; *Union Labor Advocate*, VII (September, 1907), 8–12; Jane Addams, *Twenty Years at Hull-House* (New York: Macmillan Co., 1910), p. 338.

[39] *Chicago Tribune*, October 3, 8, 10, 28, 31, November 1, 5, 1906; *Chicago Record-Herald*, October 31, November 5, 29, 1906; Dreier, *op. cit.*, p. 293.

[40] *Chicago Record-Herald*, May 19–28, 1907; *Chicago Tribune*, May 19–28, 1907; *Chicago Daily Socialist*, May 19–28, 1907; *Union Labor Advocate*, VII (June, 1907), 8–9; *Public*, X (June 29, 1907), 300; Dreier, *op. cit.*, pp. 29–31. After the matter was brought to court, largely at Robins' expense, the school board members were reinstated in December, 1907. See Ickes to Robins, December 17, 1907.

[41] *Chicago Record-Herald*, May 23, 24, 1907; Daniel Kiefer to Robins, May 27, 1907; Margaret Robins to Jane Addams, November, 1906, in Dreier, *op. cit.*, p. 31; Addams, *op. cit.*, pp. 328–39. The cautious position of Jane Addams is difficult to explain. Her own account of the affair is confusing, but she was concerned over the loss of financial support for Hull-House; she opposed too close co-operation with the Teachers' Federation, and she did not want to risk the loss of her position on the school board. She did take a stand on many other controversial issues, and Robins had a great deal of respect for her. See Robins to Medill McCormick, September 5, 1914.

settlement, as Graham Taylor and Jane Addams well knew. Raymond Robins believed the risk was worth while, that only through playing a role in public affairs and taking a stand on controversial issues could anything really be accomplished. In six years in local politics he had learned that good government in the ward meant little if there was not good government in the city, that municipal reform was closely connected to state and national reform. In order to broaden the scope of his reform efforts he resigned in 1907 as head resident of Northwestern Settlement. He did not, however, resign from the settlement movement, for to him the settlement movement meant reform.[42]

After 1907, Raymond Robins was often in the national limelight. He was one of the leading campaigners for William Jennings Bryan in 1908, one of the leading Progressives in 1912. He ran reluctantly for senator on the Progressive ticket in Illinois in 1914, and was the chairman of the National Progressive convention in 1916. He devoted a great deal of his time and money to supporting the cause of organized labor and to various religious activities, including a round-the-world tour for the Men and Religion Forward Movement. He also crusaded for peace and for prohibition. Throughout his life he kept in close contact with settlement workers and with the settlement movement. For many years he and his wife continued to live in the little cold-water flat on Chicago's West Side, midway between two settlement houses. Robins' tenement home in the slums symbolized his belief in the settlement idea. It symbolized his conviction that every reform attempt, local, national, or international, should be based, in part at least, on local neighborhood experience with ordinary people.

The historian or the social worker who looks upon the early settlement movement as only local in its influence, and who thinks of the early settlement worker as idealistic, impractical, and untrained, would do well to examine the career of Raymond Robins. In the words of Charles Merriam, he was "a political crusader, a practical evangelist, a statesman of broad democratic sympathies . . . a man without whom Chicago would have been much duller and much worse."[43]

MADISON, WISCONSIN

Received June 2, 1958

[42] R. Robins to E. Robins, July 5, 1914. Robins had tried to resign in 1905, but had stayed on until 1907 when he was replaced as head resident by Harriet Vittum.

[43] Charles Merriam, *A More Intimate View of Urban Politics* (New York: Macmillan Co., 1929), p. 210.

SOCIAL SETTLEMENTS AND IMMIGRANT NEIGHBORS, 1886–1914

GEORGE CARY WHITE

THE residents of social settlements were "among the first Americans to appreciate the cultural heritage which foreigners bring to the new country, the first to combat that cheap notion of assimilation which exacts of the foreigner that he abandon what constitutes his distinct contribution to American life —his best traditions."[1] This sweeping assertion was made in 1911 by the head worker at Madison House in New York City. The historical facts reveal that it was an accurate, even though modest, statement of the part played by the settlement movement in originating a conception of the immigrant and his place in American society which stood in sharp contrast to the prevailing views of the period before World War I.

Today the concept of cultural pluralism seems to offer the most satisfactory description of the ethnically diversified sources of our heritage. The interpretation "denies the assumption that there is an American culture fixed once and for all by our colonial ancestors. It assumes that our culture is variegated and dynamic, and that all immigrant groups have contributed to its enrichment."[2]

For the earliest expressions of this idea, commentators are likely to turn to the essays of Horace M. Kallen and Randolph S. Bourne, which were published in 1915 and 1916, respectively.[3] Yet a review of the earlier literature on immigration reveals that the settlement workers were the pioneers in recognizing and appreciating the positive significance of the pluralistic nature of our culture, and that they were literally the first representatives of the English-speaking group purposefully to seek out the alien and to communicate with him on an intimate basis. Out of this friendly intercourse came an appreciation for immigrant heritages and an effort to bridge the gap of ignorance and misunderstanding which then separated the foreign-born from the native-born.

KNOWLEDGE ABOUT THE IMMIGRANT

Workers in social settlements were in a strategic position to know the immi-

[1] Henry Moscowitz, "Music School Settlements," Survey, XXVI (June, 1911), 462.

[2] Clyde V. Kiser, "Cultural Pluralism," Annals of the American Academy of Political and Social Science, CCLXII (March, 1949), 129. For a more extensive statement of this idea see E. George Payne, "Education and Cultural Pluralism," chap. xxvii in Francis J. Brown and Joseph S. Roucek (eds.), Our Racial and National Minorities (New York: Prentice-Hall, 1937), pp. 759–69. Some leaders in the field of intergroup relationships have taken exception to the divisive implications of cultural pluralism as it is sometimes defined. Stewart G. Cole has, for example, preferred the term "cultural democracy" as descriptive of a process in which heritages are preserved in an emerging cultural unity and, more recently, has written of a "dynamic democracy" in which are recognized "the distinctive value of every culture group, and . . . the necessity of weaving the democratic interests of every individual and group into a harmonious national life" ("Intercultural Education," Religious Education, XXXVI [July-September, 1941], 131–45; and, in collaboration with Mildred Wiese Cole, Minorities and the American Promise [New York: Harper & Bros., 1954], p. 154).

[3] Horace M. Kallen, "Democracy versus the Melting-Pot," Nation, C (February, 1915), 190–4, 217–20; and Randolph S. Bourne, "Trans-National America," Atlantic Monthly, CXVIII (July, 1916), 86–97.

Social Service Review 33 (March 1959): 55–66

grant and to grasp the significance of the problems of group relationship which his presence was creating. For this purpose, no other agency of the broader community was so fortunately situated or so favorably oriented in philosophy and basic objectives.

It is true, of course, that the political machine often successfully cultivated the loyalty of the bewildered and unfriended stranger, but it did so out of selfish interest in exploiting his vote. The public school, even when it served a non-English-speaking neighborhood, was remote from the indigenous life of the area and functioned as an outpost of the dominant culture. Its aim was to "Americanize," to emancipate the child from his immigrant parents, rather than to recognize and dignify Old World traditions. The native-born who dictated the policies of the public educational system expected it to serve as the great "melting pot"; and educators pointed with satisfaction to the thoroughness with which immigrants' children were, through the influence of the school, being weaned away from any loyalty to the ways of their mothers and fathers and were becoming "Americans to the core."[4] The Protestant churches, representing in large part the religious interests of the native Americans, alienated the great mass of immigrants by a misdirected missionary zeal. Their somewhat tactless attempts at conversion made little headway among those who were devoted to the Roman Catholic, Jewish, or Greek Orthodox faiths in which they had been reared.[5]

The social settlement did not labor under these handicaps. Like many of the public schools and Protestant missions it was generally located in or near some area in which the immigrants were thickly congregated. What was significant about the settlement, however, was not only its physical proximity to the foreign-born but the motivation which led to its establishment. The essence of the settlement idea was "residence." This implied the cultivation of permanent neighborly contacts with those who lived in the vicinity of the house and the development, as one worker put it, of that "sense of identification with others" which comes from living among them.[6] Moreover, settlement workers were eager to adapt their services to community needs and, by utilizing the inherent resources of the groups with which they were in daily association, they endeavored to encourage democratic participation and self-help. It was at least their intention to base their activities not upon preconceived ideas but upon the careful study of the life of the neighborhood.[7]

FORMULATION OF THE PROBLEM
OF IMMIGRATION

Such was the relationship between settlement and immigrant. That the ideal was seldom, if ever, completely achieved is entirely probable. Yet the very at-

[4] A survey of the annual proceedings of the National Education Association justifies the conclusion that in these years educators were insensitive to the peculiar needs of children who were but one generation removed from the Old World.

[5] Gaylord S. White, "The Protestant Church and the Immigrant," *Survey,* XXII (September, 1909), 846–48; Leroy Hodges, "The Church and the Immigrants: A Record of Failure and the Remedy," *Missionary Review of the World,* XXXV (March, 1912), 167–72.

[6] William Jewett Tucker, "The Work of the Andover House in Boston," *Scribner's Magazine,* XIII (March, 1893), 362.

[7] David Blaustein, "The Inherent Cultural Forces of the Lower East Side," *Fifteenth Annual Report of the University Settlement Society of New York, 1901,* pp. 20–25.

tempts of settlement workers to relate themselves with insight and perceptivity to the members of alien groups who were generally ignored or misunderstood bore fruit. Out of these efforts emerged an appraisal of the basic problem of immigration and a method of approaching that problem which differed markedly from the popular attitudes and practices of the period.

Public opinion in those years was in general divided between two extreme views of the outcome of culture contact between immigrant and native groups. One view optimistically held that immigrants and their children were experiencing a radical transformation, abandoning with few regrets the remnants of their European backgrounds and adopting without hesitation the sentiments and behavior patterns of the Americans of old stock. An opposite view pessimistically predicted the submergence of the "American way of life" by alien customs and manners introduced by the rising flood of southern and eastern Europeans. It was held, in fact, that these elements of the "New Immigration" were inherently inferior, both biologically and culturally, to their predecessors of presumably Anglo-Saxon, Teutonic, and Celtic stock who settled the colonies or arrived here in the "Old Immigration." But the philosophy of the settlement movement as it interpreted the role of the immigrant was not in harmony with either of these widely held theories.

Jane Addams, for example, did not agree with the idea that ethnic differences were automatically disappearing, nor did she see any justification for the fear that this civilization was being imperiled by the coming of immigrants from southern and eastern Europe. She believed that the fundamental problem created by immigration was that of finding a new basis for unity in a heterogeneous society and of conserving Old World traits that would add elements of strength and beauty to American life. There was, in her judgment, no reason for expecting that out of the diversified elements of the population there would eventually develop a "consciousness of homogeneity," founded upon a common fund of historical experience and a uniformity of belief and behavior. Accepting the fact of a pluralistic culture, she insisted that the sense of community had to be based not upon similarities but upon an acceptance of differences, "a respect for variety." This implied not merely a toleration of the ways of alien groups but an appreciation for the customs and traditions which the immigrant had brought with him to the New World.[8]

In her judgment, however, native Americans were then far from achieving this measure of understanding. They were making little if any effort to bridge the wide gulf of apparent cultural difference that separated them from the newcomers. In fact, although a million immigrants were entering the country every year, virtually no attention was being paid to them. It was as if the older settlers did not even "perceive these immigrants, did not even know that they were here, or whence they came or whither they were going."[9]

The absence of social intercourse between the new arrival and the old resident meant to Jane Addams that the

[8] "Recreation as a Public Function in Urban Communities," *American Journal of Sociology,* XVII (March, 1912), 615–19.

[9] "Immigrants: Report of the Committee," *Proceedings of the National Conference of Charities and Correction, 1909,* p. 213.

organic unity of the society had been grievously impaired. For the foreign-born this had resulted in isolation from the broader community and its social and cultural resources; for the native-born it had fostered a willingness to accept the immigrant as a laborer or a factory worker but an inability to appreciate his "long reserves of experience in lines such as we do not have."[10]

Native Americans needed, therefore, to "discover" their immigrant neighbors: to value their heritages and recognize their potentialities. Yet little progress was being made in this direction for, as Jane Addams explained, the sources to which the native Americans might have turned for enlightenment were offering no help. The political administrators of the state were making no efforts to further understanding of the immigrant, nor were the scholars suggesting any method by which "to discover men, to spiritualize, to understand, to hold intercourse with aliens and to receive of what they bring."[11] One needed, in fact, to go "man-hunting" among groups of newly arrived immigrants and to point out the "sweetness and charm" of their ancient customs.[12]

It became, therefore, the duty of the social settlement to forward this process of discovery. Gaylord White, head worker of Union Settlement in New York City, regarded this as a vitally needed service in an urban community. He saw

that the absence of understanding and vital contact among the various segments of the population was responsible for the fact that each group was ignorant of the conditions of other groups and of the aspirations and values which governed their behavior.

Summing up the experiences of the quarter of a century since the founding of Neighborhood Guild, White identified some of the many ways in which settlement workers were trying to close this gap in the social ranks. He pointed to their efforts to secure firsthand information about the conditions under which their foreign-born neighbors were living and working and to disseminate this knowledge through publication and the presentation of testimony before legislative bodies and commissions. These research and educational services of the settlements not only threw light upon the problems of sanitation, housing, and industry which had been made more acute by the crowding of immigrants into the cities; they also gave currency to the idea that every immigrant group was capable of making valuable additions to "the sum total of our composite American character." Indeed, White added, "if we are to profit by these contributions, some group of people must have the insight to recognize such elements of value and the skill to draw them forth and preserve them."[13]

This function went beyond the accumulation and dissemination of facts about the immigrant. It involved a very definite effort to encourage a closer fellowship between native and alien and to disclose to the native the cultural resources of the alien. Robert A. Woods,

[10] "Work and Play as Factors in Education," *Chautauquan,* XLII (November, 1905), 251; and "The Subjective Necessity for Social Settlements," in Plymouth, Massachusetts, School of Applied Ethics, *Philanthropy and Social Progress* (New York: Thomas Y. Crowell & Co., 1893), pp. 4–5.

[11] "Recent Immigration: A Field Neglected by the Scholar," *Educational Review,* XXIX (March, 1905), 246–47.

[12] *Newer Ideals of Peace* (New York: Macmillan Co., 1907), p. 64.

[13] "The Social Settlement after Twenty-five Years," *Harvard Theological Review,* IV (January, 1911), 58–60.

head of South End House in Boston, saw the settlement as a center in which there could be brought forth "for local public appreciation the skill of hand, the heirlooms, the training in native music or drama, which the different types of immigrants have brought with them."[14] He pictured the worker as a person "able to appreciate the distinctive genius of each type and to sympathize with its traditions." Under such circumstances and leadership, the house became "common ground" where representatives of all groups met and mingled together and where prejudices were "discountenanced."[15] As Woods expressed it, such intergroup contact encouraged a reciprocity of influence among the foreign-born and the native-born. Thus the "American spirit," vitally affecting the life of the immigrant neighborhood, was in turn affected by the constructive forces of that life. "The loyal American," Woods explained, "honoring and seeking to preserve much in the genius of each nationality, will thus stimulate each racial type to seek for what is worthy in all the others."[16]

This line of thought was far removed from the popular conception of a melting pot into which, as many believed, immigrants of all nationalities were being poured and from which they were emerging completely transformed and remolded in the image of the American type. Anticipating later interpretations

of cultural pluralism and cultural democracy, Woods argued that as the nation was a "federal union" in the political sense so it must be in "its racial character and its type of civilization." For this reason it was an appropriate objective of social work to encourage "the building up of a natural federation among all our different racial groups, which will in reasonable degree preserve all that is valuable in the heredity and traditions of each type, but will link all types together into a universal yet coherent and distinctively American nationality." The settlements were forwarding this process by "bringing to light all the best characteristic traits and intellectual inheritances" of the various ethnic groups and by "recognizing and protecting these qualities." Looking to the future, Woods maintained that these efforts would contribute significantly to the "variety and resources of our future national life."[17]

But settlement leaders did not contemplate any encouragement of national disunity. As Woods saw it "every phase of immigrant culture" should be "not only respected but fostered." Yet in the long run the different "immigrant types" were to be brought together on the basis of common living standards and common vocational and recreational interests.[18] Another commentator anticipated a "fusion of the best in the cultural inheritance of the foreigner with the finest fruits of our native civilization."[19] And a third expressed the belief that it was a desirable aim of social policy to "receive, incorporate, amalgamate freely, effec-

[14] "The Neighborhood in Social Reconstruction," *American Journal of Sociology*, XIX (March, 1914), 587.

[15] "University Settlements: Their Point and Drift," *Quarterly Journal of Economics*, XIV (November, 1899), 77–78.

[16] "Assimilation: A Two-Edged Sword," chap. xii in R. A. Woods (ed.), *Americans in Process: A Settlement Study* (Boston and New York: Houghton Mifflin Co., 1902), p. 382.

[17] "Social Work: A New Profession," *International Journal of Ethics*, XVI (October, 1905), 30.

[18] "The Neighborhood in Social Reconstruction," *op. cit.*, pp. 586–87.

[19] Henry Moscowitz, *loc. cit.*

tively and generously . . . these varying elements of temperament, tradition, nationality" and to integrate in our total culture "all that is best in Saxon, Norman, Slav, and Celt."[20]

RECOGNITION OF CONTRIBUTIONS

These general views were supported by a specification of the cultural and personal assets of immigrant groups. Among the foreign-born, settlement workers found capacities for artistic and emotional expression and for constructive participation in the life of a democratic society.

No one wrote on this theme with greater feeling than did Jane Addams who was convinced that close at hand in the immigrant colonies lay rich resources of art and culture. In the public festivals and historical pageantry of the various nationality groups she saw vast reservoirs of corporate emotional expression waiting to be tapped. If the immigrant's spontaneous manifestations of sentiment and tradition were sympathetically encouraged, she was certain that they would bring drama and color to the drabness and ugliness of the city environment. She declared with characteristic sensitivity:

Nothing is more beautiful than the gay celebrations in the Italian quarter in Chicago on Garibaldi's birthday. Nothing is brighter than the march of the mutual benefit societies along the streets . . . the Greeks parade, blowing their pipes and flinging their banners in honor of their immortal heroes over our dirty Chicago streets just as they flung them out over the Acropolis.[21]

As for the artistic activities of the immigrants, she welcomed them as materials for a richer folk culture than this country had ever known. Jane Addams argued:

Were Americans really eager for a municipal art, they would cherish as genuine beginnings the tarantella danced so interminably at Italian weddings; the primitive Greek pipe played throughout the long summer nights; the Bohemian theatres crowded with eager Slavophiles; the Hungarian musicians strolling from street to street; the fervid oratory of the young Russian preaching social righteousness in the open square.[22]

Desirable attributes of national character were also counted among the virtues of various foreign-born groups. The opinions expressed by settlement workers regarding the Italian immigrant are illustrative of a generally high estimate of the newcomer of whatever ethnic origin. Describing the Italians whom she had met through her settlement activities at Denison House in Boston, Vida Scudder praised their initiative, keen curiosity, mental alertness, enthusiasm for abstract ideas, and desire to take an active part in the political and social affairs of the community.[23] Dr. Jane Robbins, one of the pioneer leaders in the settlement movement in New York City, wrote in similar vein of the "gifts" which the Italian immigrants were bringing to the New World: their "gracious and dignified manners," affectionate nature and strong love for children, their "sense of beauty" which found expression in the humblest surroundings, their "manual dexterity and mechanical ability," and

[20] Mari Ruef Hofer, "The Folk Game and Festival," Charities and the Commons, XVIII (August, 1907), 561–62.

[21] "Immigrants: Report of the Committee," op. cit., p. 214.

[22] The Spirit of Youth and the City Streets (New York: Macmillan Co., 1909), pp. 101–2.

[23] "Experiments in Fellowship: Work with Italians in Boston," Survey, XXII (April 3, 1909), 47–51.

their "temperateness in eating and drinking."[24] The capacity of the Italian immigrants for artistic expression and their love of music and poetry were applauded by Mary E. McDowell, head resident of the University of Chicago Settlement.[25] Another worker expressed the belief that the "American type" could be greatly improved by the incorporation within it of such Italian characteristics as "delight in simple pleasures, an appreciation for other things than mere financial success, a sense of beauty, a natural kindliness and social grace." She warned that "it rests with us whether we shall recognize these qualities, foster them, and assimilate them, or, by persistently ignoring and despising them, stamp them as undesirable, unAmerican, and mould the Italian immigrant in our own image."[26]

In assessing the potentialities of immigrant groups, particular attention was given to the strong democratic sentiments and political idealism which these new citizens were bringing with them to the United States. In their urban colonies evidences were found not only of elemental kindliness and altruism but of a practical capacity for organized mutual aid.[27] Unfortunately, however, the community was, in the opinion of Jane Addams, failing to draw upon these forces for good because of the American tendency to "crush the most promising bits of self-government

and self-expression" by establishing an "imperialism of virtue" and asserting a sense of political and moral superiority.[28] A knowledge of the Old World backgrounds and the New World experiences of the immigrant was needed, she argued, not only as a basis for development of public policies which would affect the newcomers but as a necessary step toward the utilization of their native proclivities.[29]

In the light of such favorable appraisals, it is not surprising that it became a major objective of settlement policy to safeguard immigrant heritages by encouraging their retention and by pointing out their values to old-stock Americans.

CONSERVATION OF HERITAGES

To the achievement of these objectives much of the work of the settlement was directed. The extensive literature dealing with the program at Hull-House offers valuable source material for a description of these endeavors carried on under imaginative leadership and with comparatively ample resources. Many other houses may not have been so fortunately staffed or equipped. It is certain, however, that the work at Hull-House illustrated a pattern that was widely followed, with

[24] "Italian To-Day, American To-Morrow," *Outlook*, LXXX (June 10, 1905), 383–84.

[25] "The Children of Our Cities," *Journal of Proceedings, National Education Association, 1896*, pp. 491–92.

[26] Lilian Brandt, "A Transplanted Birthright: The Development of the Second Generation of Italians in our American Environment," *Charities*, XII (May, 1904), 499.

[27] Grace Abbott, "The Immigrant and Municipal Politics," *Proceedings of the Cincinnati Conference for Good City Government and the Fifteenth Annual Meeting of the National Municipal League, 1909*, p. 152; Jane Addams, "Problems of Municipal Administration," in Howard J. Rogers (ed.), *Congress of Arts and Sciences, Universal Exposition, St. Louis, 1904* (Boston and New York: Houghton Mifflin Co., 1906), VII, 448.

[28] "Problems of Municipal Administration," *op. cit.*, p. 444.

[29] "Recent Immigration: A Field Neglected by the Scholar," *op. cit.*, pp. 255–56.

allowances for flexible adaptation to the community setting and to the backgrounds of neighbors.

Programs, both recreational and educational, met a variety of needs and interests. Among the most popular were the dramatic events staged by various nationality groups, usually in their native languages. These performances sometimes attracted audiences from every section of the city. Much emphasis was placed upon the cultivation of the talents of the children of immigrants and the settlement music school became a popular educational venture. The celebration of national holidays and other events significant in the history of immigrant groups publicly dramatized their ideals and sentiments and contributed to the development of a sense of solidarity between the settlement and its neighbors. Gymnastic activities provided the foreign-born with an opportunity to develop their traditional skills. Even the instruction in English not only met the immediate practical needs of the unschooled immigrant but offered the more advanced adult student an opportunity to develop his powers of self-expression in the description of colorful or personally meaningful aspects of his European past. It is not to be assumed, however, that organized activities were the only media for intergroup experience. Much was also accomplished through the informal gatherings that made each house a center for more intimate fellowship between the foreign-born and the American-born. This was particularly true in those instances in which volunteer leaders of groups and clubs came into personal touch with immigrants and their children.[30]

One of the most impressive demonstrations of intergroup education was the Hull-House Labor Museum.[31] This project, which attracted nation-wide attention in the early years of the century, provided an opportunity for foreign-born craftsmen to practice and transmit to their children their skills as spinners, weavers, potters, glass-blowers, wood-carvers, and metal-workers. Broader aims were not overlooked, however, for it was hoped that the activities of the Museum would give native Americans an opportunity to become more familiar with the creative efforts of immigrant workers.

In addition to providing shop facilities and equipment, the Museum was open for public inspection at regular intervals. A weekly demonstration of spinning and weaving by foreign-born women from the neighborhood was an established feature of the program. Products and primitive implements were placed on display. Lectures on industrial history were offered. And the arts and crafts activities of the settlement as a whole were integrated with the work of the project.

[30] Robert A. Woods and Albert J. Kennedy, *Handbook of Settlements* (New York: Charities Publication Committee, 1911), p. 59; Victor von Borosini, "Our Recreation Facilities and the Immigrant," *Annals of the American Academy of Political and Social Science,* XXXV (March, 1910), 365; and Jane Addams, "Hull House (Chicago)," in *The New Encyclopedia of Social Reform,* ed. William D. P. Bliss *et al.* (1908), p. 588; *Twenty Years at Hull-House* (New York: Macmillan Co., 1910), pp. 256, 436–37, 443–44; "The Objective Value of a Social Settlement," in Plymouth, Massachusetts, School of Applied Ethics, *op. cit.,* p. 35; "Hull-House and Its Neighbors," *Charities,* XII (May, 1904), 450–51.

[31] In this and the succeeding paragraph the references are to Jane Addams, *Twenty Years at Hull-House,* pp. 235–40, 243–46; *Newer Ideals of Peace,* pp. 203–5; and "The Humanizing Tendency of Industrial Education," *Chautauquan,* XXXIX (May, 1904), 270–71.

Explaining the general educational significance of the Museum, Jane Addams ventured the hope that those who were associated with it, either as artisans or as visitors and observers, would be able to perceive that, beneath diversities in language, religion, and political experience, the processes of industry were among all peoples essentially the same in their evolutionary development. When she looked at history from the "industrial standpoint," she believed that it became "cosmopolitan" in its implications and that differences of race and nationality "inevitably" fell away.[32] "Perhaps," she observed, "this experiment may claim to have made a genuine effort to find the basic experiences upon which a cosmopolitan community may unite at least on the industrial side."[33]

There is no evidence that the example of Hull-House in establishing its Labor Museum was followed by other settlements. On the other hand, the development of classes and interest groups in the arts and crafts was a common practice. Even closer to the aim of the Museum were the public exhibitions of hand-made products and objects of art which were often sponsored by settlements and other community agencies and groups, including organizations of the foreign-born themselves.

Such projects were extremely popular for a variety of reasons. As educational devices, they disclosed to the general public tangible evidences of the skills and artistic sensibilities of immigrants and helped to correct the popular conception that they were incapable of doing anything except performing the hardest manual labor. These exhibitions revealed, in fact, that the newcomers did not leave behind them either their love of beauty or their ability to produce it.[34]

Gathered together in a single display these creations of immigrant skill and artistry must have made a strong impression upon the visitor. Among the items that might have been found in a typical exhibit were colorful peasant costumes; embroideries and laces; ceremonial robes and altar cloths; artistic representations in painting and sculpture; elaborate floor and wall mosaics; delicate items of jewelry and painted china; useful products of the cabinetmakers' skill; work in brass, copper, and wood; hand-made textiles; and even toys and dolls.[35]

Often the planning and staging of an exhibition was a joint enterprise which involved the co-operation of community groups, native-born as well as foreign-born, who shared the same aesthetic interests. These projects also served, as one writer expressed it, to forward "the conservation of the artistic possibilities of our composite nation" by encouraging the foreign craftsman to continue in the New World the practice of pursuits in which he had become so proficient in his homeland.[36] Beyond

[34] Adelene Moffat, "The Exhibition of Italian Arts and Crafts in Boston," *Survey*, XXII (April, 1909), 51–53.

[35] "Immigrant Arts at Greenwich House," *Charities and the Commons*, XX (May, 1908), 146.

[36] Moffat, *op. cit.*, 51. An outgrowth of these efforts was the establishment in New York City of the Guild of Settlement Industries to stimulate the productive activity of immigrant craftsmen by providing them with a place where their products could be displayed and sold. Woods and Kennedy, *op. cit.*, p. 190.

[32] "The Hull-House Labor Museum," *Chautauquan*, XXXVIII (September, 1903), 60–61; and *Twenty Years at Hull-House*, p. 237.

[33] *Newer Ideals of Peace*, p. 204.

these more or less immediate objectives, some saw the prospect of fostering the growth of a New World art which would derive its superiority from the amalgamation of the finest aptitudes of each immigrant group with those of the Americans of old stock.[37]

DEFINITION OF THE ROLE
OF PUBLIC AGENCIES

Settlement workers did not expect that their own efforts would be sufficient to solve the problems that they recognized. The houses were too few in number and their means were too limited to perform a task in social engineering which involved the entire complex organism of city life. The residents thought of themselves as originators and experimenters whose primary responsibilities were identifying needs and demonstrating the most effective ways of meeting them. But only as these functions were shared by publicly supported agencies did it seem likely that the challenge would be adequately met. Hence it was to the municipal recreation programs and the public schools that settlement workers looked for the development of community-wide opportunities for intergroup activities. It was their hope that, if facilities and leadership could be more extensively provided, the foreign-born and their children would be encouraged to participate and that others would have an opportunity to share experiences with immigrants and witness their capacities for physical, artistic, and emotional expression.

Some progress was made in this direction in the years before the outbreak of World War I. Under the sponsorship of the municipal recreation authorities in Chicago, intercultural play festivals were held in which representatives of various nationality groups, dressed in native costumes, presented programs of folk songs, dances, and gymnastic exercises. The playgrounds and field houses in park areas adjacent to immigrant neighborhoods were opened for use by organizations of the foreign-born. The facilities of these centers were freely used by nationality societies, both fraternal and social, and by athletic and gymnastic, dancing, choral, and dramatic groups.[38] Graham Taylor, founder and resident warden of Chicago Commons, expressed what must have been the approval of settlement workers generally when he pointed out that these recreational centers were demonstrating the possibility of uniting the people of the city through their play pursuits.[39]

Even greater possibilities were seen in the use of the public school buildings. Settlement workers urged that they be opened to the entire community during the hours when classes were not in session. They believed that the school should be the focal point for neighborhood life. There all groups should be welcome to take part in activities that would reflect their native interests. To Jane Addams the schools, as well as the recreation centers, offered unparalleled opportunities for intercultural interpretation particularly through the use of their facilities for the celebration of national holidays, the observance of

[37] V. Svarc, "The Culture which the Slav Offers to America," *Charities,* XIV (July, 1905), 881; Henry Moscowitz, "The East Side in Oil and Crayon," *Survey,* XXVIII (May, 1912), 273.

[38] Guy L. Shipps, "Utilizing Neighborhood Groups," *Proceedings of the National Conference of Charities and Correction, 1914,* pp. 401–6.

[39] "City Neighbors at Play," *Survey,* XXIV (July, 1910), 548–59.

the birthdays of national heroes, and the holding of seasonal festivals.[40] John Dewey, then at the University of Chicago, joined the settlement workers in insisting that the schools should serve as social centers. Greatly impressed by the work at Hull-House with which he was in close contact, Dewey pointed to the Labor Museum as an illustration of what could be accomplished if the schools were to provide similar opportunities for the work of immigrant craftsmen.[41]

The intercultural activities of the school were not, however, to be confined to adults and to the evening hours. In their daily contacts with immigrant neighbors, settlement workers were making disquieting discoveries about the strained relationships between native-born children and their foreign-born parents. Eagerly embracing New World ways and standards, these young people were often found to be out of sympathy with and sometimes actually contemptuous of the alien customs of their mothers and fathers. The source of much of this conflict could be found in the general influences of the environment. It was also believed that the public schools, far from cultivating in the child a respect for his parents, were actually contributing to the alienation of the second from the first generation. Settlement workers, for this reason, urged that changes be made in teaching methods and materials for the purpose of fostering a reconciliation between the immigrants and their native-born offspring.

It was this reorientation of educational policy which Jane Addams had in mind when, at the annual conference of the National Education Association in 1908, she urged teachers and school administrators to "take hold of the immigrant colonies . . . bring out of them their handicrafts and occupations, their traditions, their folk songs and folk lore, the beautiful stories which every immigrant colony is ready to tell and translate." It was hoped that in this fashion children, through their activities in the schools, would come to prize the cultural contributions which their parents had brought with them to America.[42]

No claim is made that the ideas and action programs that grew out of settlement experience during the years of our heaviest immigration won any mass acceptance. Before 1914, public opinion was divided, in large part, between the melting pot idea and the views of the immigration restrictionists. During and immediately after World War I the Americanization movement won nationwide support in its effort to obliterate the immigrant's devotion to his past and to remake him according to what was thought to be the American pattern. The passage of the Immigration Quota Act of 1924 was a triumph for the hostile critics of the New Immigration.

On the other hand, we may rightfully award to the pioneers in the settlement movement the distinction of having been the first to see the immigrant not as passive raw material but as a positive contributor to the enterprise of nationbuilding. Foreshadowed in their observations about the immigrant are

[40] *The Spirit of Youth and the City Streets,* pp. 98–100.

[41] "The School as Social Center," *Journal of Proceedings, National Education Association, 1902,* p. 377.

[42] "The Public School and the Immigrant Child," *Journal of Proceedings, National Education Association, 1908,* pp. 101–2.

views that are commonplace in informed circles today. The correspondence between the ideas reviewed above and current conceptions of cultural pluralism and cultural democracy is not accidental. Nor is there any accident about the similarity of the activities of the settlements in the earlier decades and much of our modern work in intergroup relations.

The attitudes and methods that originated in the social settlements influenced philosophy and practice in group work and casework, gave impetus to the progressive education movement, and provided inspiration for many of our earlier efforts in intercultural education. The major impact of the settlement movement has been felt among professional workers in education and social service who have sought to translate democratic and humanitarian ideals into practical measures and programs. This has been true in many areas of our community life. It has been particularly true in the area of native-immigrant relationships.

Department of Sociology
Hollins College

Received August 5, 1958

CHICAGO SOCIAL WORKERS AND BLACKS IN THE PROGRESSIVE ERA

STEVEN J. DINER

Chicago, Illinois

This essay explores the relationship between social workers and blacks in Chicago between 1900 and 1920. In a city peopled by some thirty different nationalities, leading social workers discovered many similarities between poor blacks and poor immigrants, but they were impressed as well by the unique problems faced by black people because of racial discrimination. Both the charity and settlement wings of social work sought to discover in these years the place of blacks in a pluralistic society.

Are American blacks another group in a pluralistic society, or do they constitute a people apart? This question, so hotly debated nowadays, was posed a half-century and more ago by social workers engaged in a war against poverty. If for no other reason than perspective, it is useful to examine the relationship between social workers and blacks during the Progressive Era.

Chicago is a fitting place to examine this relationship under a microscope. In 1910, Chicago's population was 77 percent immigrant or first-generation American. Of some thirty groups, blacks—then called Negroes or colored people—ranked tenth according to the 1910 census, less numerous than Germans, Irishmen, or Italians, for example, but more numerous than Greeks, Dutchmen, or French Canadians (39: 95, 614). In 1920, as a result of the great migration during World War I, Chicago's black population of 108,000 ranked seventh (40:108–9, 378–81).

By then, in the city of Jane Addams, social work was well developed. Modern social work derived from a merger of the scientific charity and social settlement movements which began in the

The writer has expressed appreciation to Professor Arthur Mann, of the Department of History of the University of Chicago, whose critical reading of successive drafts of this article strengthened it immeasurably.

last decades of the nineteenth century. Charity workers had emphasized individual self-help as a means of combatting poverty, while settlement workers called for changes in the social environment (20:18–22). By the outbreak of World War I, however, Chicago's charity and settlement workers had joined together in groups like the Juvenile Protective Association, the Chicago School of Civics and Philanthropy, the United Charities of Chicago, the League for the Protection of Immigrants, and the Chicago Urban League.

The central purpose of these and other social work activities was to eliminate poverty among all of Chicago's ethnic groups. Yet the poverty of one group—blacks—stood out. Migrants from the American South, black people experienced the same difficulties as foreign-born Americans in adjusting to northern urban life. But blacks, in addition, suffered special handicaps because of their skin color. Whether or not these handicaps were sufficient to render blacks a separate group is a question which puzzled Chicago social workers throughout the Progressive Era.

CHARITY: SELF-HELP

Chicago charity workers thought that poverty could best be minimized through hard work and individual initiative, rather than through changes in the social environment. To diagnose cases effectively, and thereby encourage such initiative, they sought to discover the extent of poverty within each of the city's ethnic groups and the group influences which either encouraged or discouraged pauperism.

The two major charity agencies before 1908—the Chicago Relief and Aid Society and the Chicago Bureau of Charities—manifested this keen interest in ethnicity. The Chicago Relief and Aid Society, in its annual reports, broke down by nationality the total number of families aided during the year. "Colored" were not listed separately until 1905, when the list of ten nationalities was expanded to fourteen. Similarly, in its 1898–99 report, the Chicago Bureau of Charities listed "Negroes" along with thirty-two other groups whose members had received aid (11:7). Case summaries commonly noted nationality; phrases like "a sober and industrious African family" or "an Italian widow with seven children" were typical (11:16–17). Several meetings of the General Advisory Committee of the Bureau of Charities in 1907 were devoted to "the discussion of foreign families" (19k:45–46; 19m:66–67, 69–70; 19n:78–79).

This concern with ethnicity continued after these two agencies joined in 1908 to form the United Charities of Chicago. A list of nationalities of children served by its Mary Crane Nursery appeared in most of the annual reports. Local charity districts were described by the ethnicity of their residents. The 1915–16 report listed the nationalities of all families aided between 1913 and 1916 (38:12). Negroes were included in all of these calculations.

Co-operation, a journal published weekly from 1900 to 1908 by the Chicago Bureau of Charities, printed news about charitable work and discussed social issues. Charity workers' attitudes toward blacks and other groups were elaborated here.

No person better exemplified charity's goal of fostering individualism within an ethnic group than did Booker T. Washington. *Co-operation* printed numerous reports of his lectures and his work at Tuskegee and illustrated the progress of the black race through self-help. One item described the "Negro Potato King," J. G. Groves, who began by renting nine acres and became one of the most prosperous farmers in Kansas. Mr. Groves was quoted: "I think . . . our [his and his wife's] success shows that a negro can and will make his way in the world if given a chance. If we could start with but seventy-five cents and succeed as we have, other people of our race can do the same thing" (19h: 157). Another item noted the recommendation of a committee of African Methodist Episcopal clergymen that "all colored pastors shall deliver discourses on the benefits of honesty, sobriety, industry, and morality" (19e: 319). Still another described the 1908 formation by Chicago blacks of the Lincoln Law and Order League in order to provide their race with "training in thrift, industry, orderly habits, and elementary decency" (19o:285–86).

The journal ran an article which pointed out that "the 'negro problem' is being solved in Norfolk, Virginia and the solution is along the line of industrial training." Quoting a report of a Norfolk organization, the Southern Industrial Classes, the article explained that Negro parents "never tired of coming to see what their children were learning and would sit for hours interested spectators of the cooking classes":

They wandered into the mothers' meetings to learn all about it, and showed by their constant attendance their deep interest in this new departure for their children. In a single generation these women had lost the practice of those domestic arts which made the cooks and seamstresses of the slavery period so celebrated. But the tradition remained and they gladly embraced for their children the opportunity of which they had been deprived [19g: 43–44].

Co-operation also praised Booker Washington's remedy for discrimination. One issue described the plight of a respectable black minister who was unable to obtain housing on Chicago's North Side. It noted that he revolted against the fact that "persons of undoubted worth should be shunned and be made to feel that character went for nothing and that the color of their skin was a reproach to them." However, the minister gave Booker Washington's advice, that the black man acquire property so that "his dual position, that of man of character plus man of property will command respect and honor from the whites" (19c:145–46). Institutions designed to "uplift" the black race invariably received favorable notice. Among these were the Frederick Douglass Center settlement, the Institutional Church and Social Settlement, and the Home for Aged and Infirm Colored People.

Several differing "scientific" findings on the "Negro question" were discussed in the journal. One issue summarized a report of the Georgia Prison Commission defending the system of leasing black convicts "because among other things, it was better adapted for the negro convict population which has to be out of doors when it works." A later article stated that Negro prisoners'

health was not adversely affected by indoor work in the Virginia State Penitentiary. Noting the discrepancy with the earlier article, it pointed out that the Georgia Federal Prison now had "colored and white convicts working side by side in many occupations outdoor and in-door." "After a sufficient time has elapsed," it announced, "comparisons as to the relative healthfulness of different occupations upon white and colored men will be possible" (19d: 174).

Co-operation favorably reviewed Joseph Telinghast's *The Negro in Africa and America,* published in 1902 by the American Economic Association. The book's thesis was that blacks, coming from an uncivilized continent, were unable to compete successfully with the world's most advanced race:

The rapidity with which an uncivilized people may be lifted, or may lift themselves, to the plane of an advanced civilization is still undetermined. To realize that many characteristics of the American Negro are part of his inheritance from Africa, and were bred into the race there through long generations, may perhaps strengthen the patience and forebearance of those who seek to expedite his progress [19b:3–4].

A *Chicago Tribune* article, reprinted, argued the advantages of racial segregation in the Chicago public schools (19f:342). The writer of another item described the clean building, sanitary bathroom facilities, and reasonable rents in a New York model tenement for blacks. The tenement's greatest inadequacy was lack of play space for children—"If only a large basement playroom could have been provided for the poor little darkies" (19j:363–64).

Occasionally, articles in *Co-operation* expressed outrage at the treatment of blacks in the South. One piece depicted the horrible conditions of prisons for black children who committed minor offenses, and urged that the "making of beasts out of men and then killing and torturing them because they are beasts can scarcely be commended as creditable to a boasted civilization" (19*a*:5–6). On another occasion, the journal expressed disapproval of a proposed Kentucky law that would have forced Berea College, a private interracial institution, to cease teaching blacks and whites together. The institution, they argued, had been mixed since its inception in 1849 and had had no difficulties serving its interracial clientele (19*h*:87).

In many ways, *Co-operation*'s attitudes toward blacks mirrored its attitudes toward immigrants. The editors were enthusiastic about the self-help activities of all groups. Thus, articles on the "German Home for the Aged," the "Jewish Home for Girls," the "French Society," a "Polish Summer School," a "settlement in Chinatown," were common. On the negative side as well, the racial stereotyping exemplified by *Co-operation*'s praise of the "cooks and seamstresses of the slavery period" or its compassion for those "poor little darkies" had immigrant equivalents. The Irish, one article noted, suffered from "the tendency to drink, a degree of shiftlessness and [a] too mobile character" (19*m*:67). Italian characteristics included "uncleanliness; strong clannishness which allows falsehoods . . . to be told non-Italians but calls for truth when communication is had with other Italians; gentleness of manner coupled with naïvete" (19*k*:45). The journal's outrage at gross mistreatment of blacks in the South was equaled by its outrage at the abuse of newly arrived immigrants. Nevertheless, no item compared blacks with either immigrants col-

lectively or with a particular immigrant group, although many compared immigrant groups with each other.

To the extent that *Co-operation* was representative, organized charity in these early years assumed, without putting it in so many words, that Negroes faced racial discrimination in addition to the social and economic problems faced by Chicago's foreign populations. Whatever the problems, however, charity had a definite remedy for them— hard work and individual initiative.

LOUISE DE KOVEN BOWEN

Louise deKoven Bowen, a woman active in Chicago social work, combined the charity and settlement outlooks. The granddaughter of one of the city's early settlers, she was born in Chicago in 1859. She attended Dearborn Seminary and in 1886 married a successful silk manufacturer and banker, who died in 1911. She inherited a substantial fortune from both her husband and her grandfather. Independently wealthy from the start, Mrs. Bowen donated large sums to social agencies and joined many social work organizations.

Louise Bowen entered public life through the Chicago Bureau of Charities and was vice-president of United Charities until just before her death. She became active in Hull-House programs shortly after the settlement was founded, although she was never a resident, and her friendship with Jane Addams led her into social reform. She was treasurer of Hull-House from 1894 to 1935 and president from 1935 to 1944, and she also crusaded for protection of youth, elimination of vice, women's suffrage, and public health. She donated over a million dollars to Hull-House alone (7; 13; 18).

Mrs. Bowen's work with the Juvenile Protective Association led her to an active interest in Chicago's blacks. She headed this organization from its inception in 1907. Founded by prominent civic leaders, it investigated cases of alleged mistreatment, supervised areas where youth congregated, employed probation officers for the Juvenile Court, and studied the causes of juvenile delinquency. While investigating the condition of boys in the county jail, the association discovered that "1/8 of the boys and nearly 1/3 of the girls and young women who had been confined in the jail" were Negroes. Struck by this apparently high rate of juvenile delinquency, the Association set out to ascertain the causes and soon "found itself involved in a study of the industrial and social status of the colored people of Chicago." The School of Civics and Philanthropy participated in the study, and Mrs. Bowen wrote the final report, *The Colored People of Chicago,* published in 1913 (6).

Much of the report documented discrimination against blacks in employment, business colleges, certain labor unions, homes for the dependent, and recreational facilities, and by the police and the courts. Mrs. Bowen argued, in a typically environmental analysis, that Negro mothers and children were forced to work because their race faced discrimination in better-paying jobs. Furthermore, Negroes paid more than any other group for comparable housing, and many Negro families defrayed high rents by taking in lodgers, who were a bad influence on the children. These conditions strained family life, thereby encouraging delinquency. Moreover, she argued, recreational facilities in black areas were inadequate,

and the vice district—that part of the city where vice was tolerated—was situated in Negro residential areas.

Yet if Mrs. Bowen's analysis was environmental, her proposed remedies were not quite consistent with typical settlement thinking. Instead of proposing changes in the social environment, Mrs. Bowen simply demanded that blacks be judged according to their individual worth. The public, she argued, should not assume that all Negroes were "bad" simply because one Negro commits a crime, and the press should not emphasize race when a Negro is a suspect (6). While no settlement worker would have quibbled with these suggestions, references to "good" and "bad" Negroes implied that individuals rather than the social environment were responsible for criminality, a notion more akin to charity thinking. In this respect Mrs. Bowen's report drew from both charity and settlement outlooks.

Mrs. Bowen recognized the similarities and differences between blacks and immigrant groups. *The Colored People of Chicago* went to great lengths to highlight the special problems of blacks alone. In discussing crime rates, prostitution, housing, salaries, labor unions, recreational opportunities, or treatment by the police, Mrs. Bowen always contrasted blacks with the city's entire white population. Yet, she noted, "the needs of the two classes of people [blacks and immigrants] are similar in many respects, implying lack of adjustment rather than lack of ability." Her report compared blacks with another ethnic group only once, when it asserted that the birth rate of both southern Negro migrants and rural Italian peasants declined sharply when "they move to the city and become prosperous" (6). Seven years later, Mrs. Bowen addressed herself directly to this question. Speaking to a meeting of the National Urban League, she stated:

We are not apt to think of the negro as an immigrant, but in reality he occupies the same position as does the foreigner who comes to us from other shores, except that the negro's position is more difficult, for he is subjected to racial discrimination, and while no limitations are imposed upon the children of the immigrant, this unfortunately, is not true of the children of the negro [22:630].

Louise Bowen showed genuine concern for Chicago's Negro population. She supported equal treatment of Negroes and on one occasion publicly defended the employment of a Negro physician by the Municipal Tuberculosis Sanitarium (14). She was among the few Chicagoans in the Progressive Era for whom the plight of blacks was of major interest.

SETTLEMENTS: ENVIRONMENTALISM
AND CULTURAL PLURALISM

Chicago's leading settlement workers were national figures. The commanding personality, of course, was Jane Addams, whose compassion for Negroes came naturally. Conscious of her father's abolitionist background, Miss Addams opposed nearly every injustice of which she was aware. Her thinking on Negroes mirrored her social philosophy: belief in democracy, love of humanity, respect for the indigenous culture of all people. She acquired keen insight into ethnic differences through her work at Hull-House. Miss Addams recognized racial friction as a problem faced by many ethnic groups, Negroes included. Hull-House residents described their neighborhood in 1911 as one in which Greek "migration into a

territory comfortably settled by Irish and Bohemians brought racial friction" (52:54).

Nevertheless, Miss Addams perceived better than any of her colleagues that blacks faced very special problems. Slavery, she wrote, deprived Negroes of their African inheritance. For example, in comparing the relative success of Italian and Negro girls in the cities, she suggested:

Italian fathers consider it a point of honor that their daughters shall not be alone upon the street after dark, and only slowly modify their social traditions. The fathers of colored girls, on the other hand, are quite without those traditions and fail to give their daughters the resulting protection. If colored girls yield more easily to the temptations of a city than the Italian girls do, who shall say how far the lack of social restraint is responsible for it? The Italian parents represent the social traditions which have been worked out during centuries. . . . The civilizations in Africa are even older than those in Italy and naturally tribal life everywhere has its own traditions and taboos which control the relations between the sexes and between parents and children. But of course these were broken up during the period of chattel slavery for very seldom were family ties permitted to stand in the way of profitable slave sales [4:397–98].

Furthermore, Miss Addams argued, Negroes faced residential segregation and economic and political discrimination. "Complete segregation of the Negro in definite parts of the city," she asserted, "tends in itself to put him outside the immediate action of that imperceptible but powerful social control which influences the rest of the population" (4:396). She blamed this state of affairs on "national indifference" to the spirit of the Emancipation Proclamation. "How far are we responsible," Miss Addams asked, "that their [Negroes'] civil rights are often rendered futile, their political action curtailed, their equality before the law denied in fact, industrial opportunities withheld from them and, above all, that for twenty-five years they have been exposed to the black horrors of lynching?" (1:566). Friction necessarily resulted, she stated, "when one race is forced to demand as a right from the other those things which should be accorded as a courtesy" (4: 398). Furthermore, Miss Addams argued that America's treatment of non-whites was part of a "world-wide yielding to race antagonism," partaking of the "growing self-assertion of the so-called 'superior' races who exact labor and taxes from black and yellow men with the easy explanation of 'manifest destiny'" (1:565).

If race oppression distinguished Negroes from immigrants, the national consequences of stifling any group were always the same, according to Miss Addams. American democracy, she believed, must allow every group to express its indigenous culture (2). She decried attempts to force Negroes or immigrants into an "Americanized" mold:

What has been and is being lost by the denial of opportunity and free expression on the part of the Negro, it is now very difficult to estimate; only faint suggestions of the waste can be perceived. There is, without doubt, the sense of humor, unique and spontaneous, so different from the wit of the Yankee, or the inimitable story telling prized in the South; the Negro melodies which are the only American folksongs; the persistent love of color expressing itself in the bright curtains and window boxes in the dullest and grayest parts of our cities; the executive and organizing capacity so often exhibited by the head waiter in a huge hotel or by the colored woman who administers a complicated household; the gift of eloquence, the mellowed voice, the use of rhythm and onomatopoeia which is now so often travestied in a grotesque use of long words.

Much more could be added to this list of positive losses suffered by the community which puts so many of its own members "behind the veil." It means an enormous loss of capacity to the nation when great ranges of human life are hedged about with antagonism. We forget that whatever is spontaneous in a people, in an individual, a class or a nation, is always a source of life, a well-spring of refreshment to a jaded civilization. To continually suspect, suppress and to fear any large group in a community must finally result in a loss of enthusiasm for that type of government which gives free play to the self-determination of a majority of its citizens [1:566].

Jane Addams worked on behalf of blacks through the National Association for the Advancement of Colored People (NAACP) and the Chicago Urban League. Few blacks lived near Hull-House, although prominent blacks often spoke at the settlement. Miss Addams was confronted with antiblack discrimination at the Progressive Party convention of 1912. She was distressed by Teddy Roosevelt's exclusion of all rival black delegations from the South. Roosevelt maintained this "lily-white" stance in the hope of carrying southern states. Miss Addams and several other prominent progressives appealed unsuccessfully to the Resolutions Committee to reverse this action. Faced with a dilemma of conscience, Miss Addams almost left the convention (27; 29:801). In an article for *Crisis*, the NAACP magazine, Miss Addams explained her grounds for supporting Roosevelt. She argued that the Republicans paid lip service to race equality but did nothing for the Negro. While many delegates at Republican conventions were Negro, they were tools of party managers, as there were no real Republican organizations in southern states. On the other hand, if the Progressive Party was successful, she argued, a wide variety of reforms would be enacted, and the ethical spirit of reform would lift the question of race relations to a higher level (3).

Miss Addams's closest Hull-House associates shared her interest in blacks. Julia Lathrop, Sophonisba Breckinridge, and Grace and Edith Abbott were the most prominent. All these women began their social service careers at Hull-House, all were academically trained, all were environmentalists, and all were anxious to gather social data. None was black, and none worked in neighborhoods with a substantial black population. However, through their writings and activities they grappled with the problems of black people. All of them eventually taught at the Chicago School of Civics and Philanthropy. They believed that reform would come only if the nation were confronted with hard data demonstrating social and industrial misery. They discovered the problems of blacks through studies of urban poverty and because of their alertness to differences among ethnic groups.

Sophonisba Breckinridge headed the School of Civics department of social investigation, and Edith Abbott was her assistant. Together they analyzed many facets of Chicago life. One study, published in 1912, concluded that juvenile delinquency was highest among children of immigrants and Negroes. Immigrant delinquency, they argued, resulted from the cross-pressures of American and old-world customs. Negroes, they found, were "barred from the complete enjoyment of many so-called common rights," and this was an equally negative influence on the young. Furthermore, they noticed a direct relationship between high population density, characteristic of immigrant slums, and a high rate of delinquency. A ward-by-ward analysis showed that, in spite of a somewhat lower population density, the Negro Fourteenth Ward had very high delinquency, but the authors noted that this ward showed evidence of poverty and neglect. "In no wards," they wrote, "are there found greater dilapidation and poorer sanitary conditions within the homes" (10:55–56, 151–53).

This delinquency study showed blacks and immigrants facing a common problem, but a housing study by Breckinridge at about the same time concluded that Negroes faced special difficulties. Negroes of all incomes had difficulty acquiring adequate housing, she discovered, whereas only poor immigrants lived in inadequate dwellings. Housing available to Negroes was scarce, and it was more dilapidated than that occupied by any other group. In addition, like Mrs. Bowen, Miss Breckinridge found that the vice district was located in Negro residential areas. She discovered that Negroes paid "from $2 to $4 a month more than the immigrant is paying for an apartment of the same size in a better state of repair" (8).

Research projects were not the only way these women learned about blacks. The federal Children's Bureau, headed by Julia Lathrop, reported on the administration of the first federal child labor law. The 1921 report noted problems in obtaining proof of age for Negro children applying for work certificates under the law (41:49–52). A case book compiled by Breckinridge for use by social work students included some cases of black families (9:399–417, 826–28). Miss Breckinridge was also instrumental in obtaining stipends to train two Negro social workers at the School of Civics, but did not succeed in getting funds to make the program permanent (42a).

Graham Taylor, of Chicago Commons, and Mary McDowell, of the University of Chicago Settlement, also wrote about blacks. Taylor, trained as a minister, first gained notice through his work in the slums of Hartford, Connecticut. In 1888 he was appointed to the faculty of Hartford Seminary. He came to Chicago in 1892 to head the new department of Christian sociology at Chicago Theological Seminary, where he taught for most of his career. He also taught at the University of Chicago and founded the School of Civics. He founded and headed Chicago Commons, a settlement house on Grand Avenue near Morgan Street (45:21–82). The Commons neighborhood housed a variety of ethnic groups, but few blacks.

Unlike his colleagues in the settlement movement, Taylor never compared Negroes and immigrants in his writings. As editor of *The Commons*, a social work journal, he printed a few articles on the "Negro question," noted or reviewed books about Negroes, and described activities of Negro institutions. One of his own articles praised the "expert work" done in "the American black belt by the American Missionary Association and under Booker T. Washington at Tuskegee" (35:465). During the Chicago packinghouse strike of 1904–5, Taylor had some sharp words about Negro strikebreakers. Referring to the problems created by the importation of Negroes, Taylor urged settlement of the strike before the "entire community is faced with perils and burdened with loss incomparably greater than either side had at stake" (28: 394).

Taylor was critical of the conditions

which led to the Springfield race riot of 1908. Arguing that blacks needed special help, he complained:

It is a sorry comment u   American civilization that no better use has ˻ ˼n made of our resources of law, education ana religion than to have allowed that population [Springfield blacks] to become in large part so depraved. . . . Not only is this most helpless part of our population largely left to its own feeble resources for self-help, but the vicious and criminal conditions of the districts in which both the better and the worse Negroes can only find shelter are forced upon all alike and their children too, indiscriminately [34].

He lauded a proposed YMCA for Chicago blacks on the South Side and praised philanthropist Julius Rosenwald for his support of the project (37; 42b). In a 1912 article, Taylor described a "southern social awakening" and reported the "absolute honesty with which speakers from the south faced the critical questions relating to the Negro" (36). A few years later he described the antipathy of white laborers to the influx of Negroes into northern cities and the worsening living conditions in the Negro neighborhoods (42c).

Taylor, like Miss Addams, believed that America's foreign populations strengthened American culture. "Rich and varied," he wrote, "are the heritages which all foreign-born bring with them from the old world to the new" (33:234). Unlike Miss Addams, however, Taylor did not also applaud the potential contribution of Negroes. He apparently saw America's Negroes as a problem, a "depraved" people whom society was obliged to uplift and treat humanely.

Mary McDowell's outlook differed from Taylor's. Her father had been a steel plant manager in Cincinnati who moved his family to Chicago after the Civil War. Miss McDowell worked at Hull-House until 1894 when, at the suggestion of Jane Addams, she was named to head the new University of Chicago Settlement in the ethnically diverse immigrant neighborhood behind the stockyards. Before going to the settlement, Miss McDowell had organized clubs for Negro women, but there were few blacks living near the settlement (51:1–24).

During the packinghouse strike of 1904–5, black strikebreakers were brought into her neighborhood. She sympathized with the strikers, and was upset by the worsening social conditions in the neighborhood:

Before this strike the Irish and Germans were the uplifting influences in the yards district. These lift the Poles and Lithuanians. If the strike fails, and these must go, leaving the criminal and negro population to become the base while the ignorant Lithuanian peasant and imported Greek becomes the only element of uplift, the social problems of the stock yards become at once hopeless [24:406].

This acute sensitivity to the roles played by various ethnic groups in her community characterized Miss McDowell's thinking. She placed Negroes on the bottom of the ladder of group achievement. She thought Negroes poorer and more ignorant than the Greeks and Lithuanians, but she expected them to move up the ladder as they, like other groups, learned the ways of the city.

To aid them in the climb, Miss McDowell urged the stockyard unions to admit Negroes, and she frequently lauded the union's role as ethnic mediator. It "established a fellowship of workers, it broke up a feud between blacks and whites, it broke down the barrier of prejudice between the different nationalities," she wrote (23:

400). Reflecting in 1922 on the history of organized labor, she noted that, as successive ethnic groups turned to unionization, a newer group was used to break strikes. "The Negro has now arrived at the place to which the immigrant has slowly come, and will have to learn," she wrote, "as the immigrant learned, that he was being exploited when he replaced the native and English-speaking groups" (26:72). Miss McDowell's work for blacks included membership on the boards of the Chicago NAACP and the Frederick Douglass Center.

Shortly before her retirement, Mary McDowell summed up her hope for America:

[President Masaryk of Czechoslovakia] saw in our heterogeneous community the same possibilities that he sees today in his new republic with its conflicting nationalities. He shared with us his faith that tolerance and good understanding will in time, there as here, bring about what Switzerland has ever been able to develop—a nation of different peoples, even with different languages, but with a common purpose. . . . Surely this is worth fighting for; a civilization that will give every group—black and white, Jew and Gentile, people of all nations—freedom and tolerance. . . . I now see a new civilization developing that we must work out in good understanding and good will [25:60].

Here we have a major tenet of the settlements' creed. The settlement leadership of Chicago subscribed to this doctrine of cultural pluralism, but was not of one voice on how blacks fit the design. Graham Taylor omitted Negroes; Mary McDowell saw them as one more group struggling to win self-respect, but underestimated their special problems; Jane Addams believed their potential contribution to American culture certainly equaled that of any other group, but recognized that their handicaps were more devastating than those of immigrants.

SOCIAL SERVICE FOR BLACKS

Although Chicago's best-known settlements did not serve those neighborhoods in which most black people lived, several settlements were opened in black quarters. Most of these projects were initiated jointly by social workers and black community leaders.

Mrs. Celia Parker Woolley was the best-known white engaged in settlement work among Chicago's blacks. Born in Toledo in 1848, she studied at Coldwater Female Seminary and married a physician while there. The Woolleys came to Chicago in 1876. From 1893 to 1898 Mrs. Woolley served in turn as minister of the Unitarian Church of Geneva and the Independent Liberal Church of Chicago. After 1898 she was active as a lecturer and writer until 1904, when she founded the Frederick Douglass Center, an interracial settlement at Thirtieth Street and Wabash Avenue. From that time until her death in 1918, the Center was her major activity (53).

The year before Mrs. Woolley began work on the Douglass Center, she criticized northern as well as southern racism. The greatest injustice, she argued, was being done to "the educated colored people in our midst . . . who are as wise and good as their white neighbors, whose tastes and habits are the same," but who nevertheless face social ostracism because of their skin color (57:135–36). This concern remained at the heart of Mrs. Woolley's thinking. White society, she insisted, must judge Negroes by the standards by which it judges whites.

The Douglass Center's by-laws reflected Mrs. Woolley's concern. The Center sought:

> To promote just and amicable relations between the white and colored people, to seek to remove the disabilities from which the latter suffer in their civic, political and industrial life, to encourage equal opportunity irrespective of race, color or other arbitrary distinctions.
>
> To establish a center of friendly help and influence in which to gather needful information and for mutual co-operation to the ends of right living and higher citizenship.

In describing the goals of the Center in 1904, Mrs. Woolley appealed to middle-class Negroes:

> The center will not be a place in which to foster weakness or the sense of grievance, but to promote industry, honesty and thrift in all those seeking our aid and counsel, to develop a deeper sense of obligation, "the responsibility of the superior" among the more favored members of society, and to encourage individual worth and attainment on all lines among all classes and kinds of people [55].

The Frederick Douglass Center was located on the border of the "black belt" so as to attract a racially mixed clientele. Prominent among its programs were interracial teas and forums. Other projects included a women's club, domestic science classes, religious services, a boys' club and athletic association, and a library. The Center also disseminated "enlightened information" about Negroes (21; 30:103–5).

Mrs. Woolley campaigned actively for equal treatment for Negroes. In a letter to the editor of *Survey* in 1910, she criticized an article that had accused Atlanta Negroes of transmitting tuberculosis. Mrs. Woolley charged the writer with lack of compassion for Negroes suffering from the disease and attributed the high tuberculosis rate among Negroes to the fact that they were forced to live in "the poorest quarters, with few or none of the usual privileges in the way of water, light and fresh air" (56). In 1912, Mrs. Woolley, like Jane Addams, supported Roosevelt for President. She wrote to Miss Addams at the convention and praised her "powerful and courageous action on the Negro question." She later justified her own support for Roosevelt on the ground that he offered a better hope for Negroes than either of the other two candidates (43).

At an Emancipation Proclamation celebration in 1913, Mrs. Woolley called upon the white man "to emancipate himself from that race arrogance and belief in his own inherent superiority and right of rule which is today the greatest obstacle in the Negro's path" (58:5). In a review for *Survey* she criticized Charles McCord's *The American Negro as a Dependent, Defective, and Delinquent* and cited prominent authorities in contradiction to the author's bold racist assertions (54). Mrs. Woolley also worked to reverse Cook County Hospital's policy of not hiring Negro nurses (42d; 42e).

Mrs. Woolley's activities appealed mostly to educated middle-class blacks. Significantly, the Douglass Center, which came late in her career, was her only involvement in social work. In New York, Mary White Ovington had begun her career in an immigrant settlement and from there had gone on to establish a settlement among poor blacks. She became a leading figure in the struggle for the betterment of black life. Mrs. Woolley, in contrast, had little interest in the conditions of poor blacks. She admonished American society for barring Negroes who had all the refinements and abilities of middle-class whites from social and economic equality, but she failed to see Chicago's

poor Negroes as victims of industrialization and urbanization. Mrs. Woolley embraced neither environmentalism nor cultural pluralism, and in this regard she was not in the mainstream of Chicago's settlement movement. Her emphasis on Negroes who were "as wise and good as their white neighbors" and her failure to comment on Afro-American culture suggest that Mrs. Woolley conceived the ideal Negro as a white man in black skin.

The most prominent black worker at the Douglass Center was Mrs. Fannie Barrier Williams. Born in Brockport, New York, of a free Negro family, she came to Chicago in the 1880s. She gained note as a public speaker and journalist before beginning work at the Frederick Douglass Center. Her husband, S. Lang Williams, was a prominent lawyer who served as secretary of the Douglass Center (30:66–70). The Williamses were leading Chicago supporters of Booker T. Washington.

Mrs. Williams's racial views paralleled those of Mrs. Woolley. She emphasized the achievements of "respectable" Negroes, and she was careful to distinguish the educated and successful of her race from the impoverished masses. In speeches delivered before the founding of the Douglass Center, Mrs. Williams demanded equal treatment for blacks and insisted that "every moral imperfection that mars the character of the colored American" was due to slavery. However, she emphasized the accomplishments of successful Negroes. "There are thousands of men and women everywhere among us," she stated in one speech, "who in twenty-five years have progressed as far away from the non-progressive peasants of the 'black belt' of the South as the highest social life in New England is above the lowest levels of American civilization" (49:703, 705).

Mrs. Williams's emphasis did not change after she started to work at the Frederick Douglass Center. She wrote that the Center was "not organized to do slum work in what may be called the black belt of Chicago, but to be a center of wholesome influences to the end that well-disposed white people may learn to know and respect the ever increasing number of colored people who have earned the right to be believed in and respected." The "best whites and blacks," she insisted, were involved in the Center (48). In an analysis of social bonds in the South Side Negro district, Mrs. Williams characterized the central section as an area where "there is scarcely a single ray of the light of decency" (50:44).

Mrs. Williams organized women's clubs at the Douglass Center and became an important figure in the national movement for colored women's clubs. Her writings on the club movement stressed the achievements of educated Negroes and the debasing effects of slavery on Negro morality. Slavery had been particularly harmful to the black woman, she argued, because it "made her the only woman in all America for whom virtue was not an ornament and a necessity." She suggested that a controversy in the National Federation of Women's Clubs over the admission of black women had aided her race because it brought to the public's notice "the best things among colored women and the best women" (47:197, 227).

The Frederick Douglass Center aside, the only successful settlement in the middle of a black neighborhood was the Wendell Phillips Center at West Lake and Washington Streets.

Whereas the impetus for the Douglass Center came from a white woman, the Wendell Phillips settlement was founded in 1907 by a group of twenty blacks. It provided blacks with services similar to those provided for the poor by settlements in other neighborhoods.

Wendell Phillips served blacks alone. Its interracial board of directors included Sophonisba Breckinridge and Louise Bowen. The two black students at the Chicago School of Civics and Philanthropy, Sophia Boaz and B. H. Haynes, lived at the settlement and did their field work there. Both women were granted certificates from the School in 1913 and stayed at the settlement for several years, Miss Haynes as head resident and Miss Boaz as her assistant.

Wendell Phillips ran a wide variety of classes and clubs for children and adults. The center was also a community meeting place. Miss Haynes described it as a "center from which real constructive social work may be done for the betterment of conditions among the colored people of the West Side" (42*f*).

Some black church leaders in Chicago also initiated social work projects. Reverdy Ransom was the first to do so. He came to Chicago in 1896 and in 1900 founded the Institutional Church and Social Settlement at Thirty-eighth Street and Dearborn Avenue. He and his successor, Archibald Carey, developed a full program of social services, including a day nursery, a kindergarten, a mothers' club, an employment bureau, a print shop, and a gymnasium. Ransom was friendly with Jane Addams and other social workers and called Institutional "not a church in the ordinary sense . . . [but] a Hull-House or Chicago Commons founded by Negroes for the help of people of that race" (30: 95–96). He left Chicago in 1904 and for many years thereafter fought for Negro rights.

Richard Wright, Jr., another church leader, also started a settlement for Chicago blacks. A graduate of the University of Chicago Divinity School, Wright, like Ransom, was a militant. In 1905 he founded Trinity Mission north of Twenty-second Street. However, Wright soon left Chicago, and the project folded shortly thereafter (30:106; 5:106–24). Finally, Mrs. Ida Wells-Barnett, a prominent black woman, founded a settlement for blacks in 1910. The Negro Fellowship League on State Street functioned for about three years but could not raise enough money and was forced to close (30: 106).

CLIMAX: THE URBAN LEAGUE AND
THE 1919 RIOT

By the time war broke out in Europe, Chicago social workers had done some thinking about the status of blacks in their city. Their thoughts were underscored by the founding of the Chicago Urban League in 1916 and were rendered urgent when a bloody race riot engulfed Chicago in 1919.

Social workers and social work programs dominated the Chicago Urban League from the start. Leaders of the National Urban League, based in New York, took the initiative in organizing the Chicago branch. In 1915 and 1916, these leaders traveled to Chicago and spoke with key people about establishing a Chicago branch. Sophonisba Breckinridge was a member of the national League board; she and Edith Abbott were active in the early discussions.

The Chicago Urban League was officially founded on December 11, 1916. Present at the organizational meeting were, among others, A. Kenyon Maynard, resident at Chicago Commons and faculty member at the School of Civics and Philanthropy; Mrs. Alice Caldwell, of the Charity Section of the City Federation; Arthur Gould, of the Juvenile Protective Association; and Mrs. Catherine Briggs, of United Charities. Jane Addams, Celia Parker Woolley, and Amelia Sears, superintendent of the Juvenile Protective Association, were also chosen to serve on the Executive Board. Other League members included Sophia Boaz, Louise deKoven Bowen, Mary McDowell, and Graham Taylor (16a:2, 15–16; 31: 26–30).

The first annual report of the League illustrated how completely the organization's outlook rested on the experience of Chicago social workers during the preceding years. Robert Park, University of Chicago sociologist and first president of the League, asserted in the opening sentence of the report that "the problem of the Negro in Chicago is, on the whole, one with the problem of the immigrant." Blacks and immigrants shared problems of "work and wages, health and housing, the difficulties of adjustment of an essentially rural population to the conditions of a city environment." Park argued that, in addition, Negroes faced racial discrimination and were restricted in choice of employment regardless of educational level (16a:3–5).

The League provided blacks with the services that social workers daily provided for poor people of all nationalities. The Department of Investigation and Records collected data, and the Bureau of Information dispensed data. The League coordinated existing social service agencies serving blacks, and it employed a trained caseworker. An Employment Bureau sought jobs for newly arrived migrants, and the League also tried to locate housing for new arrivals. The Children's Department dealt with juvenile delinquency and sought to protect black youngsters from mistreatment. After 1918, the League supervised the Wendell Phillips Settlement directly. Finally, the League urged Negroes to obtain professional training in social work at the School of Civics (16). The principles underlying the League's program—emphasis on environment and adjustment to new conditions, coordination of social services, quest for social data, stress on common problems with immigrants, and recognition of the special problems of discrimination—had been developed by Chicago social workers well before the Urban League began.

Social workers responded quickly to the bloody Chicago race riot of 1919, and the lesson of the riot was not lost on them. In a *Survey* article Graham Taylor analyzed its causes—insufficient and unsuitable housing for the industrial classes in Chicago, the personal immorality fostered by the vice district, and the ties of Chicago's two Negro aldermen to white politicians (32). Mary McDowell, shocked by the riot, later wrote: "The race riots ... brought to the consciousness of thoughtful, unprejudiced citizens the fact that it is not possible to have a well-governed city with a segregated group within its boundaries." Shortly after the riot, she was instrumental in forming the Interracial Cooperative Committee to coordinate work of all women's clubs in matters of race relations (51:176, 182). Harriet Vittum, head resident of Northwestern University Settlement, commented that "during the last ten or fifteen years of her active service the race-relations campaign was probably Miss McDowell's most compelling interest" (44:25).

During and immediately after the riot, a number of social workers participated in a joint Emergency Committee, headed by Robert Park, which arranged legal aid for arrested blacks. The Chicago Federation of Settlements urged Illinois Governor Frank O. Lowden to appoint a special commission on the causes of the riot. A meeting of leading Chicagoans on August 1, attended by Graham Taylor, Mary McDowell, and Harriet Vittum, repeated the request (15; 46:46, 61).

The commission was created, and Graham Romeyn Taylor and Charles S. Johnson were named to direct its research. Taylor, son of Graham Taylor, had grown up and worked in Chicago Commons and had served on the editorial staff of *Survey*. Johnson was a graduate student under Robert Park and director of research for the Chicago Urban League. Their staff consisted of about eighteen researchers, mostly social workers. They analyzed housing data previously collected by social agencies and studied the files of the Chicago Urban League. They also collected new data.

The commission's final report discussed in detail Chicago race relations and the status of the city's blacks. Many of its findings corroborated earlier studies by social workers. The report denied that Negroes were biologically inferior. It pointed to the existence of anti-Negro discrimination in employment, housing, labor unions, and the courts; it denounced the role of the press in prejudicing people against Negroes; and it suggested that the police did not treat blacks fairly. However, the report contained no contrasts between blacks and immigrants, and it did not discuss black culture (12).

DISCUSSION: THE BURDEN OF COLOR

Chicago social workers in the Progressive Era were not of one mind in their outlook toward blacks; neither did they propose a single program to aid black people. But they shared a desire to eliminate poverty, and this led them to a concern for Chicago's black population.

To most Chicago social workers, blacks were one of many poor ethnic groups. Like the city's foreign-born peoples, blacks faced overcrowding, exploitation, low wages, and wretched housing. Black migrants from the rural American South were no less alien to the northern city than immigrants.

Yet, because they thought in pluralist terms, Chicago social workers perceived the special problems of blacks. People with black skin suffered the most from prejudice in jobs, education, and recreation, and their housing was not only the most segregated but also the most likely to be in the vice district. The crucial differences, however, were not those of degree but those of kind. Slavery, noted Jane Addams, robbed Negroes of traditions and restraints that enabled immigrant groups to adjust, however slowly and imperfectly, to the city. Whereas the children of the foreign-born could achieve success and escape the ancestral slum, Sophonisba Breckinridge noticed that blacks were

relegated to a subordinate status irrespective of achievement. By the end of World War I, as the 1919 riot dramatized, blacks were a group apart.

Of course, some social workers had believed that all along. For Graham Taylor, blacks fell into one category and immigrants into another. If *Cooperation* talked about blacks and immigrants in a similar way, it still placed blacks in a separate category. Celia Parker Woolley and Fannie Barrier Williams, crusaders against discrimination, did not address themselves to immigrants at all. The best indicator of the uniqueness of blacks, however, was the creation of black settlement houses. Their founders assumed that black people needed separate institutions of their own.

Nevertheless, the most influential figures on the Chicago scene, Taylor excepted, struggled to discover the place of blacks in a pluralistic society. The outlook of Jane Addams and Mary McDowell, of Sophonisba Breckinridge, Edith Abbott, and Louise deKoven Bowen, dominated the Chicago Urban League.

All of this has a modern ring. Then, as now, American society was ethnically diverse. A half-century and more ago, Chicago's social workers recognized that blacks were part of a multi-ethnic society. They recognized, too, that blacks were special in their disabilities. These social workers were among the first to perceive that blacks, in contrast to immigrant groups, might constitute a caste in northern urban life.

Received October 9, 1969

REFERENCES

1. Addams, Jane. "Has the Emancipation Proclamation Been Nullified by National Indifference?" *Survey* 29 (February 1, 1913): 565–66.

2. ———. "Immigration: A Field Neglected by the Scholar." *Commons* 10 (January 1905): 9–19.

3. ———. "The Progressive Party and the

Negro." *Crisis* 5 (November 1912): 30–31.

4. ———. *The Second Twenty Years at Hull-House.* New York: Macmillan Co., 1930.

5. Bardolph, Richard. *The Negro Vanguard.* New York: Rinehart & Co., 1959.

6. Bowen, Louise deKoven. *The Colored People of Chicago.* Chicago: Juvenile Protective Association, 1913. [Pages unnumbered.]

7. ———. *Growing Up with a City.* New York: Macmillan Co., 1926.

8. Breckinridge, Sophonisba P. "The Color Line and the Housing Problem." *Survey* 29 (February 1, 1913): 575–76.

9. Breckinridge, Sophonisba P., ed. *Family Welfare Work in a Metropolitan Community: Selected Case Records.* Chicago: University of Chicago Press, 1924.

10. Breckinridge, Sophonisba P., and Abbott, Edith. *The Delinquent Child and the Home.* New York: Charities Publication Committee, 1912.

11. Chicago Bureau of Charities. *Fifth Annual Report, 1898–99.*

12. Chicago Commission on Race Relations. *The Negro in Chicago: A Study of Race Relations and a Race Riot.* Chicago: University of Chicago Press, 1922.

13. *Chicago Daily News,* November 11, 1953.

14. *Chicago Examiner,* January 30, 1917.

15. Chicago Historical Society. Lea Taylor MSS. Chicago Federation of Settlements, Minutes, 1919.

16. Chicago League on Urban Conditions among Negroes. *Annual Reports, 1917–20.* (a) *First Annual Report, 1917.*

17. Chicago Relief and Aid Society. *Forty-fourth Annual Report, 1900–1901.*

18. *Chicago Sun Times,* November 11, 1953.

19. *Co-operation.* (a) September 21, 1901; (b) November 1, 1902; (c) May 9, 1903; (d) May 30, 1903; (e) October 3, 1903; (f) October 24, 1903; (g) February 6, 1904; (h) March 12, 1904; (i) May 14, 1904; (j) October 28, 1905; (k) February 9, 1907; (m) March 2, 1907; (n) March 9, 1907; (o) September 5, 1908.

20. Davis, Allen F. *Spearheads for Reform: The Social Settlements and the Progressive Movement.* New York: Oxford University Press, 1967.

21. "Frederick Douglass Center." *Journal of Social and Civic Chicago* 3 (January 1913): 10; 3 (March 1913): 12.

22. Humphrey, Mary E., ed. *Speeches, Addresses, and Letters of Louise deKoven Bowen,* vol. 2. Ann Arbor: Edwards Bros., 1937.

23. McDowell, Mary. "At the Heart of the Packingtown Strike." *Commons* 9 (September 1904): 397–402.

24. ———. "The Community's Interest in the Stockyards Strike: The Inside View of an Outsider." *Commons* 9 (September 1904): 402–6.

25. ———. "How the Living Faith of One Social Worker Grew." *Survey* 60 (April 1, 1928): 40–43, 57–60.

26. ———. "The Negro in Industry." *The World Tomorrow* 5 (March 1922): 72–73.

27. *New York Tribune,* August 6, 1912.

28. "Private versus Public Cost of a Strike." *Commons* 9 (September 1904): 393–94.

29. Roosevelt, Theodore, to Raymond Robins, August 12, 1914. In *The Letters of Theodore Roosevelt,* vol. 7, edited by Elting E. Morison, pp. 796–802. Cambridge, Mass.: Harvard University Press, 1954.

30. Spear, Allan H. *Black Chicago: The Making of a Negro Ghetto, 1890–1920.* Chicago and London: University of Chicago Press, 1967.

31. Strickland, Arvarh H. *History of the Chicago Urban League.* Urbana, Ill., and London: University of Illinois Press, 1966.

32. Taylor, Graham. "Chicago in the Nation's Race Strife." *Survey* 42 (August 9, 1919): 695–97.

33. ———. "Developing the American Spirit." In *America and the New Era,* edited by Elisha M. Friedman, pp. 231–46. New York: E. P. Dutton & Co., 1920.

34. ———. "The Riot in Lincoln's City." *Charities and the Commons* 20 (August 29, 1908): 627–28.

35. ———. "Social Tendencies of the Industrial Revolution." *Commons* 9 (October 1904): 459–68.

36. ———. "The Southern Social Awakening." *Survey* 28 (September 14, 1912): 744–45.

37. ———. "Washington's Day for Citizenship." *Survey* 25 (February 25, 1911): 880–81.

38. United Charities of Chicago. *Annual Report, 1915–16.*

39. United States. Census Bureau. *Abstract of the Thirteenth U.S. Census, 1910, with Supplement for Illinois.*

40. ———. *Abstract of the Fourteenth U.S. Census, 1920.*

41. United States. Department of Labor. Children's Bureau. *Administration of the First*

Federal Child Labor Law. Washington, D.C.: Government Printing Office, 1921.

42. University of Chicago Library. Julius Rosenwald papers. (*a*) Sophonisba Breckinridge to Graham Taylor, October 11, 1912; (*b*) Graham Taylor to Julius Rosenwald, January 3, 191[1]; (*c*) Graham Taylor, "To Safeguard Incoming Negro Labor," undated clipping; (*d*) Celia Parker Woolley to Charlotte Johnson, November 27, 1912; (*e*) Celia Parker Woolley to Julius Rosenwald, November 27, 1912; (*f*) "Wendell Phillips Settlement" folder.

43. ———. Microfilm of Jane Addams correspondence in the Swarthmore College Peace Collection. Celia Parker Woolley to Jane Addams, August 7, 1912, and October 8, 1912.

44. Vittum, Harriet. "Foreword to 'Prejudice' by Mary McDowell." In *Mary McDowell and Municipal Housekeeping: A Symposium,* edited by Caroline Hill. Chicago: Millar Publishing Co., 194——.

45. Wade, Louise. *Graham Taylor, Pioneer for Social Justice, 1851–1938.* Chicago and London: University of Chicago Press, 1964.

46. Waskow, Arthur. *From Race Riot to Sit In, 1919 and the 1960s.* Garden City, N.Y.: Anchor Books, 1967.

47. Williams, Fannie Barrier. "Club Movement among Colored Women." In *The Colored American from Slavery to Honorable Citizenship,* edited by J. W. Gibson and W. H. Crogman, pp. 197–231. Atlanta, Ga.: J. L. Nichols & Co., 1903.

48. ———. "The Frederick Douglass Center." *The Southern Workman* 35 (June 1906): 334–36.

49. ———. "The Intellectual Progress of the Colored Women of the United States since the Emancipation Proclamation." In *The World's Congress of Representative Women,* edited by May Wright Sewall, pp. 696–711. Chicago and New York: Rand, McNally & Co., 1894.

50. ———. "Social Bonds in the 'Black Belt' of Chicago." *Charities and the Commons* 15 (October 7, 1905): 40–44.

51. Wilson, Howard. *Mary McDowell, Neighbor.* Chicago: University of Chicago Press, 1928.

52. Woods, Robert, and Kennedy, Albert. *Handbook of Settlements.* New York: Charities Publication Committee, 1911.

53. "Woolley, Celia Parker." In *The Book of Chicagoans, 1917,* p. 745. Chicago: A. N. Marquis Co., 1917.

54. Woolley, Celia Parker. Review of *The American Negro as a Dependent, Defective, and Delinquent,* by Charles McCord. *Survey* 35 (October 9, 1915): 52.

55. ———. "The Frederick Douglass Center, Chicago." *Commons* 9 (July 1904): 328–29.

56. ———. "Negro Contagion." *Survey* 23 (January 8, 1910): 505.

57. ———. *The Western Slope.* Evanston, Ill.: William S. Lord, 1903.

58. ———. "The White Man's Emancipation." *Journal of Social and Civic Chicago* 2 (February 1913): 5, 8.

Consensus for Reform: The Mothers'-Pension Movement in the Progressive Era

Mark H. Leff
Chicago, Illinois

Mothers' pensions, the precursor of today's aid to families with dependent children, achieved remarkable legislative success. Only workers in some private social agencies actively opposed this trailblazing assertion of governmental welfare responsibility. The movement synthesized common concerns about children, widows, and the home during the Progressive era. This consensus for reform permitted and sometimes encouraged the behavioral demands and the hostility to indigent males that still characterize the welfare system.

Scoring its first statewide victory in Illinois in 1911, the mothers'-pension movement swept forty states in less than a decade. No plank of the social-justice platform, with the possible exception of workmen's compensation, mustered a better legislative record. Drawing upon historic American concerns with children, widows, and the home, mothers' pensions incorporated the major strains of progressivism. Moral reformers and economic-efficiency buffs, women's clubs and labor unions, middle-class do-gooders and relief recipients, New Freedom advocates and New Nationalism partisans, all jumped onto the bandwagon. Their clash with unconvinced charity workers and half-dormant conservatives was a mismatch.

The startlingly narrow scope of this consensus highlights the economic and social limitations of early-twentieth-century reform. Mothers' pensions (also called widows' pensions or mothers' aid) were paltry long-term cash provisions for children without employable fathers, contingent upon their mothers' acceptance of middle-class behavioral norms. The program thus promised to be cheap and morally uplifting, while raising no specter of dissolute male misfits lining up for their monthly liquor money.

In 1935, the aid-to-dependent-children provisions of the Social Security Act tendered federal guidelines and financial support to state mothers'-aid agencies. This program has earned as great a consensus in its opposition as had formerly been secured in its favor. Yet popular principles regarding welfare have changed little; they still encompass reliance upon local administration, the rejection of a right to public aid, and the imposition

Social Service Review 47 (September 1973): 397–417

of "suitable home" criteria. Today's "welfare mess" is, in no small part, a product of yesterday's welfare maxims.

The Development of Mothers' Pensions

The case for mothers' pensions was airtight in terms of contemporary concerns. Seeing in children "infinite possibilities for good," Progressives believed that "in the child and in our treatment of him rests the solution of the problems which confront the State and society today" (27: 280; 29: 1). But interest in children was not unique to progressivism. In the 1860s and 1870s, sympathy for war orphans, supplemented by a belief in the value of differential treatment of children and adults, had resulted in state campaigns to remove orphans and other children from almshouses and to place them in institutions. By the turn of the century, dissatisfaction with the "products" of orphanages, combined with objections to institutional regimentation, artificiality, and inability to dispense individual care, elicited substantial popular opposition. "Even a very poor home," it was said, "offers a better chance for [a child's] development than an excellent institution" (10: 186). By 1909, children's-home societies in twenty-eight states furthered the foster-home movement (5: 317).

The widow, too, was an object of public sympathy. She could scarcely be held accountable for the death of her husband; yet the disintegration of the extended family in urban America often left her with pitifully little to fall back on. While it was expected that married women would not be gainfully employed (only 5–10 percent of them were), almost one-third of all widows found it necessary to hold jobs (12: 196). It became a cliché to warn that "to be the breadwinner and the home-maker of the family is more than the average woman can bear." The results, it was said, were that "the home crumbles" and that "the physical and moral well-being of the mother and the children is impaired and seriously menaced" (47: 809). Aid to prevent this disintegration was distinguished from other relief because it buttressed traditional family roles: "Women and children ought to be supported, and there is no sense of degradation in receiving support" (25: 351).

The role of government in public relief aroused more controversy. Late in the nineteenth century, social workers and private charities challenged public outdoor-relief programs, and succeeded in abolishing or curtailing them in most major cities (6: 40). Yet, by 1900, new state laws regulating private children's institutions reasserted the government position. Boards of public welfare were established in a number of midwestern cities, beginning in Kansas City in 1908 and reaching Chicago soon thereafter. Their proponents asserted that relief was a public responsibility rather than a private service, that relief needs had grown too large to be met by private resources, and that public agencies could apply the lessons of efficiency and scientific philanthropy as competently as private ones.

Many private agencies thus came to fear a preemption by government. Realizing that their failure to preserve the home was the chink in their armor, they established nurseries, along with job-placement services for widows. However, they still encouraged many widows to send some of their children to orphanages in order to provide adequate family support. A few charity institutions (particularly Jewish ones) disregarded the admonitions of scientific philanthropy that assured relief would be pauperizing, and began to give regular monetary aid to widows. Other organizations pointed out that regular private charity showed little commitment to meeting this need, and focused their efforts on widows' pensions alone.

Around the turn of the century, public aid for dependent children in their own homes had been proposed as an alternative to public outdoor relief and private charity. In 1898, the New York legislature passed a bill granting widowed mothers in New York City an allowance equal to the state expenditure for institutionalizing their children (44: 182). However, the mayor of New York City, pressured by the interests of private charity, convinced the governor not to sign the bill. In 1906, the juvenile courts in some California counties liberally interpreted laws to furnish county aid to children in their own homes, and in 1910 the attorney general of New Jersey took a similar step. Oklahoma in 1908 established "school scholarships," paid from educational funds to children of widows; and in the early months of 1911 Michigan enacted a comparable law for indigent children. None of these laws explicitly recognized state responsibility for support of dependent children in their own homes. Nevertheless, it is clear that the public distinguished widows' aid from other public relief.

Probably the greatest spur to the subsequent passage of mothers'-pension laws was the 1909 Conference on the Care of Dependent Children. President Roosevelt opened the conference by discussing the plight of the widow unable to support her children. "Surely in such a case," he urged, "the goal toward which we should strive is to help that mother, so that she can keep her own home and keep the child in it; that is the best thing possible to be done for that child. How the relief shall come, public, private, or by a mixture of both, in what way, you are competent to say and I am not" (51: 36). In the debate that followed, several members called for public mothers' pensions. In rebuttal, a vocal minority desperately defended children's institutions. The fourteen conference resolutions, which reflected the most advanced ideas on child welfare of the time, laid the foundation for several future reforms. The creation of the Children's Bureau, for example, was one result of this conference. But the resolution relating to mothers' pensions attracted the most attention:

Home life is the highest and finest product of civilization. It is the great molding force of mind and of character. Children should not be deprived of it except for urgent and compelling reasons. Children of parents of worthy character, suffering from temporary misfortune and children of reasonably efficient and deserving mothers who are without the support of the normal breadwinner, should, as a rule, be kept with their parents, such aid being given as may be necessary to maintain suitable homes for the rearing of the children. This aid should be given by such methods and from such sources as may be determined by the general relief policy of each community, preferably in the form of private charity, rather than of public relief. Except in unusual circumstances, the home should not be broken up for reasons of poverty, but only for considerations of inefficiency or immorality [51: 9–10].

This resolution, though expressing a preference for privately funded mothers' pensions, catalyzed the drive for public legislation. Soon a stream of people declared their advocacy of pensions for mothers. With the passage of the first mothers'-pension laws, this stream became a flood.

The legislative breakthrough came with the passage of two mothers'-pension provisions in 1911. Missouri's statute, confined to Kansas City, was sponsored by Judge E. E. Porterfield of the Jackson County (Kansas City) juvenile court. The statewide law in Illinois benefited from lobbying efforts by the Chicago-based National Probation League (a recently formed organization primarily geared toward probation as an alternative to prison or reformatories for child and adult offenders); it also drew support from Judge Merritt Pinckney of the Cook County juvenile court, whose participation in the 1909 conference had reinforced his interest in mothers' pensions. As judges, both men had found it distasteful to separate children from their unsupported mothers on grounds of poverty, and they believed that many delinquent children became "bad" because their working mothers could not care for them.

Although 1912 was an off year for most state legislatures, momentum gathered in a Colorado referendum victory led by Denver juvenile court judge Ben Lindsey, and in several municipal and county ordinances adopting mothers' pensions. In 1913, the floodgates burst. Of the forty-two state legislatures in session, twenty-seven considered mothers'- pension legislation and seventeen passed it. Twenty states, sixteen of them in the West or Midwest, had now enacted mothers'-pension laws (see table 1). By 1915, the number had grown to twenty-nine; in 1919 it reached thirty-nine, plus Alaska and Hawaii. By this point, the mothers'-pension movement ceased to be a national concern. The next fifteen years were a mopping-up operation that gathered in the two remaining western and New England states, the District of Columbia, and five of the seven remaining southern states.

This "wildfire spread of widows' pensions," many commentators contended, exceeded that of any other social or humanitarian idea of their era (57: 87). Mothers'-pension provisions usually carried by near-unanimous tallies; opposition successes depended on preventing the bills

Table 1
Passage of Mothers'-Pension Laws, by Time Period and Region

Time Period	Region			
	Northeast	Central	South	West
1911–13	Massachusetts New Hampshire New Jersey Pennsylvania	Illinois Iowa Michigan Minnesota Missouri* Nebraska Ohio South Dakota Wisconsin		California Colorado Idaho Nevada Oregon Utah Washington
1914–19	Connecticut Maine New York Vermont	Indiana Kansas North Dakota	Arkansas Delaware Florida Maryland Oklahoma Tennessee Texas Virginia West Virginia	Alaska Arizona Hawaii Montana Wyoming
1920–31	Rhode Island		Alabama District of Columbia Kentucky Louisiana Mississippi North Carolina	New Mexico

*Law not made statewide until 1917.

from coming to a vote. Referendums, too, proving no contest, won by majorities of more than two to one in both Colorado and Arizona.

The enactments resulting from this popular upsurge exhibited broad similarities. Funding and administration of the laws was locally based. Administrative duties usually fell to juvenile courts, a recent Progressive attainment. Their existing bureaucracy and responsibility for dependent children, along with their dissociation from both outdoor relief and private charity, made them a natural choice for this function. Almost every statute established a maximum allowable monthly pension, which ranged from nine dollars to fifteen dollars a month for the first child and four dollars to ten dollars a month for additional children. To be eligible to receive this pension, a mother had to be "a proper person, physically, mentally and morally fit to bring up her children" (53: 22). Pensions could usually be granted only for children under the age of fourteen or sixteen. The state-residency requirement was one to three years; two states required the mother to be a United States citizen. Most states did not restrict eligible recipients to widows alone; pensions were occasionally authorized for women whose husbands had deserted them, were confined to mental hospitals or prisons, or were physically or mentally incapacitated. Only Michigan specifically included unmarried or divorced mothers, though several laws were general enough to include fathers. Rarely, however, were such opportunities exploited, since they were usually the result of legislative imprecision or fear that the law would otherwise be declared unconstitutional. All states required proof of extreme poverty, along with an agreement to cease or limit employment upon receipt of a pension.

But the rudimentary measures instituted between 1911 and 1919 had already forged one of the major contributions of the social-justice movement to the New Deal's formulation of the welfare state.

The Formation of the Consensus

The alignment of forces contesting mothers'-pension proposals was unique in the history of American reform. Even persistent conservative foes of social-justice legislation muted their criticism. In their stead, the vanguard of the social-justice movement itself rose in opposition to mothers' pensions. Swept aside by a movement that had advanced beyond their original reform intentions, a phalanx of prominent charity workers turned against many of their colleagues and most of their disciples.

Charity-worker opposition to widows'-pension legislation emanated from the perceived threat to the agencies that employed them and to their cult of scientific philanthropy. Only in the 1920s did mothers' pensions gain widespread social work support. By that time, as administrators, social workers had molded the program to suit their casework approach.

The social service profession polarized over what has been called "the well-nigh universal disagreement between settlements and organized charity on the question of widows' pensions" (60: 380). Nowhere was this better illustrated than in New York City, where every major private charity in the state opposed the 1913 widows'-pension bill, while the Association of Neighborhood Workers, which represented the settlement houses of New York City, publicly favored it. Settlements had always been more prone than private charities to attribute individual problems to social ills and to seek government aid to make necessary economic and environmental changes.

Some advocates of mothers' pensions, such as Robert Hebbard and Jacob Billikopf, held positions on boards of public welfare or in other governmental relief organizations that were less likely to resent an expanded public-aid role. The failure of private charity to find adequate funding for widows'- aid experiments led charity workers such as Hannah

Einstein and Homer Folks to favor a mothers'-pension law. A number of social work leaders, such as Mary Simkhovitch, Lillian Wald, Jane Addams, and Florence Kelley, counted themselves among the early proponents of pensions for mothers, as did the Abbott sisters and Julia Lathrop to a lesser extent. (All seven of these women were either former or active settlement workers.) Yet this support was usually tempered by fear of reversion to pre-scientific-philanthropy methods. Thus, no spokesman for this group emerged, and most of these social welfare leaders played minor or inactive roles in widows'-pension campaigns.

Most leading charity workers felt keenly threatened by the attack upon private philanthropy's hegemony. "Who are these sudden heroes of a brand new program of state subsidies to mothers?" asked Edward T. Devine, general secretary of the New York Charity Organization Society and the most vocal antagonist of mothers' pensions. "Who are these brash reformers who so cheerfully impugn the motives of old-fashioned givers, of the conscientious directors of charitable institutions, of pious founders of hospitals and all manner of benefactions?" (13: 182–83). Opposition to widows' pensions permeated almost every private charity agency and orphanage in the country. Charity-organization societies contributed the four major opponents of mothers' pensions: Edward Devine, Josephine Shaw Lowell, Frederic Almy, and Mary Richmond. Charity workers led the attack in New York, Massachusetts, Pennsylvania, and other states with strong charity interests. (The latter did not include the western and midwestern states, which were to be the most fertile ground for the new laws.)

In their assault upon mothers' pensions, charity workers used two main lines of argument: a defense of orphanages and private charity and a restatement of the truths of scientific philanthropy. Especially in the debates on mothers' pensions in the 1909 conference, social workers such as Edward Devine and directors of children's institutions had acclaimed the benefits of institutional care for even nondelinquent children whose parents supported them but were not a "pure, moral influence" (51). This argument had little currency in later mothers'-pension debates. But numerous social workers defended private charity throughout this period, contending that few children were separated from their parents on grounds of poverty alone ("inefficiency" of the mother, for example, might be the justification), and that private charity could finance wider private widows'-pension programs if they did not have to compete against government (one problem, though not stated explicitly, was that impoverished widows and children were good drawing cards for funds).

The philosophy of scientific philanthropy underpinned the case against public grants for dependent children. Opposition was particularly fierce in cities that had succumbed to intense private-charity pressure to dismantle their public outdoor-relief systems. The widow's plight had served as a justification for the maintenance of government relief; the reemergence of this image thus presented a special threat. Defending their hard-won position, charity workers depicted mothers' pensions as "a step backward, a reversal of policy" (38: 489). Government was deemed incapable of learning the lessons of scientific philanthropy: it would be subject to corruption and political interference; it would fail to realize the importance of attracting competent trained administrators; and it would not provide adequate supervision. Combined with the subversive and fiercely assailed belief that certain forms of regular relief were a right, the result would be "pauperization," a "pathological parasitism" that would "inevitably create a new class of dependents" (7: 174; 13: 180). It was a scandalous mistake to give recipients cash rather than certain basic necessities; with pensions averaging twenty-three dollars a month for some families, "temptations come to spend money recklessly or foolishly" (7: 164). Moreover, mothers' pensions were "an insidious attack upon the family, inimical to the welfare of children and injurious to the character of parents." Not only did pensions encourage desertion in those few states that granted them to deserted families, but they failed to invoke the "great principle of family solidarity, calling upon the strong members of the family to support the weak" (13: 177; 16: 453).

Few detractors of widows' pensions emerged outside the social service community. A number of social-insurance advocates (many of whom were charity workers who rallied to this alternative as the mothers'-pension movement gained momentum) expressed their fear that the pension campaign would divert interest from more basic reforms. This opposition, however, derived from different assumptions than might be supposed. These workers were leery of the imputation of a primary governmental responsibility for the alleviation of poverty. Social insurance, many of them felt, was "only a cooperative form of self-help"; no "self-respecting worker" would want it to become "a subsidy either from employers or from consumers" (13: 180–81).

Unlike much social legislation, mothers'-pension programs were neither expensive nor disruptive to productive efficiency. They thus posed no threat to wealthy conservatives, who were disinclined anyway to exert their political muscle on the wrong side of motherhood. The infrequent public attacks trod familiar ground. Widows'-pension expenditures, it was predicted, would irrepressibly soar. Poor widows from other countries or other states would descend upon states with new laws to make a quick pittance. The greatest danger, of course, was socialism. It was warned that the guiding philosophy of mothers' pensions was "not alms, but their right to share"—a principle that "represses the desire for self-help, self-respect, and independence," and leads to old-age pensions, free food for the unemployed, and state socialism (26: 103). But such objections seldom surfaced. Some conservative newspapers led campaigns against such laws, but, except for the referendum fight in

Colorado, these too seem to have been rare. Even the large number of juvenile-court judges who opposed aid to dependent children chose the strategy of nonenforcement in preference to public disputes with their reformist colleagues.

Support for mothers' pensions was neither so limited nor so reticent. Approval was widespread despite the polycentricity of the mothers'-pension movement, which had no national coordinating committee or national leader.

Juvenile-court judges had initially spearheaded widows'-pension drives. They had been pivotal in the passage of the first three state mothers'-pension laws, and they were important advocates of later dependent-children provisions in New York, Wisconsin, and California. But the role of these judges in legislative campaigns waned as the growing strength of the movement was catalyzed by the first few state laws.

Progressive politicians played a less readily definable role. Many consider the years from 1911 to 1915 to be the pinnacle or culmination of progressivism. Especially in those western and midwestern states that proved the most fertile ground for widows' pensions, this legislation was frequently accompanied by statutes on child labor, working conditions and minimum wages for women and children, or workmen's compensation, which drew more upon a concern for women and children than is now generally realized. Mothers' pensions dovetailed neatly with other reformist drives: they compensated certain families inadequately protected by accident-insurance laws, and they made child-labor restriction and compulsory education less onerous to families of widowed mothers.

Yet mothers' pensions were not a central political concern. The belief that public aid and other social services were a local responsibility rendered them a dead issue on the national level. Before the 1930s, the scattered mothers'-pension bills proposed in Congress (starting in 1914) received little consideration, while aid-to-dependent-children planks emerged in the national platforms of only two minor parties. Despite the widespread Progressive support for mothers' pensions, which transcended party boundaries, this program rarely even merited mention in the party platforms of states that enacted such laws. In Wisconsin, where a mothers'-pension provision was urged in the 1912 Republican state platform, proposed in 1913 by a Republican governor and overwhelmingly passed later that year by a Republican legislature, this law ranked near the bottom of the Republicans' list of accomplishments in their 1914 state platform. More typically, state platforms did not advocate mothers'-pension legislation until its enactment; the follow-up was either continued silence, self-congratulation, or calls for its expansion and support.

Political figures, however, were not divorced from the widows'-pension movement. Mothers'-pension partisans claimed support from Theodore Roosevelt, Robert LaFollette, and Louis Brandeis (31: 10; 45). A 1923 campaign biography cited Calvin Coolidge's past support for mothers' pensions as evidence of his Progressive nature (59: 27). In his December 1925 message to Congress, Coolidge proposed an aid-to-dependent-children law for the District of Columbia—a belated action that Congressman La Guardia termed "the only human touch in the President's message" (50). Alfred E. Smith was perhaps more deserving of the credit he received on this score in his campaign biographies, for he delivered a heart-rending 1915 widows'-pension speech, which received wide coverage in New York newspapers, and he helped guide the law through the legislature. Some gubernatorial messages dealt with mothers' pensions, and some state legislators publicly discussed their advocacy of pensions, but on the whole, politicians remained followers rather than molders of public opinion.

Progressive newspapers and magazines participated more actively in the mothers'-pension movement. Beginning in 1907 with the arrival of Theodore Dreiser as its editor, the *Delineator,* a crusading mass-circulation women's fashion magazine, had championed foster homes as an alternative to institutional care for dependent children. By 1912, the *Delineator* became a forceful advocate for mothers' pensions and even sent a lecturer around the country to promote this cause. William Hard, a young Rooseveltian Progressive who had formerly headed the Northwestern University Settlement House, turned the *Delineator's* regular column on women and children into a journalistic campaign for mothers'-pension laws. Hard was also a member of the heavily packed New York commission whose 1914 report was probably the most uncompromising defense of mothers' pensions and the most forthright attack on the ineffectiveness of private charity ever delivered by a public body (34).

Another member of this commission was Sophie Loeb, a thirty-seven-year-old staff reporter for the *New York Evening World,* a Democratic paper with strong ties to the Wilson administration. Loeb launched a personal crusade, through her columns and through lobbying efforts, to secure a New York child welfare law. To her belongs much of the credit for both the appointment of the previously mentioned New York mothers'-pension commission and the 1915 passage of the mothers'-pension law. She soon became president of the board that administered this law, and later used her position as president of the Child Welfare Committee of America to foster the passage of dependent children laws and to urge their funding and enforcement.

Other Progressive newspapers and magazines, though not so intimately involved in the activities of the mothers'-pension movement, contributed to its success. The Scripps-McRae and Hearst chains both conducted editorial campaigns for widows' pensions, as did a number of locally based papers. The legislation found acceptance throughout the spectrum of Progressive magazines; it received endorsement from such journals as *Outlook, Nation,* and *Public.*

Labor also gave some encouragement to mothers'-pension laws. In the early 1900s, the concept of widows' pensions had been associated, rightly or wrongly, with labor interests. In 1911, the American Federation of Labor endorsed a federal mothers'-pension resolution (1: 357–58). However, only in the middle 1920s, when it supported a mothers'-aid bill for the District of Columbia, did the AFL Executive Council play an active role in promoting mothers'-pension legislation.

Labor's slighting of mothers' pensions was more a matter of priority than of neutrality. Certain state federations of labor testified in favor of proposed mothers'-pension statutes, and a number of supporters of these laws (such as Secretary of Labor Wilson and the Socialist party) could be classified as sympathetic to labor. Other social-justice legislation, such as workmen's compensation and child labor, was of greater importance to labor, but mothers' pensions did not pass unnoticed.

Social-insurance advocates who were not charity workers were also likely to favor mothers' pensions. By asserting a public responsibility that entailed an enlarged government-welfare role, and by picturing private charity as an inadequate and improper repository for this function, the mothers'-pension movement borrowed and reinforced two of the main pillars of the case for social insurance. Thus, a number of social-insurance proponents, such as Ben Lindsey and Isaac Rubinow, held that these pensions would "prove at least a good entering wedge for those social and industrial-insurance laws that must come in time as the public is educated to their necessity" (24: 716). There was a difference in emphasis among these advocates, however. Those directly involved in the mothers'-pension campaign, such as William Hard and the New York widows'-pension commission, averred that comprehensive social insurance lacked sufficient support to be adopted in the near future, and contended that mothers' pensions might prove an essential part of a social-insurance package anyway. Those less involved in the movement decried the meagerness of the grants, and contended that the law's reliance on requirements of moral "fitness" and the means test betrayed it as a prisoner of charity concepts. Yet both groups looked forward to building upon the success of what they considered to be at least a partial corrective for an existing social ill.

Women made up the principal component of the mothers'-pension movement. Around the turn of the century, women's organizations began to flourish under leadership that helped to direct the latent energies of middle-class women into reform channels. The politicization of the woman's role built upon society's concession of feminine expertise on child welfare matters; women were thus ritualistically appointed to mothers'-pension commissions, and occasional statutes even required their appointment as administrators.

Although the more militant wing of the suffrage movement feared that mothers' pensions might damage the cause of sexual equality by glorifying the woman's place at home, supporters of women's suffrage generally favored mothers' pensions. Moreover, the legislatures that most easily and quickly approved mother's pensions were usually those actively considering women's suffrage or chosen by a sexually unrestricted electorate. After women were enfranchised in Oregon in 1912 (a widows'-pension law was passed the next year), the *Portland Oregonian* pointed out that "neither Senators nor Representatives are opposing any measures which will tend to be of assistance to the women."[1] In other states, too, the achievement of the franchise gave impetus to the enactment of new statutes on schools, public morality, women's working conditions, and child welfare. The second decade of the twentieth century may have marked the height of political influence for women. Legislators, apprehensive of the female vote, did what they could to mollify suffrage advocates and to mitigate the threatened wrath of newly enfranchised women. But as they learned in the 1920s that the only thing they had to fear was fear itself, the influence of women's pressure groups declined accordingly.

The two main women's organizations, the General Federation of Women's Clubs (whose membership may have exceeded 1 million) and the National Congress of Mothers and Parent-Teacher Associations (which had recently initiated the PTA movement and later was subsumed under it), lent considerable support to mothers'-pension drives. These organizations attracted principally middle-aged, middle-class, poorly educated married women (36: 48–49; 41: 293). These women sensed a waning influence in an emerging industrial system that created a new social hierarchy, new social conditions, and altered values. Their reaction, spurred by increased leisure and Victorian role consciousness, was to impose upon that system the values of home, family, and moral purity that women had long been charged with defending. The same group of resolutions that endorsed mothers' pensions was also likely to condemn comic pages, cigarettes, intemperance, and "the extravagant dress now in vogue among school girls," or to urge motion-picture censorship, an alliance between the church and the schools, and tougher divorce laws.

At least on a national level, the Congress of Mothers was far more vocal and determined in its support for widows' pensions than was the unwieldy and cautious General Federation of Women's Clubs. The federation, after a vague endorsement in 1912, left action on mothers' pensions to the discretion of the local clubs. The mothers' congress, on the other hand, passed a mothers'-pension resolution at virtually every convention after 1911, and claimed that every state affiliate had worked for this legislation. Often in conjunction with local women's clubs, local mothers' congresses and PTAs launched "study classes" or special committees on widows' pensions, presented bills on this subject to their state

1. *Portland Oregonian,* quoted in Alice Stone Blackwell's letter to the editor, *New York Times,* May 18, 1913, sec. 3, p. 6.

houses, lobbied in favor of mothers'-pension laws, or placed their members on commissions to examine proposed statutes. The Congress of Mothers in Massachusetts and Oregon perhaps gave the greatest boost to this legislation. Clara Park (wife of sociologist Robert Park), who led the state campaign of the Massachusetts Congress of Mothers, drafted the mothers'-pension-commission bill of 1912 and then served on the commission. After lobbying efforts and a statewide letter-writing campaign organized by the Congress of Mothers, a mothers'-pension bill carried the legislature in 1913. In Oregon, the mothers' congress drafted a widows'-pension bill, which it sent to every legislator, newspaper, and Grange in the state. By the end of the campaign, the bill carried with only one dissenting vote (20: 248). The mothers'-pension movement had found an effective unofficial campaign headquarters.

Several other women's organizations also actively sought mothers'-pension legislation. The National Consumers' League (a more militant group, whose predominantly female membership tended to be younger, less likely to be married, better educated, and of a higher social station than other women's groups) and its secretary, Florence Kelley, worked in favor of mothers'-pension laws and other legislation oriented toward women and children. Members of the Women's Suffrage League of Virginia were largely responsible for the passage and later funding of a widows'-pension law in that state (23: 51). In Tennessee, the Women's Christian Temperance Union joined forces with women's clubs and PTAs to push through the 1915 statute. Special "Mothers' Pensions Leagues," such as one formed by a "group of young women" in Allegheny County, Pennsylvania, cropped up in several states (26: 100–101). Promotion of mothers' pensions was indeed women's work, and upon that work rested much of the success of this reform.

The preceding description of proponents of mothers' pensions is not comprehensive—an inevitable result of the diffuse nature of this movement—but at least a few of the more important remaining groups should be mentioned. Quite likely to be forgotten in most analyses are the potential recipients themselves. The *Jewish Courier* and *Dziennik Zwiazkowy*, two Chicago newspapers whose immigrant base made them more legitimate spokesmen for the poor than most other sources, both demanded mothers'-pension statutes (8; 9). *Dziennik Zwaizkowy* also pointed out that some women considered it degrading to appeal for relief from the county agent or private charity, while they viewed a pension as a sort of right. This situation was bemoaned by opponents of widows' pensions and lauded by its advocates.

As a general rule, organizations with a special concern for improving treatment of widows and children supported this legislation. Child-labor and compulsory-education reformers furthered mothers' pensions in the hope of nullifying the potent argument that many widows would be unable to support their families without their children's earnings. Even certain fraternal organizations (which in Britain resisted proposed contributory widows'- and orphans'-pension schemes for fear of losing financial support for their own programs) labored for mothers' pensions in a number of states. Apparently uncowed by such a limited noncontributory proposal, they argued that states should follow the example of the fraternal pension plans for widows of former members.

Finally, the most intriguing supporter of this legislation was Henry Neil, the self-styled and widely proclaimed "father of the mothers'-pension system" (21; 31: 10; 56: 404).[2] Judge Neil, as he called himself (he was a former teacher and author who had served as a justice of the peace), gained public exposure through the interviews he arranged with various newspapers, which dutifully declared his paternity to their readers. Available evidence fails to substantiate this reputation. Yet Neil, as secretary of the National Probation League, organized mothers'-pension leagues and apparently helped draft several state mothers'-pension provisions. He also garnered support from a number of northern newspapers and legislators, and provided information to those interested in existing laws.

The support of such wide-ranging reformers as Frederic Howe and Rabbi Stephen Wise has not even received mention in this paper, and the contributions of many other prominent Progressives have been neglected. But these omissions should not significantly detract from an understanding of the widows'-pension movement. No individual or group of individuals was vital to it. The consensus that it created depended largely on the ease with which it meshed with developing American attitudes. By adopting the name "widows' pensions," it even exploited the public support given to pensions for families of war veterans.

The most frequent argument of mothers'-pension advocates (especially women's groups and women's magazines), and the one that best demonstrates the moral base of this reform, was an indictment of orphanages and a corresponding sanctification of "a mother's love" and of the home. Spokesmen often bolstered their pleas for mothers' pensions with portrayals of juvenile-courtroom scenes, with "children clinging to a mother's skirts or sobbing in the mother's arms" as she unwillingly relinquished them to an orphanage in order to support them (39: 142–43). Pension proponents depicted institutions as factories for "human machines" in which the "good innocent child" was "obliged to associate with undesirable children," and in which some children died or were mentally debilitated for lack of the "most sacred thing in human life—a mother's love" (32: 2–4; 40: 208). "Only in the home, and from his own mother," it was asserted, could a child "receive the love and personal care necessary to his complete development" (32: 3). In effect, the state was designated the promoter of the woman's hallowed position as rearer of her children.

2. See also *Chicago Tribune*, August 15, 1939, p. 18.

A few advocates carried this role even further by making a rather tenuous connection between Theodore Roosevelt's fear of "race suicide" and the need for mothers' pensions. The emancipated, childless working woman was branded as a "sexless female." Mothers' pensions were an honorable recognition of "the real woman . . . the one who marries and is glad of it, who brings children into the world and loves them" (28; 48). By assuring women that even in widowhood they could support their children, mothers' pensions might encourage families to have the four-child quota that Roosevelt set for them.

If any argument underlay the thrust of the mothers'-pension campaign, it was that private charity was neither an adequate nor an appropriate substitute for certain governmental welfare functions. Mothers'-pension crusaders avowed that "poverty is too big a problem for private philanthropy," or that "private charity, in this particular matter of the widowed mother, is today a failure" (30: 3; 34: 32). Angered further by private charity's antagonism to their attempts to use the government to meet this need, attacks sometimes became more vituperative. Characterizing scientific-philanthropy methods as "the third Degree" and the "blood red tape of private charity," some supporters of mothers' pensions particularly denounced the "reactionary" Russell Sage Foundation and charity-organization societies (commonly branded the "Charity Trust") (49: 152).[3] Charity workers, accustomed to wearing the white hats on social-justice questions, were not to emerge from this controversy unperturbed or unchanged.

Mothers'-pensions proponents also rebuked private philanthropy through their distinction between charity and the "right" to a mothers' pension. They insisted that the paternalism and opprobrium attached to charity must not be carried over to the pension. Some contended that, since society itself bore partial responsibility for the husband's death (either because he had been unable to earn sufficient wages or because his death was due to preventable disease or accident—a likely possibility for a man who was young enough to leave school-age children), society should alleviate the widow's poverty. Almost all their proponents depicted mother's pensions as payment for a service rather than as a dole. A mother caring for her children, they said, made a greater contribution to society than if she engaged in some other employment. The widows'-pension recipient, then, could be compared with a civil servant: "He is paid for his work; she for hers. And she should be paid by those for whom she does it—all the citizens of the state, not the subscribers to the charities" (19: 108). This view constituted a novel attitude toward American welfare recipients; a request for aid no longer constituted evidence of inefficiency or moral turpitude.

This assertion of a state responsibility involved a quantum jump in the line dividing the roles of public and private welfare agencies. As

3. *New York Times*, March 2, 1913, p. 3.

the restriction circumscribing governmental action came into question, so did the axiom of scientific philanthropy that private relief would necessarily be better administered than public relief. Private charity was never to recoup the premier position that it had held in the beginning of the twentieth century.

Such bold departures from the conventional wisdom on public welfare policy tend to overshadow more basic continuities. The justification of the pension in terms of the widow's service to society (along with the understanding that mothers' pensions were a child welfare measure that ceased when the children reached a certain age, regardless of the financial situation of the mother) proved double-edged, precluding male participation while providing the rationale for "supervision" of the mother's "job" performance. Through their rhetoric and their preference for juvenile courts and special boards as administrative agencies, mothers'-pension proponents made it clear that aid to dependent children was to be "utterly segregated from public poor law outdoor relief" (18: 187). This concern stemmed naturally from the attitudes of poor-relief administrators, who often shared with charity workers a grudging officiousness. But it also arose from an objection to "placing the mother upon the same plane with drunkards and worthless people" (33: 18). Moreover, certain supporters of widows' pensions censured poor-relief authorities for failing to stress the "obligation" of the recipient of a pension "to bring up her children as right-thinking, right-minded, useful American citizens" (52). Though this complaint fails to account for the demand for public widows' pensions, it does underscore an overriding administrative reality in dependent-children programs. Scientific-philanthropy standards often became mothers'-pension guidelines. As much as mothers'-pension proponents tried to differentiate their concept of supervision from that of private charity, their distinctions did not ring true. Their investigators, they asserted, would not be the "meddlesome," "policing," "I-am-responsible-for-your-general-development-as-a-human-being" type (2: 21; 17: 105; 22: 122). Instead they would offer "only kindness, help, advice" (2: 21). They would be "family friends" who would "educate the mothers more and supervise them less" (21: 122, 127). Perhaps, William Hard even suggested, this sort of compulsory "instruction" might be good for all mothers (17: 104).

Although it would be unfair to equate the operation envisioned by mothers'-pension advocates with the practices of the social caseworkers who obtained an ever-tightening grip on this program, it is clear that these investigators were anything but unmeddlesome good friends. A number of jurisdictions (usually the ones that supplied either no grants or very meager ones) applied no supervision at all, but some mothers'-pension agencies vigorously injected themselves into the lives of their "pensioners." Use of tobacco and lack of church attendance were evidence of being an "unfit" mother (53: 43). Families were forced to move from "neighborhoods whose morality was questionable" (3: 15). Investigators "visited" to enforce home cleanliness and rules against male boarders (26: 109). The eviction of incapacitated husbands could be ordered if they were deemed "a menace to the physical and moral welfare of the mother or children" (53: 22). Mothers were obliged to prepare monthly budgets showing how they spent their pensions and met such requirements as "nourishment, no extras," or "warm clothes, not fancy" (54: 7). The Massachusetts Board of Charity was quite forthright in its statement of objectives: "The public authorities can make adequate relief a powerful lever to lift and keep mothers to a high standard of home care" (53: 35). More revealing, though less abrasive, is the observation of the chief probation officer of the Cook County Juvenile Court: "For the children of mothers with right motives and willingness to accept and follow kindly and intelligent advice, the system has been of great benefit" (11: 73).

Mothers'-pension advocates forecast a range of gains in social stability or morality. By protecting the home "against any theories of collectivism" and by showing government's concern with evident social needs, this legislation would serve as a bulwark against radicalism (48: 31). Since "neglected children almost invariably become delinquent children," and since neglect was linked to the necessity for the mother to work and the "dangerously low standard of living" of the family, widows' pensions were touted as an anticrime measure (34: 33; 46: 460). Pensions would also mitigate the poverty that drove dependent mothers and daughters to prostitution. Child labor would be reduced, for the mother would not need the earnings of her children to support the family. A similar argument applied to school attendance, especially since "the absence from home of wage-earning mothers contributes largely towards truancy" (42: 432).

Thus, widows' pensions were "a plain business proposition . . . to the end that [the children] become intelligent, industrious and respectable citizens and add to the industrial prosperity of the community" (38: 150; 58: 21). Implicit was an assumption that financial support would foster a value scheme that would transform poor children into upstanding men and women. But most mothers'-pension adherents were not averse to framing this expectation of family rehabilitation as a demand.

The Legacy of the Mothers'-Pension Movement

The legacy of the mothers'-pension movement meets neither past hopes nor present concerns. Especially in the early years of the law, most counties refused to enforce it, claiming that within their boundaries there were no cases to which it was applicable or that poor-relief authorities could do a better job.[4] At no point before the enactment of the Social Security Act did more than half the counties in the United States provide

---

4. Judge W. C. DeWolf, quoted in the *Institution Quarterly* (37: 12).

mothers' pensions. There were also regional and urban-rural disparities. Per capita mothers'-pension expenditures in 1930 ranged from three cents in Louisiana to eighty-two cents in New York. Coverage was weighted heavily toward northern industrial states and against southern agrarian states (a pattern that survives today) (55: 8, 14–15). Within states, cities made far greater per capita expenditures than rural areas.

Nothing receded like the mothers'-pension movement after its legislative success. Like most Progressive reformers, mothers'-pension advocates proved more vigilant in promoting passage of the law than in monitoring its administration and assuring its adequate financial support. Pensions never reached a sufficient level for families to support themselves without resorting to supplementary public or private aid. Less than one-third of all eligible families, the Children's Bureau estimated in 1931, received any pension at all (4: 30). Widows were favored over other categories of dependent mothers; they received over four-fifths of the aid (55:11). Blacks particularly faced discrimination; they received only 3 percent of the total pensions, with a number of counties and some southern states barring them totally from their programs (55: 13, 26, 27). With the exception of this question of racial bias (which aroused little interest among supporters of aid to dependent children), these practices did not square with the rhetoric of the mothers'-pension campaign.

This rhetoric did, however, condone other shortcomings. Strictures against aiding families with unemployed but able-bodied fathers excluded some of the most impoverished families. Paradoxically, this restriction may also have caused some increase in desertion, thereby damaging the middle-class family structure that mothers'-pension advocates were intent on promoting. Mothers'-pension proponents were also sparing in employing their insight that home life suffered from the lack of an assured adequate income. Instead, they permitted, and sometimes encouraged, the imposition of the same behavioral demands that had characterized the private charity system that they maligned. These demands vitiated their concept of mothers' aid as a right, and stymied their attempt to remove stigma from the pension. Aid to dependent children became the government program most associated with official harassment and suspicion.

Yet the impact of mothers'-pension legislation had a large positive component. The past practice of juvenile court-martials, with poverty as the charge and family separation as the sentence, was abandoned. On the eve of the Social Security Act, the number of children aided by mothers' pensions rivaled the total in foster homes and orphanages combined (15: 770). The widows'-pension program had burgeoned impressively, far faster than almost any other type of government expenditure (35: 1267). In 1931, the appropriation for mothers' pensions exceeded $33 million, distributed among more than 90,000 families with over 250,000 dependent children (55: 8, 14). Despite a budgetary crisis severe enough to cut back or to terminate a number of mothers'-pension programs during the Great Depression, mothers'-aid families were "the aristocrats of our relief population" (43: 491). For all their flaws, mothers'-pension programs made appreciable inroads into the poverty of a significant number of people.

The United States traveled a solitary road in its halting and hazardous trek to the welfare state. Although mothers'-pension adherents occasionally referred to European social-insurance schemes, they cited them more as precedents than as models. No other major industrial nation had such a special concern for its children and such a fear of providing assistance to indigent men. Thus, the United States was the world leader in mothers' pensions and a world laggard in social insurance.

The legacy of the mothers'-pension movement, though, went beyond the passage of one unique piece of child welfare legislation. It laid a foundation for later contentions that government had the responsibility to establish welfare as a right, independent of the compassion, altruism, and paternalism of the "better" members of society. It shattered the view of income support as a mere adjunct to more direct programs of social control. It undermined the prestige of private charities to such an extent that they never again so confidently asserted their prerogative to define the government-welfare role. The United States had reached a preliminary recognition of poverty as a public problem requiring governmental remedies.

Received November 7, 1972

References

1. American Federation of Labor. *Report of Proceedings of 31st Annual Convention, November, 1911.* Washington, D.C.: Law Reporter Printing Service, 1911.
2. Appo, Alice Maxwell. "House Bill No. 626." *Colliers* 49 (August 1912): 20–21.
3. Bogue, Mary F. *Administration of Mothers' Aid in Ten Localities.* Children's Bureau Publication no. 184. Washington, D.C.: Government Printing Office, 1928.
4. Bradbury, Dorothy E. *Four Decades of Action for Children: A Short History of the Children's Bureau.* Washington, D.C.: Government Printing Office, 1956.
5. Bremner, Robert H., ed. *Children and Youth in America: A Documentary History.* 2 vols. Cambridge, Mass.: Harvard University Press, 1971.
6. Brown, Josephine Chapin. *Public Relief, 1929–1939.* New York: Henry Holt & Co., 1940.
7. Carstens, C. C. "Public Pensions to Widows with Children." In *Selected Articles on Mothers' Pensions,* edited by Edna D. Bullock, pp. 159–75. White Plains, N.Y.: H. W. Wilson Co., 1915.
8. Chicago. Regenstein Library, University of Chicago. Special Collections. Box 23. "An Inaudible Tragedy," editorial, *Sunday Jewish Courier,* March 15, 1914.
9. ———. Box 32. "Pensions for Poor Mothers," editorial, *Dziennik Zwiazkowy,* November 24, 1911.

10. Conyngton, Mary. *How To Help*. New York: Macmillan Co., 1909.
11. Cook County, Illinois, Family Court. "Report of Chief Probation Officer." *Annual Report*. Chicago, 1913. Pp. 67–73.
12. Davis, Lance E., et al. *American Economic Growth*. New York: Harper & Row, 1972.
13. Devine, Edward T. "Pensions for Mothers." In *Selected Articles on Mothers' Pensions*, edited by Edna D. Bullock, pp. 176–83. White Plains, N.Y.: H. W. Wilson Co., 1915.
14. Epstein, Abraham. *Insecurity*. New York: Random House, 1938.
15. Frank, Lawrence. "Children and Youth." In *Recent Social Trends in the United States*, prepared by President's Research Committee on Social Trends, pp. 751–800. New York: McGraw-Hill Book Co., 1933.
16. Glenn, Mrs. John M. "Relief of Needy Mothers in New York." In *Proceedings of the Forty-first National Conference of Charities and Correction*, pp. 452–53. Fort Wayne, Ind.: Fort Wayne Printing Co., 1914.
17. Hard, William. "Financing Motherhood." In *Selected Articles on Mothers' Pensions*, edited by Edna D. Bullock, pp. 91–97. White Plains, N.Y.: H. W. Wilson Co., 1915.
18. ———. "General Discussion." In *Selected Articles on Mothers' Pensions*, edited by Edna D. Bullock, pp. 183–88. White Plains, N.Y.: H. W. Wilson Co., 1915.
19. ———. "Moral Necessity of 'State Funds to Mothers.'" In *Selected Articles on Mothers' Pensions*, edited by Edna D. Bullock, pp. 98–108.
20. Hayhurst, Elizabeth. "How Pensions for Widows Were Won in Oregon." *Child-Welfare Magazine* 7 (March 1913): 248–49.
21. "Henry Neil: Pension Agent." *Survey* 29 (February 1913): 559–61.
22. Howe, Frederic, and Howe, Marie. "Pensioning the Widow and the Fatherless." In *Selected Articles on Mothers' Pension*, edited by Edna D. Bullock, pp. 118–39. White Plains, N.Y.: H. W. Wilson Co., 1915.
23. James. Arthur W. *Virginia's Social Awakening*. Richmond, Va.: Garrett & Massie, 1939.
24. Lindsey, Ben B. "The Mothers' Compensation Law of Colorado." *Survey* 29 (February 1913): 714–16.
25. Lowell, Josephine Shaw. "Children." In *Children and Youth in America: A Documentary History*, edited by Robert H. Bremner, 2: 349–52. Cambridge, Mass.: Harvard University Press, 1971.
26. Lubove, Roy. *The Struggle for Social Security, 1900–1935*. Cambridge, Mass.: Harvard University Press, 1968.
27. Mason, Martha Sprague, ed. *Parents and Teachers*. New York: Ginn & Co., 1928.
28. "Mothers' Pension Bills." *Hearst's Magazine* 23 (June 1913): 970–71.
29. National Congress of Mothers and Parent-Teacher Associations. *Triennial Hand Book, 1911–1914*. [Chicago]: Danforth & Webster Printing, n.d.
30. "Needy Widows in the State of New York." *Survey* 32 (April 1914): 1–3.
31. Neil, Henry. "Mothers' Pensions Campaigns in Many States." *Newer Justice* 4, no. 1 [1913]: 9–10.
32. New Haven, Connecticut. Yale University Law Library. Leila Osborne, "Mothers' Pensions," speech at "Forum," February 1915.
33. ———. M. J. Quinn, "Mothers' Pension Bill," speech at "Forum," February 1915.
34. New York State Commission on Relief for Widowed Mothers. "Report, 1914." In *Selected Articles on Mothers' Pensions*, edited by Edna D. Bullock, pp. 32–39. White Plains, N.Y.: H. W. Wilson Co., 1915.
35. Odum, Howard. "Public Welfare Activities." In *Recent Social Trends in the United States*, prepared by President's Research Committee on Social

Trends, pp. 1224–73. New York: McGraw-Hill Book Co., 1933.

36. O'Neill, William L. *The Woman Movement.* New York: Barnes & Noble, 1969.

37. "One Year of Mothers' Pensions in Illinois." *Institution Quarterly* 5 (December 1914): 8–18.

38. "Pensions to Widows—Discussion." *Proceedings of the Thirty-ninth National Conference of Charities and Correction,* pp. 485–98. Fort Wayne, Ind.: Fort Wayne Printing Co., 1912.

39. Pinckney, Merritt. "Public Pensions to Widows." In *Selected Articles on Mothers' Pensions,* edited by Edna D. Bullock, pp. 139–52. White Plains, N.Y.: H. W. Wilson Co., 1915.

40. Porterfield, Edward E. "How the Widow's Allowance Operates." *Child-Welfare Magazine* 7 (February 1913): 208–10.

41. Reigel, Robert E. *American Women: A Story of Social Change.* Rutherford, N.J.: Fairleigh Dickinson University Press, 1970.

42. "Resolutions Adopted by Third International Congress on the Welfare of the Child." *Child-Welfare Magazine* 8 (June 1914): 431–34.

43. Rubinow, I. M. *The Quest for Security.* New York: Henry Holt & Co., 1934.

44. Schneider, David, and Deutsch, Albert. *The History of Public Welfare in New York State, 1867–1940.* Vol. 2. Chicago: University of Chicago Press, 1941.

45. "State News—Massachusetts." *Child-Welfare Magazine* 6 (February 1912): 209–11.

46. "State News—Oregon." *Child-Welfare Magazine* 7 (August 1913): 459–60.

47. "The Conservation of the Home." *Outlook* 108 (December 1914): 809–10.

48. "The Mothers' Congress." *Child-Welfare Magazine* 6 (September 1911): 30–31.

49. Tishler, Hace Sorel. *Self-Reliance and Social Security 1870–1917.* Port Washington, N.Y.: Kennikat Press, 1971.

50. U.S., Congress, House. *Congressional Record,* 69th Cong., 1st sess., 1926, 67, pt. 4: 3566.

51. U.S., Congress, Senate. *Conference on Care of Dependent Children: Proceedings,* 60th Cong., 2d sess., 1909, S. Doc. 721.

52. ———. Committee on the District of Columbia. *Mothers' Aid in the District of Columbia: Hearings on S. 120 and S. 1929,* 69th Cong., 1st sess., 1926, p. 85.

53. U.S., Department of Labor, Children's Bureau. *Laws Relating to "Mothers' Pensions" in the United States, Denmark, and New Zealand.* Children's Bureau Publication no. 7. Washington, D.C.: Government Printing Office, 1914.

54. ———. *Conference on Mothers' Pensions: Proceedings.* Children's Bureau Publication, no. 109. Washington, D.C.: Government Printing Office, 1922.

55. ———. *Mothers' Aid, 1931.* Children's Bureau Publication no. 220. Washington, D.C.: Government Printing Office, 1933.

56. Warner, Hoyt L. *Progressivism in Ohio, 1897–1917.* [Columbus]: Ohio State University Press, 1964.

57. "Wildfire Spread of Mothers' Pensions." In *Selected Articles on Mothers' Pensions,* edited by Edna D. Bullock, pp. 87–89. White Plains,N.Y.: H. W. Wilson Co., 1915.

58. Wisconsin, State Board of Control, ed. *Aid to Dependent Children.* [Madison], 1919.

59. Woods, Robert A. *The Preparation of Calvin Coolidge.* Boston and New York: Houghton Mifflin Co., 1924.

60. Woods, Robert A., and Kennedy, Albert J. *The Settlement Horizon.* New York: Russell Sage Foundation, 1922.

Prelude to Welfare Capitalism: The Role of Business in the Enactment of Workmen's Compensation Legislation in Illinois, 1905–12

Joseph L. Castrovinci
Chicago, Illinois

The first modern, comprehensive welfare programs in the United States appeared on the state level during the Progressive era. Workmen's compensation, which was adopted in Illinois in 1911, was a particularly popular innovation. It was eagerly supported by reformers, but even more so by businessmen. The latter, beset by a dramatic increase in work-related injuries, saw compensation as a way to reduce the attendant rise in insurance costs and economic uncertainties. Labor also endorsed compensation, although reluctantly and belatedly. The refusal of businessmen to support further reform led to the failure of other Progressive proposals, many of which were enacted by later reform movements such as the New Deal and the Great Society.

Twentieth-century welfare capitalism traces its origins to the social justice concerns of the Progressive era. These years, which stretch from 1890 to World War I, are traditionally seen as ones in which Americans sought to relieve the suffering of the poor by enacting comprehensive, forward-looking measures to limit the hours of work; prohibit child labor; provide recreational facilities for the urban masses; regulate working conditions; and enact a minimum wage, widows' pensions, and workmen's compensation.

Several factors fostered the emergence of welfare capitalism. Rapid industrialization in the late nineteenth century brought fabulous wealth to some and poverty to many. This widening gap between rich

Social Service Review 50 (March 1976): 80–102

and poor generated social tensions which convinced many of the need for remedial action. Among these were large numbers of the nation's intellectuals, who had recently founded professional societies such as the American Economic Association and the American Political Science Association, which vastly increased their influence and sense of self-awareness. For the first time, lawyers, sociologists, economists, and political scientists were using their skills to define and publicize social ills, suggest corrective legislation, and staff new, problem-solving government bureaus.

In a similar manner workers, speaking through the American Federation of Labor (AFL) and its affiliates, began to seek state assistance in certain areas. This represented a break with tradition, as the AFL, long fearful that such aid would weaken unions, had adhered to a policy of laissez faire. But during the Progressive era, reform programs which entailed affirmative governmental action, such as widows' pensions and a ban on child labor, began to win the approval of unions. Workers and professionals often fought together for such legislation.

But to categorize the struggle for welfare capitalism as one of labor and reformers versus business is mistaken, for the latter also fought for such programs. Confronted early in this century with economic uncertainties which threatened to overwhelm them, businessmen endorsed and even formulated many of the demands normally associated with labor and reformers, hoping thereby to restore a stability lost in the frenzy of turn-of-the-century competitive activity. The passage of workmen's compensation legislation in Illinois provides an illustration of this phenomenon, as businessmen supported it as a way to reduce instabilities engendered by the antiquated system of common-law liability and block the more fundamental changes sought by others.

Slowly the welfare state replaced traditional notions about the proper role of the state in the economy. These notions, usually identified as laissez faire, are more accurately labeled mercantile, for government in the United States has always freely aided business enterprise. The transformation effected by the Progressives was to create programs under which all segments of society began to receive benefits. Though no longer the sole recipients of government largess, businessmen were nonetheless able to block many of the reformers' demands. This was the consequence of their refusal to endorse legislation perceived as inimical to their interests. As a result, the United States in the Progressive era took but a first step on the road to the welfare state. Further measures, such as social security, a national minimum wage, and health insurance, would have to await later reform movements such as the New Deal and Great Society.

Reforming the Common Law

Along with widows' pensions, workmen's compensation was the most widely adopted reform of the Progressive era. One historian has dubbed the first two decades of this century the "Era of the Liability Commission"[1] because they witnessed the creation of forty state-sponsored bodies to examine the problem of work-related injury.[2] Between 1900 and 1920, the federal government and forty-three states enacted compensation laws.[3] Rarely in American history had a legislative proposal gained such general acceptance so quickly.[4]

The reasons for this were the rapid increase in on-the-job accidents late in the nineteenth century; inadequacies in the common law, the legal system under which one sought redress for them; and the agreement of normally antagonistic political forces on the need for reform. Since advocates of workmen's compensation had to expose the shortcomings of the common law, it is to this subject that we must first turn our attention.

The common law required people to conduct themselves and manage their property in ways not likely to harm others. Thus, even in the heyday of laissez faire, employers had to furnish safe workplaces and inspect and repair them when necessary to prevent injury. They also had to hire reasonably intelligent and careful workers and assign them only to those tasks suited to their apparent capacity. All this, supposedly, freed employees from undue concern about job safety. In the event of injury, however, the doctrines of contributory negligence, assumption of risk, and fellow servant frequently absolved employers of liability.

The most cursory examination revealed the need for change. An injured worker, for example, could never be sure if he had a legitimate basis for making a claim. In the absence of an out-of-court settlement, he could secure compensation only by suit, a costly and lengthy affair. One typical study revealed that of the awards granted for industrial accidents in 1903, only 16 percent were paid in that year, 37 percent in the second year, 20 percent in the third year, 14 percent in the fourth year, and 16 percent in the fifth and succeeding years.[5] The problem was obvious: "At the moment when panic is greatest, the strain most intense, when aid is needed, when children are taken from schools and put to work, the present system withholds assistance unless the family is willing to blindly accept the terms that are offered."[6] Were an award granted, moreover, its size was rarely based on the severity of the injury;[7] there was no guarantee it would ever be collected, as employers might refuse to honor the decision or might have gone out of business. An employee uncooperative enough to sue might also be dismissed.[8]

These difficulties derived from the common law, which was compiled by the magistrates of a preindustrial society where work-related
dangers were obvious even to the most unthinking. It was founded on
an image absurd in an age of factory labor; namely, that of a man
"who never relaxes his vigilance under the influence of monotony,
fatigue, or habituation to danger, never permits his attention to be
diverted, even for a moment, from the perils which surround him,
never forgets a hazardous condition he once observed, and never
ceases to be on the alert for new sources of danger."[9]

Critics also found the common law inadequate to the needs of an
economy which stressed the division of labor and the use of complex
machinery. Typical was its failure to provide for the adjudication of
disputes arising out of "uncaused accidents." In simple agricultural or
commercial pursuits, or in manufacturing done in the home, almost
all injuries were traceable to precise causes; but in factories, upward
of one-half were due not to negligence but to hazards inherent in the
trade.[10] Workers injured under such circumstances usually went uncompensated. A second problem concerned older workers long employed at a job which suddenly, through increased mechanization,
became more hazardous. Not truly free to resign, the law left them
unprotected. Third, the impersonal nature of employer-employee
relations aggravated otherwise routine problems. Hitherto, master
and servant had known and worked directly with each other, but in
large factories this was not the case. Employers hesitated to compensate employees with whom they were not acquainted, for fear of encouraging malingering, self-mutilation, and the like. Suit, with its
attendant expense, delay, and ill-feeling, was often the only recourse.

Enter the State

In 1905, the General Assembly of Illinois created a commission to
consider the question of work-related injuries and suggest corrective
legislation. Two years later the commission issued a report calling for
the creation of a voluntary but comprehensive system of private insurance to compensate workers injured on the job, irrespective of
cause. In exchange for this fixed, guaranteed sum, employees would
forego the right to sue employers for larger amounts. The plan thus
abrogated the common law in places of employment covered by it.
Here we have the essence of the theory behind workmen's compensation: all businesses are intrinsically hazardous and hence should provide insurance to employees; while on the job, workers act at the
behest of their employer and thus are partially his responsibility;

employers and employees, as partners in a joint venture, rely for success on the well-being of each other; and the state owes compensation to its citizens as part of its duty to further the common good.[11]

The commission urged compensation as beneficial both to workers and businessmen. The former needed it because they "have no longer ownership and control of the instruments of production, no voice in the management process, no vote in shaping the physical conditions under which they must toil, and share none of the profits of the business."[12] If injured, their lack of capital and property doomed them to penury. The report also recognized the hardships the common law imposed on business, among them jury decisions so "inconsistent and capricious"[13] that no advance provision for them could be made.

In its proposed bill, modeled after one adopted in Great Britain several years before,[14] the commission urged that compensation plans be inspected by the state superintendent of insurance, to whom copies of policies and quarterly reports of income and outgo would be submitted. Death benefits were to equal at least three years pay or $1,000, whichever was greater, with the sum adjusted according to the number of dependents; and total disability benefits were to be at least 50 percent of the worker's wages and continue for four years after his death. Each contract was to provide separately for partial disability payments. The bill obligated employers to pay at least half the premium, with employees to pay the remainder. It also required employees to notify supervisors of injury within a specified period of time and submit to any necessary medical exams. The bill allowed insurance companies to terminate coverage of workers who resigned their positions. Disputes were to be settled by arbitration, but benefits were automatically forfeited for injuries caused by deliberate employee misconduct. The bill did not relieve employers from liability for accidents due to failure to observe safety ordinances.

As with many such reports, this plan was never implemented, largely because of labor opposition.[15] However, it placed the issue of accident insurance before the public, thereby serving an educatory function which paved the way for a second commission, established in 1910.

The latter body met under circumstances far more favorable to reform. Several months earlier, at Cherry Hill, Illinois, a mine explosion killed almost 300 men and left 200 women and 1,000 children without means of support.[16] The public outcry was immense and combined with the influence of reform drives overseas and in other states to make the adoption of some kind of insurance all but inevitable.[17]

The commission, which consisted of twelve members, six each from labor and business, sought to devise an equitable and effective method of providing compensation to accident victims. Its report repeated many of the assertions of the earlier one but differed in the depth and breadth of its research. It solicited opinions from 1,200 employers, 1,700 labor leaders, 200 judges and attorneys, and studied 5,000 industrial accidents.

Statistics illustrated the large and growing number of uncaused accidents, the extortionate size of attorney fees, the lengthy delay in collection of awards, and the need to improve factory safety. The fact that only 42 percent of all premium payments under employer's liability went for medical care attested to the waste in existing private plans; the balance went for legal expenses (10 percent), investigation of claims (10 percent), and administration (38 percent). A study of 614 fatal cases showed that while twenty-four were resolved in and 386 out of court, 204 remained unsettled.[18] Most awards were pitifully small. The average court settlement for the death of a skilled railroad worker, for example, was $2,078; those settled out of court averaged $1,457, and 12 percent went uncompensated.[19] For railroad laborers, the average court settlement was $936, for miners, $294.[20] Similar studies were conducted for other trades. The report concluded:

> The present system is unjust, haphazard, wasteful, the cause of enormous suffering, of much disrespect for law, and of a badly distributed burden on society. . . .
> The popular notion that the workingman, or his family in the event of his death, has a chance to secure comfortable damages, was utterly refuted by an examination of the facts. . . .
> While fire, deterioration of plant, and financial loss are insured against, and insurance, whatever form it may take, is charged to the cost of production, no account has thus far been taken in America of the deterioration of the.human machine. . . ."[21]

The commission explored the fate of injured workmen and their dependents. One study of 147 Cook County families showed that only forty-three still had any income, averaging a mere $6.88 per week.[22] The remainder were totally dependent on charity. One case concerned a "widow with four daughters who finally gave up the struggle to make ends meet and embarked upon a career of immorality."[23]

The report attacked the common law as unfair to employers. If uninsured, it left them vulnerable to suit; if insured, rates were set such that less hazardous plants subsidized more hazardous ones, thereby making the installation of safety devices and the removal of dangerous conditions unprofitable.[24] Enacting accident insurance was seen as tantamount to guaranteeing safe factories, as it would give employers an incentive to secure low-rate, preferred-risk status. Correspondence from American consular officials in Europe was cited to prove that business there did not find compensation particularly burdensome.

For reasons discussed later, the commission's labor members split, those from the Illinois Federation of Labor (IFL) favoring compensation, those from the Chicago Federation of Labor (CFL) opposing it. When representatives from the latter resigned in protest over the impending adoption of a compensation plan, the governor appointed members of the IFL to replace them, and deliberations resumed. Early in 1911, the commission presented the general assembly with a compensation bill which was adopted by a near-unanimous vote and signed by the governor in May.

The law, modeled on those of Europe,[25] made insurance through private companies compulsory for hazardous trades such as construction, mining, and transportation; voluntary in all others; and abrogated the common law once in effect. In cases of fatal injury, benefits were four times the worker's annual wage but not less than $1,650 or more than $3,000. Employees injured on the job collected from seven to twelve dollars weekly as long as needed, with the total amount not to exceed the maximum death benefit. Various sums were fixed for loss or incapacitation of body members. As in the 1907 bill, such policies were subject to state inspection. Employers were to bear the cost of insurance.

The plan proved popular with labor and capital. It went into effect on May 1, 1912, and within one year over 90 percent of the state's manufacturers had opted for coverage. Though free to do so, no employee has ever rejected benefits under the law in order to sue for a potentially larger sum.[26] Illinois thus became among the first two or three states to adopt a workmen's compensation program.

Business: The Quest for Stability

American businessmen have traditionally been the recipients of government largess, laissez-faire protestations notwithstanding. In colonial times, for example, states and localities extended bounties, franchises, and subsidies to favored entrepreneurs. The new republic fostered commerce through a national bank, tariffs, and internal improvements. Even in the late nineteenth century, laissez-faire's golden age, government granted land and other benefits to many industries. Thus, when confronted early in this century with a huge increase in job-related accidents, the indemnification of which threatened the financial stability of many companies, businessmen naturally turned to the state for a solution.

From their viewpoint, the manner in which common-law court decisions were made was highly unsatisfactory, even dangerous, and needed to be replaced by the more predictable system of automatic compensation. Jury awards, for example, varied enormously in size, often set according to the employer's ability to pay rather than the severity of the injury.[27] Verdicts in favor of workers were becoming more common and their amounts increasing to $5,000, $10,000, and even $25,000,[28] sums for which many firms could not get insurance.[29] Statistics indicated an increase in the percentage of injuries for which claims were made and which were brought to trial and appeal.[30] In the past, higher courts could be relied on to reduce or reverse such verdicts, but this was no longer the case.[31] My own survey of some 600 Illinois appellate court decisions shows that from 1905 to 1910 they ran about two to one in the employee's favor.

Another problem with the common law was the high cost of litigation. An employee suing for compensation spent from 30 to 60 percent of his award on lawyer's fees,[32] even more if he appealed an unfavorable decision because such required on the average the services of three to six attorneys.[33] Employers, who were often criticized for treating injured workers heartlessly, would have preferred that the full amount be spent on relief.[34] Singled out for particular criticism were "ambulance chasing" lawyers who, eager to collect fees, prodded workmen into filing suit.[35]

The waste involved in private insurance was also irritating. Nationally, in 1908, premiums totaled $22 million, of which only one-quarter reached incapacitated workers, the remainder having been spent on administration, investigations, sales drives, and profits.[36] One hundred and forty-one Illinois firms reported in 1910 that they had spent $100,000 for accident insurance, of which only $25,000 was awarded to workers.[37] By contrast, the 1911 legislation would have returned $84,000 and lowered rates by creating incentives for the removal of unsafe conditions.[38]

By requiring that disputes be settled by suit, the common law injected hostility into employer-employee relations and constituted "one of the greatest causes of class hatred and antagonism."[39] Such was the natural outcome of trials which pitted workers against their employers. The latter often felt compelled to contest every claim, noting "the peculiarities of the laws covering employer's liability and the still more peculiar methods employed in their application, would in many instances be to invite financial disaster, and in the case of smaller manufacturers with limited capital, financial annihilation, were he to yield to the unfair, the unjust, and often outrageous demands made for damages resulting from injuries."[40]

Employers also feared the effect of a failure to achieve "responsible reform." A 1910 survey by the National Association of Manufacturers

(NAM) of 13,000 businessmen showed that over 99 percent were in favor of automatic compensation[41] as a way to reduce the waste and hostility engendered by the common law and avoid having the problem "settled for us with a vengeance by the agitator and the demagogue."[42] The NAM insisted, "the employer or insurance man who in the present day and age is obstructive or even inactive in developing equitable workmen's compensation laws, and above all in preventing accidents, is not a progressive or desirable member of his class."[43] Specifically, it expressed concern that the employer's three common-law defenses, already whittled down by a plethora of child-labor, factory-safety, and maximum-hour laws, might be removed completely. In 1909, for example, Illinois passed its first comprehensive factory safety bill, which included rules for proper ventilation, safeguarding power machines, and constructing sufficient exits and stairways. Employers violating this statute were open to suit and feared that more legislation like it would result in a nightmare of endless litigation and ever-mounting fines. Significantly, employers on the 1910 commission refused to accept changes in the common law without prior passage of a compensation plan, while several labor representatives fought for abolishing the defenses first.[44]

The Illinois Manufacturers Association (IMA), the state's leading business organization and spokesman for about 1,000 of its largest corporations, was an early and vocal proponent of compensation. In 1905, protesting that the existing system left employers "unable to extend the most rudimentary evidences of common humanity," it called for change but offered no specific remedy.[45] In 1909, it began to agitate for compensation;[46] and in 1910, in the wake of Cherry Hill, President LaVerne Noyes announced that the IMA had promised Governor Charles S. Deneen to support compensation, "secured the creation of an employers liability commission, rounded up sentiment among manufacturers for a fair bill, gave the state [commission] three of its most able men, who contributed their valuable time and wisdom, and used its influence to secure honest and fair provisions in a bill to be submitted to the General Assembly."[47]

The IMA mounted a campaign to secure the plan's passage. It distributed a record amount of literature to members requesting information on their needs and interests in compensation legislation, held meetings to explain provisions of the bill, and cooperated in securing facts needed by the commission and the general assembly.[48] Never before, the organization reported in 1911, had it exerted itself so strenuously on behalf of a piece of legislation.[49]

The general assembly, under the impression that the IMA supported the proposal,[50] approved it and a companion bill, sponsored by labor, abolishing the employer's common-law defenses. At this point, the IMA, favoring compensation in principle but objecting to the benefit schedule as too high,[51] reversed its stand and urged the veto of both bills. The issue was now in the lap of the governor.

Charles S. Deneen was a progressive Republican. In the 1890s he acquired a reputation for courage and integrity when, as Cook County prosecuting attorney, he, in Lincoln Steffens's words, "convicted so many rich men that there was a Banker's Row of cells in the jail."[52] In 1904, he ran for governor on a platform which endorsed the extension of civil service, direct primaries, and stronger pure food and drug and factory inspection laws.[53] Once in office, he enjoyed good rapport not only with reformers but with business, labor, and Bryan democrats.[54]

Deneen endorsed compensation in his annual messages to the legislature.[55] In 1910 he introduced into the general assembly a model plan devised by the National Civic Federation. This failed, and when presented in May 1911 with both an employers' liability and a compensation bill, he signed only the latter since it more clearly expressed the wishes of a majority of the commission members.[56]

As noted earlier, almost all IMA members opted for coverage.[57] In 1912, in order to lower insurance rates, the association formed its own mutual insurance company which by 1922 was writing more than $500,000 in premiums annually and had assets of over $1 million.[58] In 1955, the IMA offered this retrospective praise to the compensation act: "It has meant (1) that a complex, highly technical subject has been kept from becoming a political football; (2) that a stability has been maintained in Illinois which has not been possible in many other states; and (3) that substantial savings have been made in workmen's compensation."[59]

Insurance companies also favored compensation, though not as actively as the NAM, in order to thwart efforts at establishing government plans. Edson Lott, president of the United States Casualty Company and an active spokesman for the Liability Insurance Association, whose members included giants such as Aetna and Travelers, warned that state policies would be perverted into political tools. He denounced reformers advocating such changes for compulsively needing to "blow their own horns [and] cry out against that which is and for that which is not, otherwise they would be out of the spotlight."[60] The Workmen's Compensation Publicity Bureau's P. Tecumseh Sherman cautioned that state insurance would be corrupt, inefficient, and encourage malingering: "sentiment, not justice, will rule in the settlements."[61]

Opposed to extending employer liability, which would make it "manifestly impossible to fix the rates with any certainty," private insurance companies also favored compensation because it made "the amount of [awards] directly ascertainable when once the question of responsibility has been established."[62] In the words of one actuary:

"Companies have nothing to lose and everything to gain by the enactment of a workmen's compensation law."[63]

The insurance associations advocated government regulation of compensation plans as a way to check possible abuses by member companies. Frank E. Lawson, vice-president of the Fidelity and Casualty Association of New York, for example, endorsed the creation under state aegis of rate-making associations to set minimum charges which would cover overhead and provide a fair return. Competition, he cautioned, was dangerous in this field, as it made insurers insolvent and secured unfairly low rates to favored customers.[64]

These factors help to explain why compensation was adopted in 1911, while many equally pressing social problems, such as those of the unemployed, the sick, and the aged, went unattended. Accident insurance was a highly attractive reform to employers. It short-circuited the drive, as in the case of the 1909 Illinois factory safety code, to abrogate their common-law defenses. It relieved them of the expenses of litigation and private insurance. It substituted a fixed, limited charge for an unpredictable, potentially ruinous one. It operated in a manner "summary, expeditious, free from formalities and inexpensive."[65] It circumvented courts and juries whose decisions increasingly ran counter to the interests of capital. It did not require a new payroll cost but only an increase in existing overhead.[66] It served to pacify employees and public opinion. And it could be implemented in a manner congenial to private insurers. Such advantages did not attend reforms in the areas of medical, unemployment, or old age insurance, and thus employers did not back them. Changes there had to await the Great Depression.

A New Element in the Political Equation: Progressive Reformers

Reformers agreed with businessmen on the need for workmen's compensation, although their reasons differed. They were eager to enact welfare programs because of their belief that only regularized bureaucratic procedures could achieve social justice and cope with the problems of urban-industrial life. In earlier times, friends and relatives and informal devices such as fraternal associations could tide people over times of financial hardship. But in the modern world, the Progressives noted, such recourses were often unavailable or unreliable. For that reason, the state had to help the aged, ill, handicapped, unemployed, and those injured on the job. Workmen's compensation was an important part of their program because it would aid workers, reduce entrepreneurial risk, insure social harmony, prevent the breakup of families, and challenge the ethic of individualism.

One reformer who endorsed these views was Charles Richmond Henderson, a Baptist minister, chaplain, and professor of sociology at the University of Chicago and member of many professional and social action organizations. He decried the frequency with which businessmen and reformers fought each other and sought a union of "the more generous industrial leaders" and "practical scholars" to promote social welfare.

> It is the duty of the ethical theorist to show that the self-interest of the manufacturer and landlord do not secure the public welfare in any city in this country, and that it is precisely this self-interest, narrowly conceived, which prevents rational legislation. . . . It would be interesting to know what a factory would be worth in a community where "sentiment" had died of asphyxia and where the interest of one class was left to determine the terms on which industry should be conducted. . . . Without strong ethical feeling organized for common action, the meanest employer sets the pace for all those who really desire to be honorable and fair.[67]

Henderson felt the duty of the scholar was "to select out the facts which will help generous and genial industrial leaders to promote the common welfare and especially the welfare of those who are employed by them and over whom their commanding position as leaders has given them great power."[68] He also held the belief that sociology existed to solve social problems: "To assist us in the difficult task of adjustment to new situations, God has providentially wrought out for us the social sciences and placed them at our disposal."[69]

A prolific writer long active in the drive for social insurance, Henderson gave the cause a theoretical base in a series of twelve articles published in the *American Journal of Sociology* from 1907 to 1909. Insurance, he noted, was of no use to the rich, who did not need it—nor to the poor, who were too weak to benefit from collective action and required other forms of aid. The great mass of Americans, however, clearly required coverage; no longer owning any instruments of production, unable to accumulate savings, and without a voice in management, their meager financial resources doomed them to penury if they became ill or incapacitated. In Henderson's words: "No statistics which can be gathered can visualize the conditions of constant dread of suffering and pauperism which are the hourly torment of thoughtful workmen. . . . The aim of social insurance is not only to keep the wolf from the door, but to keep him so far away that he cannot destroy sleep with his howls."[70]

Henderson insisted that private insurance was inadequate, in part because it covered no more than 10 or 15 percent of injuries.[71] Fraternal societies, operating without competent actuaries, set rates oblivious to age, sex, or working conditions. "The majority of the members of the brotherhoods have made themselves believe that the law of gravity, the multiplication table, and economic forces and laws may be set at defiance if only men love each other enough."[72] Since most of these voluntary societies were small and locally organized, a large accident or epidemic might easily bankrupt them. The absence of scientific rates created an incentive for younger, healthier, more cautious men to avoid such plans. If members moved or changed jobs, they lost their investment. Such policies were also unsatisfactory as they were narrowly interpreted, vaguely worded, and covered only rare diseases.[73] Union plans were inadequate because those most in need of coverage—low-paid workers in high-risk trades—could least afford it. Workers hesitated to purchase union-sponsored coverage for fear that their funds might instead be spent secretly on strikes.[74] Last, the high overhead of private insurance made it too expensive for many.

Henderson spoke of the psychological benefits of insurance. Guaranteed compensation would foster the "manly virtues"[75] and engender worker self-respect by obviating reliance on charity. Wages hitherto spent on "drink and other useless consumption" would be used for insurance. Workers resuming employment after extended illness would do so only when fully recovered—which, in the long run, would produce fewer absences—and without the discouragement attendant to having spent their savings and gone into debt.

Henderson appreciated the advantages to employers of compensation. He denounced as "unscientific" jury verdicts which gave full benefit of the law to employees. Opposing reforms designed merely to expand employers' liability, he sought compensation in part to counter them[76] and to create a conservative, contented, sober, and faithful workforce. "Condition of bodily vigor, of comparative contentment and serenity of mind, of freedom from irritating and depressing despair in the prospect of incapacity to earn a living temporarily or permanently, is an asset of the first importance in the process of continuous manufacturing. . . . Human workers, with sound bodies and varied wants, are at once our first factor in large production, and our largest market for goods made. A million such civilized customers are better than several millions of savages or all the spendthrifts in the world."[77] Another reason for Illinois to adopt compensation was because the state which offered the best welfare programs to its workers would "swiftly and surely" attract those of the highest quality.[78] Henderson also knew that many employers could not afford liability insurance—the cost of which was "beyond belief"—yet compromised their credit if without it.[79] Compensation was the only solution.

Henderson thus sought insurance for work-related injuries for two reasons. It would serve humanitarian ends by obviating suffering and economic uncertainty, and practical ends by attracting better workers and reducing the risks and high costs imposed on capital by an antiquated legal system. He was able to fight for his ideas as a member of the 1905 commission, where one author has said of his work: "Because of his extensive knowledge, the other commission members looked to Henderson for leadership. He drew up the lines of inquiry, formulated the major decisions the commission would have to make, and furnished the other members with bibliographies on workmen's insurance and copies of the laws passed in Europe and the other . . . states."[80] Henderson also headed the Committee on Workmen's Insurance of the National Conference of Charities and Correction and wrote its model compensation act.[81]

A second such reformer was Ernst Freund, law professor at the University of Chicago, author of many books and articles on labor legislation, and head of the Illinois branch of the Association for the Advancement of Labor Legislation (AALL), which was heavily involved in the drive for compensation.

The AALL was established in 1906 as the American section of the International Association for Labor Legislation. While its membership remained small, consisting of about 200 social scientists, among them Richard T. Ely, John R. Commons, and I. M. Rubinow, its influence was large. It assisted in the creation of many industrial commissions and the drafting and enactment of numerous early compensation laws. In its work, the AALL stressed the role of the expert who "in contrast to any other segment of society, combined broad knowledge of and allegiance to the broad community interest."[82] Seeking to apply to legislation a scientific study of cause and effect, it incorporated into many laws the best and latest research in science, hygiene, medicine, economics, sociology, and jurisprudence. Nationally, it helped transform the topic of social insurance from an abstraction into a live public issue.[83]

In the 1870s, the rise of industry and organized labor led many European nations to enact welfare programs, such as workmen's compensation, which replaced the insurance of local brotherhoods and fraternal societies. Most plans were compulsory and employer financed and called for the collection of statistics with which to chart future policy. Born and educated in Germany, a nation without a laissez-faire, limited-government tradition, Freund illustrates the way in which American reform proposals often derived from European models.

He disapproved of the common law for failing to keep pace with advancing ideals. It preserved order, authority, and property at the expense of the weak. As regards industrial accidents, for example, it discouraged preventive measures by permitting employees to sue employers for negligence only after an accident had occurred. The common law was also unsuited to an assault against injustice in that redress under it was prohibitively expensive and lengthy. Freund wrote: "Most of it developed in that atmosphere of indifferent neutrality which has enabled the courts to be impartial but also keeps them out of touch with vital needs."[84] The remedy was threefold: precise statutory definitions of employer obligations, removal of unsafe conditions, and enactment of laws which placed life before property and the welfare of the whole before that of any individual.[85]

Freund saw workmen's compensation as a major step in the right direction, as it was

based upon a new principle which perhaps should be designated as that of social solidarity. The nexus of employer and employee in a common undertaking, the inevitable risk of accident and the apportionment of loss through a system of measured benefits not aiming to give full indemnity—these are the elements of solidarity which are entirely absent from the common law principle of liability. . . . Workingmen's compensation carries no stigma or disability, and by its conditions or terms rather seems to be in the nature of the discharge of a debt that the community owes to its members, a deferred payment for previously inadequately rewarded services, or a compensation for some kind of injustice suffered.[86]

Freund was particularly interested in the constitutional problems of creating a system of compensation. The first of these was that some saw liability without fault as a violation of due process in that it required employers to make restitution for injuries for which they may not have been responsible while denying them the right to prove their innocence in court. Others saw compensation as a violation of equal protection of the laws, as it covered only certain trades. Many early compensation laws were declared unconstitutional for these reasons, as in the case of the 1902 Maryland, 1905 New York, and 1909 Montana laws.

In the 1907 model bill, which he wrote, Freund devised a solution to these problems of constitutionality by proposing a plan which, while voluntary, was so attractive as to guarantee broad acceptance. Under it, employers and employees were free to reject coverage, but at the cost of losing their common-law rights—that is, the former could no longer use their defenses, the latter could no longer sue for damages. Freund's proposal was incorporated into the 1911 Illinois law and those of many other states.

In his writings, Freund also rejected two nonconstitutional objections to workmen's compensation. To the charge that it was unfair because one group—that is, employees—would benefit while another—employers—paid, he responded: "It is reasonable that those who create or maintain the risk or danger for their own benefit should consent to the most effectual means of obviating its harmful consequences; and collective responsibility is a wise and conservative method of meeting the risk. . . . Its imposition should be allowed as a valid condition of the right of keeping a dangerous instrument."[87] To the contention that insurance is a private matter, best left free from state interference, Freund asserted that the community has a stake in averting the destitution attendant to the injury, extended illness, or death of a breadwinner. The distribution of such losses over the entire population by state insurance was in his view a legitimate use of government power.[88]

Between the formation of the first commission in 1905 and the passage of compensation legislation in 1911, Freund made four additional major contributions to the cause of workingmen's insurance in Illinois. He wrote annual reports on the progress of labor legislation in the general assembly, describing the bills introduced, their strengths and weaknesses, and the support each generated. A specialist in constitutional law, he became Chicago's leading expert on reform legislation: many bills submitted to the general assembly were first scrutinized by him as to wording, effectiveness, and constitutionality.[89] In 1909, after hearing that Illinois was about to begin a major public works project, he drew up a compensation policy for those employed on it. The plan, which was approved by the legislature, was state funded and provided benefits for three years' wages in the event of death, six months' for total disability.[90] Last, as head of the Illinois Association for Labor Legislation, Freund collected and disseminated information on workmen's compensation. In 1909, for example, he proposed that any legislation meet the following standards: that employers furnish necessary medical care for a reasonable period; that disability benefits equal two-thirds of the employee's wages but not less than five or more than twenty dollars per week; that partial disability benefits equal two-thirds of the difference between wages before and after injury; that widow's benefits be 35 percent of wages, with an additional 10 percent for each child under eighteen; that coverage be compulsory and the common law abrogated; and that a special accident board settle disputes arising under the law.[91]

The State, Businessmen, and Reformers

Businessmen and reformers united to secure passage of the 1911 compensation law. Business, it appears, was the more important force. Reformers like Henderson and Freund and groups such as the AALL sought not only compensation but an entire range of welfare-state programs. They did not obtain them, largely because their goals meshed with those of the IMA only on the question of removing the unstable and expensive system of litigation created by the common law. In the words of Roy Lubove, "The social reformer may have justified workmen's compensation in terms of equity and social expediency, but the decisive consideration was that the major voluntary interests anticipated concrete, material advantages through the substitution of compensation for liability. This circumstance was absent in the case of all other social insurance."[92]

The final form taken by the compensation plan was suited to business needs. By one account, the injured worker, not the employer, continued to bear most of the expense, as compensation covered no more than one quarter of the cost of injuries.[93] Benefits were kept low by several devices, among them waiting periods before the receipt of benefits and small medical allowances.

The strong resemblance between the Illinois plan and that of the National Association of Manufacturers, with which the IMA was affiliated, provides further proof that the bill was congenial to capital. The NAM's plan was compulsory for all workers making under $1,800 annually, the Illinois plan for all workers in some trades, voluntary in others. To prevent insolvency, Illinois required the inspection of policies by the state superintendent of insurance, while the NAM required the purchase of a second policy to guarantee the soundness of the first. Should both policies fail, the state government in which the company was located was obligated to make the payments. Each plan required employers to furnish reasonable medical and surgical care at the accident scene. The NAM urged compensation at half pay for ten years in the event of permanent incapacitation and a death benefit of from $1,200 to $3,000; Illinois required a smaller amount for permanent injury but a larger death benefit. Both encouraged accident prevention through the use of preferred-risk status. Illinois required employers to assume the cost of insurance, while the NAM urged employees to pay about one-quarter of the premium. This difference is not as important as it might at first seem, as in both cases insurance represents a labor cost and thus technically is part of the employee's wages.

Labor: Against, Then For

During these years labor, like the Progressives, began to take an active role in politics. Its leaders, such as Samuel Gompers, had hitherto been staunch defenders of laissez-faire; but this changed because of the increased use by employers of injunctions and other union-busting devices and the inability of labor to abolish wage-lowering phenomena like child labor and immigration without becoming involved in politics. As a result, in 1906 the AFL for the first time fought to defeat several of its enemies in Congress and in 1908 endorsed a presidential candidate, democrat William Jennings Bryan. Among the achievements of this new political activism was the Clayton Act of 1914, which removed labor from the jurisdiction of the Sherman Act.[94]

This policy transformation on the national level had an analogue in the attitude of Illinois unions toward workmen's compensation: they were initially opposed, seeking instead repeal of the employers' common-law defenses. Their reasons were labor's anti-welfare-state tradition; the belief of many workers that they would do better by looking to the courts for potentially large awards rather than to compensation for small, albeit guaranteed ones; and widespread ignorance about what social insurance was.[95]

Until 1910, for example, nearly every convention of the Illinois Federation of Labor urged repeal of the common-law defenses. In 1883, it supported a bill to give employees the same right to sue employers as nonemployees and to void contracts forbidding workers from suing if injured.[96] Despite lobbying efforts, this and succeeding plans failed, in part because of the inability of the federation's member unions to agree on the exact terms of a bill. The IFL fought for the defeat of the 1905 compensation bill.

At the 1910 convention, however, President Edwin Wright, a member of the second liability commission, endorsed compensation.[97] Removing the employer's common-law defenses, he noted, would net more money only to workers with good counsel able to fight up to the state supreme court. Few could do so, and awards would thus be smaller and less frequently granted than under compensation.[98] In pushing for the latter, Wright was opposed by the railroad workers, who had company insurance plans and therefore saw the proposal as superfluous, and supported by the miners—low-paid workers in a high-risk trade which generally did not provide such coverage.[99]

The ranks of labor were now split. The Chicago Federation of Labor (CFL), headed by John Fitzpatrick, saw in compensation a scheme to shift financial responsibility for accidents from employers to employees[100] and thwart abolition of the common-law defenses, which the Cherry Hill disaster had made a distinct possibility.[101] The CFL also objected to compensation because the benefits were so low that they would force recipients into penury while employers incurred costs equal to or lower than those under the old system.[102] The split between the two organizations precluded the implementation of an agreement reached after Cherry Hill to field a slate of independent labor candidates for the general assembly committed to expanded liability legislation were a satisfactory law not passed before the fall elections.[103]

During 1912, the Chicago group lobbied for a liability law, and when the commission began to endorse compensation, members John Flora of the CFL and M. J. Boyle of the Chicago Switchmen's Union objected. In July, Flora reported to the federation that the legislation being drawn up was so complicated and narrow in coverage that he "utterly opposed it."[104] In September, with the commission about to publicly endorse compensation, the two walked out. Labeling the common-law defenses "the aliases of crooks and hold-up men" which rendered employers "practically immune under the law" while permitting them to live off "blood money, pure and simple,"[105] Boyle and Flora reiterated the need to secure liability legislation prior to the enactment of compensation. Asserting that Cherry Hill had exposed "the interests and their jack-pot method of juggling legislation which failed to heed the demands of the toilers of the state,"[106] they urged rejection of the commission proposals.

In opposing compensation, the Chicago Federation of Labor and its ally, the Railway Trainmen's Union, emphasized that death benefits under compensation were limited to $1,500 to $3,500 but were upward of $10,000 under expanded liability. They also stressed that repeal of the defenses would for the first time force industry to concern itself with job safety, as "it would make it so expensive for employers to kill their workmen that every safety appliance known to science will be installed."[107] President W. C. Carter of the Brotherhood of Locomotive Firemen noted: "Workmen's compensation would see a great increase in deaths and injuries. My purpose in all legislation is to prevent deaths and injuries rather than to secure compensation. It is much better that the law remain as it is if under the present law thousands of lives and limbs are saved. A few hundred dollars to the widows and orphans of a man killed in a railroad wreck by defective machinery is no exchange for the life and service of that man to his family."[108] Many also feared that the lower maximum death benefit for single men would cause them to be hired in preference to married men.

In January 1911 the Chicago federation reintroduced a liability bill in the general assembly and ordered its lobbyists "not to countenance or waste any time or effort for the passage of said Workmen's Compensation bill."[109] In May, however, it agreed not to oppose compensation in exchange for a promise from "friends of the Governor and his allies"[110] that the liability bill would also pass. Both were thereupon approved in the legislature by near-unanimous margins, but later in the month, in what may have been a violation of the earlier pledge, Governor Deneen signed the compensation bill while vetoing the liability bill.

The Chicago federation came quickly to accept the program, however. In 1912, it published a pamphlet outlining the law's defects but expressed a willingness to give it a fair trial.[111] In 1913, it showed support for the plan by agreeing to participate with the IMA and the IFL in an effort to revise it. The main achievement of this conference was the creation of a quasi-judicial board empowered to adjudicate disputes arising under terms of the law, thereby obviating a good deal of litigation.

An Emerging Welfare State

A crucial problem confronting Americans at the turn of the century was to restore an equity lost under the common law because of the advent of large-scale industry. The huge increase in job-related accidents, the instability they brought to business conditions, the lengthy and costly delay in determining awards, and the arbitrariness of many court decisions made change imperative.

Businessmen, seeking to reduce risk, led the move for reform because employers' liability had become too expensive and capriciously enforced. The Progressives acted for broader reasons. Aware of the enormous problems industrialization and urbanization had brought, they sought to restore security to workers' lives by replacing outmoded family and fraternal ties with state-sponsored welfare and insurance programs. They fought for comprehensive change to insure people against injury, unemployment, sickness, and the infirmities of old age. Labor initially opposed reform, fearful that a welfare state would weaken the allegiance of workers to their unions. Their view changed, however, as the intractable nature of problems like child labor and the injunction made political involvement imperative.

By 1911, the vast majority of Illinois public opinion makers favored workmen's compensation. The desire of the Progressives to go further, however, was blocked by the refusal of business to endorse such changes. In this sense, capital was the force which most fully achieved its goals: it secured compensation while blocking further reform. In the words of Illinois State Federation of Labor President Edwin Wright, "I say to you frankly that there has never been a time since we started trying to get a compensation law enacted that if we hadn't got an agreement with the employers affected by it we would have been able to get a single bill through."[112]

Although the additional changes on the Progressive agenda were postponed, workmen's compensation represented a major breakthrough to welfare capitalism. No longer were businessmen the virtually sole recipients of government aid, as workers and reformers had united to secure programs in their own interest. Others would build on this breakthrough during later reform movements, such as the New Deal and the Great Society.

Notes

1. Harry Weiss, "Employers' Liability and Workmen's Compensation," in *A History of Labor in the United States, 1896–1932*, ed. John R. Commons (New York: Macmillan Co., 1935), p. 572.

2. Ibid., p. 573.

3. James Weinstein, *The Corporate Ideal in the Liberal State, 1900–1918* (Boston: Beacon Press, 1968), p. 61.

4. Weiss, p. 575.

5. *Report of the Employer's Liability Commission of the State of Illinois* (Chicago: Stromberg, Allen & Co., 1911), p. 14; hereafter cited as *Report*, 1911.

6. Ibid., p. 195.

7. George W. Angerstein, *The Employer and the Workmen's Compensation Act of Illinois* (Chicago: Hawkins & Loomis, 1923), p. 40.

8. I. M. Rubinow, *Social Insurance* (New York: Henry Holt & Co., 1913), p. 97.

9. Roy Lubove, *The Struggle for Social Security* (Cambridge, Mass.: Harvard University Press, 1968), p. 48.

10. *Report*, 1911, p. 9; Angerstein, p. 8.

11. Clarence W. Hobbs, *Workmen's Compensation Insurance* (New York: McGraw-Hill Book Co., 1939), pp. 44–45.

12. *Report of the Industrial Insurance Commission to the Governor of Illinois* (Chicago: Phillips Brothers, 1907), p. 4.

13. Ibid., p. 7.

14. Ibid., p. 9.

15. Illinois Bureau of Labor Statistics, *Labor Legislation in the 46th General Assembly* (Springfield, Ill.: State Printers, 1911), p. 13.

16. "Town of Orphans Calling for Help," *Chicago Tribune* (November 15, 1909).

17. *Report*, 1911, p. 142.

18. Ibid., p. 91.

19. Ibid., p. 18.

20. Ibid., p. 138.

21. Ibid., p. 9.

22. Ibid., p. 203.

23. Ibid.

24. Ibid., p. 169; I. M. Rubinow, *A Standard Accident Table* (Boston: Spectator Co., 1915), p. 4.

25. *Report*, 1911, p. 9.

26. Angerstein, p. 38.

27. Charles Richmond Henderson, "Industrial Insurance. II. Local Relief Societies," *American Journal of Sociology* 12 (March 1907): 188.

28. Rubinow, *Social Insurance*, p. 169.

29. Henderson, p. 188; Rubinow, *Social Insurance*, p. 167; *Report*, 1911, p. 14.

30. Rubinow, *Social Insurance*, p. 169.

31. Ibid., p. 166.

32. Fred C. Schwedtman, *Co-operation or—What?* (New York: National Association of Manufacturers, 1912), p. 14.

33. Earl R. Beckner, *A History of Labor Legislation in Illinois* (Chicago: University of Chicago Press, 1929), p. 449.

34. Rubinow, *Social Insurance*, p. 98.

35. Henry L. Rosenfield, *Cooperation and Compensation versus Compulsion and Compromise in Employers' Liability* (New York: Workmen's Compensation Publicity Bureau, 1911), p. 3.

36. *Report,* 1911, p. 37.
37. Ibid., p. 167.
38. Ibid., p. 14.
39. Angerstein, p. 9.
40. Schwedtman, p. 14; Rubinow, *Social Insurance,* p. 98.
41. Rosenfield, p. 2.
42. Schwedtman, p. 2.
43. Ibid., p. 6.
44. *Report,* 1911, p. 74.
45. *Annual Report of the Illinois Manufacturers Association for 1905* (Chicago: Illinois Manufacturers Association, 1905), p. 15.
46. *Annual Report of the Illinois Manufacturers Association for 1909* (Chicago: Illinois Manufacturers Association, 1909), p. 40.
47. *Annual Report of the Illinois Manufacturers Association for 1910* (Chicago: Illinois Manufacturers Association, 1910), p. 3.
48. Ibid., p. 35.
49. Ibid.
50. *Annual Report of the Illinois Manufacturers Association for 1911* (Chicago: Illinois Manufacturers Association, 1911), p. 66; hereafter cited as *IMA Report, 1911.*
51. Ibid., p. 37.
52. Lincoln Steffens, *The Autobiography of Lincoln Steffens,* 2 vols. (New York: Harcourt Brace & Co., 1931), 2: 132.
53. "Deneen Campaign in Lively Finish," *Chicago Tribune* (November 3, 1908).
54. "Even Foes of Deneen Predict His Election," *Chicago Record Herald* (November 2, 1908).
55. Illinois Bureau of Labor Statistics (n. 15 above), p. 68.
56. *IMA Report, 1911,* p. 5.
57. Ibid., p. 67.
58. Alfred Kelly, "A History of the Illinois Manufacturers Association" (Ph.D. diss., University of Chicago, 1938), p. 97.
59. Illinois Manufacturers Association, *Workmen's Compensation in Illinois* (Chicago: Illinois Manufacturers Association, 1955), p. 1.
60. Edson Lott, *Politics versus Workmen's Compensation Insurance* (Hartford, Conn.: Liability Insurance Association, 1916), p. 2.
61. P. Tecumseh Sherman, "Invasion of the Insurance Field by the State," in *Addresses Made at the Fifth Annual Meeting of the Liability Insurance Association* (Hartford, Conn.: Liability Insurance Association, 1911), p. 45; hereafter cited as *Addresses.*
62. S. H. Wolf, "Is the State to Compensate Injured Workmen?" in *Addresses,* p. 50.
63. Frank E. Law, "State Insurance of Workmen's Compensation for Accidents," in *Addresses,* p. 30.
64. Ibid., p. 32.
65. Hobbs (n. 11 above), p. 68.
66. Quoted in Lubove (n. 9 above), p. 49.
67. Charles Richmond Henderson, "Businessmen and Social Theorists," *American Journal of Sociology* 1 (January 1896): 391.
68. Ibid., p. 395.
69. Steven Diner, "A City and Its University" (Ph.D. diss., University of Chicago, 1972), p. 92.
70. Charles Richmond Henderson, "Industrial Insurance. I. The Extent and Nature of the Demand for a Social Policy of Workingmen's Insurance," *American Journal of Sociology* 12 (January 1907): 472.
71. Charles Richmond Henderson, "To Protect the Workers," *Chicago Daily News* (November 1, 1906).
72. Charles Richmond Henderson, "Industrial Insurance. IV. The Insurance of Fraternal Societies," *American Journal of Sociology* 13 (July 1907): 36.
73. Charles Richmond Henderson, "Industrial Insurance. VI. Private Insurance Companies," *American Journal of Sociology* 13 (November 1907): 366–67.
74. Charles Richmond Henderson, "Industrial Insurance: Benefit Features of Trade-Unions," *American Journal of Sociology* 12 (May 1907): 366.
75. Charles Richmond Henderson, "Industrial Insurance. VIII. Insurance Plans of Railroad Corporations," *American Journal of Sociology* 13 (March 1908): 609.

76. Charles Richmond Henderson, "Industrial Insurance. V. The Employers' Liability Law," *American Journal of Sociology* 13 (September 1907): 170.

77. Henderson, "Extent and Nature," pp. 484–85.

78. Ibid., p. 484.

79. Henderson, "Employers' Liability Law," p. 188.

80. Diner (n. 69 above), p. 77.

81. Among the other organizations of which Henderson was a member were: Society for Social Hygiene, Civic Federation of Chicago, Chicago Vice Commission, University of Chicago Settlement, City Unemployment Commission, Society for School Extension, City Club Labor Committee, Infant Welfare Society, and the Educational Committee on Child Philanthropy. He also served as president of the National Conference on Charities and Correction and the National Prison Association.

82. Lubove (n. 9 above), p. 32.

83. Ibid., p. 35.

84. Ernst Freund, *Standards of American Legislation* (Chicago: University of Chicago Press, 1917), p. 48.

85. Ibid., p. 93.

86. Ibid., pp. 24, 111.

87. Ernst Freund, *Police Power* (Chicago: Callaghan & Co., 1904), p. 460.

88. Ibid., p. 464.

89. Diner, p. 86.

90. Ernst Freund to State Senator Frank P. Schmidt, April 14, 1909, Ernst Freund Papers, Department of Special Collections, Joseph Regenstein Library, University of Chicago.

91. Ernst Freund, *Standards for Workmen's Compensation* (New York: Macmillan Co., 1914), p. 3. Among the other reform organizations of which Freund was a member were: the Immigrants' Protective League; City Club; Short Ballot Association; Citizens Committee on the Garment Workers Strike; and Advisory Board, Illinois Committee for Social Legislation. Freund also served in 1915 as president of the American Political Science Association. This discussion of reformers and organizations supporting workmen's compensation is by no means exhaustive. Among the innumerable other advocates of compensation were Florence Kelly; Jane Addams; Graham Taylor; the magazines *Survey* and *Outlook;* and the United Charities of Chicago, the City Club of Chicago, the Industrialists Club of Chicago, the Chicago Board of Charities, and the National Conference on Social Work.

92. Lubove, p. 49.

93. Ibid., p. 57.

94. See Marc Karson, *American Labor Unions and Politics* (Carbondale: Southern Illinois University Press, 1958).

95. Beckner (n. 33 above), p. 437.

96. Eugene Staley, *A History of the Illinois State Federation of Labor* (Chicago: University of Chicago Press, 1930), p. 51.

97. Ibid., p. 59.

98. Ibid., p. 61.

99. Ibid., p. 64.

100. Chicago Federation of Labor, "Minutes of the Executive Council Meetings for 1910," Chicago Federation of Labor Papers, the Chicago Historical Society, p. 5; hereafter cited as CFL "Minutes."

101. *Report,* 1911, p. 23.

102. CFL "Minutes," p. 6.

103. *Report,* 1911, p. 32.

104. CFL "Minutes," p. 7.

105. *Report,* 1911, p. 31.

106. Ibid., p. 32.

107. Staley, p. 257.

108. *Report,* 1911, p. 225.

109. CFL "Minutes," p. 9.

110. Ibid., p. 5.

111. Staley, p. 260.

112. Kelly, p. 70.

Isaac Max Rubinow: Pioneering Specialist in Social Insurance

J. Lee Kreader
Evanston, Illinois

The United States' first major theorist of social insurance, Isaac Max Rubinow, was a dedicated fighter in the frustrating campaign for comprehensive social insurance during the Progressive era. While partly fitting the profiles that historians have drawn of typical Progressive reformers, Rubinow—an immigrant, a Jew, and a socialist—also represents aspects of Progressivism which historians have neglected. After a respite in the 1920s, Rubinow renewed his efforts for social insurance early in the 1930s. The New Deal asked little of his advice in preparing the Social Security Act of 1935; nevertheless, Rubinow welcomed social security as the long-delayed beginning of an inclusive American system of social insurance.

Isaac Max Rubinow (1875–1936) was a groundbreaking theorist and a tireless fighter for American social insurance. In his mammoth *Social Insurance, with Special Reference to American Conditions* (1913) and in his lifelong outpouring of other books and articles, he explained the unfamiliar term "social insurance" to Americans. Without comprehensive social insurance, he warned, working-class victims of industrial life would slip into permanent poverty. A key member of several reform and professional associations in the Progressive era, Rubinow lobbied for model legislation to expand American social insurance in many directions.

Workmen's compensation laws guaranteeing minimal financial benefits to laborers injured in industrial accidents represented the greatest Progressive achievement in social insurance. By 1920 forty-three states had enacted compensation legislation.[1] By then thirty-nine states had also passed widows' and orphans' pension laws providing subsistence incomes to the needy wives and children of dead

Social Service Review 50 (September 1976): 402–25
© 1976 by The University of Chicago

workers.[2] In the Progressive years, Rubinow and fellow advocates of more comprehensive social insurance vainly urged the United States to follow Europe's example and further protect laboring people against illness, old age, and unemployment.

Despite their efforts, American social insurance remained under-developed until the New Deal. Even social security, finally adopted in 1935, was less comprehensive than the system Rubinow had articulated in 1913.

Although two recent historians of the American "struggle for social security" have praised Rubinow as "a remarkable man"[3] and "the outstanding American theoretician of social insurance,"[4] no one has yet studied Rubinow's busy career in the Progressive era. Rubinow's phenomenal energy and dedication to social insurance make his story in these years appealing in itself. With his drive, he could have created the appearance of a social movement single-handedly.

Yet the man and his work have broader significance. Examination of Rubinow's ethnic, economic, social, and intellectual background reveals sources of reform impetus in the Progressive years which historians have overlooked or oversimplified. Rubinow's influence in reform organizations and his reputation as an important social theorist further bespeak receptivity, tolerance, and breadth in the Progressive mind. Finally, his failure until the 1930s to convince Americans of the need for more extensive social insurance marks one boundary of Progressive accomplishment.

The Immigrant as Expert

Isaac Rubinow came to New York City from Moscow in 1893 when he was seventeen years old. Like his parents and four older brothers, he fled rising persecution of Jews in the Russia of Tsar Alexander III.[5] The son of a wealthy Jewish textile merchant, Rubinow had been among the few fortunate Jews in Russia. Imperial regulations dating back to Catherine the Great had confined the vast majority of Russian Jews to a Pale of settlement along the western and southern borders of the Russian empire. Early in his reign, however, Alexander II, liberator of the Russian serfs, relaxed restrictions on Jewish settlement, allowing certain favored groups—including "merchants of the first guild"—to live in major Russian cities. There, the tsar hoped, they would invest their wealth and talents to the advantage of all Russia.[6] Rich enough to qualify as a merchant of the first guild, Rubinow's father moved with his family to Moscow in 1883.[7]

Until that time, the Rubinows had lived in Grodno, a town of the

Pale in the Grodno province of Lithuania. In the years following
Isaac's birth there in 1875, tobacco and textile factories appeared in
his native province. Jewish entrepreneurs and a large pool of Jewish
labor, confined to the towns and cities by the May Laws of 1882,
participated importantly in the industrial growth.[8]

The congestion and poverty of Jews were far greater in Lithuania
than anywhere else in the Pale.[9] Yet Russian Jews had routine contact
with Russian Gentiles, and Rubinow wrote that "the mingling with
persons who speak other tongues" gave the average Jew knowledge of
both Yiddish and Russian. Wealthier, better-educated Jews like the
Rubinows even spoke Russian at home.[10]

By the time they joined the tiny Jewish minority in Moscow, the
Rubinows had already been partially assimilated into the larger Russian society. Between 1885 and 1892, young Isaac's sensitivities expanded still further during study at the Petri-Pauli-Schule, a German
gymnasium in Moscow.[11] His adaptability served him well when Alexander III, who had long opposed Alexander II's assimilative policy,
expelled most Jews from the cities of Russia and pushed the
Rubinows to New York City.[12]

Rubinow stayed in touch with Russia after emigrating. From 1897
to 1917 he served as an American correspondent to several Moscow
and Saint Petersburg newspapers; from 1898 to 1915 he contributed
to the publications of the Russian Ministry of Finance. In 1907 the
Ministry of Finance awarded him a medal in recognition of his "distinguished service to commerce and agriculture."[13] That same year he
wrote a lengthy article for American readers on *The Economic Condition of the Jews in Russia* in which he analyzed the data on Jews from the
1897 census of the Russian empire. He took pains to break the
stereotype of the Russian Jew as a rich, parasitic merchant and to
underscore statistically the poverty and occupational diversity of Jews
in his native land.[14] Until the outbreak of the Russian Revolution,
Rubinow corresponded with Russian friends, including Jewish revolutionaries seeking to end the persecution of their people.[15]

Although conscious of his Jewish heritage, Rubinow opposed ethnic exclusiveness. In a 1905 article on "The Economic Condition of
the Russian Jew in New York City," he stressed the economic and
social diversity among Russian Jews there. Acknowledging the poverty of the great majority of these immigrants, he singled out the
sweatshop as their "essential economic problem." Yet unlike other
Jewish writers, he considered the sweatshop a question for society at
large, not a "specifically Jewish" issue.[16] A Jewish associate wrote: "His
[Rubinow's] work and his ideas . . . kept him rather aloof from purely
Jewish movements. He . . . thought of the solution of Jewish problems
in terms of the solution of social problems."[17]

Not raised an orthodox Jew, Rubinow confessed he had little Jewish learning; Jewish friends, however, believed he had the next best thing, "Jewish feeling."[18] More than mere feeling, he had an informed appreciation for the Russian Jews' traditions of mutual assistance. He wrote approvingly, for example, of *khevras*, associations of Jewish artisans whose ancient origins "must be sought in the rites of the Jewish religion." Originally set up for communal prayer, *khevras* gradually acquired charitable functions, and finally, under the impact of industrialism, they established sick benefit funds.[19] Rubinow also described Jewish communal organizations in the towns of the Pale to which the tsar delegated authority to collect taxes to support the Jewish communities' charitable institutions.[20]

Aware of these traditions from childhood on, Rubinow saw in them—and in similar customs of other European laboring people —the deepest roots of the movement for state-supported social insurance.[21] Europe had a head start over the United States in social insurance; Rubinow's equal familiarity with Europe and the United States distinguished him among American theorists of social insurance.

For Rubinow, like many educated Russian Jews, socialism was an important intellectual heritage. In Russia, socialism and the Jewish labor movement intertwined with the Jews' efforts to improve their legal standing.[22] The Jewish labor movement arose in Rubinow's native Lithuania in the 1880s and 1890s, recruiting members among the impoverished Jewish workmen and leaders among the young Jewish intelligentsia—some of whom had encountered Marx's ideas during university education outside Russia.[23] Rubinow noted "the very widespread tendency of the educated minority to organize secret classes for the instruction of adult working men and women . . . with secret socialist and other propaganda."[24] Freed by emigration from any direct role in the Jews' struggle in Russia, Rubinow nevertheless remained a Marxian.

Marx's broad generalizations gave Rubinow powerful insights into industrial society in the United States. Like most immigrant socialist intellectuals in New York City, Rubinow was an evolutionary socialist, believing that America's maturation into a cooperative society was inevitable. The fully developed cooperative state might be far distant, but in the meantime portions of it could grow up alongside remnants of capitalism. After all, as Rubinow reasoned in the *International Socialist Review* in 1903, an early stage of capitalism just emerging from the South's feudal slave society coexisted with the North's full-blown capitalism.[25]

Rubinow was a flexible Marxian. In *Was Marx Wrong?*, a socialist pamphlet published in 1914, Rubinow used statistics to argue that American experience had fulfilled all of Marx's prophecies except one, the increasing misery of the proletariat. Unperturbed, Rubinow wrote: "We are not pledged to follow 'in his [Marx's] steps' because they were 'his steps,' except in so far as our study of present day conditions justifies us in retaining his view of the economic development of capitalist society."[26]

Well prepared for college by his eight-year course in the gymnasium and already fluent in English, Rubinow entered Columbia University as a junior the autumn after arriving in New York City. Ambition for their sons' higher education may have been one of the elder Rubinows' chief reasons for leaving Russia. Earlier in the nineteenth century, Russian Jews had been permitted to receive advanced instruction, but beginning late in the 1880s, Alexander III severely restricted Jewish enrollment in Russian gymnasiums and universities. Rubinow earned his A.B. from Columbia University in 1895.[27]

After a year's postgraduate study in biology, he enrolled in New York University Medical College.[28] Ten years later, Rubinow candidly explained: "Medicine has remained one of the favorite professions [of Russian Jews in the United States]. The laxity of entrance requirements, the awe of a doctor's title the Russian Jew brings from the old country, and the easy success of the older members of the profession have all contributed toward the popularity of this vocation."[29] Rubinow practiced medicine in the ghettos of New York City from 1899 to 1903.[30]

In America as in Russia, Rubinow was wealthier and far better educated than most other Jews. His medical practice taught him about poverty. He learned how poor health and poverty fed on each other. Horrified by the conditions in which working-class mothers gave birth to their children, he later wrote that these wretched deliveries first awakened his interest in social insurance.[31] Eager to pursue his social insights, in 1900 Rubinow again enrolled in Columbia University, this time as a part-time graduate student in the School of Political Science. He studied economics, statistics, sociology, and political philosophy. A seminar conducted by Edwin R. A. Seligman, a leading specialist in public finance,[32] expanded Rubinow's curiosity for the neglected field of social insurance.[33]

In 1903 he gave up medical practice altogether and took the first of several posts in the federal bureaucracy in Washington, D.C. Rubinow first served as a U.S. Civil Service Commission examiner, but finding this work monotonous, he left it after only a year.[34] Between 1904 and 1907 he worked as an expert in economics and statistics in the Bureau of Statistics of the U.S. Department of Agriculture. Here he wrote a series of monographs on Russian wheat.[35]

Yet his interest lay in workmen's, not agricultural, problems. In 1904 he had published his first scholarly articles on workmen's insurance; he transferred to the Bureau of Statistics of the U.S. Department of Commerce and Labor in 1907.[36] When the Bureau of Labor

Statistics of the Department of Commerce and Labor, reacting in 1908 to a deepening American concern over industrial accidents, began a study of European workmen's insurance legislation, it picked Rubinow and two others to direct the research.

Rubinow was splendidly qualified for his new position; it drew on his concern for laborers, his knowledge of Europe, and his training in statistics. In 1909 the three produced the giant, two-volume *Twenty-fourth Annual Report of the Commissioner of Labor*, which became a standard reference for the social insurance movement in the Progressive era.[37] In 1911 Rubinow left government employment. He received his Ph.D. from Columbia in 1914, submitting as his dissertation the portions of the *Twenty-fourth Annual Report* which he alone had prepared—the sections on Italy, Russia, and Spain.[38]

Throughout these formative years, Rubinow came to consider himself an expert, both in knowledge of European social insurance and in statistical ability. "Childish preference for home-made plans to imitations of European systems"[39] and "preposterous abuse of statistical data" annoyed him.[40] He had adapted quickly to the United States, calling himself an American and writing lively English prose sprinkled with quotations from American literary figures and allusions to American history.[41]

Rubinow counted himself a socialist, not a Progressive. As a socialist, he said he stood for "reforming, remaking, radically changing our social institutions." Not content merely to await the fully developed socialist state, Rubinow admittedly worked for interim improvements.[42] If in the true sense of the word he was a "reformer," Rubinow insisted that Progressives were not reformers at all. "They are afraid of a change—a new patch on an old hole—that is as far as their social vision goes. Social reformers, indeed! Social conservators—that is more accurate. And, as a matter of fact, is this not admitted? Doesn't our progressive movement continually and boastfully emphasize its conservative character?"[43]

Yet Rubinow exhibited several traits which historians have considered typical of Progressive reformers. With his double professional training in medicine and social science, he ideally represented the assertive "new middle class" determined to reorder American life to which Robert Weibe has ascribed much of the momentum of Progressivism. He mastered the new field of statistics; he worked in the expanding federal bureaucracy. Weibe's observation that "the expert who timed his entry properly and presented his plans cleverly could become the indispensable man" applied well to Rubinow, especially after he left the Bureau of Labor Statistics.[44]

Rubinow displayed other traits which partially fit older profiles of Progressives. Urban and comfortably middle class, his background in these respects was like that of the average Progressive in Richard

Hofstadter's *Age of Reform*.[45] Willing to learn from Europe, Rubinow resembled other reformers who looked to Europe for guidance—the social thinkers, settlement workers, and municipal socialists Arthur Mann has described.[46] Infused with a deep sense of social justice, Rubinow's career had that moral tone which Hofstadter, Mann, and others have observed in Progressivism.[47]

But Rubinow was a socialist. His moral vision was rooted in the cooperative ethic of Marxism and the ancient Jewish tradition of communal responsibility, not the competitive ethic of capitalism or the Protestant social gospel more commonly associated with Progressivism. Moreover, unlike Hofstadter's typically native-born Progressive, Rubinow was an immigrant. Those historians who have described the immigrants' role in Progressive reform have seen only the laborers' protest against miserable working and living conditions.[48] Rubinow was no laborer. He was an immigrant intellectual who constantly compared the plights of American and European workers.

Rubinow's career reveals the broad base of Progressivism and the thin line between Progressivism and evolutionary socialism. More particularly, a brief study of Isaac Rubinow in the Progressive era uncovers important contributions to Progressive social welfare thought from sources not generally cited: Jews, socialists, and intellectuals from immigrant families.

The Expert as Reformer

Between 1911 and America's entry into World War I, Rubinow fought for social insurance on many fronts. A gifted and prolific writer, he wrote lengthy theoretical works explaining social insurance and shorter journal articles advocating it. Energetic and adaptable, he worked through several lobbying and professional organizations to advance its cause.

On the theoretical level, he wrote *Social Insurance, with Special Reference to American Conditions*, published in 1913. In *Social Insurance*, Rubinow reworked lectures he had originally presented at the New York School of Philanthropy and drew heavily on the research for the *Twenty-fourth Annual Report*. *Social Insurance* provided a new framework for understanding all social insurance laws in Europe and the United States. Previous works, including the *Twenty-fourth Annual Report*, had examined social insurance country by country; Rubinow's compared countries by categories of social insurance. The major categories were insurance against industrial accidents, sickness, old age, invalidity, death, and unemployment.[49] Though these hazards

faced all workmen, or a statistically predictable portion of all workmen, Rubinow showed that the average worker could not accumulate
sufficient savings to meet such catastrophes. Inadequate financial reserves, not weak character, turned an unlucky worker into a pauper.[50]

Rubinow's solution was social insurance, which "when properly developed, is nothing if not a well-defined effort of the organized state
to come to the assistance of the wage-earner and furnish him something he individually is quite unable to obtain for himself."[51] To
Rubinow, in the best, most "properly developed," social insurance,
the state reduced the cost to workers as far as possible by forbidding
profit on sale of the insurance, by assuming the cost of administering
it, or, best of all, by shifting its entire cost to sectors of society better
able to afford it. Finally, Rubinow insisted that social insurance be
compulsory so that even those workmen unwilling to pay a small,
subsidized premium would participate.[52]

Social Insurance, which Rubinow deemed a "pioneering" effort,[53]
received a favorable critical reception. Reviewers praised its clarity,
expertise, and timeliness—appearing as it did at the peak of the
workmen's compensation movement. A mixed review in the *Boston
Transcript,* however, complained that "too much space is given to the
European condition."[54]

In its implication that the United States could not learn much from
Europe, this remark represented a repeated criticism of the American
social insurance movement. As Roy Lubove explained in *The Struggle
for Social Security,* the state's involvement and compulsion, so crucial to
Rubinow's theory of social insurance, seemed alien to Americans, who
traditionally equated democracy with limited state activity and voluntary associations.[55] Others argued that, since American workmen
earned higher wages than their European counterparts, they did not
need the protection of social insurance. These critics overlooked the
correspondingly higher prices Americans paid for food and shelter.[56]

From Rubinow's viewpoint, a residue of voluntarism weakened the
twenty-four workmen's compensation laws in force in the United
States when *Social Insurance* appeared. To skirt the constitutional objection that compensation insurance violated a worker's right to sue
an employer for damages in an industrial accident, over twenty of the
laws were "elective." At hiring, employer and employee could elect, in
the event of an accident, to waive the employer's liability option and
use the compensation procedure.[57] Rubinow protested that this device let some employers avoid the compensation system altogether.

That most employers opted for compensation did not mean,
moreover, that they had their workers' interests at heart. It most often
meant, according to Rubinow, that they could buy compensation
coverage from insurance companies more cheaply than they could
buy liability insurance. The compensation laws provided for appal-

lingly low settlements; liability settlements, though less frequent, usually had been much higher. Therefore, liability coverage was more expensive.[58] Rubinow believed that compensation ironically benefited employers more than workers.

Rubinow felt that the United States had accomplished almost nothing in the other areas of social insurance by 1913. The seventeen state widows' and orphans' pension laws, which began appearing in 1911, he conceded, were "a step towards, if not quite yet a measure of, social insurance."[59] Because they provided no automatic payments to a workman's widow and children—they required proof of a widow's financial need and moral fitness to raise her children—Rubinow classified these laws as public relief, not genuine social insurance against death.[60]

"A convinced enthusiast of progressive and radical labor legislation,"[61] Rubinow threw himself into efforts to expand American social insurance. He was not exclusively a theorist. "I would not miss the opportunity of doing . . . propaganda, which I consider no less important than the effort to impart accurate information," he proclaimed.[62] Knowing that European social insurance systems had been enacted piece by piece, he expected the same pattern to hold in the United States.

In professional and scientific journals like the *American Economic Review*, the *Journal of Political Economy*, the *American Labor Legislation Review*, and *Survey*, he published hundreds of articles advocating social insurance. From 1911 to 1916 he served as a contributing editor to *Survey*, a professional magazine for social workers.[63] In *Survey* he reexplained his theories and applied them to recent developments in the social insurance movement. Responding to critics who feared that social insurance would make American workers lazy, he admitted that social insurance, like private insurance, could be abused. However, Rubinow asked, since no one wanted to abolish fire insurance because it encouraged an occasional arsonist, did opponents really block social insurance for fear of a loafer or two? Behind the worry over "malingering," Rubinow saw employers who actually objected to contributing to social insurance. Rubinow suggested that people genuinely concerned about malingering study European mechanisms to minimize it. Thirty years' experience with social insurance had not demoralized the European working class.[64]

Rubinow might have been expected to work for social insurance through the Socialist Party of America, of which he had been a member since its founding in 1901.[65] In 1914 Rubinow deemed himself as representative a member of the party as it was possible to find.[66] He could easily have interpreted the expanded state activity in behalf of workers that was implicit in social insurance as a step toward the cooperative society. More concretely, in 1904—about the time

Rubinow discovered his interest in social insurance—the Socialist Party of America's platform called for the most comprehensive social insurance ever requested by an American political party.[67]

Socialist Meyer London, elected to the U.S. House of Representatives from the Lower East Side of New York, convened hearings on social insurance before the House Committee on Labor in 1916. In his testimony, Rubinow claimed that the Socialist Party of America still favored social insurance.[68] Afterward, however, he stressed that witnesses from every political party had spoken in support of social insurance[69] and that social insurance was not socialism simply because many socialists favored it. "Social insurance [he wrote] is not a philosophical theory for the radical reorganization of modern society on new collectivist principles. . . . Social insurance is a very practical, matter-of-fact movement to utilize the resources of existing society in an effort to eliminate . . . extreme poverty or destitution in modern society by attacking the problem at its sources."[70]

Morris Hillquit, leading theorist of evolutionary socialism in the Socialist Party of America, agreed that social insurance had little in common with socialist theory. To Hillquit, it was more a prop for capitalism than a step toward socialism.[71] In Social Insurance, Rubinow noted the ambiguity and left the question of social insurance's proper classification hanging: "The fact that both the extreme reactionaries and the extreme revolutionaries are dissatisfied with . . . [the] general effects of social insurance upon the class relations in modern industrial society, surely furnishes some wholesome food for reflection."[72]

Rubinow also knew that socialist rhetoric frightened an American electorate. "If there were any assets in revolutionary phrases they would have been captured and assimilated by the Progressives by this time," he wrote in 1914.[73] Rubinow did not weaken the appeal of social insurance by crediting it to socialism. In 1912, while a member of the Socialist Party of America, Rubinow helped write the Progressive party platform, preparing the social insurance portions of the plank on social and industrial justice.[74]

Like de Tocqueville almost a century before, Rubinow understood a "fundamental difference in the history of social legislation in Europe and the United States." In Europe, the government or the beneficiaries of a proposal initiated the change. In America, "such legislation usually starts as a 'reform movement' initiated by private individuals and groups. Not only the government but even the social group directly concerned often remains indifferent or even antagonistic to the proposal for a long time. It takes [for example] an American Association for Labor Legislation . . . through education, propaganda, wire-pulling and sometimes unesthetic lobbying, to pass an act. . . ."[75]

In 1906, Rubinow was a founding member of the American Association for Labor Legislation (AALL), a group largely composed of social science professionals—many of whom were affiliated with major American universities.[76] After many "somnolent" years as "an appendage to the International Association for Labor Legislation," the AALL joined the workmen's compensation movement around 1911.[77] Rubinow recognized that economic self-interest led employers and business organizations like the National Association of Manufacturers to support compensation; he saw that low compensation settlements partly stemmed from the employers' natural desire to buy the lowest-priced insurance possible.[78] Yet he and his fellow experts seemed convinced that, if only they made the right "scientific" suggestions, compensation laws could be improved and the next phases of social insurance could be better planned. Exasperated, Rubinow complained that "many errors have been committed which but repeat the errors of the early history of the compensation movement in Europe, and others which nothing but the grossest ignorance of the underlying problem can explain."[79] The AALL's *American Labor Legislation Review* published papers on social insurance, while the state branches of the AALL drafted and lobbied for bills.[80] California, Kentucky, Massachusetts, Montana, and Utah called Rubinow as a consultant to their compensation boards.[81]

The experts in the AALL saw social insurance from varying perspectives. John R. Commons and John B. Andrews, for example, stressed that compensation gave employers a financial motive to improve safety conditions in their factories. "Safety first" became a major goal of compensation to them. While Rubinow hoped that the United States could lower its world-record number of industrial accidents, he knew that even in a safe factory a minimum number of accidents were statistically inevitable. For him, preventing destitution resulting from interruptions in a worker's earning power remained the essential purpose of any social insurance.[82] However, the varying emphases were not divisive in these heady years when the AALL believed that prejudice against government involvement in income maintenance had been overcome by the compensation movement and that the United States stood on the brink of creating a comprehensive system of social insurance.[83]

After leaving the Bureau of Labor Statistics in 1911, Rubinow directed the statistical department of the Ocean Accident and Guarantee Corporation, an insurance company selling casualty compensation insurance to employers. Most state laws did not set up state insurance funds; instead, they required employers to purchase compensation insurance from commercial companies. The sudden advent of compensation legislation caught the casualty companies poorly prepared to sell the new insurance. Their biggest headache was figuring out how much to charge for the coverage. While working at Ocean Accident and Guarantee, Rubinow used his statistical skill to solve the problem.

Rubinow reasoned that the "pure premium," the actual cost of the insurance after subtracting agents' commissions and the insurance company's administrative expenses, depended on three factors: the accident rate, the relative degrees of seriousness among accidents, and the compensation scale prescribed by any given state. It was a simple matter to acquire the states' scales. In his *Standard Accident Table as a Basis for Compensation Rates,* published in 1915, Rubinow provided statistically reliable estimates for the other two factors. He determined accident frequency from the sketchy accident reports submitted to casualty companies by their industrial policyholders. He then turned to European accident records to learn which proportion of those accidents was likely to be extremely serious and which proportions would be progressively less serious.[84] The result was "something akin to the standard mortality table in life insurance," and almost every casualty insurance company in the United States adopted it quickly. By 1915, Rubinow boasted that his table laid "the foundation of almost all compensation insurance rates . . . in force in this country."[85]

Publication of the "Rubinow Standard Accident Table" gave him an immediate reputation throughout the casualty insurance world and stimulated further scholarly inquiry in the field. In 1914 Rubinow organized and became first president of the Casualty Actuarial and Statistical Society of America (CASSA), a society for "the promotion of the study of statistics and actuarial science as applicable to the lines of insurance business . . . known as 'casualty insurance.' "[86] The CASSA, a professional organization which published a journal full of learned articles, did not lobby like the AALL. "Associates" had to pass an examination in algebra, geometry, trigonometry, calculus, bookkeeping, statistics, and the like. "Fellows," the voting members, had to pass an additional examination on calculation of premiums which included a section on the history of social insurance.[87] While the organization took no official stand on pending legislation, President Rubinow assumed that additions to social insurance were imminent and that insurance experts should not again be caught unprepared by new legislation. More specifically, in his presidential address of October 1915, he urged casualty actuaries to prepare for health insurance.[88]

In 1912 the AALL established a Social Insurance Committee of which Rubinow was a busy member. This committee made the strategic decision to push health insurance as "the next step in social progress."[89] Other branches of social insurance seemed less immediately attainable. Unemployment insurance was relatively new even in Europe, and consideration of retirement benefits raised controversy over whether they should be insurance or "gratuitous government pensions." Health insurance, on the other hand, seemed a logical extension of compensation; the line between work-related and other illness had always been difficult to draw.[90]

To avoid the variation from state to state which made compensation legislation so confusing, the Social Insurance Committee drew up a model health insurance bill which the AALL's branches offered to state legislatures. It required compulsory coverage of all wage workers—except domestics and seasonal workers—who earned less than $100 each month. It provided medical benefits for workers and their families, a cash benefit equal to two-thirds of the wages lost due to illness, and a $50 funeral benefit. The state paid 20 percent of the program's cost, while employers and employees each paid 40 percent. The insurance came through state insurance funds, not commercial companies. Finally, the standard bill left details of delivery of medical care up to local health insurance associations representing contributing employers and employees. Local associations and certified local physicians were to choose the styles of inpatient and outpatient service most suitable for their area. In its provision for local autonomy, the standard bill most closely resembled German precedent.[91]

While the AALL lobbied for its bill in several states, other national organizations joined the health insurance movement. Even the American Medical Association (AMA) assumed that health insurance was just around the corner; in 1916 the AMA set up its own Committee on Social Insurance to gather information on health insurance and to see that proposed legislation protected doctors' economic interests and avoided "conflict . . . [and] bitterness between the profession and the public."[92] Although the AMA would lobby, it would do so to safeguard its professional interests, not necessarily to advance health insurance. Like the CASSA, the AMA resolved to be ready for health insurance.

Utilizing Rubinow's double training in medicine and social science, the AMA hired him as executive secretary of its Committee on Social Insurance. Rubinow seemed further suited for the position with the publication of his *Standards of Health Insurance* in 1916. Like the AMA, Rubinow recognized the potential problems in adjusting doctors' private practices to a system of state health insurance. Some doctors feared an invasion of privacy in the proposed relationship with a local health insurance association. Others worried that local associations would offer unrealistically low reimbursement to doctors; this had been the unhappy case in Germany.

Under Rubinow's supervision, the Committee on Social Insurance tried to reassure physicians through a series of seven pamphlets on social insurance distributed throughout the profession. In the sixth pamphlet, Dr. Alexander Lambert, Theodore Roosevelt's personal physician and a member of the social insurance committees of the AALL and AMA, defended the standard bill as providing "a well balanced scheme by which the quarrels and friction produced under the health insurance laws of the old world are avoided."[93] Neither professionally nor financially as secure as Dr. Lambert, other American doctors remained skeptical. The seventh pamphlet provided a statistical analysis of the American medical profession. It showed that most physicians earned modest incomes compared with other professionals and raised the "suspicion" that the explanation lay in the "inability for the masses of the population to pay satisfactorily for the medical services they need."[94] Elsewhere Rubinow directly suggested that health insurance, like compensation before it, would mean more money in doctors' pockets. Balancing his appeal to doctors' self-interest with an appeal to their social conscience, Rubinow hoped to persuade them to support health insurance.[95]

He failed. The more American doctors heard about health insurance, the less they liked it. The national administration of the AMA moved from mild objectivity toward health insurance to a pronounced and sustained hostility.[96] Preoccupied with medical problems raised by the American entry into World War I, in May 1917, the AMA cut off the committee's funds.[97]

Meanwhile, Rubinow accepted the invitation of California Governor Hiram Johnson to help his state's Social Insurance Commission prepare the country's first state report on social insurance. The 1917 report prompted the California legislature to submit to referendum a state constitutional amendment sanctioning health insurance. In 1918 California voters rejected the amendment by a two-to-one margin.[98] Elsewhere the movement fared no better. Rubinow's strenuous eight-state speaking tour for health insurance early in 1917 had little effect.[99] Few state proposals based on the standard bill got beyond the legislative committee stage. Only three states—New York, Massachusetts, and New Jersey—introduced bills. None passed.[100]

Writing twenty years later, Rubinow explained the collapse of the health insurance movement. He dismissed World War I and the Red Scare as alibis, certain that a deeply rooted movement would have withstood the blow of borrowing a major feature—the provision for local autonomy—from the German enemy. More central to the failure was opposition from key economic groups. Doctors opposed it. Employers and taxpayers, together responsible for 60 percent of the program's cost, objected for economic reasons. Casualty insurance companies, which had just begun issuing small amounts of health insurance, resented the provision for state insurance. Life insurance companies joined them in complaining about the small funeral allowance. More surprisingly, wage earners, the proposed beneficiaries, rejected the plan. While rank and file resisted a deduction from already slim paychecks, leaders of organized labor protested on ideological grounds. The plan was "un-American." Individualistic American workers simply wanted healthier conditions and wages high enough to enable them to purchase private medical care.[101]

Samuel Gompers, influential head of the American Federation of Labor, was particularly outspoken in his criticism of health insurance.[102] Furthermore, he suspected "intellectuals" and other "saviours of Labor" of trying to "dominate the labor movement with their panaceas. . . ." Gompers was doubly distrustful because many of these intellectuals worked as government "experts" and perhaps only wanted to create more jobs for specialists in the government bureaucracy.[103]

New Deal Breakthrough

After the AMA disbanded its Committee on Social Insurance, Rubinow briefly directed the Bureau of Social Statistics in the Department of Public Charities of New York City. He also headed a study for the Federal Trade Commission. In July 1918, he accepted Walter Lippmann's invitation to take over direction of the economic department of an inquiry into European conditions being made by the United States government to prepare for the eventual peace conference.[104] Then, in 1919, Rubinow surprised Jewish friends by moving to Palestine—at the urging of American Jewish leader Henrietta Szold—to head the American Zionist Medical Unit.[105] He stepped into social welfare work sponsored by organized Judaism, never to return full time to the struggle for American social insurance.

Rubinow considered his four years in Palestine as important as his work for social insurance. He set up hospitals, infant welfare stations, school medical services, and a rural medicine program. The physicians, like the rest of his staff of up to 500 people, worked for fixed salaries. Though he concluded that "all doctors, no matter where they come from, are equally difficult,"[106] Rubinow relished his chance to experiment with an alternative to private medical practice. He had deliberately soft-pedaled his "theories of organized social medicine" during the unsuccessful fight for health insurance of the United States.[107]

Rubinow and his family returned to the United States in 1923. Over the next thirteen years, he worked for several Jewish social service organizations. From 1923 to 1928 he headed the Jewish Welfare Society of Philadelphia, editing *Jewish Social Service Quarterly* between 1925 and 1929. He disliked the psychiatric orientation dominating social work in the 1920s and asked that social workers remember the objective causes of poverty.[108]

After brief tenure as executive director of the Zionist Organization of America (1928–29), Rubinow became secretary of the Independent Order of B'nai B'rith (1929–36) and moved to Cincinnati, Ohio, where the order had its headquarters. In these later capacities, he fought the world's spreading anti-Semitism.[109] He did not regard the battle against anti-Semitism as an entirely new departure; he recognized the connection between economic insecurity and hostility among social groups, arguing that effective social insurance eased social friction.[110]

Rubinow maintained his commitment to social insurance, though he could devote only scraps of stolen time to its cause. He occasionally called for "a social insurance revival" in the pages of *Survey Midmonthly;* in 1930 he chaired a conference at the University of Chicago to draft model old-age insurance legislation; and he remained a member of the organized social insurance movement.[111]

The movement fractured in the 1920s. Commons and Andrews now dominated the AALL and advocated an "American plan" of social insurance. Unlike Rubinow, they thought the health insurance movement had suffered from too close an identification with Europe.[112] Younger colleagues at the University of Wisconsin, including Paul Rausenbusch and his wife, Elizabeth Brandeis Rausenbusch, daughter of Supreme Court Justice Louis Brandeis, assisted Professor Commons in detailing the American plan.[113]

Passed by Wisconsin in 1931, the nation's first unemployment insurance law embodied their thinking. The law required each employer gradually to build up an independent reserve fund to be tapped by workers he discharged. Commons and his associates reasoned that an employer's obligation to maintain a minimum balance in his fund penalized the employer who allowed excess unemployment in his operation. The inefficient employer had to replace the money his former employees withdrew in unemployment benefits.[114] Rubinow criticized the "Wisconsin Plan"—a direct descendant of "safety first"—for emphasizing prevention of unemployment at the expense of actuarial soundness. Doubting that individual employer reserves could adequately meet the claims against them, Rubinow favored contributions from workers as well as employers and the added security of a single state pool to which all employers and employees contributed. He further questioned an individual employer's power to prevent unemployment stemming from problems in the general economy.[115]

In 1927, Abraham Epstein founded a rival to the AALL, the

American Association for Old-Age Security. Though he remained a member of the AALL, Rubinow became vice-president of the new group. As Epstein's organization broadened its concerns beyond old-age insurance—in 1933 it changed its name to the American Association for Social Security—it sharpened its challenge to the AALL and its emphasis on prevention. Epstein, like Rubinow, believed that social insurance could never eliminate all the dangers workers faced. Both insisted that the proper job of social insurance was to protect workers against unavoidable interruptions in their income.[116] Though Epstein and Rubinow were warm friends, Rubinow regretted that their names so frequently appeared side-by-side in print. "Our silver shirt friends," Rubinow wrote to Epstein, ". . . will insist that social insurance is definitely a Jewish conspiracy."[117]

The Great Depression renewed the nation's interest in social insurance. Rising unemployment stimulated the search for alternatives to Wisconsin's system. As chief actuary and chairman of the Committee on Research of the Ohio Commission on Unemployment, Rubinow published his long-standing theories of unemployment insurance in 1932. Immediately after release of the commission's report, nicknamed the "Ohio Plan," bills based on its principles were introduced in seventeen state legislatures. Eventually, state pools replaced employer reserves in every state.[118]

Although Rubinow kept up contact with socialist friends, his commitment to socialism faded throughout the 1920s. Disillusioned by the Russian Revolution, he increasingly rejected Marxian analysis.[119] In a 1931 letter to Norman Thomas, head of the Socialist Party of America, Rubinow praised Thomas's courage in "brushing aside so many old shibboleths of the so-called classic Marxian theory, as the labor theory of value, or economic interpretation. . . ."[120] Finally, Rubinow felt the political stigma of socialism more keenly than ever. *Was Marx Wrong?* hampered his work for the Ohio unemployment commission, though Rubinow complained that his Ohio Chamber of Commerce critics had not even read the pamphlet and "didn't know whether I said the old fellow was right or wrong."[121] Rubinow contributed to Thomas's 1932 presidential campaign fund, but he declined to preside at a Cincinnati meeting at which Thomas was to speak. The Ohio legislature was then considering his unemployment insurance bill; he did not want to hurt the bill's chances. "I hope you do not consider this . . . pussy-footing," he apologized to the organizer of the Thomas appearance.[122]

As always, Rubinow valued social insurance over socialism. He spent "sleepless nights" between 1931 and 1933 writing a second comprehensive book on social insurance, *The Quest for Security* (1934).[123] Determined not to repeat the mistake in *Social Insurance* of appealing only to "professors, college instructors and college seniors,"

Rubinow deliberately discarded all "the so-called scientific parapher-nalia . . .—references, quotations, footnotes, chronologies, diagrams," and, difficult as it was for a statistician like Rubinow, "even statistical tables."[124] He had learned that experts need popular support to change society.

In the closing pages of *The Quest for Security*, Rubinow also stressed the importance of a national leader in building support for social insurance. "Will it be Bismarck, Lloyd George and—Franklin D. Roosevelt?" the book asked.[125] Rubinow sent a copy of *The Quest for Security* to Roosevelt's wife, Eleanor, asking her to bring its last few pages to the president's attention.[126] The New Deal had tinkered enough with the national economy by 1934 for Rubinow to suggest the previously "preposterous" and "unconstitutional" "possibility of direct social insurance legislation by Congress to cover all of the coun-try with old-age pensions, health insurance or unemployment insurance."[127]

Coincidentally, *The Quest for Security* appeared on the very day Roosevelt announced his commitment to national social insurance.[128] The president appointed a cabinet-level Committee on Economic Security, chaired by Labor Secretary Frances Perkins, to draft a bill. The committee, in turn, asked social insurance experts for help.[129] Although Perkins and Rubinow had exchanged ideas on unemploy-ment insurance while Perkins was industrial commissioner of New York's Department of Labor, Perkins did not often seek Rubinow's counsel now.[130] The committee only asked Rubinow to make one brief trip to Washington, D.C., to lead a round-table discussion on old-age security.[131] The committee similarly slighted Abraham Epstein.[132] Perkins instead looked to Wisconsin, selecting Edwin Witte, a student of John Commons and director of Wisconsin's Legis-lative Library, to direct the work of the committee and its advisory council.[133] Writing resignedly to his son early in 1935, Rubinow ob-served that the "Brandeis-Commons-Rausenbusch-Andrews-Perkins combination is pretty hard to break."[134]

Roosevelt had warned Perkins to steer clear of consultants who might be "too theoretical."[135] The Wisconsin group, however, was no less theoretical than Rubinow and Epstein. Perhaps in bypassing Rubinow, Roosevelt acted to head off congressional criticism of social security as socialistic. During Senate hearings on the bill, Senator Thomas P. Gore of Oklahoma goaded Secretary Perkins, asking, "Isn't this a teeny-weeny bit of Socialism?"[136]

Nevertheless, Roosevelt recognized Rubinow's contribution. Dur-ing Rubinow's final illness in 1936, Roosevelt sent him a copy of *The Quest for Security*, inscribed by the president instead of the author. Roosevelt explained "this reversal of the usual process, in view of the great interest I have had in reading your book."[137]

Rubinow welcomed the Social Security Act, which became law shortly before his death. He regretted its omission of health insurance, its exclusion of many workers, its inadequate provision for mothers with dependent children, and its failure to supplement workers' and employers' contributions to old-age and unemployment insurance with funds from the federal treasury. But he was mellow; he accepted the act, with its flaws, as a long-overdue beginning which could be amended later.[138]

Social insurance at last had popular appeal. Prominent politicians joined spokesmen for the social insurance movement and national leaders of Judaism in mourning Rubinow's death in September 1936. Among his honorary pallbearers were New York Governor Herbert H. Lehman and New York City Mayor Fiorello LaGuardia. Rubinow was buried in Workmen's Circle of Mount Carmel Cemetery.[139]

Perspectives on Progressivism

Rubinow was not the only Jewish reformer-intellectual to contribute to Progressivism. E. R. A. Seligman in economics, Louis Brandeis in Law, Walter Weyl and Walter Lippmann in journalism and political theory, Rabbi Stephen Wise in religion, and Lillian Wald in settlement work all flourished during the Progressive era. All came from backgrounds similar to Rubinow's.

Though not conventionally religious, all were propelled by a "deep vein of Hebraic . . . idealism," a belief in the brotherhood of man.[140] All came from financially comfortable, urban families. All were highly educated, many having studied in Europe. Some were socialists; all took socialist analysis seriously. All were the children or grandchildren of immigrants.[141]

A changing America demanded the very qualities these earnest, well-educated Jews supplied: social vision not straitjacketed by individualism, insight into industrialism, familiarity with cities, knowledge of Europe, and technical expertise. Local, state, and federal governments often asked their advice. While they by no means represented the totality of Progressivism, they contributed impressively to forward-looking, Progressive social thought.

Rubinow's career highlights Progressivism's intellectual as well as its ethnic inclusiveness. Rubinow first published his advanced theories in the Progressive era, theories which were aired so thoroughly that even the AMA assumed that health insurance would indeed be the "next step in social progress." This reveals a fair degree of breadth and ideological tolerance in the Progressive mind. In the 1920s,

Americans ignored the foreign-born, socialist, Jewish statistical expert who asked them to learn from Europe.

Yet essentially, Rubinow received only a hearing in the Progressive era. He came to realize that the health insurance movement had attracted little support beyond the "narrow circles" of professional social workers, university professors, economists, and social scientists. "Energetic, largely self-appointed," Rubinow and his colleagues tried to make up in "enthusiasm and literary ability what . . . [they] lacked in numbers."[142] They failed, and their failure is evidence of the limited Progressive accomplishment in social justice. Experts charted the ideal course of society, but they did not change it. The success of workmen's compensation depended on business support; a coalition of economic interests killed health insurance. However open-minded Progressivism was, it had a traditional, capitalist heart.

Notes

I wish to thank Arthur Mann of the University of Chicago Department of History for his counsel throughout the preparation of this article.

1. Roy Lubove, *The Struggle for Social Security, 1900–1935* (Cambridge, Mass.: Harvard University Press, 1968), p. 54.

2. Ibid., p. 99.

3. Forrest A. Walker, "Compulsory Health Insurance: ' The Next Great Step in Social Legislation,' " *Journal of American History* 56, no. 2 (September 1969): 295.

4. Lubove, p. 34.

5. Neva R. Deardorff, "Isaac Max Rubinow," in *Dictionary of American Biography*, ed. Robert L. Schuyler (New York: Charles Scribner's Sons, 1958), 22:585; and Rubinow to F. Akston, January 24, 1934, Isaac M. Rubinow Papers, Labor-Management Documentation Center, M. P. Catherwood Library, Cornell University, box 3, fol. 7.

6. Abram Leon Sachar, *A History of the Jews* (New York: Alfred A. Knopf, 1930), pp. 311, 316.

7. Isaac M. Rubinow, *The Economic Condition of the Jews in Russia*, repr. from *Bulletin of the Bureau of Labor* (Washington: U.S. Department of Commerce and Labor, 1908), p. 489; and Rubinow, *Studies in Workmen's Insurance: Italy, Russia, Spain* (New York: Faculty of Political Science, Columbia University, 1911), vita.

8. Rubinow, *The Economic Condition of the Jews in Russia*, pp. 492, 536.

9. Ibid., p. 571.

10. Ibid., pp. 576–78.

11. Deardorff, p. 585; and Rubinow, *Studies in Workmen's Insurance*, vita.

12. Sachar, pp. 317–18; and Rubinow, *The Economic Condition of the Jews in Russia*, p. 492.

13. Rubinow to G. Derby, January 18, 1926, Rubinow Papers, box 18, fol. 11.

14. Rubinow, *The Economic Condition of the Jews in Russia*, pp. 498–500.

15. Oscar Leonard, "Dr. Rubinow Comes Home: A Reminiscence," *B'nai B'rith Magazine* 51, no. 1 (October 1936): 5.

16. Isaac M. Rubinow, "The Economic Condition of the Russian Jews in New York City," in *The Russian Jew in the United States: Studies of Social Conditions in New York, Philadelphia, and Chicago*, ed. Charles S. Bernheimer (Philadelphia: J. C. Winston Co., 1905), pp. 116–17.

17. Leonard, p. 5.

18. Edward E. Grusd, "Isaac Max Rubinow: 1875—1936," *B'nai B'rith Magazine* 51, no. 1 (October 1936): 4.

19. Rubinow, *The Economic Condition of the Jews in Russia*, pp. 530–31.

20. Ibid., p. 572.

21. Isaac M. Rubinow, *The Quest for Security* (New York: Henry Holt & Co., 1934), p. 597.

22. Rubinow, *The Economic Condition of the Jews in Russia*, p. 550.

23. S. M. Dubnow, *History of the Jews in Russia and Poland from the Earliest Times until the Present Day*, vol. 3. *From the Accession of Nicholas II until the Present Day*, trans. I. Friedlaender (Philadelphia: Jewish Publication Society of America, 1920), pp. 55–56.

24. Rubinow, *The Economic Condition of the Jews in Russia*, p. 581.

25. David Shannon, *The Socialist Party of America: A History* (New York: Macmillan Co., 1955), pp. 11–13; and Isaac M. Rubinow, "The Industrial Development of the South," *International Socialist Review* 3, no. 9 (March 1903): 513–29.

26. Isaac M. Rubinow, *Was Marx Wrong? The Economic Theories of Karl Marx Tested in the Light of Modern Industrial Development* (New York: Cooperative Press, 1914), p. 58.

27. Rubinow, *Studies in Workmen's Insurance*, vita, and *The Economic Condition of the Jews in Russia*, p. 567.

28. Rubinow to Derby (n. 13 above).

29. Rubinow, "The Economic Condition of the Russian Jews in New York City," p. 106.

30. Rubinow to Derby (n. 13 above).

31. Isaac M. Rubinow, *Standards of Health Insurance* (New York: Henry Holt & Co., 1916), p. 138.

32. Joseph Dorfman, *The Economic Mind in American Civilization*, vol. 3, *1856–1918* (New York: Viking Press, 1949), pp. 254–56.

33. Isaac M. Rubinow, *Social Insurance, with Special Reference to American Conditions* (New York: Henry Holt & Co., 1913), pp. iii–v.

34. Rubinow, *Studies in Workmen's Insurance*, vita; and Grusd, p. 4.

35. Deardorff, pp. 585–86.

36. Rubinow, *Studies in Workmen's Insurance*, list of publications; and Rubinow to Derby (n. 13 above).

37. Deardorff, p. 586.

38. Ibid.; and Rubinow to Derby (n. 13 above).

39. Rubinow, *Social Insurance, with Special Reference* . . . , p. 189.

40. Rubinow, *Was Marx Wrong?* p. 51.

41. Ibid., p. 62; and Rubinow, *The Economic Condition of Jews in Russia*, p. 578.

42. Rubinow, *Was Marx Wrong?* pp. 59–60.

43. Ibid., p. 60.

44. Robert H. Wiebe, *The Search for Order, 1877–1920* (New York: Hill & Wang, 1967), pp. 173–75.

45. Richard Hofstadter, *The Age of Reform: From Bryan to F.D.R.* (New York: Vintage Books, 1955), p. 144.

46. Arthur Mann, "British Social Thought and American Reformers of the Progressive Era," *Mississippi Valley Historical Review* 42, no. 4 (March 1956): 672–92.

47. Holfstadter, p. 15.

48. J. Joseph Huthmacher, "Urban Liberalism in the Age of Reform," *Mississippi Valley Historical Review* 49, no. 2 (September 1962): 231–41.

49. Rubinow, *Social Insurance, with Special Reference* . . . , pp. iii–viii.

50. Ibid., pp. 8–9.

51. Ibid., p. 11.

52. Ibid., pp. 10–11.

53. Rubinow, *The Quest for Security*, p. 607.

54. Clara E. Fanning and Mary K. Reely, eds., *Book Review Digest, 10th Annual Circulation* (New York: H. W. Wilson Co., 1915), p. 466.

55. Lubove, pp. 1–24, passim.

56. Rubinow, *Standards of Health Insurance*, pp. 14–15.

57. Rubinow, *Social Insurance, with Special Reference* . . . , p. 175.

58. Ibid., p. 179.

59. Ibid., p. 438.

60. Ibid., p. 436.

61. Rubinow to J. R. Commons, January 27, 1909, in *Microfilm Edition of the Papers of the American Association for Labor Legislation, 1905–1943*, ed. Mary S. Arluck (Glen Rock, N.J.: Microfilming Corp. of America, 1973), reel 1.

62. Rubinow, *Social Insurance, with Special Reference . . .* , p. vi.

63. "Isaac Max Rubinow," in *Biographical Encyclopaedia of American Jews*, ed. Leo M. Glassman (New York: Maurice Jacobs & Leo M. Glassman, 1935), 1:462.

64. Isaac M. Rubinow, "The Specter of Malingering," *Survey* (October 25, 1913), pp. 97–98.

65. Lubove, p. 194.

66. Rubinow, *Was Marx Wrong?* p. 6.

67. Kirk H. Porter and Donald Johnson, comps., *National Party Platforms, 1840–1960* (Urbana: University of Illinois Press, 1966), pp. 111, 123, 128, 142.

68. Lubove, p. 194.

69. Isaac M. Rubinow, "Health Insurance: The Spread of the Movement," *Survey* (July 15, 1916), p. 408.

70. Isaac M. Rubinow, *Social Insurance*, Social Insurance Series, pamphlet 5 (Chicago: Council on Health and Public Instruction of the American Medical Association, 1917), p. 5.

71. Lubove, p. 194.

72. Rubinow, *Social Insurance, with Special Reference . . .* , p. 499.

73. Rubinow, *Was Marx Wrong?* p. 61.

74. Rubinow to Derby (n. 13 above).

75. Rubinow, *The Quest for Security*, p. 604.

76. Lubove, pp. 29–30.

77. Rubinow, *Social Insurance, with Special Reference . . .* , p. 161.

78. Ibid., p. 162.

79. Rubinow, *Standards of Health Insurance*, p. 8.

80. Rubinow, *Social Insurance, with Special Reference . . .* , pp. 161–62.

81. Rubinow to Derby (n. 13 above).

82. Lubove, pp. 42–43.

83. Rubinow, *Standards of Health Insurance*, p. 8.

84. Isaac M. Rubinow, *A Standard Accident Table as a Basis for Compensation Rates* (New York: Spectator Co., 1915), pp. 7–8.

85. Ibid., pp. 12–13.

86. Casualty Actuarial and Statistical Society of America, *Proceedings* (November 7, 1914), p. 2.

87. Ibid., pp. iv, ix–x.

88. Isaac M. Rubinow, "Address of the President," Casualty Actuarial and Statistical Society of America, *Proceedings* (October 22 and 23, 1915), p. 8.

89. Rubinow, *The Quest for Security*, p. 208.

90. Rubinow, *Standards of Health Insurance*, pp. 5–6.

91. Rubinow, *The Quest for Security*, pp. 208–9; Walker (n. 3 above), pp. 294–95; Committee on Social Insurance, "Health Insurance: Tentative Draft of an Act," *American Labor Legislation Review* 6, no. 2 (June 1916): 239–68; Alexander Lambert, chairman, "Report of Committee on Social Insurance," *Journal of the American Medical Association* (June 17, 1916), pp. 1951–85; and Alexander Lambert, *Medical Organization under Health Insurance*, Social Insurance Series, pamphlet 6 (Chicago: Council on Health and Public Instruction of the American Medical Association, 1917), pp. 1–15.

92. Lambert, "Report of Committee," p. 1951.

93. Lambert, *Medical Organization*, pp. 13–14.

94. *Statistics of the Medical Profession in the United States*, Social Insurance Series, pamphlet 7 (Chicago: Council on Health and Public Instruction of the American Medical Association, 1917), p. 94.

95. Isaac M. Rubinow, "Social Insurance and the Medical Profession," *Journal of the American Medical Association* (January 30, 1915), pp. 381–86.

96. Rubinow, *The Quest for Security*, pp. 213–14.

97. Rubinow to Derby (n. 13 above).

98. Ibid.

99. Isaac M. Rubinow, "20,000 Miles over the Land," *Survey* (March 3, 1917), pp. 631–35.

100. Walker (n. 3 above), pp. 298–99.

101. Rubinow, *The Quest for Security*, pp. 210–14.

102. Ibid., p. 531.

103. Samuel Gompers, "Advice Welcome—Intrusion Never," *American Federationist* 22 (November 1915): 974, quoted in Lubove, p. 15; Gompers, " 'Intellectuals,' Please Note," *American Federationist* 23 (March 1916): 198–99, quoted in Lubove, p. 15; and Gompers, "Labor vs. Its Barnacles," *American Federationist* 23 (April 1916): 268, quoted in Lubove, p. 15.

104. Rubinow to Derby (n. 13 above).

105. Lubove, p. 41.

106. Rubinow to J. B. Andrews, August 5, 1922, *Microfilm Papers of the American Association for Labor Legislation* (n. 61 above), reel 27.

107. Rubinow to Derby (n. 13 above).

108. Deardorff, p. 587; and Isaac M. Rubinow, "Needed: A Social Insurance Revival," *Survey Midmonthly* (May 15, 1926), pp. 233–34, 283.

109. Deardorff, p. 587.

110. Isaac M. Rubinow, "Social Security and Intergroup Relations," unpublished, August 1935, Rubinow Papers, box 25, fol. 1.

111. Rubinow, "Needed: A Social Insurance Revival," pp. 233–34, 283; and Isaac M. Rubinow, ed., *The Care of the Aged: Proceedings of the Deutsch Foundation Conference, 1930* (Chicago: University of Chicago Press, 1931), passim.

112. Lubove, pp. 113–14.

113. L. D. Brandeis to Rubinow, March 31, 1932, Rubinow Papers, box 3, fol. 1.

114. Lubove, pp. 169–71.

115. Isaac M. Rubinow, "Ohio versus Wisconsin: Conflict or Compromise?" unpublished, Rubinow Papers, box 1, fol. 13.

116. Lubove, pp. 142–43; and Deardorff, pp. 586–87.

117. Rubinow to A. Epstein, August 8, 1934, Rubinow Papers, box 4, fol. 1.

118. Lubove, pp. 171–73; and Deardorff, p. 586.

119. Deardorff, p. 587.

120. Rubinow to N. Thomas, July 29, 1931, Rubinow Papers, box 11, fol. 3.

121. Rubinow to B. R. Brickner, January 24, 1933, Rubinow Papers, box 3, fol. 1.

122. Rubinow to M. D. Brite, October 3, 1932, and November 10, 1932, Rubinow Papers, box 3, fol. 1.

123. Isaac M. Rubinow, "Social Security—Promise or Program" (lecture delivered at the New York State Conference on Social Welfare, Buffalo, New York, October 23, 1935), Rubinow Papers, box 27, fol. 2.

124. Rubinow, *The Quest for Security*, pp. iv–v.

125. Ibid., p. 606.

126. Rubinow to Eleanor Roosevelt, June 25, 1934, Rubinow Papers, box 27, fol. 13.

127. Rubinow, *The Quest for Security*, p. 629.

128. Rubinow, "Social Security—Promise or Program" (n. 123 above).

129. Frances Perkins, *The Roosevelt I Knew* (New York: Harper Colophon Books, 1964), pp. 281–82.

130. Correspondence of Rubinow and Perkins, March 11, 1932–November 2, 1934, Rubinow Papers, box 16, fol. 14.

131. E. E. Witte to Rubinow, November 7, 1934, Rubinow Papers, box 1, fol. 12.

132. Rubinow to S. E. Sobeloff, November 13, 1935, Rubinow Papers, box 20, fol. 3.

133. Perkins, p. 285.

134. Rubinow to Raymond Rubinow, January 11, 1935, Rubinow Papers, box 28, fol. 17.

135. Perkins, p. 285.

136. Ibid., p. 299.

137. *New York Times* (September 3, 1936).

138. Rubinow, "Social Security—Promise or Program" (n. 123 above); and Rubinow to Sobeloff (n. 132 above).

139. *New York Times* (September 5, 1936).

140. R. L. Duffus, *Lillian Wald: Neighbor and Crusader* (New York: Macmillan Co., 1938), p. 1.

141. Joseph Dorfman, "Edwin Robert Anderson Seligman," in *Dictionary of American Biography*, ed. Robert L. Schuyler (New York: Charles Scribner's Sons, 1958), 22: 606–9; Joachim O. Ronall, "Seligman," in *Encyclopaedia Judaica*, ed. Cecil Roth and Geoffrey Wigoder (Jerusalem: Macmillan Co., 1971), 14: 1130; Alpheus T. Mason, *Brandeis: A Free Man's Life* (New York: Viking Press, 1946), passim; Maurice Weyl et al., *Walter Weyl: An Appreciation* (Philadelphia: By the Authors, 1922), passim; John Luskin, *Lippmann, Liberty and the Press* (University: University of Alabama Press, 1972), pp. 1–28; Morton Mayer Berman, "Stephen Samuel Wise," in *Encyclopaedia Judaica*, 16:566–68; Carl Herman Voss, *Rabbi and Minister: The Friendship of Stephen S. Wise and John Haynes Holmes* (New York: World Publishing Co., 1964), passim; Duffus (n. 140 above), passim; and Lillian Wald, *The House on Henry Street* (New York: Henry Holt & Co., 1915), passim.

142. Rubinow, *The Quest for Security*, p. 214.

Women and the Anti–Child Labor Movement in Illinois, 1890–1920

Lynn Gordon
Chicago, Illinois

Industrialization, urbanization, and immigration brought problems as well as benefits to Americans living around the turn of the century. People were especially alarmed by the pressures on family life, and what they saw as its disintegration. Yet profound mistrust existed between labor and business, rich and poor, upper and working classes, so that attempts to help families never led anywhere. A very special group of women, college educated and seeking meaningful work, drew together other women from all levels of society, formed child welfare organizations, proposed legislation, and lobbied for its passage. Regulation of child labor became their most important project. Between 1890 and 1903, three major laws were passed to limit the kinds of work children could do, and a State Department of Factory Inspection was set up to watch over young employees.

Passed between 1893 and 1903, Illinois's major child-labor laws were largely due to the pressure and skill of women reformers. As early as the 1870s, organized labor, business leaders, and the press worried publicly about child labor, but they failed to form an effective coalition or develop concrete proposals to deal with the problem. Two decades later, led by Hull House, the women succeeded in both respects.

Hull House residents Jane Addams, Florence Kelley, and others skillfully circumvented class conflicts, persuading working-, middle-, and upper-class women to join organizations that formed a child welfare movement. Working together in the National Woman's Trade Union League, the Chicago Women's Club, the National Congress of Mothers, the Illinois Child Labor Committee, and the Consumers' League, women publicized the problems of children, and enlisted support from male legislators, school officials, and judges for the regulation of child labor.

Social Service Review 51 (June 1977): 228–48

Reformers proposed a whole battery of laws to get children out of factories and into schools, provide them with recreational areas, and set up vocational education programs. They also saw workmen's compensation and mothers' pensions as ways of benefiting children. Making the future of America the basis of their appeal, they said the United States needed healthy, well-educated citizens prepared to take their places in the urban, industrial order. Thus the proper socialization of all children, and especially immigrants, was an urgent national priority.

1870–90: Recognition of a Problem

In 1873, Chicago's largest daily, the *Tribune,* lamented: "We are getting to be a community of strangers. No one expects to know . . . half the audience at the church or theatre, and as to knowing one's neighbors, that has become a lost art."[1] Certainly the years 1870–90 saw rapid changes in the city. The population increased 268 percent, with 77.9 percent of foreign parentage. Before the 1870s immigrants came from western and northern Europe; the new arrivals were southern Italians, Poles, Bohemians, Croatians, Slovakians, Lithuanians, and Greeks. The black population doubled. All groups faced overcrowding and housing shortages.[2] These physical changes plus rapid industrialization and periodic depressions led to social tensions, strikes, and violence culminating in the 1886 Haymarket Riot and the 1894 Pullman strike. The middle and upper classes identified all workers with strikers, calling them dangerous radicals and anarchists. In turn, native and foreign-born laboring people developed a profound mistrust of the "establishment." Thus when Chicago's trade unionists called for the regulation of child labor, other groups acknowledged the problem but refused to support their call for legislation.

In 1879 Thomas Morgan of the Chicago Trades and Labor Assembly (later the Chicago Federation of Labor) appeared with other union leaders before the Illinois House of Representatives Special Committee on Labor to ask for compulsory education laws and prohibition of wage labor by children under fourteen. They argued that child labor depressed wages, took jobs away from adults, deprived young people of educational opportunities, menaced their health, and fostered juvenile delinquency.[3]

Morgan and his wife Elizabeth, both officers of the Trades and Labor Assembly, were British socialists who had come to America in the 1870s. They led the labor unions' fight against child labor. The *Chicago Evening Post* said of Elizabeth Morgan: "The child labor and sweating system have been the study of her life, and when a Congressional Committee came to Chicago to investigate sweaters, she was the only representative of labor who appeared before it."[4] The Morgans found, however, that they could not solve the problem of child labor solely with union support.

Middle- and upper-class attitudes toward female child labor may be found in a series of articles in the Chicago *Times*. Published in the summer of 1888, they were advertised as: "Life among the Slave Girls of Chicago. Let Romance Rest—Give Truth a Hearing. No need to draw upon the imagination nor to indulge in fiction. A dreadful, damnable reality is presented to this community. European methods introduced developing and expanding here, whereby the marrow is ground out of the bones, the virtue out of the souls and the souls out of the bodies of the miserable, ill-fed, half-starved, underpaid, insulted, roughly-treated and unprotected working girls."[5]

The girls' lot was pictured graphically if too dramatically by reporter "Nell Nelson" who worked for a time in Chicago's sweatshops. The *Times* concluded that female child labor menaced the American family: "but worse than broken shoes, ragged clothes, filthy closets, poor light, etc, was the cruel treatment . . . robberies of a gentle life . . . murder forever the sweet faith that belongs to woman's nature."[6]

Prominent businessmen quoted by the newspaper agreed. One executive said that factory girls only worked for "pin money" and that their parents could well afford to keep them in school. What would become of the working class if the women labored in factories instead of learning to make leftovers of a veal roast and to darn socks?[7]

The articles, and the many "Letters to the Editor" inspired by the series, showed no awareness that financial necessity caused young girls to work. Readers' solutions to the child labor problem called for domestic science courses to make school more meaningful, and placement of the girls as maids in wealthy families. They admitted that servants had little free time, low social status, and small wages, but still felt service was more educative and respectable for a future homemaker than factory work.[8]

The only letter writer recommending legislation to improve working conditions and limit child labor was John Peter Altgeld, reformer and future Illinois governor. His comments prefigured the ideas of Progressive reformers in the mid-1890s: "While legislation not backed by public sentiment may be a dead letter, public sentiment produces definite and lasting results only through legislation. Moral suasion and the benign influence of religion are beautiful, but unfortunately in all ages there have been men who went straight from the sanctuary into the world, and plundered and trampled on the weak, and, what is more, they lost neither their seats nor their influence in the temple. So that after all it is legislation that protects the lowly."[9]

The new immigrants from southern and eastern Europe had a bad image for encouraging child labor, yet the foreign language press consistently opposed it. *L'Italia* condemned the "inhuman practice indulged in by some of our compatriots" of sending ten-year-old boys onto the streets to shine shoes. The youths often picked their clients' pockets to make enough money to satisfy their employers. The latter, said *L'Italia*, were "brutal, ignorant, uneducated Beasts."[10] Other newspapers complained that child labor harmed the immigrants' image with native Americans.[11]

A public consensus existed, then, that child labor harmed not only young people but the larger society. Only trade unionists, however, wanted corrective legislation, and they lacked broad-based support and skilled lobbying techniques to get it.[12] The middle and upper classes approached the problem with condescension, lack of understanding, and fears about any social legislation proposed by workers. Only the efforts of the remarkable Hull House women brought these groups together for successful social action.

The Women of Hull House[13]

Jane Addams and Ellen Gates Starr inaugurated an era of social action in Illinois with the 1889 founding of Hull House. Leading residents at the social settlement included Florence Kelley, Julia Lathrop, Sophonisba Breckinridge, Grace and Edith Abbott, and Dr. Alice Hamilton. Through their efforts, and with the patronage of wealthy society, Hull House became a neighborhood cultural center and an international gathering place for planning social reform.

Each resident worked on projects to benefit children and family life. Florence Kelley was most prominent in the drive to regulate child labor. Julia Lathrop, instrumental in setting up the juvenile court system in Illinois, became the first chief of the U.S. Children's Bureau. Grace Abbott supported birth registration to facilitate the carrying out of compulsory education laws and administered enforcement of the first federal child labor statute (1916) for the Children's Bureau. Sophonisba Breckinridge and Edith Abbott collaborated on social science studies of women, the family, and employment. Jane Addams did everything and inspired everyone.

The Hull House residents fit Richard Hofstadter's profile of early twentieth-century reformers: native Protestants from locally prominent families who feared erosion of their status by new groups in American life.[14] We must add to this picture, however, if we hope to understand the Hull House women. They came from small towns and families with a reform tradition. All had unusually close relationships with fathers who inspired them to care for worlds beyond the household. They had attended college and faced serious conflicts choosing careers upon graduation. These additional data provide insights into their interest in a child welfare movement.

Florence Kelley grew up in Philadelphia, but the others were not raised in large, urban areas. The Abbott sisters were brought up in Grand Island, Nebraska; Sophonisba Breckinridge lived in Lexington, Kentucky, and the Lathrop and Addams families were from Rockford and Cedarville, Illinois. The lure of the big city drew them all to Chicago, but they brought with them the celebrated rural values of neighborliness and visiting, so important in the social settlement movement. Significantly, Kelley spent much less time going to meetings and acting as a local organizer than the rest. Primarily she conducted social investigations for the state and federal governments, and served as an officer in national welfare organizations.

The fathers of these women were active in public life, often for reformist causes. Many had Quaker ancestors. Othman Abbott was a lawyer, politician, and Civil War veteran. William Lathrop, also a lawyer, helped to start the Republican party in Illinois and served in both the state legislature and the United States Congress. The Breckinridges were a nationally distinguished family. Sophonisba was the great-granddaughter of John Breckinridge, Kentucky senator and attorney-general of the United States under Thomas Jefferson. A cousin, John C. Breckinridge, ran against Lincoln for the presidency in 1860. Her father, a Confederate colonel, was also a prominent local lawyer. Florence Kelley's father, nicknamed "Pig Iron" Kelley, fought in Congress for a protective tariff on metals, believing that it would guarantee high wages for workers and security for their families. His daughter absorbed his concern for the working class.[15]

In *Twenty Years at Hull House*, Jane Addams spoke of her father with the greatest respect, affection, and devotion. John Addams had been a friend of Abraham Lincoln, an Illinois legislator, and an important man in his town. He had opportunities to become senator or governor but, to his wife's disgust, declined. His daughter paid warm tribute to him in the following passage:

> Of the many things written of my father in that sad August in 1881, when he died, the one I cared for most was written by an old political friend of his who was then editor of a great Chicago daily. He wrote that while there were doubtless many members of the Illinois legislature who during the great contracts of the wartime and the demoralizing reconstruction days that followed, had never accepted a bribe, he wished to bear testimony that he personally had known but this one man who had never been offered a bribe because bad men were instinctively afraid of him.[16]

In some cases the family's activist tradition extended to the female members. Kelley's Quaker Aunt Sarah Pugh, an abolitionist, refused to use the products of slave labor, sugar and cotton, in her home. Julia Lathrop's mother Adeline, class valedictorian at Rockford Female Seminary, was a suffragist and local cultural leader, as was Elizabeth Abbott, mother of Grace and Edith. The Hull House women had close, inspirational relationships with their parents, especially their fathers, who encouraged them to study, discuss issues, and take an active interest in the world.

All the residents had been part of the first generation of American women to attend college in significant numbers. Florence Kelley went to Cornell University; Sophonisba Breckinridge to Wellesley;. Julia Lathrop to Vassar; Jane Addams to Rockford Seminary; Edith Abbott to the University of Nebraska; and Grace Abbott to Grand Island College. The college experience was inspirational, intellectual, and communal. Jane Addams said that Rockford students were very conscious of their obligation to carry on the traditions of the pioneer missionaries who founded the seminary. The missionary fervor pervaded, although for many, like Addams, it was a secularized spirit.[17] She mentioned that one of the students' favorite quotations came from Thomas Carlyle: " 'Tis not to taste sweet things but to do noble and true things that the poorest son of Adam dimly longs."[18]

Most of the future reformers spent their immediate postcollege years drifting, dissatisfied and frustrated, confronted with the classic dilemma of the educated woman. In the nineteenth century women chose between family and career; few combined the two. The traditional Victorian view of woman credited her with enormous moral and spiritual influence, but for the most part restricted this influence to her home. By inspiring her husband and children to be noble, patriotic, pure, religious, thrifty, and responsible in their contacts outside the home, she uplifted the social order. She was "the better half"—a bulwark against the crass materialism created by industrial and commercial opportunity. Most women accepted these ideas; even today some feminists think women are innately more sensitive, compassionate, and better suited to deal with people than are men.

Bryn Mawr's president Martha Carey Thomas rejected the "homebody's" role for women; she directed her students into academic and professional careers; many did not marry. Statistics from Wellesley, Smith, and Vassar for the late nineteenth century show that many of their graduates too did not become wives and mothers.[19]

For the Hull House group the choice was particularly difficult. Their families, including those previously supportive and encouraging fathers, expected them to use their education only in the home. The women themselves believed that mothers exercised the essential influence over their children and should not work. Florence Kelley argued that female teachers made poor models for young girls because they never performed little homely chores like making toast and cocoa in front of their students. She wanted required domestic science courses in the schools. Otherwise women would be tempted to work in factories instead of taking proper care of their families.[20]

Yet the pull of the outer "man world" was strong. Only Kelley of the Hull House group actually did marry and have children, and she was divorced when she began her social reform activities. Her three children lived with friends and relatives most of the time before they entered college. Kelley, Addams, Lathrop, and Breckinridge all studied law or medicine, attempting to become professionals. Jane Addams, however, developed an illness leading to collapse while attending medical school. Kelley was denied admission to the University of Pennsylvania law school because of her sex. Colonel Breckinridge wanted his daughter to uphold the family honor, but he didn't want her to be a lawyer. Only when she wept did he permit her to take the Kentucky bar exam. Not surprisingly, she never practiced law.

This period of doubt and despair following college demoralized all. Jane Addams, traveling in Europe and very unhappy, talked of seeing other young women from her social class caught endlessly in "the snare of preparation,"[21] and never accomplishing anything useful. Julia Lathrop worked as her father's secretary. By 1895 Sophonisba Breckinridge's family feared for her mental health.

By looking beyond the Hofstadter profile, then, it becomes clear how the social settlement movement grew from the needs of these women, as well as in response to social conditions. Settlement work for child welfare allowed them to use their knowledge, develop special professional skills, and yet be "feminine" because they worked on behalf of children and families. They could remain happily within their "sphere" because they extended it. Settlement life also satisfied desires for an intellectual, communal environment like college.[22]

Jane Addams felt and often said that settlement work benefited reformers far more than the people they tried to help.[23] Yet their services to society went far beyond self-serving individual acts of good will. By persuading disparate groups to work together to carry out a child welfare program they reassured Americans that social problems could be attacked and that the social order was reformable without revolution.

Formation of a Reform Coalition

Reformers appreciated the benefits of industrialization but worried about the pressures of modern urban life on families, particularly among the working classes and immigrant groups. The city offered children constant temptations to steal and to indulge in "adult" pleasures. Technological change made skills obsolete, putting people out of work perhaps permanently. The breadwinner had no financial protection against accident, and his family received little if he died. Lack of income often forced women and children into factories. When children worked, they often developed health problems, and their lack of education meant trouble for future generations of Americans. Immigrant children frequently lacked respect for parental authority because their mothers and fathers weren't "American" enough. Jane Addams concluded: "The family has been called the 'fountain of morality,' the source of law, the necessary prelude to the state itself; but while it is continuous historically, this dual bond must be made anew a myriad times in each generation, and the forces upon which its formation depend must be powerful and unerring. It would be too great a risk to leave it to a force whose manifestations are intermittent and uncertain. The desired result is too grave and fundamental."[24]

Reformers who wished to strengthen the family focused on the child, key to the future. To allow him to be abused or neglected was not merely a personal injustice but endangered the future of the country. The Republic needed self-governing, enlightened, healthy citizens. If the family cannot raise children properly, the state and the schools must step in. Advocates of social legislation carefully pointed out that the dollar cost of social action was not large compared to what could eventually become a dreadful burden on society.

The human product of our industry is an army of toiling children undersized, rachitic, deformed, predisposed to consumption if not already tuberculous. Permanently enfeebled by the labor imposed upon them during the critical years of development, these children will inevitably fail in the early years of manhood and womanhood. They are now a long way on the road to become suffering burdens upon society, lifelong victims of the poverty of their childhood and the greed which denies to children the sacred right of school life and healthful leisure.[25]

How much better it would be, said child welfare proponents, to spend the money now to enforce compulsory education and child labor laws, give scholarships to children so they could attend school, provide parks and playgrounds for innocent amusements, set up vocational education courses in the schools, and compensate injured workers so that mothers could stay home and properly raise their children.

The Hull House residents believed that "the people" should work together against "the bad guys." Jane Addams disliked organized philanthropy because it did not promote social change but represented only the vague good wishes of the upper classes. She praised social reform plans by trade unionists as moral because they represented united class action, and she urged the middle and upper classes to join in.

> An exaggerated personal morality is often mistaken for a social morality. ... A man who takes the betterment of humanity for his aim and end must also take the daily experiences of humanity for the constant correction of his process. He must not only test and guide his achievement by human experience but he must succeed or fail in proportion as he has incorporated that experience with his own. ... It is necessary to know of the lives of our contemporaries, not only in order to believe in their integrity, which is after all but the first beginnings of social morality, but in order to attain to any mental or moral integrity for ourselves or any such hope for society.[26]

Nothing pleased Addams more than the use of social settlements as neighborhood centers. *Twenty Years at Hull House* contains many descriptions of people working together. Italian-Americans entertained Irish-Americans at a successful party.[27] Business and working men held conferences, which Addams said might have prevented Haymarket had they been undertaken earlier. She complained that people did not realize that the settlement house stood neither for capital nor for labor, but for cooperation.[28]

Florence Kelley became a socialist in Europe in the 1880s and worked with the Socialist party in New York City. In *Modern Industry* she stated that the only real solution to industrial problems was cooperative ownership of the means of production.[29] Yet her activities spoke far more of the conciliatory reformer than the doctrinaire radical. She said that Europeans never understood her brand of "American" socialism,[30] though she herself did not explain it. Her socialist comrades kicked her out of the New York party, and she never worked with them again. Perhaps Kelley failed as a radical because she tried to reconcile class differences instead of seeing them as inevitable.

The Hull House residents, then, believing that coalition was a moral imperative, as well as a practical necessity for passing legislation, became the links between upper-class high society women and female labor leaders. Reformers joined the most exclusive Chicago women's clubs and labor organizations as well. Upper- and working-class women, following their example, became members of each other's groups and formed new ones together, like the National Woman's Trade Union League (NWTUL). Some of the women drawn together and into social action by the settlement workers became outstanding figures in their own right.

Agnes Nestor, a leader in the female gloveworkers' union, described a Hull House meeting in support of striking stockyard workers in her autobiography. She joined the NWTUL, noting that it was an organization "begun at the top." Yet she praised the "social justice, unselfishness, great vision, and high courage" of reformers Jane Addams and Mary Eliza McDowell.[31] Nestor worked with Ellen Henrotin, Sophonisba Breckinridge, and Edith Abbott on legislative proposals for compulsory education, an eight-hour day for women, and regulation of child labor. She also served on a committee to advise the federal government on the administration of the Smith-Hughes Act promoting vocational education.

Margaret Dreier Robins came from a wealthy New York family. She and her husband Raymond, both social workers, moved to Chicago and lived for a time at Hull House. As the frequent president of the NWTUL, she joined working-class women in social action programs.[32]

Margaret Angela Haley grew up on a farm in Joliet, Illinois. She taught in rural schools and studied for one semester with Francis Parker at the Cook County Normal School before becoming a Chicago public school teacher. In 1901 Haley began a thirty-year career as the business agent and president of the Chicago Teachers' Federation. Her organization belonged to the Chicago Federation of Labor from 1902 to 1917, and she herself joined the NWTUL. Haley supported child labor legislation, laws to improve women's working conditions, direct primaries, and women's suffrage and fought against sexist policies of the National Education Association.

Ellen Martin Henrotin was president of the General Federation of Women's Clubs, wife of a Chicago bank president, and author of *The Social Status of European and American Women* (1887). Women's clubs had been founded as middle- and upper-class cultural organizations, but leaders like Henrotin pushed them into reform programs by persuading the membership that working women and children needed their help. By the turn of the century most women's clubs had "Industrial Committees" to draft and lobby for social legislation. When the Chicago Woman's Club sent delegates to NWTUL meetings, Agnes Nestor commented: "Only now can we appreciate the distance we have come."[33]

Alzina Stevens, a printer and typesetter, became active in women's labor groups in the 1880s. She organized for the Knights of Labor in Ohio and attended the 1892 Populist party convention. Stevens came to Chicago in 1892 and moved into Hull House. Critical of those with a sentimental attachment to labor, she nevertheless worked very well and closely with the reformers. Florence Kelley appointed her assistant factory inspector in 1893. She lobbied for a stronger child labor law and for compulsory education. In 1899, just before her death, she became the first probation officer of the Cook County Juvenile Court.

Wealthy and socially prominent Louise DeKoven Bowen turned down Jane Addams's request in 1891 that she serve as president of the Hull House Women's Club. Pleading pregnancy, she sent Addams a check instead, saying that she feared "Miss Addams would think her a useless member of society."[34] Later Bowen became Hull House's most devoted supporter, contributing her time and money generously until her death in 1954. Bowen was also vice-president of United Charities and a leader in the woman's suffrage movement. Most important, she formed and presided over the Juvenile Protective Association, an umbrella organization for many child welfare projects.

Led by these women, and staffed by lesser-known volunteers, reform groups mounted effective campaigns to get legislation benefiting children. The story of the movement to regulate child labor in Illinois shows the successful operation of the coalition.

The Coalition in Operation: 1893–1903

The Hull House reformers, led by Florence Kelley and Jane Addams, used this women's coalition to push for child labor legislation. In 1892 Kelley suggested an investigation of the sweating system and child labor in Chicago to the Illinois Bureau of Labor Statistics. She and Elizabeth Morgan undertook this job, along with a study of Chicago's slums, for the federal government. Their reports showed a preponderance of women and children in the garment trade; only 25 percent of the workers were male adults.[35]

After hearing the evidence, the 1893 Illinois legislature appointed its own committee to make a personal investigation. Fearful that this was intended as a gesture to pacify labor and provide legislators with a junket to the big city, Kelley and Morgan took charge of the committee and led the men on a tour of the sweatshops. A Chicago newspaper reported that a senator actually refused to enter one workplace, lest he take germs home to his children.[36]

As a result of the committee's report, the Illinois Senate proposed a bill to regulate child labor. Jane Addams described the lobbying efforts of reformers on behalf of the bill: "Before the passage of the law could be secured, it was necessary to appeal to all elements of the community, and a little group of us addressed the open meetings of trade unions and benefit societies, church organizations, and social clubs nearly every evening for three months. Of course the most energetic help as well as intelligent understanding came from the trades-unions."[37] She also asked Ellen Henrotin and the General Federation of Women's Clubs for assistance: "We insisted that well-known Chicago women should accompany this first little group of Settlement folk who with trades-unionists moved upon the state capitol in support of factory legislation."[38]

Thus the skills of reformers in gathering information and people together, the power of labor, the prestige of prominent Chicago women, and the support of Governor Altgeld secured practically unanimous passage of the State Factory Inspection Bill of 1893 (108 to six in the House, forty to zero in the Senate).[39]

The law stated that: (1) no child under fourteen could work in any factory, workshop, or manufacturing establishment; (2) children fourteen–sixteen seeking employment needed an affidavit of age from a parent or guardian; (3) employers were required to keep a file of affidavits and a posted list of all employees aged fourteen–sixteen (called a wall register); (4) state factory inspectors could demand a physical fitness certificate from any working child who appeared unwell; (5) females and children could not work more than eight hours a day, or forty-eight hours a week; (6) a state department of factory inspection consisting of a chief, a deputy, and ten assistant inspectors would enforce the new law.

There was no organized, sustained, articulate opposition to the 1893 law, or to the two that followed in 1897 and 1903. Businessmen founded the Illinois Manufacturers' Association (IMA) in 1894 to oppose the eight-hour day for women, not the regulation of sweatshop conditions and child labor. Examination of extant IMA records shows that its officers often urged the membership to block proposed labor legislation, but never when it concerned child workers.[40] Florence Kelley said that the IMA wrote secret letters to individual businessmen saying that the law was unconstitutional and offering support to those who broke it, but no evidence exists to substantiate her claim.[41] Many businessmen actively supported child welfare laws, and those who did not would probably not have argued against them publicly. During the Progressive Era, child welfare legislation became so popular that opposition was almost unpatriotic. Then too, many industries no longer employed children, and their use continued to decline.[42]

Two groups of manufacturers resisted enforcement, if not passage, of the new statute. The garment sweaters, who employed the largest numbers of children, consistently broke the law. Inspectors complained that the fly-by-night nature of sweatshop operations made it impossible to police them. Shut down in one location for repeated violations of the law, they opened next day in another.[43] They never formed a block against reforms, but counted on quietly evading the law. The small size of the inspection staff helped sweaters get away with this. The glass manufacturers broke the law and openly opposed further legislation. They used child labor extensively and were powerful enough to effect Florence Kelley's dismissal as chief factory inspector in 1896.[44]

Parents, especially immigrant parents, often resisted enforcement of the child labor laws. They were the despair of reformers who never understood that resistance to schooling came from a desire to keep children close to "old country" values and from a lack of understanding about the value of education in America. Often immigrant parents did not realize that the work in an American factory differed from the work children performed in Europe, such as picking oranges in the family grove.[45] Settlement workers often denied that children's wages were an important source of family income and insisted that parents kept them out of school only from stubbornness, laziness, and stupidity.[46]

At the suggestion of Henry Demarest Lloyd, Governor Altgeld asked Florence Kelley to head the inspection department. She selected Alzina Stevens for her deputy, and ten others for assistant inspectors. They issued annual inspection reports for 1893–96 that have become classics in social welfare literature. The reports listed all inspections, violations, and results of court cases. Graphs, tables, and charts showed the extent of child labor in Illinois. The department was also responsible for health and safety inspections, but Kelley's famous commentaries on the statistics always dealt with child labor.

She said that the affidavit system worked well: "Although some affidavits are undoubtedly false, hundreds of parents have withdrawn their children from work, rather than forswear themselves."[47] She complained, however, that doctors issued fitness certificates with only cursory examinations of the children.[48] Kelley cited cases showing the bad effects of child labor on health and morals, and proving that child workers lacked education and preparation for adult life. Many working children, illiterate in English, drifted from one job to another without learning vocational skills. Teachers and principals failed to enforce compulsory education laws, expelled unruly students, and did not update their curriculum.[49]

Florence Kelley thought that fourteen–sixteen year olds should not work at all. Since employers continued to hire children in this age bracket despite the difficulties of the affidavit, health certificate, and wall register procedure, she recommended tougher legislation. Sixteen should be the minimum age for employment, English literacy required for any job, and night work for minors prohibited. All mercantile establishments, not just factories, should be under the law. She asked for more inspectors and for staff physicians to eliminate the department's dependence on unethical doctors.[50] Kelley also wanted parents who swore to false affidavits punished for perjury, saying that the behavior of immigrant parents greedy for their children's wages was "sordid."[51]

The 1893–96 reports documented the battle of the State Department of Factory Inspection with the Illinois Glass Company. Glass manufacturers said they needed child labor. Inspectors told them either to use older children or make technological changes. Most fell in line, but Illinois Glass, the largest firm, held out until Governor Altgeld ordered a special investigation of the Alton, Illinois, firm in 1895. Inspectors found no wall register, no affidavits, and a "defiant disposition" at Alton.[52] Adult workers at Illinois Glass said it was easier and safer to work with children over fourteen, but the company preferred younger boys because it could pay them less. Kelley said that town officials forced poor families to send their children to work in the glass factory, rather than giving them relief. Schools already too crowded to accommodate factory children had no plans for enlargement.[53] By 1896 the annual factory inspection report said that the Illinois Glass Company no longer employed children illegally, but the staff continued to watch the firm closely.

Bills incorporating Kelley's recommendations were proposed but not passed by the legislature. In 1895, however, a Child Labor Commission was appointed, which asked the Chicago Civic Federation, part of the unofficial child welfare coalition, to write a new law. The Federation's Industrial Committee, chaired by Deputy Inspector Stevens, investigated child labor in mercantile establishments. The report said that children who worked in department stores faced constant temptations to steal. A long working day meant that they returned home at hours when the streets were unsafe. Poverty, not greedy parents, was the cause of most child labor, but children's wages were so low that they rarely contributed significantly to the family's support. Children under fourteen should be removed by law from department stores and required to attend school. Such a law would also help adults by making more jobs available for them.[54]

A new child labor bill passed the 1897 General Assembly forty to one in the Senate, 120 to zero in the House.[55] This law put department stores, offices, and laundries under the provisions of the 1893 act. Hours for all working children were restricted to ten a day, sixty a week. Dangerous and "immoral" occupations (unspecified in the law) were prohibited to those under sixteen.

Florence Kelley was not able to enforce the new law. When John Tanner became governor in 1896, he assured the public that Kelley would retain her post. Yet to the indignation of the Chicago press, he replaced her with Louis Arrington, a resident of Alton and former employee of the Illinois Glass Company.[56] That ended Kelley's active influence in Illinois. She moved to the Henry Street Settlement in New York City and continued to work against child labor as the secretary of the National Consumers' League. The Illinois reform coalition, however, continued to press for further legislation.

Arrington's factory inspection reports, 1897–1901, contained mostly statistics and little commentary. He did recommend taking the power to issue affidavits away from parents, requiring working places to improve sanitary conditions, requiring English literacy of working children, regulating "street trades," and adding doctors to the inspection staff.[57] No legislation, however, passed during this period.

In 1901–2 Chief Inspector and reformer Edgar T. Davies investigated and condemned the affidavit system, saying that it encouraged parents to lie about their children's ages.[58] His report interested a number of child welfare organizations which set up the Cook County Child Saving League and proposed to regulate child labor further and send young workers to school. Members of the league included Edwin G. Cooley, superintendent of Chicago schools; Hastings H. Hart, president of the Child's Home and Aid Society; E. P. Bicknell, general superintendent of the Chicago Bureau of Charities; Jane Addams; Harriett Van der Vaart, head of Neighborhood House Settlement and member of the Industrial Committee of the State Federation of Women's Clubs; Judge R. S. Tuttle, Juvenile Court of Cook County; George Thompson, legislative committee of the Illinois Federation of Labor; T. D. Hurley, president of the Visitation and Aid Society; W. L. Bodine, ex-officio superintendent of compulsory education; and Davies as chairman.[59]

The league's bill eliminated the old affidavit system. Instead, children wishing to work needed a statement of age and classroom attendance from school authorities. Working hours were again reduced to eight a day, forty-eight a week, and night hours (during which work by children was prohibited) were extended. Reformer Charles Chute said that if the proposed law passed the legislature, Illinois would have "one of the best bodies of protective legislation for children to be found at that time in any State."[60] The bill disappointed Davies, though, who had wanted English literacy required for a work permit.[61]

The determined opposition of the glass manufacturers made a great deal of lobbying necessary for the 1903 bill to pass. Representatives from charitable organizations, settlement houses, the Illinois State Federation of Labor, and juvenile reform groups went to Springfield to debate the glass industry before the House Committee on Labor and Industrial Affairs. No record of the debates has survived, but Margaret Haley commented on them in her unpublished autobiography. She reported her argument with Mr. Levis of Illinois Glass. Levis said that boys in school learned nothing that would help them in the working world, whereas factory work trained them for jobs. Agreeing that the schools' curriculum needed revision, Haley maintained that child workers changed jobs so often they failed to learn skills. Also, they did such menial work that when technological change eliminated their jobs, children were left with no training to earn their living.[62]

The bill passed eighty-five to one in the House and thirty-eight to zero in the Senate.[63] Davies called Jane Addams the "moral force" behind the new law, and praised her assistance in setting up the revised affidavit procedures in the schools.[64]

The Decline of Reform: 1904–17

Although the separate elements of the reform coalition increased their influence after 1903, the 1903 law was the last major child labor statute of the Progressive Era in Illinois. Yet not only the influence but the visibility of the coalition had widened.

The Chicago and Illinois Federations of Labor consistently supported child labor reform and became more powerful and effective between 1903 and 1917. The State Federation in particular benefited from the swift, nationwide expansion of the American labor movement, the purging from its ranks of "undesirable radicals," successful legislative efforts, and the affiliation of Illinois coal miners.[65] In 1906 the State Federation and the NWTUL unofficially joined forces. Agnes Nestor, Mary Eliza McDowell, Jane Addams, and Ellen Henrotin pushed the ISFL to support bills aiding women and child workers.[66] Labor's lobbying techniques also improved. In 1913 unions set up a permanent Joint Labor Legislation Board in Springfield. Reformers looked to the board for assistance. In 1916, Barney Cohen, former ISFL president, became chief state factory inspector.

Reformers also received help from newly formed national organizations—the Consumers' League (1899) and the National Child Labor Committee (1903). Both groups lent their names, resources, and journals to state efforts. Harriett Van der Vaart, Jane Addams, Florence Kelley, and Edgar Davies wrote about child labor in Illinois for these national periodicals. In 1908 the National Child Labor Committee held its annual meeting in Illinois, providing the coalition with much publicity.[67]

The Chicago Industrial Exhibit of 1907 was a showcase for child welfare groups. Exhibitors represented women's clubs, labor unions, and government departments. Among the sponsors were the Illinois Woman's Trade Union League, Illinois Consumers' League, Chicago Tuberculosis Institute, Chicago Woman's Club, Chicago Geographical Society, State Department of Factory Inspection, Chicago Federation of Labor, University of Chicago Settlement, Northwestern University Settlement, Hull House, Chicago Commons, Neighborhood House, Department of Health of Chicago, Visiting Nurses' Association, and the Industrial Committee of the City Club. Charles Henderson and other University of Chicago faculty spoke, national organizations lent support, and Chicago businessmen donated supplies and money. Displays included charts, posters, pictures, and graphs on industrial conditions. Papers presented there were later published.[68] A similar exhibit was held in 1911.[69]

In 1916 the Greek newspaper *Saloniki,* encouraged by the owner of a shoeshine parlor, campaigned to help bootblacks working for Greek employers. *Saloniki* said that bootblacks should have reasonable working hours so they could attend school, thereby causing native Americans to think well of the Greek community. Grace Abbott addressed Greek businessmen and bootblacks at a Hull House meeting, and many of the employers present agreed to close their shops on Sundays and holidays so the boys could rest and study. Two or three times a week young bootblacks would be allowed to go to night school.[70]

Yet with all its publicity and support, the coalition could only block attempts to destroy existing legislation; proposals for new laws failed. In 1911 the National Alliance for the Protection of Stage Children tried to get special, more liberal work permits for child actors. Jane Addams, the Mothers' Congress of Illinois, the Illinois State Federation of Labor, and the Illinois Child Labor Committee lobbied vigorously, and the bill was defeated. The reformers' own bill, however, for stricter regulation of children working in street trades, also failed to pass. In 1915 the Illinois Committee on Social Legislation, representing many organizations of the reform coalition, asked the legislature to raise the minimum age for certain kinds of work. For the first time, violent opposition to a child labor bill led to its defeat.[71]

Oscar Nelson, chief state factory inspector in 1915, assumed that manufacturers engineered the defeats. Yet when his office surveyed businessmen, an overwhelming majority favored further regulation, even prohibiting work for those under fourteen.[72] Why, then, the sudden reluctance of the legislature to regulate child labor? In the absence of legislative debates from that time, no definitive answer exists, but there are some probabilities.

In a recent essay, Selwyn Troen has suggested that technological advances between 1900 and 1920 put many children out of work. The adoption, for example, of the pneumatic tube, cash register, and conveyor belts in department stores eliminated the need for cash boys and girls. Typewriters and dictating machines required more skilled office workers. Child labor regulation and inspection systems may also have promoted technological change, as in the Illinois glass factories. In any case, more and more of the employable young stayed in school and went on to high school.[73] Progressive social reformers wanted more laws and tougher school attendance requirements, but the sense of crisis had passed, and with it went much of their political support.

Furthermore, the reformers' basic tenet that the state should step in because parents had failed offended many, especially immigrants, who saw American society and schools drawing their children away from community values. Some said that further legislation would infringe too much upon proper parental authority and personal liberties. In the 1920s those opposed to the federal child labor amendment used the parental rights argument.[74]

The professionalization of the elements of the coalition, described by Robert Wiebe in *The Search for Order,* also led to a decline in effectiveness. Lawrence Cremin has said that the progressive education movement, a coalition of professional educators and reformers, lost its vitality and lay support as teachers became more organized.[75] As each group in the child welfare movement developed and concentrated on its own specific interest, it lost support from the general public for common causes.

In the 1920s labor, for example, organized, unionized, and negotiated for wages rather than social reform legislation. Middle- and upper-class women joined suffrage organizations. None of the women's rights groups was very broadly based; some had a strong nativist element, excluding working-class and immigrant women. The Woman's Party, pushing for full equality, threatened protective legislation for working women, widening the distance between social classes. The Hull House women continued to work for the old organizations and support the familiar causes, but with many of their earlier goals already achieved, and the coalition breaking up, they could accomplish little in the way of more social legislation. The public had lost not only its sense of crisis but its interest in continuing reform.

Conclusion

Apart from the actual effects of social legislation, the coalition's achievement lay in promoting the idea that children's rights may transcend parental authority. How far the state should go to define and protect those rights continues to be controversial.

Most importantly, the coalition helped prevent further polarization in a tense and troubled time by showing that groups need not have profound empathy to cooperate. Women in particular formed functional bonds that temporarily ignored class, and learned to work together outside their homes.

Aside from their contributions to society, the personal growth and fulfillment of the Hull House reformers was great. They began their adult lives confused and purposeless. By the first decade of the twentieth century their confidence, energy, compassion, and determination had made them a generation of heroines.

Notes

1. Bessie Louise Pierce, *A History of Chicago* (New York: Alfred A. Knopf, 1957), 2:63.

2. Ibid., chap. 2.

3. Illinois Special Committee on Labor, *Report to the House of Representatives* (Springfield, Ill.: Weber, Magie & Co., 1879), p. 50.

4. *Chicago Evening Post* (undated interview, box 2), Thomas J. Morgan Papers, University of Chicago.

5. "Slave Girls of Chicago," *Chicago Times* (July 29, 1888).

6. Ibid. (August 1, 1888).

7. Ibid. (August 25–28, 1888).

8. Ibid.

9. John Peter Altgeld, *Live Questions* (New York: Humboldt Publishing Co., 1890), p. 71.

10. *L'Italia* (December 17, 1892), *Foreign Language Press Survey,* Chicago Public Library.

11. *Foreign Language Press Survey of Chicago, 1890–1925* (Works Progress Administration), Chicago Public Library.

12. Eugene Staley, *History of the Illinois State Federations of Labor* (Chicago: University of Chicago Press, 1930), pp. 146–49.

13. Biographical data on Sophonisba Breckinridge, Margaret Haley, Ellen Henrotin, Julia Lathrop, Agnes Nestor, Margaret Robins, and Alzina Stevens came from relevant articles in *Notable American Women, 1607–1950,* ed. Edward James, 3 vols. (Cambridge, Mass.: Belknap Press of Harvard University Press, 1971). The articles on Jane Addams, Florence Kelley, and Grace Abbott are also useful.

14. Richard Hofstadter, *The Age of Reform: From Bryan to FDR* (New York: Alfred A. Knopf, 1955).

15. Florence Kelley, "My Novitiate," *Survey Graphic* (April 1927), pp. 31–32.

16. Jane Addams, *Twenty Years at Hull House* (New York: Signet, New American Library, 1960), p. 39.

17. Ibid., p. 46.

18. Ibid., p. 47.

19. Barbara M. Cross, ed., *The Educated Woman in America* (New York: Classics in American Education Series, Columbia University Press, 1962), pp. 30–45, 145–75.

20. Florence Kelley, *Modern Industry* (New York: Longmans, Green & Co., 1914), pp. 96–97.

21. Addams, pp. 60–74.

22. John P. Rousmaniére, "Cultural Hybrid in the Slums: The College Woman and the Settlement House, 1889–1894," in *Education in American History,* ed. Michael Katz (New York: Praeger Publishers, 1973).

23. Addams, pp. 90–100.

24. Jane Addams, *The Spirit of Youth and the City Streets* (New York: Macmillan Co., 1912), p. 34.

25. Illinois State Department of Factory Inspection, *Annual Report* (1893), pp. 12–13.

26. Jane Addams, *Democracy and Social Ethics* (New York: Macmillan Co., 1902), pp. 176–77.

27. Addams, *Twenty Years,* pp. 248–49.

28. Jane Addams, "The Objective Value of a Social Settlement," in *The Social Thought of Jane Addams,* ed. Christopher Lasch (New York: Bobbs-Merrill Co., 1965), pp. 60–61.

29. Kelley, *Modern Industry,* pp. 35–36.

30. Kelley, "My Novitiate," p. 35.

31. Agnes Nestor, *Women's Labor Leader* (Rockford, Ill.: Bellevue Books, 1954), p. 70.

32. See articles on Haley, Henrotin, Robins, and Stevens in *Notable American Women* (n. 13 above).

33. Nestor, p. 76.

34. Louise Bowen to Jane Addams, December 1891, Bowen Scrapbooks, Chicago Historical Society.

35. Illinois Bureau of Labor Statistics, *Seventh Biennial Report* (1892), and U.S. Commissioner of Labor, *Seventh Special Report* (1892).

36. *Chicago Tribune* (February 10–14, 1893).

37. Addams, *Twenty Years,* p. 150.

38. Ibid., p. 151.

39. Illinois General Assembly, *House Journal* (Springfield, Ill.: Phillips Brothers, 1893), p. 1097, and *Senate Journal,* p. 892.

40. Illinois Manufacturers' Association Papers, Illinois Manufacturers' Association, 135 So. LaSalle, Chicago (courtesy of Mr. Thomas Reid).

41. Florence Kelley, "I Go to Work," *Survey Graphic* 58 (June 1, 1927): 301.

42. Selwyn Troen, "The Discovery of Adolescence by American Educational Reformers, 1880–1920," in *Schooling and Society,* ed. Lawrence Stone (Baltimore: Johns Hopkins University Press, 1976).

43. Illinois State Department of Factory Inspection, *Annual Report* (1895), p. 13.

44. Janet Jean Zuck discusses this incident in "Florence Kelley and the Crusade for Child Labor Legislation in the United States, 1892–1932" (M.A. thesis, University of Chicago, 1946), pp. 40–43. She uses stories from the *Chicago Record,* the *Chicago Times-Herald,* and the *Social Democrat* for late August and early September of 1897.

45. Addams, *Twenty Years,* p. 149.

46. A common theme in Florence Kelley's writings; see esp. the *Annual Reports* of the State Department of Factory Inspection for 1893–96.

47. Illinois State Department of Factory Inspection, *Annual Report* (1893), p. 8.

48. Ibid., pp. 9–10.

49. Illinois State Department of Factory Inspection, *Annual Report* (1894), pp. 13–15.

50. Illinois State Department of Factory Inspection, *Annual Report* (1895), pp. 8–26.

51. Illinois State Department of Factory Inspection, *Annual Report* (1893), p. 14.

52. Illinois State Department of Factory Inspection, *Annual Report* (1895), p. 15.

53. Ibid., pp. 15 ff.

54. Report of the Child Labor Commission (written by the Chicago Civic Federation) is printed verbatim in the Illinois State Department of Factory Inspection, *Annual Report* (1896), pp. 18–21.

55. Illinois General Assembly, *House Journal,* p. 875, and *Senate Journal,* p. 1113.

56. Zuck, p. 41.

57. Illinois State Department of Factory Inspection, *Annual Report* (1900), pp. 4–28, and (1901), pp. 5–6.

58. Earl R. Beckner, "History of Illinois Labor Legislation" (Ph.D. diss., University of Chicago, 1927), pp. 227–29.

59. Ibid., p. 230.

60. Charles L. Chute, *Survey* (May 27, 1911), p. 332.

61. Beckner, p. 236.

62. Margaret Haley MSS (unpublished autobiography), Chicago Historical Society, box 32, folder 2, pp. 95–96.

63. Illinois General Assembly, *House Journal,* p. 1161, and *Senate Journal,* p. 999.

64. Illinois State Department of Factory Inspection, *Annual Report* (1903), p. xxiii.

65. Staley, pp. 179–83.

66. Ibid., p. 273.

67. Addams, *Twenty Years,* p. 214.

68. *Handbook of the Chicago Industrial Exhibition* (March 11–17, 1907).

69. Chicago School of Civics and Philanthropy, *Child in the City,* (Chicago: Hollister Press, 1912).

70. *Saloniki* (December 25, 1915–April 8, 1916), *Foreign Language Press Survey,* Chicago Public Library, Chicago, Ill.

71. Beckner, pp. 240–47.

72. Illinois State Department of Factory Inspection, *Annual Report* (July 1, 1914–June 30, 1915), pp. 30–43.

73. Troen (n. 42 above).

74. Beckner, p. 244; see also Walter Trattner, *Crusade for the Children: A History of the National Child Labor Committee and Child Labor Reform in America* (Chicago: University of Chicago Press, 1970).

75. Lawrence Cremin, *The Transformation of the School* (New York: Alfred A. Knopf, 1961).

The Chicago Playground Movement: A Neglected Feature of Social Justice

Benjamin McArthur
Chicago, Illinois

Among the problems plaguing cities at the turn of the nineteenth century was that of inadequate play areas for children. Chicago became the first city to remedy this situation on a large scale. Its famous network of playground parks provided the model for similar projects in other cities. The movement for playgrounds was part of the Progressive's quest for social justice. Social welfare workers, civic organizations, and local business and professional men united on an issue they all deemed important. Playgrounds, it was hoped, by preserving the health and morals of the child, solidifying the home, and inculcating a democratic ethos, would help ensure an orderly society.

The duke of Wellington is said to have remarked that the battle of Waterloo was won on the playing fields of Eton. Apocryphal or not, the remark reflects a judgment about play similar to American beliefs. Americans share the feeling that play imparts values necessary for a successful life—teamwork, self-sacrifice, and a competitive spirit.

Playgrounds had their origin in the same era that baseball became the national pastime, Walter Camp promoted intercollegiate football, and bicycling became the rage. The 1880s and 1890s marked the beginning of America's love affair with sports and outdoor recreation. For the first time many Americans discovered the pleasures of exercise. The playground movement emerged as a part of the new emphasis on strenuous living.

But, in addition to being a cultural phenomenon, playgrounds sprang from a social movement. The campaign for playgrounds and small parks was as much a manifestation of the Progressive spirit as widows' pensions, workmen's compensation, and anti-child-labor laws.

Social Service Review 49 (September 1975): 376–95
© 1975 by The University of Chicago

Those elements of the "quest for social justice" have been investigated. No one, however, has put the drive for public playgrounds in the perspective of the Progressive Era.[1]

The neglect is surprising in view of what the playground movement achieved. In 1890, only one public playground existed in the entire United States. By 1917, as a result of the playground movement, 481 cities maintained 3,944 playgrounds.[2] The Playground Association of America, founded in 1906, worked diligently to promote the establishment of playgrounds across the country. It included such Progressive notables as Jane Addams, Joseph Lee, Robert Woods, and Lilian Wald; the honorary president was Theodore Roosevelt and the honorary vice-president, Jacob Riis. Its journal, *The Playground*, heralded the benefits of organized play.

Chicago stood preeminent both in the magnitude of its problem and in the scope of its solution. On the eve of the twentieth century, only a handful of playgrounds served Chicago's over one-half million children. Within five years Chicago had the most ambitious program of small park and playground construction anywhere. Setting the standard against which other cities were measured, Chicago enables one to grasp the dynamics of the American playground movement as a whole. And through the playground movement one can more fully understand the Progressive sense of social justice.

Inception and Evolution

In the early 1890s, Jacob Riis described a visit he made to a West Side Manhattan school. Children played in the basement, a dark, foulsmelling, gas-lit room. Because teachers conducted classes upstairs, children had to do the impossible—play quietly. The basement was their only playground.[3] Scenes like this one could be found in other American cities. Not only were children deprived of adequate play areas during school hours—after school they had no place to go except the streets. Streetcorner gangs with nothing better to do found an outlet for their energy by stealing from pushcarts and baiting policemen. And children who escaped the lure of gang life did not always escape the wheels of a passing wagon. Not surprisingly, the primary reason for early playgrounds was to take children off the streets.[4]

As in so many other social welfare measures, Europe pioneered in playgrounds. Dr. Marie Zakerzewska, on a visit to Berlin in the 1880s, noticed that the public parks provided sandpiles for children to play in. Her letter to the Massachusetts Emergency and Hygiene Association in 1885 resulted in what is generally regarded as the beginning of the playground movement. That year sand gardens, opened just three hours a day, were established in Boston. The idea became so popular that in 1898 the Massachusetts legislature approved a $500,000 appropriation for the Boston Park Commission to build playgrounds. Within three years the city had ten playgrounds. The Boston movement got its impetus from the Massachusetts Emergency and Hygiene Association and from Joseph Lee, philanthropist and head of the Massachusetts Civic League, who spent his life working for playgrounds.[5]

Earlier even than Boston, New York City, in 1887, received legislative approval to spend $1 million a year acquiring small parks and playgrounds. It wasn't until 1895, however, that the city made plans for two small parks on the Lower East Side. When the Outdoor Recreation League, headed by Charles Stover, heard that the parks were to be the conventional shrub and grass type, they took a survey among local residents. Results showed that the people wanted a playground. Hence, in 1899, the Outdoor Recreation League cleared the debris from the Seward Park site and equipped a playground. The popularity of the Seward Park playground persuaded the New York Park Commission to take over its operation in 1893 and make plans to build others.

The children of New York also benefited from the tireless work of two men, Jacob Riis and Luther Gulick. Riis's special burden lay with school playgrounds. By 1899 New York had thirty-one schoolyard playcenters, a tribute to his efforts. Luther Gulick, philosopher of the play movement and cofounder of the Camp Fire Girls, set up the Public School Athletic League to encourage interschool athletics among all boys, not just the talented few.

Besides Boston and New York, Philadelphia experimented early with playgrounds. There the Culture Extension League both promoted playgrounds and shared with the city the expenses of what in 1898 was said to be the most complete playground in the country. Baltimore, Washington, D.C., and Pittsburgh were other cities in the forefront of playground development.[6]

Chicago shared the problems of other industrial cities. Jane Addams described conditions: "The streets are inexpressibly dirty, the number of schools inadequate, sanitary legislation unenforced, the street lighting bad, the paving miserable and altogether lacking in the alleys and smaller streets, and the stables foul beyond description. Hundreds of houses are unconnected with the street sewer. The older and richer inhabitants seem anxious to move away as rapidly as they can afford it."[7]

Chicago had a precedent for action. Washington and Jackson Parks, designed by the famous landscape architects Olmsted and Vaux, had been among the finest in the nation when opened in the

1870s. And, on the North Side, Lincoln Park provided outdoor recreation. But these parks had two shortcomings. First, Chicago had grown tremendously since the 1870s when most park building had been done. Though large, both Washington and Jackson Parks were on the South Side, too far away for most people to enjoy. Those huddled in West Side ghettos and the stockyards district had no access to recreation areas. Second, parks of the nineteenth century reflected the formal-gardens idea. They were places in which to stroll leisurely and appreciate the beauty of flowers and well-trimmed hedges. The ubiquitous "keep off the grass" sign discouraged children from having fun. Jackson and Lincoln Parks did get tennis courts in the 1880s, and horse racing on the boulevards was permitted. But these suited recreational tastes of adults, not children.

Chicago playgrounds had their beginnings in the social-settlement movement. The first model playground in America opened at Hull-House on May Day, 1894.[8] Florence Kelley had become disturbed over a particularly rundown tenement next to Hull-House. In a letter to the newspaper, Kelley mentioned by name the owner of the property, A. E. Kent and Son. The son, William Kent, who later became a well-known Progressive congressman from California, came out and inspected the building. His decision to let Hull-House have the property resulted in the building being torn down and the playground replacing it. Thereafter, Kent maintained a lifelong interest in the playground movement.[9] The Hull-House playground provided for a wider age group of children than had the Boston sand gardens. Little children had swings, a maypole, paving blocks, and sandpile. Older children played handball and softball.

Mary McDowell's University of Chicago settlement also pioneered in playgrounds. Located in the rough-and-tumble stockyards district, it had an ethnically varied population. The local alderman gave Miss McDowell twenty-five dollars to try to devise a way to keep the neighborhood boys out of mischief. She bought a swing and a sandbox and put them on a vacant lot. The incipient playground was so successful that she went to Boston to study their playgrounds. After returning she added more apparatus. In 1896, the community celebrated its grand opening with a great "festival of play," featuring folk dancing and singing of many nationalities.[10]

Most Chicago settlements had some sort of playground facility: Graham Taylor's Chicago Commons, Northwestern University settlement, Forward Movement settlement, Olivet Institute, and Association House.[11] Generally, these had a sand bin, wood paving blocks to build with, swings, seesaws, and sometimes ladders or climbing ropes. Play leaders organized activities, and in some ethnic neighborhoods they taught German, Russian, Scandinavian, and Japanese national games.[12]

Second City children also found friends in the Chicago Women's Club. In 1898 it set up a Vacation School Committee (VSC) to provide children with activities during the summer months, seeking to preserve their health and morals. An important part of children's activities, the VSC realized, was supervised play. So, with $1,000 appropriated by the city council, the VSC maintained playgrounds in six schoolyards. In their annual report, the committee claimed to have been the initiators of the movement for playgrounds in the Chicago public schoolyards. Though they overstated their case a bit—the West End District of the Associated Charities actually opened the first schoolyard playground in 1897 at Washington School—the vacation schools did much to popularize them.[13]

These playgrounds, with all manner of games and activities, proved immensely popular, except with school janitors. Summer months had traditionally been their time to take it easy around the school. The school playgrounds invaded their privacy and increased their work load. Happily, by 1900 the committee could report that these troubles had been ironed out and that the janitors were going out of their way to help.[14] But these were just summer playgrounds, and only in a few schools. The board of education had yet to see the value of playgrounds for all schools during the entire year.

Both social-settlement and vacation-school workers urged the municipal financing of playgrounds.[15] The first step in the transition from voluntary association to municipal control came in 1898, when the Chicago City Council subsidized the VSC playgrounds. To finish the task, however, more people had to become aware of the need. Three events raised the consciousness of Chicagoans.

The first hearing on playgrounds before an influential audience was at a banquet of the Chicago Real Estate Board in October 1897. Congressman Henry Boutell digressed from his topic of parks and boulevards to emphasize the need for playgrounds in the poorer sections of town. His ideas did not take immediate effect, but subsequently the Merchant's Club of Chicago, an organization of prominent businessmen, interested itself in the movement and donated money for the purchase of land.[16] A more immediate jump in municipal playground interest came as a result of Jacob Riis's visit to Chicago in 1898. Giving a talk before the Municipal Science Club at Hull-House on the need for playgrounds, he made such a vivid impression on the members that a delegation of the committee went to Mayor Carter Harrison asking him to act on the matter.[17] The result was the Special Park Commission (SPC). Set up in 1899, it inquired into Chicago's need for small parks and playgrounds and formulated a policy for their development.[18] The SPC maintained its independence from the three park boards already existing in Chicago. Its twenty-one members, nine aldermen and the rest from business and the professions, served without compensation.

The SPC received impetus from a later speech by Jacob Riis, in 1898, at a Merchant's Club dinner. With twenty-one specially invited aldermen present, Riis gave a stereopticon presentation of New York slums and how playgrounds could relieve urban blight. Once again Riis struck a responsive chord in his audience. After the program ended, the aldermen expressed enthusiasm about playgrounds.[19]

The city council initially granted the SPC a generous $100,000 to buy land and build their playgrounds. Almost immediately, however, the council realized it could not afford that much and cut the appropriation to $11,500. The sum dipped to $10,000 in 1901 and rose slowly to $22,000 in 1905. This lack of support by the city forced the SPC to look elsewhere for funds. They issued, in 1905, a pamphlet called *A Plea for Playgrounds.* It graphically portrayed Chicago's need for recreation facilities and appealed to all good Chicago citizens for help. The police, health department, and juvenile court all attested to the salutary effects playgrounds would bring.[20] The appeal failed. Despite having distributed 5,000 copies to those citizens best able to give, by the end of the year only $105 had been raised.[21]

Nonetheless, the SPC's efforts were not completely in vain. By 1905, with the council's appropriations, they operated nine playgrounds; the Chicago Commons playground on Grand Avenue became a part of the municipal system the same year, and other settlement playgrounds received apparatus.

SPC playgrounds offered the usual assortment of games and activities for young children. But they went beyond the settlement playgrounds in their emphasis on organized competitive games. Teams representing various playgrounds played one another in baseball, football, basketball, and track. A Municipal Playground Athletic League was set up to test the all-around ability of the participants. It had three divisions: for boys aged 12–14, 15–17, and 18 and over. Older youth now found themselves attracted to playgrounds.[22]

The social-settlement, vacation-school, and SPC playgrounds broke the ground. Yet, as much as these three, playground construction in Chicago resulted from the vision and hard work of J. Frank Foster, general superintendent of the South Park District since 1890. At a time when park superintendents generally saw their role as custodians of beauty, Foster envisioned parks alleviating the negative conditions of urban life. As early as 1895, he planned recreational features, outdoor gymnasiums, swimming pools, and field houses —things incorporated in the small parks ten years later.[23] He got a chance to implement his ideas when the SPC saw that they could not build many playgrounds on their stringent budget. They proposed that a more efficient plan would be to use the park boards already in existence, since they had the power to tax for park revenue.

Chicago's three park districts, the South, West, and Lincoln Park Districts, were created by the Illinois Legislature in 1869. Independent of the municipal government, they could tax residents in their own district and issue bonds for the construction and upkeep of parks. The governor appointed the seven commissioners of the West and Lincoln Park Boards, leading to a mixture of politics with park policy. Neither board offered any new answers to the problem of urban recreation.[24]

The judges of the Circuit Court of Cook County named the five South Park commissioners. The South Park Commission (South PC) had a tradition of honest and innovative men on its board, such as Henry Foreman, one of the organizers of the Chicago Stock Exchange and the Chicago Real Estate Board. Foreman was president of the South PC in 1903, when it decided to take up the challenge of building small parks. The South PC had a distinct advantage over the other two park boards; the loop lay within its territory, ensuring adequate financing. Before the enlargement program could be undertaken, the South PC required authority from the legislature to purchase additional land wherever needed, and a $3 million bond issue had to be submitted to the residents of the district. Both passed, the bond issue with an overwhelming 80 percent of the vote.[25]

Having liked Frederick Law Olmsted's plans for Washington and Jackson Parks, the South PC contracted with his firm to draw up plans for the new playground parks. The locations for the parks were carefully studied and the needs of individual neighborhoods canvassed. The commission discovered that 350,000 people, over half the population of the South Park District, had no convenient access to parks. This, in some of Chicago's worst slums.

Initial plans had been laid in 1903. By 1905, fourteen small playground parks dotted the South Side of Chicago. The names of the parks honored giants of Chicago's past: Cornell Square, Ogden Park, Palmer Park, Armour Square. The parks varied in size from ten-acre squares to the 322-acre Marquette Park. They reflected a dramatic departure from previous park theory. They combined beauty with utility, marking the beginning of a concept now generally accepted in all city parks—that they must be useful as well as ornamental.

What were the distinctive features of the playground parks? They provided facilities for young and old, men and women. Besides being a place for physical activity, they attempted to meet social needs. For children under ten there were the usual playgrounds with sandbox, wading pool, and other apparatus. For children over ten and adults, the parks offered both indoor and outdoor gymnasiums, one each for men and women, complete with locker rooms. An outdoor swimming pool and plunge bath were in each park (swim suits were available from the attendant free of charge). Qualified gymnasium instructors directed activities.

The playground-park directors made special efforts to provide for working boys and young men, lest they completely lose the play spirit, by setting aside evenings and weekends for them and for young married couples. Records for 1907 showed that attendance totaled 15,774 at the indoor gymnasiums. Of this number, 9,461 were boys and 6,313 were girls; 6,928 of the patrons worked and students numbered 8,846. Categorized by age, 9,467 were under age sixteen; 6,307 were sixteen and over.[26]

Social activities centered around the field houses. These were conceived as being complete neighborhood centers, with rooms for local clubs and organizations and an assembly hall allowing for large gatherings and lectures. For the hungry, a lunch counter served meals at cost. A branch of the public library was included in three of the recreation centers. All of these facilities were free "to any person who conducts himself or herself properly."[27]

The South PC system led the way, and by its success the playground cause moved ahead throughout Chicago. In an editorial, the *Chicago Record-Herald* favored increased park expansion: "The fundamental truth regarding park building is that it cannot be overdone."[28] The West and Lincoln Park Districts, though less innovative, were pulled along in the current toward providing small parks and playgrounds. The West Park Board opened two parks in 1908 and one in 1909. They planned them along the lines of the South Park's, with swimming pools, gymnasiums, and field houses.[29] The Lincoln Park Board started work on their first playground park, Seward Park, in 1907. Opened July 4, 1908, it became an immediate success. By 1910, Stanton, Hamlin, and Welles Parks plus Lake Shore playground added to the North Side's recreation picture.[30] At the beginning of 1916, the city of Chicago had fifty-five playgrounds or playground parks under municipal administration. That year marked a shift in policy from concentrating on building new playground parks to using public schoolyards as the focus of playground development.

There had always been a lively debate over the desirability of uniting playgrounds and public schools or of keeping them separate. The advocates of separation pointed to the board of education's indifference, bordering on hostility, toward the responsibility of maintaining playgrounds in schoolyards. They emphasized that playground supervision needed expert administration. The trend in public administration, they pointed out, was toward control by a commission of specialists in the field. Further, recreation was for all ages, not just school children. To these objections, proponents of union stressed that play is primarily an educational function—an extension of the school. Positive contact between student and teacher could be increased through recreational time together. And by identifying play with his school hours, the child would gain a new appreciation for learning.[31]

Ultimately, placing playgrounds in schoolyards came to be the accepted answer. Children spent much of the day in school; during these hours municipal playgrounds were virtually deserted. In an age concerned with efficiency and rationality, the linking of playgrounds to schools seemed the efficient and rational thing to do. After much prodding, the Chicago Board of Education finally acceded to having the SPC establish forty playgrounds in schoolyards during 1916. In 1921, the schools took over administrative control of them.[32]

The sand gardens, an idea imported from Germany, had become something new in America. When, in 1908, J. Frank Foster visited Germany and found playgrounds there to be nothing but bare patches of land, he observed: "Europe affords examples of parks of nearly every character except the play park, which, in its complete development, is an American product of the present decade."[33]

Chicago playgrounds developed haphazardly; several municipal bodies proceeded at different rates in their own way. Yet, had there been just one park commission for the entire city, it is likely that inertia might have retarded growth even more. The conservative nature of the city council, school board, and West and Lincoln Park Boards inhibited innovation. It took someone to move ahead and show the feasibility and practical benefit of playgrounds. Under vigorous leadership by men such as J. Frank Foster and Henry Foreman, the South PC revealed what could be done. The rest of Chicago, indeed the rest of the nation, followed in the path laid out by them.

People and Ideas

To find out what kind of people involved themselves in the playground movement, one can look to the Chicago Playground Association (CPA). Appropriately enough, the CPA originated at Hull-House. A group of interested people organized in 1907 to serve as host to the national convention of the Playground Association of America.[34] But they had long-range plans as well. They believed that a voluntary association working alongside the park boards and SPC would give impetus to the movement.[35] They proposed a three-pronged attack: (1) investigate city conditions and playground needs, (2) help form neighborhood cooperating committees to stir up playground sentiment among residents and secure playgrounds in their districts, and (3) secure immediate use of vacant lots for playgrounds.[36]

The CPA had eighteen directors, fourteen men and four women. In a general way, they may be classified into three groups: businessmen, professionals, and welfare workers. There were six businessmen: three bankers, two manufacturers (one of whom was Harold McCormick, son of Cyrus, and an International Harvester director), and Livingston Wells Fargo, an American Express executive. Five professionals served as directors: well-known juvenile court judge Julian Mack and Jens Jensen, the noted landscape architect, plus a lawyer, architect, and civil engineer. As might be expected, there was a good representation of welfare workers, six in all. There were both social-settlement people (Jane Addams, Mary McDowell, Amalie Hofer) and charity workers (Sherman Kinglsey and Ernest Bicknell). In addition, Henry Thurston, director of the Juvenile Protective League, worked with the CPA.[37] One more director, Anita McCormick Blaine, does not fit in any of these three categories. Yet she, as a McCormick, a philanthropist, and leader in Chicago society, added more prestige to an already star-studded cast.

The composition of the CPA holds no surprises. The same types of people who participated in other Progressive reform movements were here also.[38] That many reformers came from high social and economic status may not mean that they were any more concerned with the poor than other Americans were, or that they became involved because of a declining social status. It may just be that they had the time and means to follow through on those projects they thought useful. The question, rather, is why these people thought playgrounds worthwhile. In answering it, one must recapture the attitudes and popular notions of the time and isolate ideas about the city's influence on children and families, the nature and function of play in children's education, and any other sources that inspired Chicago citizens to take up the playground cause.

The spirit of the play movement was apotheosized in the first annual convention of the Playground Association of America. Graham Romeyn Taylor described its atmosphere: "There wasn't a minute when the play spirit even took a rest. It romped in at the Thursday night session when President Frederick Greely, of the playground of Chicago, introduced 'our playmates,' Miss Jane Addams, Joseph Lee and Dr. Luther H. Gulick. And it romped boisterously out late on Saturday afternoon when a whole field of 5,000 delegates, spectators and festival participants played tag with a thunderstorm. . . . The play spirit captivated everyone."[39]

The convention brought together the biggest names of the movement to deliver papers. They discussed playgrounds from many angles, and from the various papers it is possible to derive the core philosophy of the movement. The titles of just five of the eighteen papers read indicate what they thought play involved: "Play and Democracy," "Play as a School of the Citizen," "Public Recreation and Social Morality," "Relation of Play to Juvenile Delinquency," "Playgrounds in the Prevention of Tuberculosis."[40] Fundamentally, the play movement was a response to the conditions of modern urban life and the concomitant fear that it weakened the health and morals of children, destroyed the home, and undermined democracy. Reformers hoped that playgrounds would serve both as a deterrent to these evils and as a positive force to shape children's characters.

One source for the play movement lay in new educational theories. Prominent among them was that of Friedrich Froebel, who concerned himself particularly with children between the ages of three and six. At this age, "play is the purest, most spiritual activity of man." His kindergarten sought to free children from harsh discipline and encouraged their natural development through creative play.[41] G. Stanley Hall proposed another influential theory. He held that games are remnants of earlier activities of the race. What may now be just a simple footrace hearkens back to times when man had to run down his prey.[42] Philosopher of the play movement, Luther Gulick, asserted that the individual reveals himself most completely when at play. And, conversely, play has a greater shaping power on the character and nature of man than any other activity.[43]

But these theories on the nature of play were usually relegated to the more speculative minds. Arguments that held a wider appeal resided in what playgrounds could do to improve the mental and physical health of children. As opposed to the wholesomeness of country life, the city imposed artificial conditions on the individual, reducing the opportunities for exercise.[44] England was often cited as an example of the degenerative effects of industrial life. The factory system there, affording little exercise to its citizens, received the blame for England's weakness in the Boer War. Accepting this causal relationship, it was just a short step to prescribing regular exercise as an important factor in race development.[45]

A problem in poorer sections of the cities was ignorance of personal hygiene. The field houses of the South PC provided public baths to develop habits of cleanliness in children. By 1906, the director of gymnasiums for the South PC reported that many residents took weekly showers there. With conditions as they were it is not surprising that tuberculosis flourished. The scourge of TB especially devastated the cramped quarters of the cities. The battle against TB found its way into the playground arena. Henry Baird Favill, president of the Chicago TB Institute, advocated playgrounds on the grounds that a daily fresh air experience was the single most important deterrent.[46]

If the city adversely affected the physical condition of its inhabi-

tants, even more it ate away at its moral base. Jane Addams's *The Spirit
of Youth and the City Streets* was only the most eloquent of the appeals to
rectify the problem of recreation.[47] Dance halls, saloons, back-alley
gambling, and movie houses offered allurements to the youth. "But
where else were they to go for fun?" reformers asked. They answered, of course, that youth would flock to the playground parks. As
Jane Addams put it, who can imagine a boy playing craps in a stuffy
alley when there is a swimming pool a few blocks away. Statistical
proof widely cited showed that the new playgrounds reduced juvenile
delinquency in their districts.[48]

The enticements of youth also concerned the Juvenile Protective
Association. Founded in 1899, the association sought to remove temptations from children and better the conditions of their neighborhoods. Consequently, the Juvenile Protective Association helped
campaign for small parks and playgrounds. They hoped that with
proper organization and leadership children could be spared the experience of passing through the courts.[49]

Just as play, or the lack of it, could affect health and morals, it also
had implications for the democratic process. Jacob Riis told the
Merchant's Club: "It was in the minds of the men who wrote the
Constitution that our boys should play. . . . A boy robbed of his
chance to play will not be an honest and effective man—you can't
depend on him at the polls."[50] It was said that when people had spent
leisure time in dissipation, they set the stage for their fall. Democracy
depended on self-disciplined citizens who could take part in the
larger social processes. The individual character had to be strong;
since the character is formed by habits, and habits are formed in
youth, it is vital that the activities of children be of the right kind.
Organized play is necessary because it teaches children, through team
activities, the loyalty and self-sacrifice necessary for a democracy. In place of the rule of the strong found on the street, the
playground enforces rigid rules of fair play and the submission of the
self to the team. When translated into political terms, that meant
self-government, respect for the law, social service, and good
citizenship.[51]

But play, if left undirected, would not accomplish these results. At
the early playgrounds many children just stood around, not knowing
any games to play, and the bigger children took over from the
younger. Thus, the need for a play leader recurs in the literature of
the play movement. The play leaders had to be well trained, possessing certain desirable characteristics: the playfulness of a child, the
endurance of a spartan, the patience of Job, the missionary spirit of a
Jesuit, and the wisdom of Solomon.[52] They were to evoke the finer
qualities of youth. In a general letter to gymnasium instructors, the
South PC exhorted them to: "Regard your work as an instrument

with which to build character and good citizens . . . praise every tendency of a boy or girl to sacrifice himself or herself for the good of the team, show them that this is the only way to succeed—by unity of action . . . we are engaged in a work which, if properly conducted, is perhaps better calculated to raise the standard of good citizenship than any other single agency in the hands of public servants."[53] The moralism and complete assurance that their action is the correct one, so typical of Progressives, is evident here. The Playground Association of America supplied a list of qualified play leaders available for work. In Chicago, a playground training school was held one summer with courses in folk games and dancing, psychology, physical training, and rhythm.[54]

The South PC took the ultimate step by developing the playground into a complete social and recreational center for all ages—children, teens, and adults. When it first started planning its new playground parks in 1903, it still thought only of children's needs. But after investigating its territory it discovered that conditions dictated that greater measures be taken. Gymnasiums, libraries, meeting halls, and facilities for total community service were needed.[55] The uniqueness of Chicago's playground parks lay in their being complete social centers. In a sense they stood in the tradition of the social settlements —offering a place where people of the neighborhood could get together in various types of clubs, where the foundations of a real community could be laid. It would be an agency for the social redemption of the people.

Progressives feared that the city threatened the most sacred of American institutions, the family. A Chicago social worker, Amalie Hofer Jerome, wrote: "When the family splits up for its recreation, there is danger. When young people take their places apart by themselves without a wholesome influence of family life, there is danger. Only when the family stays together do we have wholesome conditions." The playground parks would serve as a gathering spot for family recreation; there they could participate together in games and dances, solidifying their relationship.[56]

Just as reformers trusted that playgrounds would strengthen family ties, they hoped they could help create bonds of unity among the constant influx of immigrants. They thought that playgrounds would serve as a catalyst in breaking down national and racial prejudices. It was not a matter of simply Americanizing the foreigner. On the contrary, some complained that the public schools taught immigrant children to despise their cultural heritage. To counteract this, the playgrounds gave opportunity for the Slav, the Italian, or the Bohemian to play his national game, to sing the fatherland's song. After a day of work under conditions of imposed conformity, immigrants found appealing the recreation centers where variety and individual

folklore were valued. Not only did they encourage children in their
cultural heritage, but an effort was made to educate the public in
appreciation of ethnic cultures. The Chicago play festivals helped
achieve this goal, as large numbers of spectators enjoyed the folk
songs and dances of the performers.[57]

Even while some argued that the industrial state stifled the play
spirit, others commended playgrounds because they would increase
the productivity of workers. This would be accomplished through two
qualities: more efficiency and better teamwork. Workers would be
more efficient because they would be healthier and vitalized, their
minds sharpened by physical activity. And by making life more enjoy-
able, workers would have a greater incentive to be efficient and produce more so that they could enjoy a greater share of life. Through
team sports, the spirit of cooperation and team play would be built
up. Competition in play would also teach children that competition is
the mainstream of business—and of life. Supervised play was essential
for every city child to "continue the stalwart, virile, work-a-day race
upon which the greatness of America depends."[58]

Arguments for playgrounds ranged from the simple to the sophisticated. At the upper end of the spectrum came one with philosophical underpinnings from William James. The trouble lay in America's
business civilization. [59] It turned its citizens into a nation of inactive
consumers. America, intellectuals felt, was getting soft. To people
such as Oliver Wendell Holmes, Jr., the Civil War had been a time
when the nation's character had been resolute and courageous to
meet the challenge. Now, in the last decade of the century, young
men of our country lacked any training ground in character. Edward
Bellamy offered a utopian society based on the martial principles of
army organization. Theodore Roosevelt went a step further and said
that a new war was essential to build "the strenuous life."

War repelled William James. Yet he agreed that something had to
be done to inspire and invigorate the nation's youth, especially the
young patrician gentlemen. What he sought was a "moral equivalent
of war"—something to call forth the enthusiasm, courage, and
self-sacrifice of war but that would be peaceful and constructive.
James's solution lay in forming an army of young men to do the
distasteful tasks—coal and iron mining, tunnel building, and the like.
From these efforts they would be prepared for the business of life.[60]

The fear that America was getting soft and James's moral equivalent of war were both applied to the play movement. In *The Playground,* an article appeared by George Johnson, "Play as a Moral
Equivalent of War." War has in the past played an important part in
the history of man, Johnson conceded. It developed heroic qualities
that saved humanity from degenerating. But war was no longer
necessary; these martial qualities could be preserved through play.

Boxing and wrestling, competitive games, all create attitudes of courage, a contempt for softness, adherence to rules, and resentment of unfairness and meanness. "It can insure us the benefits of past wars, while it takes away the moral necessity of future wars."[61]

Likewise, Joseph Lee posited "Play as an Antidote to Civilization." Man is by nature an active being who must be constantly challenged. But our industrial civilization, Lee argued, takes the store of vital energy out of its citizens. Through team play the individual can again become a significant member of the group. The ideal would be to incorporate into industry the element of team play. Until then, more playgrounds, shorter working hours, and relaxed Sunday laws for activities are desired. War should be abolished, because modern warfare no longer exercises the warlike impulse. "But to abolish war and put nothing in its place is a change of doubtful value."[62]

One more source for the playground movement in Chicago remains: the element of city pride. At the turn of the century Chicagoans took a renewed interest in the physical appearance of their town. The lake shore was secured for the public, Grant Park expanded, the Art Institute and Field Museum of Natural History built, and a grand outline for Chicago's development drafted—Daniel Burnham's Chicago Plan. When the SPC was set up in 1899, besides its playground responsibilities, it was to investigate the possibility of setting aside wooded lands in territory surrounding Chicago for a system of outer-belt parks. The Cook County Forest Preserves are the present-day legacy of their efforts. The playgrounds, then, represented just one aspect of a newly refurbished Chicago.

In general, playgrounds enjoyed a consensus of favorable opinion. There is one report, though, of a wealthy Chicago businessman threatening suit against the South PC for misusing public funds in "socialist" enterprises.[63] That line of attack had been answered a few years earlier by Frederick Bancroft, president of the Merchant's Club. After hearing Jacob Riis give his talk on the need for playgrounds at a club dinner in 1899, Bancroft got up and seconded the idea. He said: "This is not Socialism, not anarchy, not the preaching of a new course of municipal action, but it is common sense applied to actual conditions."[64]

Newspaper editorials called playgrounds "the best investment Chicago has ever made," and they proudly announced that statistics showed Chicago leading all cities in the amount of money spent. It was a fact, said the *Record-Herald*, which exemplifies the Chicago spirit at its best, "a spirit quick to see and quick to perform."[65]

The pride of Chicago, its park playgrounds, went on display during the 1907 playground convention. This meeting marked the transition of playground activity from a more or less sporadic activity to a firmly established and well-organized national movement.[66] Theodore

Roosevelt encouraged cities to send delegates to examine the new parks. From coast to coast cities responded. Chicago's influence spread as far as Japan, evidenced by the imperial consul's Chicago office requesting that reports on the subject be sent to the park-improvement department in Tokyo.[67]

Conclusion

One question remains: What can the playground movement tell us about the social justice side of Progressivism? A major debate concerning the nature of Progressivism is whether reformers were forward-looking in their aims, realizing that the industrial way of life was here to stay, or whether they attempted to turn the clock back to a simpler age. The playground movement can help resolve this dispute.

In general, playground reformers accepted industrialization and its accompanying urban way of life. They were realists who knew that the industrial tendency could not be reversed. But they could not accept the stultifying and degrading conditions of the cities. If America was to continue as a democracy, some things must be preserved from the city's contamination. Jacob Riis expressed this concern to the Chicago Merchant's Club: "Where there is no decent home there can be no manhood, no family, no patriotism."[68]

The triune of children, family, and patriotism had to be protected. It was not a matter of preserving outmoded values but of enabling Americans to move forward and make the transition into an industrial civilization as smoothly as possible. Everett Mero summarized the reformers' philosophy when he wrote: "All this line of effort has a common end: the making of life more worth living under conditions that exist; the improving of conditions so that instead of trying to escape from steel fetters of present civilization we may willingly remain in the embrace of velvet supports and guides."[69]

As previously mentioned, many Progressive reformers actively supported the playground movement: Jacob Riis, Lilian Wald, Judge Ben Lindsay, Robert Wood, Charles Evans Hughes. The list could go on. But non-Progressive types also advocated playgrounds. President Taft, for example, said: "I do not know of anything which will contribute more to the strength and morality of the generation of boys and girls compelled to remain part of urban populations in this country, than the institution in their cities of playgrounds."[70] He and the big businessmen who served as directors of the CPA cannot be counted as Progressives simply because they supported this one measure. One reason for their hearty endorsement may lie in an argument some reformers used—namely, that playgrounds helped ensure social order by providing an outlet for surplus energy and by instilling traits of self-discipline and obedience to authority. Such an appeal could get a favorable response from conservatives as well as Progressives.

Playgrounds benefited from almost universal support because they were noncontroversial. Unlike workmen's compensation, child-labor laws, and other social-welfare measures, playgrounds did not represent a drastic turn from America's legacy of individualism. Municipal control was new, but play, like education, seemed to fall naturally within the city's purview, and thus did not become a major issue. This consensus of favorable opinion about playgrounds is its most atypical aspect with regard to other Progressive welfare measures.

What can this fundamental difference tell us about the social-justice crusade? Perhaps by locating one aspect of Progressivism about which there is near-unanimous agreement, not only among paradigmatic Progressives but among all members of society, one can isolate a central tenet, a unifying theme of the age. Might not the three elements mentioned by Jacob Riis—the child, the family, and patriotism—be the key to understanding what everyone during the Progressive Era wanted? E. B. DeGroot, recreation and playground supervisor of the South Park District, observed: "However difficult it may be to unite our adult population on public issues of the day affecting the common weal, they may be unified most easily on those things which affect the interest of children. And the children's playgrounds not only help in unifying our adult population but they interpret fundamental American ideals to all concerned."[71]

All agreed on the inviolability of these three. Playgrounds, by protecting the child, unifying the home, and inculcating patriotism, helped America make the transition into an urban age.

Notes

1. Harold U. Faulkner's *The Quest for Social Justice* (Chicago: Quadrangle Books, 1959) devotes a few paragraphs to the play movement. But, as Robert Wiebe observed, Faulkner described the changes of the time "with scarcely an interpretation" (Robert Wiebe, *The Search for Order* [New York: Hill & Wang, 1967]). The best accounts of the playground movement are Henry Curtis's *The Play Movement and Its Significance* (New York: Macmillan Co., 1917), and Clarence Rainwater's *The Play Movement in the United States: A Study of Community Recreation* (Chicago: University of Chicago Press, 1922). Neither of these books places the play movement within the wider perspective of Progressivism. An article by Gerald K. Marsden, "Philanthropy and the Boston Playground Movement, 1885–1907," *Social Service Review* 35 (March 1961): 48–58, does explore one aspect of it in its Progressive context.

2. Charles Zueblin, *American Municipal Progress* (New York: Macmillan Co., 1916), p. 296, and "Playground Facts," *Playground* 12 (April 1918): 4. The journal *The Playground*

has continued under different titles. In 1931 it changed to *Recreation*, testifying to its enlarged scope. In 1966 it merged with two other magazines to become *Parks and Recreation*.

3. Jacob Riis, "Playgrounds for City Schools," *Century* 48 (September 1894): 657–66.

4. Rainwater, pp. 53–54; Curtis, p. 8.

5. Marsden, pp. 52–58.

6. Allen Davis, *Spearheads for Reform* (New York: Oxford University Press, 1967), pp. 63–64; Charles Stover, "Seward Park Playground at Last a Reality," *Charities* 10 (February 1903): 127–33; Charles Robinson, "Improvement in City Life," *Atlantic* (April 1899), pp. 524–37.

7. Jane Addams, *Twenty Years at Hull-House* (New York: Macmillan Co., 1930), p. 98.

8. Joseph Lee, *Constructive and Preventive Philanthropy* (New York: Macmillan Co., 1902), p. 173.

9. Elizabeth Thatcher Kent, *William Kent* (privately printed, 1950), pp. 95–96.

10. Howard E. Wilson, "Mary E. McDowell and Her Work as Head Resident of the University of Chicago Settlement House, 1894–1904" (Ph.D diss., University of Chicago, 1927), p. 73.

11. Yuk Sam Tom, "A Study of Social Settlements in Chicago" (M.A. thesis, University of Chicago, 1919), p. 44.

12. Charles Zueblin, "Municipal Playgrounds in Chicago," *American Journal of Sociology* 17 (September 1898): 151.

13. *Report of the Chicago Vacation School Committee of Women's Clubs* (Chicago, 1899), p. 38; Rho Fisk Zueblin, "Playground Movement in Chicago," *Playground* 1 (June 1907): 3–5.

14. *Report of the Chicago Vacation School Committee of Women's Clubs* (Chicago, 1900), pp. 39, 46–47.

15. *Report of the Chicago Vacation School Committee*, 1898, pp. 4–35.

16. Editorial, *Chicago Record-Herald* (June 20, 1907).

17. Elizabeth Halsey, *Development of Public Recreation in Municipal Chicago* (Chicago: Chicago Recreation Commission, 1940), p. 27.

18. Chicago City Council, *Proceedings*, November 6, 1899 (Chicago: John F. Diggins, 1899), pp. 1535–36.

19. *Chicago Tribune* (November 12, 1899).

20. Chicago Special Park Commission, *A Plea for Playgrounds* (Chicago: W. J. Hartman Co., 1905).

21. *Annual Report of the Special Park Commission* (Chicago, 1905), p. 6.

22. *Annual Report of the Special Park Commission* (Chicago, 1911), pp. 16–18.

23. Halsey, p. 30. Foster's source of ideas is unclear. The most likely explanation is that he was influenced by the work of Chicago settlements. No connection can be proven, however, as biographical information on Foster is scanty.

24. Rainwater, pp. 93–94, 102–3; Halsey, pp. 34–36.

25. *Annual Report of the South Park Commission* (Chicago, 1903), p. 6.

26. *Annual Report of the South Park Commission* (Chicago, 1908), p. 64.

27. Henry Foreman, "Chicago's New Park Service," *Century* 69 (February 1905): 610–20.

28. Editorial, *Chicago Record-Herald* (June 6, 1906).

29. *Annual Report of the West Chicago Park Commission* (Chicago, 1908), p. 36.

30. Halsey, p. 36.

31. The arguments pro and con were summed up in several papers presented at the American Playground Association's first annual convention in Chicago in 1907: *Papers of the Chicago Meeting, Playground Association of America, June 1907* (Chicago, 1907); also in Curtis (n. 1 above), pp. 30–50.

32. Halsey, pp. 40–41.

33. *Annual Report of the South Park Commission* (Chicago, 1909), p. 25.

34. *Annual Report of the Special Park Commission* (Chicago, 1906), p. 18.

35. Here is a curious reversal of roles. Robert Buroker, in "From Voluntary Association to Welfare State: The Illinois Immigrants' Protective League, 1908–1926," *Journal of American History* 58 (December 1971): 643–60, spoke of voluntary associations as being the training ground for similar jobs in later government organizations. In this case, members of the municipal SPC joined the CPA, a voluntary association devoted to

the same ends as the SPC. The CPA's activities were purely auxiliary to those of the SPC. No effort was made by the CPA to operate playgrounds itself.

36. Playground Association of Chicago, pamphlets (n.d.).

37. Biographical information is from John Leonard, ed., *The Book of Chicagoans* (Chicago, 1905, 1911).

38. For group analyses of two Chicago reform movements, see Buroker, and Kenneth Kusmer, "The Functions of Organized Charity in the Progressive Era: Chicago as a Case Study," *Journal of American History* 60 (December 1973): 657–78.

39. *Papers of the Chicago Meeting, Playground Association of America, June 1907*, p. 1.

40. Ibid.

41. Davis (n. 6 above), p. 44.

42. Henry Curtis, *Education through Play* (New York: Macmillan Co., 1916), p. 4; G. Stanley Hall, *Youth: Its Education, Regimen, and Hygiene* (New York: D. Appleton & Co., 1909), pp. 73–119.

43. Luther Gulick, *A Philosophy of Play* (New York: Charles Scribner's Sons, 1920), p. xiv.

44. *Annual Report of the South Park Commission* (Chicago, 1903), pp. 62–63.

45. Everett Mero, ed., *American Playgrounds* (New York: Baker & Taylor, 1908), p. 15; Otto Mallery, "The Social Significance of Play," *Annals of the American Academy of Political Science* 35 (March 1910): 153–54.

46. Henry Baird Favill, "Playgrounds in the Prevention of Tuberculosis," *Papers of the Chicago Meeting, Playground Association of America, June 1907*, pp. 31–36.

47. Jane Addams, *The Spirit of Youth and the City Streets* (New York: Macmillan Co., 1909).

48. *Annual Report of the South Park Commission* (Chicago, 1909), pp. 112–14.

49. Juvenile Protective Association of Chicago, pamphlets (Chicago, 1910–11).

50. *Chicago Record-Herald* (November 12, 1899).

51. Gulick, pp. 118–19; Stoyan Vasil Tsanoff, *Educational Value of the Children's Playground: A Novel Plan of Character Building* (Philadelphia, 1897), pp. 51–52; Gulick, pp. 261–62; Mallery, p. 156.

52. *Report of the Chicago Vacation School Committee*, 1900, p. 44.

53. Annual Report of the South Park Commission (Chicago, 1905), p. 48.

54. Chicago Training School for Playground Workers, *Prospectus* (Chicago, 1911–12).

55. Foreman (n. 27 above), pp. 610–20; *Annual Report of the South Park Commission* (Chicago, 1904), pp. 6–7.

56. Amalie Hofer Jerome, "The Playground as a Social Center," *Annals of the American Academy of Political and Social Science* 35 (March 1910): 132; *Chicago Permanent School Extension Report* (Chicago, 1909–10), pp. 14–15. In 1909 the Chicago Vacation School Committee became the Chicago Permanent School Extension Club.

57. Jane Addams, "Recreation as a Public Function in Urban Communities," *American Journal of Sociology* 17 (March 1912): 616; Victor Von Borosini, "Our Recreation Facilities and the Immigrant," *Annals of the American Academy of Political and Social Science* 35 (March 1910): 143; John Higham, *Strangers in the Land* (New York: Atheneum Publishers, 1971), pp. 121–22.

58. Mallery, p. 154; Howard Braucher, "Play and Social Progress," *Annals of the American Academy of Political and Social Science* 35 (March 1910): 114; editorial in *Journal of Education* (February 8, 1912), p. 143.

59. This discussion is based on George Frederickson's *The Inner Civil War: Northern Intellectuals and the Crisis of the Union* (New York: Harper & Row, 1965), especially chap. 14, "The Moral Equivalent of War," pp. 217–38.

60. William James, "The Moral Equivalent of War," *McClure's Magazine* (August 1910), p. 467.

61. George Johnson, "Play as a Moral Equivalent of War," *Playground* 5 (July 1912): 111–23.

62. Joseph Lee, "Play as an Antidote to Civilization," *Playground* 4 (July 1911): 110–26.

63. Halsey, p. 30.

64. *Chicago Tribune* (November 12, 1899).

65. *Chicago Record-Herald* (November 27, 1906); editorial, ibid. (January 6, 1910).

66. Graham Romeyn Taylor, "How They Played at Chicago," *Papers of the Chicago Meeting, Playground Association of America, June 1907*, p. 2.

67. *Annual Report of the Special Park Commission* (Chicago, 1910), p. 7.

68. *Chicago Record-Herald* (November 12, 1899).

69. Everett Mero, "Playgrounds Part of a General Modern Tendency," *Journal of Education* 69 (June 1909): 629–31.

70. Mero, *American Playgrounds*, p. 291.

71. *Annual Report of the South Park Commission* (Chicago, 1908), pp. 72–73.

Contributors

ROBERT H. BREMNER is a professor of history at Ohio State University. He has published extensively in the area of American social welfare history. Among his writings are *From the Depths: The Discovery of Poverty in the United States* (1956) and *American Philanthropy* (1960). He has also edited a three volume work, *Children and Youth in America* (1970–74).

JOSEPH L. CASTROVINCI wrote "Prelude to Welfare Capitalism" for a graduate seminar in history at the University of Chicago. He now works in banking.

CLARKE A. CHAMBERS is professor of American history and director of the Social Welfare History Archives at the University of Minnesota. His books include *California Farm Organizations* (1950), *Seedtime of Reform* (1963), *The New Deal at Home and Abroad* (1964), and *Paul Kellogg and the Survey* (1971).

ALLEN F. DAVIS is professor of history at Temple University. Among his publications are *Spearheads for Reform: The Social Settlements and the Progressive Movement* (1967), *American Heroine: The Life and Legend of Jane Addams* (1973), *Generations: Your Family in Modern American History* (1974 and 1978), and *Searching for Your Past* (1978).

STEVEN J. DINER is associate professor and chair of the Department of Urban Studies at the University of the District of Columbia. Among his publications are *A City and Its Universities: Public Policy in Chicago, 1892–1919* (1980) and "Scholarship in the Quest for Social Welfare: A Fifty–Year History of the *Social Service Review*" (1977).

JOHN HOPE FRANKLIN is the John M. Manley Distinguished Service Professor of History at the University of Chicago and has served as president of the American Historical Association. An eminent scholar of American black history and the history of the South, his numerous publications include *From Slavery to Freedom* (1947, 1956, and 1967), *The Militant South* (1956), *Reconstruction after the Civil War* (1961), *The Emancipation Proclamation* (1963), *A Southern Odyssey: Travellers in the Antebellum North* (1976), and *Racial Equality in America* (1976).

LYNN GORDON is instructor in history at Northern Illinois University. She has published articles on the history of college education for women.

MARCUS WILSON JERNEGAN (deceased) was professor of history at the University of Chicago from 1920 until 1937. A specialist in American colonial history, he authored several books, including *The American Colonies, 1492 to 1750* (1929) and *Laboring and Dependent Classes in Colonial America.*

BENJAMIN J. KLEBANER is professor of economics at City College of New York. He has published numerous articles, predominantly on the history of banking.

J. LEE KREADER is completing graduate study in history at the University of Chicago. The article on Isaac Rubinow was written for a graduate seminar.

MARK H. LEFF is assistant professor of history at Washington University in St. Louis.

BENJAMIN MCARTHUR is assistant professor of history at Southern Missionary College, Collegedale, Tennessee. A graduate of the University of Chicago, he has recently completed his doctoral dissertation, "Actors in American Culture: 1880–1920."

SEATON W. MANNING taught social welfare at San Francisco State College and at California State University in San Francisco.

ELEANOR PARKHURST wrote "Poor Relief in a Massachusetts Village" while studying for her doctorate in the School of Social Service Administration at the University of Chicago in the late 1930s.

RALPH E. PUMPHREY is emeritus professor of social work at Washington University in St. Louis. For many years he worked as a social welfare administrator. His publications include *The Heritage of American Social Work* (1961).

DAVID M. SCHNEIDER held various positions in social welfare administration in New York State until his retirement in 1969. His major work has been in the area of medical economics. His books include *Workers' (Communist) Party and American Trade Unions* and a two-volume *History of Public Welfare in New York State.*

NEGLEY K. TEETERS (deceased) was a leading authority on criminology. He was Hardy Professor of Sociology at Hartwick College and, before that, taught sociology at Temple University. He authored twelve books and seventy-five articles, among them *New Horizons in Criminology* (with Harry Elmer Barnes), *Hang by the Neck* (1967), *The Cradle of the Penitentiary* (1955), *Penology from Panama to Cape Horn* (1946), and *World Penal Systems* (1944).

WALTER I. TRATTNER is professor of history at the University of Wisconsin—Milwaukee. He has written extensively on the history of American social welfare. His books include *Homer Folks: Pioneer in Social Welfare* (1968), *Crusade for Children: A History of the National Child Labor Committee and Child Labor Reform in America* (1970), and *From Poor Law to Welfare State: A History of Social Welfare in America* (1974).

MARY BOSWORTH TREUDLEY taught sociology at Wellesley College until her retirement in 1952. Her books include *Prelude to the Future: The First Hundred Years of Hiram College* (1950), *The Men and Women of Chung Ho Ch'ang* (1971), and a biography of China missionary Minnie Vantrin entitled *This Stinging Exultation* (1972).

GEORGE CARY WHITE (deceased) was professor of sociology at Holliss College in California.

ELIZABETH WISNER (deceased) was dean of the Tulane University School of Social Work, where she began teaching in 1927. Her books include *Public Welfare Administration in Louisiana* (1930) and *Social Welfare in the South* (1970).

Appendix

Articles and Source Materials concerning the History of Social Welfare Published in *Social Service Review* between 1927 and 1980

"Dorothea L. Dix and Federal Aid" (Source Materials). 1, no. 1:117–37

Edith Abbott. "The Civil War and the Crime Wave of 1865–70." 1, no. 2:212–34

"Samuel Gridley Howe, 1801–76" (Source Materials). 1, no. 2:291–309

Clara E. Collett. "Some Recollections of Charles Booth." 1, no. 3:384–89

"Stephen Girard, 1750–1831" (Source Materials). 1, no. 3:470–91

Ray Strachey, "The Centenary of Josephine Butler: An Interview with Dame Millicent Garrett Fawcett." 2, no. 1:1–9

"A Physician Philanthropist in the Eighteenth Century: Benjamin Rush, 1745–1813" (Source Materials). 2, no. 2:274–303

"Benjamin Franklin's Account of an Eighteenth-Century Hospital" (Source Materials). 2, no. 3:469–86

Marcus Wilson Jernegan. "The Development of Poor Relief in Colonial Virginia." 3, no. 1:1–18

Elizabeth A. Hughes, "The History of the College Social Service Exchange." 3, no. 1:58–74

Charles Loring Brace. "An Early Adventure in Child-placing" (Source Materials). 3, no. 1:75–97

Helen A. Bonser. "Illustrations of Political Economy: An Early Example of the Case Method." 3, no. 2:243–51

Edith Abbott. "The Webbs on the English Poor Law." 3, no. 2:252–69

Josephine Shaw Lowell. "Public Outdoor Relief—Theory and Practice in 1883" (Source Materials). 3, no. 2:271–79

Edward L. Pierce. "Experience of the Overseers of the Poor" (Source Materials). 3, no. 2:280–88

Frederic H. Wines, "The County Almshouses of Illinois, 1872" (Source Materials). 3, no. 2:289–94

Percy H. Boynton. "Two Practical Idealists." 3, no. 3:405–11

S. C. Ratcliffe. "Some Illinois County Poor Relief Records, 1837–60" (Source Materials). 3, no. 3:460–75

Elizabeth Wisner. "The Louisiana Law of Family Relations." 3, no. 4:584–96

"The Wellesley Case and the Juvenile Court Movement" (Source Materials). 4, no. 1:64–81

Percy H. Boynton. "Graham Taylor—Religion in Social Action." 4, no. 3:423–26

"Thomas Eddy's Proposals regarding the Care of the Insane, 1815" (Source Materials). 4, no. 3:459–74

Percy H. Boynton. "Toward World-Consciousness." 4, no. 4:533–36

A. B. Hopkins. "Liberalism in the Social Teachings of Mrs. Gaskell." 5, no. 1:57–73

"The Establishment of 'Penitentiary Houses' " (Source Materials). 5, no. 1:74–93

Marcus Wilson Jernegan. "The Development of Poor Relief in Colonial New England." 5, no. 2:175–98

"Sir Samuel Romilly and the Abolition of Capital Punishment" (Source Materials). 5, no. 2:276–96

Marcus Wilson Jernegan. "Compulsory and Free Education for Apprentices and Poor Children in Colonial New England." 5, no. 3:411–25

"The First Public Welfare Association" (Source Materials). 5, no. 3:468–81

"Relief Work for the Unemployed in the Seventeenth Century: Thomas Firmin, 1632–97" (Source Materials). 5, no. 4:629–41

Jane Addams. "A Great Public Servant, Julia C. Lathrop." 6, no. 2:280–85

James S. Plant. "Frederick Pickering Cabot: A Modern Puritan." 7, no. 1:122–29

Jane Addams. "Julia Lathrop and Outdoor Relief in Chicago, 1893–94." 9, no. 1:24–33

Jane Addams. "Julia Lathrop's Services to the State of Illinois." 9, no. 2:191–211

Ronald C. Davison. "The Evolution of British Social Services: A Historical Summary." 9, no. 4:651–63

Margaret Creech. "Some Colonial Case Histories." 9, no. 4:699–730

Albert Deutsch. "Public Provision for the Mentally Ill in Colonial America." 10, no. 4: 606–22

Shelby T. McCloy. "Charity Workshops for Women, Paris, 1790–95." 11, no. 2:274–84

Eleanor Parkhurst. "Poor Relief in a Massachusetts Village in the Eighteenth Century." 11, no. 3:446–64

Martha A. Chickering. "An Early Experiment in State Aid to the Aged, California, 1883–95." 12, no. 1:41–50

Shelby T. McCloy. "Government Assistance during the Plague of 1720–22 in Southeastern France." 12, no. 2:298–318

David M. Schneider. "The Patchwork of Relief in Provincial New York, 1664–1775." 12, no. 3:464–94

Mary Bosworth Treudley. "An Early Council of Social Agencies." 13, no. 1:93–104

Margaret Creech. "Six Colonial 'Case Histories.' " 13, no. 2:246–62

Edith Abbott. "Grace Abbott: A Sister's Memories." 13, no. 3:351–408

Grace Abbott. "Federal Regulation of Child Labor, 1906–1938." 13, no. 3:409–30

Marshall E. Dimock. "The Inner Substance of a Progressive." 13, no. 4:573–78

Harrison Clark. "The Development and Organization of Public Labor Exchanges in Sweden." 14, no. 3:453–68

Mary Bosworth Treudley. "The 'Benevolent Fair': A Study of Charitable Organization among American Women before 1835." 14, no. 3:509–22

David M. Schneider and Albert Deutsch. "The Public Charities of New York: The Rise of State Supervision after the Civil War." 15, no. 1:1–23

Norman D. Humphrey. "Mexican Repatriation from Michigan: Public Assistance in Historical Perspective." 15, no. 3:497–513

Mabel Newcomer. "Fifty Years of Public Support of Welfare Functions in the United States." 15, no. 4:651–60

Edith Abbott. "Twenty-One Years of University Education for the Social Services, 1920–41." 15, no. 4:670–705

Virgil A. Hampton. "Provision for Soldiers' Dependents before World War I." 16, no. 4:612–29

Martha Branscombe. "The Poor Law Policy of Liability of Relatives and the New York Courts, 1784–1929." 17, no. 1:50–66

Edith Abbott. "Juvenile Delinquency during the First World War: Notes on the British Experience, 1914–18." 17, no. 2:192–212

Miriam Damick Weller. "The Development of the Federal Probation System." 18, no. 1:42–58

Howell V. Williams. "Benjamin Franklin and the Poor Laws." 18, no. 1:77–91

Frank J. Bruno. "Twenty-Five Years of Schools of Social Work." 18, no. 2:152–64

Agapita Murillo. "Public Welfare Service in the Philippines, 1898–1941." 18, no. 2:189–204

Alton A. Linford. "Responsibility of Children in the Massachusetts Old Age Assistance Program." Part I, "Legislation before 1936." 19, no. 1:61–74. Part II, "Legislation and Administration, 1936–43." 19, no. 2:218–34

Elizabeth Wisner. "The Puritan Background of the New England Poor Laws." 19, no. 3:381–90

Charitable Bequests in Early English Wills (1284–1580) and Statutes (1414–1601) to Protect Charitable Gifts" (Source Materials). 20, no. 2:231–46

Emma O. Lundberg. "Pathfinders of the Middle Years." 21, no. 1:1–34

"The Work of Thomas H. Gallaudet and the Teaching of the Deaf" (Source Materials). 21, no. 3:375–86

Harold T. Pinkett. "Records in the National Archives relating to the Social Purposes and Results of the Operation of the Civilian Conservation Corps." 22, no. 1:46–53

John G. Hill. "Fifty Years of Social Action on the Housing Front." 22, no. 2:160–79

Edith Abbott et al. "Sophonisba Preston Breckinridge." 22, no. 4:417–50

William H. Riback, "Theodore Parker of Boston: Social Reformer." 22, no. 4:451–60

Katharine F. Lenroot. "Sophonisba Preston Breckinridge, Social Pioneer." 23, no. 1:88–92

Mildred Brink Tintor. "Review of the Organizational History of the Chicago Social Service Exchange." 24, no. 2:181–97

Edith Abbott. "Grace Abbott and Hull House, 1908–21." Part I. 24, no. 3:374–94. pp. 493–518. Part II. 24, no. 4:493–518

Rachel Marks. "The Effects of Early Workmen's Compensation Legislation on the Employment of the Handicapped, 1897–1915." 25, no. 1:60–78

Eleanor K. Taylor. "The Public Accountability of Charitable Trusts and Foundations: Historical Definition of the Problem in the United States." 25, no. 3:299–319

Mary Stanton."The Development of Institutional Care of Children in California from 1769 to 1925." 25, no. 3:320–31

Elizabeth S. L. Govan. "A Community Program of Foster-Home Care: New South Wales, 1881." 25, no. 3:363–75

Peter Bachrach. "The Right to Work: Emergence of the Idea in the United States." 26, no. 2:153–64

Edith Abbott. "The Hull House of Jane Addams." 26, no. 3:334–38

Wayne McMillen. "The First Twenty-Six Years of the *Social Service Review.*" 27, no. 1:1–14

Frank R. Breul. "The Genesis of Family Allowances in Canada." 27, no. 3:269–80

Maurice B. Hamovitch. "History of the Movement for Compulsory Health Insurance in the United States." 27, no. 3:281–99

Dora Goldstine. "The Literature of Medical Social Work: Review and Evaluation." 27, no. 3:316–28

Rachel Marks. "Treatment of Delinquent Women: A Nineteenth-Century Experiment Reported in the Letters of Charles Dickens." 27, no. 4:408–18

Alex Elson. "First Principles of Jane Addams." 28, no. 1:3–11

Frances Perkins. "My Recollections of Florence Kelly." 28, no. 1:12–19

Frank T. Flynn. "Judge Merritt W. Pinckney and the Early Days of the Juvenile Court in Chicago." 28, no. 1:20–30

Lea D. Taylor. "The Social Settlement and Civic Responsibility: The Life Work of Mary McDowell and Graham Taylor." 28, no. 1:31–40

Helen R. Wright. "Three against Time: Edith and Grace Abbott and Sophonisba P. Breckinridge." 28, no. 1:41–53

Marion K. Craine. "Heritage and Prospects: Social Service in Chicago." 28, no. 1:54–64

Nicholas Kelley. "Early Days at Hull House." 28, no. 4: 424–29

Alice Channing. "The Early Years of a Pioneer School." 28, no. 4:430–40

Negley K. Teeters. "The Early Days of the Magdalen Society of Philadelphia." 30, no. 2:158–67

Robert H. Bremner. " 'Scientific Philanthropy,' 1873–93." 30, no. 2:168–73

Charlotte Towle. "Marion E. Kenworthy: A Social Worker's Reflections." 30, no. 4:446–52

Muriel W. Pumphrey. "The 'First-Step'—Mary Richmond's Earliest Professional Reading, 1889–91." 31, no. 2:144–63

James Brown IV. "Marshall Field." 31, no. 2: 179–82

Sidney E. Zimbalist. "Index-making in Social Work." 31, no. 3:245–57

C. L. Mowat. "Charity and Casework in Late Victorian London: The Work of the Charity Organisation Society." 31, no. 3:258–70

Elizabeth Wisner. "Edith Abbott's Contributions to Social Work Education." 32, no. 1:1–10

Harold A. Jambor. "Theodore Dreiser, the *Delineator* Magazine, and Dependent Children: A Background Note on the Calling of the 1909 White House Conference." 32, no. 1:33–40

Rachel Marks, ed. "The Published Writings of Edith Abbott: A Bibliography." 32, no. 1:51–56

Irvin G. Wyllie. "The Reputation of the American Philanthropist: A Historian's View." 32, no. 3:215–22

Kathleen Woodroofe. "C. S. Loch," 32, no. 4:400–413

Ralph E. Pumphrey. "Compassion and Protection: Dual Motivations in Social Welfare." 33, no. 1:21–29

George Cary White. "Social Settlements and Immigrant Neighbors, 1886–1914." 33, no. 1:55–66

Allen F. Davis. "Raymond Robins: The Settlement Worker as Municipal Reformer." 33, no. 2:131–41

Merle Curti. "Subsidizing Radicalism: The American Fund for Public Service, 1921–41." 33, no. 3:274–95

Maurice R. Friend. "The Historical Development of Family Diagnosis." 34, no. 1:2–15

James Brown IV. "Child Welfare Classics." 34, no. 2:195–202

Donald Meiklejohn. "Jane Addams and American Democracy." 34, no. 3:253–64

Kathleen Woodroofe. "Social Group Work and Community Organization in Nineteenth-Century England." 34, no. 3:309–22

Archibald MacLeish. "Jane Addams and the Future." 35, no. 1:1–5

Grace Longwell Coyle. "The Great Tradition and the New Challenge." 35, no. 1:6–14

K. Gerald Marsden. "Philanthropy and the Boston Playground Movement, 1885–1907." 35, no. 1:48–58

Roy R. Grinker et al. "The Early Years of Psychiatric Social Work." 35, no. 2:111–26

John G. Cawelti. "Changing Ideas of Social Reform as Seen in Selected American Novels of the 1850's, the 1880's, and the Present Day." 35, no. 3:278–89

Robert D. Cross. "The Philanthropic Contribution of Louisa Lee Schuyler." 35, no. 3:290–301

Benjamin K. Klebaner. "The Myth of Foreign Pauper Dumping in the United States." 35, no. 3:302–09

Dorothy G. Becker. "The Vistors to the New York City Poor, 1843–1920." 35, no. 4:382–96

Seaton W. Manning. "The Tragedy of the Ten-Million-Acre Bill." 36, no. 1:44–50

Jack R. Parsons. "The Origins of the Income-and-Resources Amendment to the Social Security Act." 36, no. 1:51–61

Clarke A. Chambers. "Social Service and Social Reform: A Historical Essay." 37, no. 1:76–90

Abram L. Harris. "John Stuart Mill: Government and Economy." 37, no. 2:134–53

Mark H. Haller. "Heredity in Progressive Thought." 37, no. 2:166–76

James Leiby. "Amos Warner's 'American Charities,' 1894–1930." 37, no. 4:441–55

Dorothy G. Becker. "Exit Lady Bountiful: The Volunteer and the Professional Social Worker." 38, no. 1:57–72

Herman Levin. "The Future of Voluntary Family and Children's Social Work: A Historical View." 38, no. 2:163–73

Samuel Mencher. "The Influence of Romanticism on Nineteenth-Century British Social Work." 38, no. 2:174–90

Walter Elder. "Speenhamland Revisited." 38, no. 3:294–302

Phyllis Atwood Watts. "Casework above the Poverty Line: The Influence of Home Service in World War I on Social Work." 38, no. 3:303–15

Benjamin K. Klebaner. "Poverty and Its Relief in American Thought, 1815–61." 38, no. 4:382–99

Genevieve C. Weeks. "Religion and Social Work as Exemplified in the Life of Oscar C. McCulloch." 39, no. 1:38–52

Arnulf M. Pins. "Development of Social Work Recruitment: A Historical Review." 39, no. 1:53–62

Jon A. Peterson. "From Social Settlement to Social Agency: Settlement Work in Columbus, Ohio, 1898–1958." 39, no. 2:191–208

Genevieve C. Weeks. "Oscar C. McCulloch: Leader in Organized Charity." 39, no. 2:209–21

Robert H. Bremner. " 'An Iron Sceptor Twined with Roses': The Octavia Hill System of Housing Management." 39, no. 2:222–31

Milton D. Speizman. "Speenhamland: An Experiment in Guaranteed Income." 40, no. 1:44–55

Verl S. Lewis. "Stephen Humphreys Gurteen and the American Origins of Charity Organization." 40, no. 2:190–201

Walter I. Trattner. "Homer Folks and the Public Health Movement." 40, no. 4:410–28

Frank Leonard. " 'Helping' the Unemployed in the Nineteenth Century: The Case of the American Tramp." 40, no. 4:429–34

Jacob Kellner and Constance Dilley Tadros. "Change in Society and in the Professions: Issues in the Emergence of Professional Social Work." 41, no. 1:44–54

Russell E. Smith. "The March of the Mill Children." 41, no. 3:298–303

Elizabeth Wisner. "The Howard Association of New Orleans." 41, no. 4:411–18

James Leiby. "Social Work and Social History: Some Interpretations." 43, no. 3:310–18

Alvin B. Kogut. "The Negro and the Charity Organization Society in the Progressive Era." 44, no. 1:11–21

Jeffry Galper. "The Speenhamland Scales: Political, Social, or Economic Disaster?" 44, no. 1:54–62

John Hope Franklin. "Public Welfare in the South during the Reconstruction Era, 1865–1880." 44, no. 4:379–92

Steven J. Diner. "Chicago Social Workers and Blacks in the Progressive Era." 44, no. 4:393–410

Robert E. Moran. "The Negro Dependent Child in Louisiana, 1800–1935." 45, no. 1:53–61

Anatole Shaffer. "The Cincinnati Social Unit Experiment: 1917–19." 45, no. 2:159–72

Gisela Konopka. "Reform in Delinquency Institutions in Revolutionary Times: The 1920s in Germany." 45, no. 3:245–58

Joseph B. Chepaitis. "Federal Social Welfare Progressivism in the 1920s." 46, no. 2:213–29

Leslie B. Alexander. "Social Work's Freudian Deluge: Myth or Reality?" 46, no. 4:517–38

Robert R. Allen, "Count Rumford: Behavioral Engineer." 46, no. 4:597–602

James B. Lane. "Jacob A. Riis and Scientific Philanthropy during the Progressive Era." 47, no. 1:32–48

Pauline Lide. "The National Conference on Social Welfare and the Black Historical Perspective." 47, no. 2:171–207

Mark H. Leff. "Consensus for Reform: The Mothers'-Pension Movement in the Progressive Era." 47, no. 3:397–417

Eric Anderson. "Prostitution and Social Justice: Chicago, 1910–15." 48, no. 2:203–28

Howard N. Rabinowitz. "From Exclusion to Segregation: Health and Welfare Services for Southern Blacks, 1865–1890." 48, no. 3:327–54

Kathleen Woodroofe. "The Irascible Reverend Henry Solly and His Contribution to Working Men's Clubs, Charity Organization, and 'Industrial Villages' in Victorian England." 49, no. 1:15–32

Harriett M. Bartlett. "Ida M. Cannon: Pioneer in Medical Social Work." 49, no. 2:208–29

Julia B. Rauch. "Women in Social Work: Friendly Visitors in Philadelphia, 1880." 49, no. 2:241–59

Benjamin McArthur. "The Chicago Playground Movement: A Neglected Feature of Social Justice." 49, no. 3:376–95

Stephen Kalberg. "The Commitment to Career Reform: The Settlement Movement Leaders." 49, no. 4: 608–28

Joseph L. Castrovinci. "Prelude to Welfare Capitalism: The Role of Business in the Enactment of Workmen's Compensation Legislation in Illinois, 1905–12." 50, no. 1:80–102

Walter L. Trattner. "The Federal Government and Social Welfare in Early Nineteenth-Century America." 50, no. 2:243–55

J. Lee Kreader. "Isaac Max Rubinow: Pioneering Specialist in Social Insurance." 50, no. 3:402–25

Steven J. Diner. "Scholarship in the Quest for Social Welfare: A Fifty-Year History of the *Social Service Review*." 51, no. 1:1–66

Michael J. Austin and Neil Betten. "Intellectual Origins of Community Organizing, 1920–1939." 51, no. 1:155–70

Lynn Gordon. "Women and the Anti-Child Labor Movement in Illinois, 1890–1920." 51, no. 2:228–48

Robert Fisher. "Community Organizing and Citizen Participation: The Efforts of the People's Institute in New York City, 1910–1920." 51, no. 3:474–90

Maurice MacDonald. "Food Stamps: An Analytical History." 51, no. 4:642–58

Barry J. Kaplan. "Reformers and Charity: The Abolition of Public Outdoor Relief in New York City, 1870–1898." 52, no. 2:202–14

Edward S. Shapiro. "Robert A. Woods and the Settlement House Impulse." 52, no. 2:215–26

Louis L. Athey. "From Social Conscience to Social Action: The Consumers' Leagues in Europe, 1900–1914." 52, no. 3:362–82

Philip Jackson. "Black Charity in Progressive Era Chicago." 52, no. 3:400–417

Emily K. Abel. "Middle-Class Culture for the Urban Poor: The Educational Thought of Samuel Barnett." 52, no. 4:596–620

Joseph L. Candela, Jr. "The Struggle to Limit the Hours and Raise the Wages of Working Women in Illinois, 1893–1917." 52, no. 1:15–34

Priscilla Ferguson Clement. "Families and Foster Care: Philadelphia in the late Nineteenth Century." 53, no. 3:406–20

Alison R. Drucker. "The Role of the YWCA in the Development of the Chinese Women's Movement, 1890–1927." 53, no. 3:421–40

J. David Greenstone. "Dorothea Dix and Jane Addams: From Transcendentalism to Pragmatism in American Social Reform." 53, no. 4:527–59

Emily K. Abel. "Toynbee Hall, 1884–1914." 53, no. 4:606–32.

Index

Abbott, Edith, 2, 3, 233, 239, 315, 316, 317, 318

Abbott, Grace, 315, 316, 317, 318, 328

Acadians, supported in Massachusetts, 102–3

Act for Settling a Ministry, 70

Addams, Jane, 216–17, 219, 220, 224, 226, 229, 231, 232, 233, 241, 312, 315, 316, 317, 318, 319, 320, 322, 335, 344

Aid to Dependent Children (ADC), 3, 244. *See also* Mothers' pensions

Almshouses, 32, 33

Altgeld, John Peter, 314, 323

American Association for Labor Legislation (AALL), 278, 298–300

American Federation of Labor (AFL), 266, 282

American Medical Association (AMA), 300–301

Apprentice Laws, in South, 190; Programs, 79, 80

Arrington, Louis, 325

Babcock, Charlotte, 22

Berea College, 229

Blacks, and Chicago social workers, 226–41; and mothers' pensions, 261; and Reconstruction, 187, 188, 191; and settlements, 231–35; social service for, 236–39. *See also* Segregation

Boaz, Sophia, 238

Boston Seaman's Aid Society, 142

Bowen, Louise De Koven, 229–31, 238, 321–22

Boyle, M. J., 283

Brace, Charles Loring, 7

Breckinridge, Robert J., 184

Breckinridge, Sophonisba, 233, 238, 239, 241, 315, 316, 317, 318

Bremner, Robert H., 179, 197

Breul, Frank R., 1

Bridgman, Laura, 9

Bryan, William Jennings, 282

Burns, Allen T., 210

Burns, Eveline M., 23

Business, role of, in workmen's compensation legislation, 272–75, 281

Carey, Archibald, 238

Carey, Matthew, 117, 119, 127, 129, 140, 143, 144, 145

Carter, W. C., 283

Cartwright, Dr. S. C., 191

Castrovinci, Joseph L., 180, 265

Chambers, Clarke A., 4, 14

Charity, private vs. public, 123, 124–27; view of, 226–29. *See also* Philanthropy

Charity organizations, 198–202, 227; among American women, 132–45; and mothers' pension movement, 250, 258; in New England, 56–57

Chicago, 180, 226–41. *See also* Hull House, Blacks and Chicago social workers

Chicago Bureau of Charities, 227, 229

Chicago Civic Federation, 325

Chicago Commons, 205–7, 223, 234

Chicago Federation of Labor (CFL), 271, 282, 283, 327

Chicago Playground Association, 341–42

Chicago Playground Movement, 181, 333–49

Chicago Relief and Aid Society, 227

Child labor, coalition for, 318–22; decline of reform of, 327–29; legislation on, 322–27; movement against, 181, 312–30; as poor relief, 38–39; the problem, 313–15

Child Labor Commission, 325

Child welfare, 79–81; educational provisions, 81–86; during Reconstruction, 190

Churches, and poor relief, 72. *See also* Vestries

Civic Federation, 205

Civil War, and need for public relief, 185. *See also* Reconstruction

Clayton Act of 1914, 282

Colonial America, 2, 29–35; Virginia, 32, 36–53. *See also* New England Poor Laws
The Colored People of Chicago, 230
Common Law, and workmen's compensation, 267–68, 272, 278–79
Compassion, 3, 5–13; institutions originating in, 8–9
Connecticut Asylum for the Deaf and Dumb, 157–61
Constitutions, of southern states after Civil War, 188
Consumers' League, 327
Cook County Child Saving League, 326
Cooper, Thomas, 129
Co-operation, 227, 228, 229
Coyle, Grace, 15, 17
Cremin, Lawrence, 329
Cultural heritage, 214; preserving, 219–23. *See also* Immigrants

Danstedt, Rudolph, 16
Davis, Allen F., 179, 203
Deaf and dumb institutions, federal aid to, 156–64, 193
Delineator, 253
Deneen, Charles S., 273, 274
Denison House, Boston, 219
Depression of 1873–78, 197
Deutsch, Albert, 173
Devine, Edward T., 250
Dewey, John, 224
Dexter, Ebenezer Knight, 57
Diner, Steven J., 180, 226
Disease, and poor relief, 60, 61. *See also* Epidemics
Dix, Dorothea, 8–9, 34, 157, 165, 169–75, 183, 192
Dreier, Margaret, 209

Economics, and poverty, 117–21
Education, for poor children, 81–86. *See also* Public education
English Poor Laws, 114, 129, 131, 160, 174; 1834 English Poor Law Reform, 32; Elizabethan Poor Laws, 30–31, 32; English Law of Settlement and Removal, 96
de l'Epée, Charles Michel Abbé, 158
Epidemics, 58–60, 71, 91, 137, 191
Epstein, Abraham, 303, 304

Favill, Henry Baird, 343

Federal aid, to deaf and dumb, 156–64; to mentally ill, 165, 169–74
Federal government, role of, 177
Female Society of Philadelphia for the Relief and Employment of the Poor, 132
Fitch, John A., 21
Fitzhugh, George, 184
Fitzpatrick, John, 282
Flora, John, 283
Foreman, Henry, 339
Foster, J. Frank, 338, 341
Franklin, Benjamin, 114
Franklin, John Hope, 177–78, 183
Frederick Douglass Center, 236, 237, 238
Freedmen's Bureau, 178, 186, 187; educational work of, 187
Freund, Ernst, 278–80
"Friendly Circle," 132, 139
Froebel, Friedrich, 343

Gallaudet, Thomas Hopkins, 158
Garment sweaters, and child labor, 323
General Federation of Women's Clubs, 255
Gilbert, Sir Humphrey, 39
Gilman, Daniel Coit, 197
Glass manufacturers, and child labor, 323, 324–25, 326
Gompers, Samuel, 281, 302
Gordon, Lynn, 181, 312
Graham, Isabella Marshall, 133
Greenhow, Robert, 120
Griscom, John, 9
Gulick, Luther, 335, 343
Gurteen, Rev. S. H., 198

Hakluyt, Richard, 39
Hale, Mrs. Sarah Josepha, 9, 142, 143, 144, 145
Haley, Margaret Angela, 321, 326
Hall, G. Stanley, 343
Hall, Helen, 15
Handicapped, special relief for, 86–89
Hard, William, 253, 259
Hatch Act, 22
Hawkins, Gaynell, 17
Haynes, B. H., 238
Health care, need for, 191, 192. *See also* Disease

Henderson, Charles Richmond, 276, 278
Henrotin, Ellen Martin, 321
Hillquit, Morris, 297
Hollander, Sidney, 15, 23
Homestead Act, 175
Hone, Philip, 118
Hospitals, for the poor, 89–93
Houses of correction, 74–79
Houses of industry, 139
Howe, Frederick, 257
Howe, Samuel Gridley, 9
Hubbard, William, 55
Hull House, 220–22, 224, 229, 312, 315–18, 336
Hull House Labor Museum, 221–23, 224
Hunter, Robert, 208

Illegitimate children, 42–43, 51
Illinois, anti-child labor movement, 312–30; workmen's compensation legislation, 265–84. See also Chicago
Illinois Association for Labor and Legislation, 280
Illinois Federation of Labor (IFL), 271, 327
Illinois Manufacturers Association (IMA), 273
Immigrants, 178; and child labor, 324; compared to blacks, 231–32; contributions of, 218, 219–20; heritage of, 220–23; knowledge about, 214–15; and settlements, 214–25
Immigration, views on, 215–19
Immigration Quota Act of 1924, 224
Indentured servant system, 40
Industrialization, and poverty, 118; and workmen's compensation, 268
Insane, care for, 192, 193; humane treatment of, 8
Institutional Church and Social Settlement, 238
Institutionalization, 74–75, 108–12
Insurance companies, and workmen's compensation, 274
Isaacs, Abraham, 206, 207

James, William, 346
Jernegan, Marcus W., 32, 36
Jerome, Amalie Hofer, 345

Juvenile court judges, pro mothers' pensions, 252
Juvenile Protective Association, 230, 344

Kellogg, Paul U., 19, 22
Kelley, Florence, 312, 315, 316, 317, 318, 320, 322, 324, 325, 336
Kentucky Deaf and Dumb Asylum, 158, 162–64
Klebaner, Benjamin J., 33, 114
Kreader, J. Lee, 180–81, 288

Labor, and mothers' pensions, 254; and workmen's compensation, 281–84; and Raymond Robins, 207, 208
Land grant colleges, 175
Land redistribution, during Reconstruction, 188–89
Lathrop, Julia, 233, 315, 316, 317, 318
Laziness, and poverty, 116
Lee, Porter, 20
Leff, Mark H., 180, 244
Lindsey, Ben, 254
Lively, Robert, 156
Loeb, Sophie, 253
London, Meyer, 297
London Charity Organization Society, 198
Lowell, Josephine Shaw, 199
Lowry, Fern, 24
Lubove, Roy, 281
Lurie, Harry L., 17

McArthur, Benjamin, 181, 333
McCord, Charles, 237
McDowell, Mary, 220, 234, 235, 240, 336
Magdalen Society, 34, 146–55
Manning, Seaton W., 34, 169
More, Thomas, 38
Marshall, Dr. C. K., 192
Mather, Cotton, 55–56, 60, 62
Malthus, T. R., 127, 130
Martineau, Harriet, 131
Massachusetts Settlement Act of 1794, 95–96
Mayo, Leonard, 28
Media, and mothers' pension movement, 253
Medical aid, 89–93
Mentally handicapped, 86–89

Mentally ill, 165, 169–74
Mohl, Raymond, 157
Morgan, Thomas, 313, 314
Morrill, Justin S., 175
Morrill Act, 175
Mothers' pension movement, 3, 180, 181; development of, 245–49; legacy of, 260–62; opposition to, 249–52; support for, 252–60
Municipal Lodging House, 208
Municipal Voters' League, 205

National Association for the Advancement of Colored People (NAACP), 232
National Association of Manufacturers (NAM), 281
National Association of Social Workers (NASW), 27
National Child Labor Committee, 327
National Congress of Mothers and Parent Teacher Associations, 255
National Consumers' League, 256
The Negro Fellowship League, 239
Neighborhood Guild, 217
Neil, Henry, 257
Nelson, Oscar, 328
Nestor, Agnes, 320
New Deal, 303–6
New England Poor Laws, 32, 54–63
New York, poor relief in, 64–94
New York Children's Aid Society, 7
New York City, poor relief in, 68–74
New York Institute for the Instruction of the Deaf and Dumb, 161
New York Society for the Prevention of Pauperism, 10
Newman, Samuel P., 127
The 1919 Riot in Chicago, 239–40
Northwestern University Settlement House, 209, 253
Nott, Dr. Josiah C., 191
Noyes, LaVerne, 273

Olmsted, Frederick Law, 339
Orphanages, 190
Orphans, 43, 52
Ovington, Mary White, 237

Paine, Robert Treat, 199
Parish system, and administration of poor relief, 40–53

Park, Robert, 239, 240
Parkhurst, Eleanor, 32, 95
Parks. See Playground movement
Parrish, Anne, 132, 135, 139
Pauperism, badge of, 67, 68; remedies for, 121–22
Pennsylvania Hospital, 11–12
Philanthropy, analysis of, 12–13; growth of, 54; moralizing about, 199; motivation for, 5–7; scientific, 197–202. See also Charity
Phillips, Willard, 129
Pierce, Franklin, 165, 169, 172
Play, direction of, 344–45; need for, 343
Playground movement, 333–49; evolution of, 334–41; ideas concerning, 344–48; people in, 341–44; and settlements, 336; Special Park Commission, 337, 338, 339
Politics, and the church, 62; and mothers' pension movement, 252
Poor, moralizing about, 136, 197, 198
Poor farms, 108–112
Poorhouses, 74–79, 193
Poor laws, 64; abolition of, 127–30; arguments against, 122–24; controversy over, 122–31; English, 30–33; in New England, 54–63; public vs. private charity, 124–27; and the sick, 60–61
Poor relief, 36–53, 64–94, 95–113; administered by vestries, 41–52; and child welfare, 79–81; in Colonial Virginia, 36–53; education of poor children, 81–86; establishment of poor farms, 108–12; for handicapped, 86–89; institutional, 74–79; in Massachusetts, 95–113; medical aid, 89–93; in New York City, 68–74; in Provincial New York, 64–94; report of committee on, 108–109; and slavery, 93–94; "warning out," 95–99
Population increase, 178
Poverty, economics behind, 117–21; moralizing about, 114–17. See also Pauperism, Poor
Pray, Kenneth L. M., 26–27
Private charity, and mothers' pension

movement, 258, 259; vs. public charity, 123, 124–27

Progressive Era, Chicago social workers and blacks during, 226–41; and mothers' pension movement, 244–62; and workmen's compensation, 265–84

Progressive reformers and workmen's compensation legislation, 275–80

Protection, 3, 5–13; institutions originating in, 9–11

Psychology, and social work, 18, 19

Public agencies, role of, 223–24

Public education, 186, 188; and the Freedmen's Bureau, 186, 187; and immigrants, 215; in the South, 184

Pumphrey, Ralph, 3, 5

Puritanism, 32, 55–63

Quakers, ancestors of Hull House women, 316, 317; involved in poor relief, 132–33

The Quest for Security, 304, 305

Railway Trainmen's Union, 283

Ransom, Reverdy, 238

Rausenbusch, Elizabeth Brandeis, 303

Rausenbusch, Paul, 303

Raymond, Daniel, 118

Recipient requirements, 137, 138

Reconstruction, 183–94

Republican party, 174, 175

Richmond, Mary, 24

Riis, Jacob, 334, 335, 337, 344

Robbins, Dr. Jane, 219

Robins, Margaret Dreier, 321

Robins, Raymond, 203–13; and Chicago Commons, 205–7; early life of, 204; and local politics, 209–10; "the oracle of the settlements," 207–8; work in Alaska, 204–5

Rubinow, Isaac Max, 5, 17, 20, 254, 288–307; biographical information on, 289–94; fight for social insurance, 294–302; in Palestine, 302

Russell Sage Foundation, 5

Sanders, Marion K., 203

Schneider, David M., 31, 32, 64

Scientific charity, 179

Scientific philanthropy, 197–202; vs. mothers' pensions, 250

Scudder, Vida, 219

Segregation, in insane hospitals, 192–93

Settlements, 179; and blacks, 231–35; creed of, 235; and immigrants, 214–25; limits of, 223–24; and playgrounds, 336; and urban reform, 203–13. See also names of individual settlement houses

Sherman Act, 282

Slavery, 40, 93–94, 231

Smallpox, 58–60. See also Epidemics

Smith, Jeremiah, 131

Social insurance, and Isaac M. Rubinow, 288–307

Social reform, and social work, 14–28

Social Security Act, 5, 8, 20, 181, 260–61

Social service, for blacks in Chicago, 236–39

Social welfare, 1–4; after Civil War, 177–82; colonial, 29–35

Social work, history of, 14–28

The South, during Reconstruction, 183–94

South End House, Boston, 218

Starr, Ellen Gates, 315

State Factory Inspection Bill of 1893 (Illinois), 323

Statute of Artificers, 37, 38

Stevens, Alzina, 321, 324

Stillman, Hannah, 134

Survey magazine, 22

Tanner, John, 325

Taylor, Graham, 206, 223, 234, 241

Teeters, Negley K., 34, 146

Temperance, and poverty, 114–17

Ten-Million-Acre Bill, 169–74

Terry, Nathaniel, 159, 160

Thomas, Martha Carey, 317

Trattner, Walter I., 34, 156

Treudley, Mary Bosworth, 33, 132

Trinity Mission, 239

Troen, Selwyn, 328

Tuckerman, Joseph, 124

Twenty Years at Hull-House, 316, 320

Unemployment, 119, 120

Union Settlement, New York, 217

versity of Chicago Settlement, 220, 234, 336
e Urban League, 24, 239–40
rban reform, and settlements, 179

Vendue, of paupers, 106
Vestries, and administration of poor relief, 41–52, 72; bequests to, 44–49
Vittum, Harriet, 240
Voluntary charity, 177

War, effect on poor relief, 73, 74
Ware, Nathanial, 122, 123
"Warning out," 95–99
Washington, Booker T., 227, 228, 234, 237
Webb, Henry, 56–57
Wendell Phillips Center, 238, 240
Wharton, Robert, 146
White, Gaylord, 217
White, George Cary, 179–80, 214
Wiebe, Robert, 329
Wiley, Calvin H., 184
Williams, Mrs. Fannie Barrier, 237, 238

Winthrop, John, 55
"Wisconsin Plan," 303
Wise, Rabbi Stephen, 257
Wisner, Elizabeth, 32, 54
Women, and anti-child labor movement, 181, 312–30; and charitable societies, 33, 34, 132–45; education of, 178; of Hull House, 315–18; in mothers' pension movement, 254–56; and settlement work, 179
Woods, Robert A., 217–18
Woolley, Mrs. Celia Parker, 236, 237
Workhouses, 74–79
Workmen's Compensation, 180, 265–84
Work relief, 139–40; economics of, 141–44
Wright, Edwin, 282, 284
Wright, Helen R., 25
Wright, Richard Jr., 239

Zakerzewska, Dr. Marie, 334
Zueblin, Charles, 209